PERSUASION

THEORY AND APPLICATIONS

Lillian L. Beeson

UNIVERSITY OF PITTSBURGH AT GREENSBURG

NEW YORK   OXFORD

OXFORD UNIVERSITY PRESS

Oxford University Press is a department of the University of Oxford.
It furthers the University's objective of excellence in research,
scholarship, and education by publishing worldwide.

Oxford   New York
Auckland   Cape Town   Dar es Salaam   Hong Kong   Karachi
Kuala Lumpur   Madrid   Melbourne   Mexico City   Nairobi
New Delhi   Shanghai   Taipei   Toronto

With offices in
Argentina   Austria   Brazil   Chile   Czech Republic   France   Greece
Guatemala   Hungary   Italy   Japan Poland   Portugal   Singapore
South Korea   Switzerland   Thailand   Turkey   Ukraine   Vietnam

For titles covered by Section 112 of the US Higher Education
Opportunity Act, please visit www.oup.com/us/he for the
latest information about pricing and alternate formats.

Published by Oxford University Press
198 Madison Avenue, New York, New York 10016
http://www.oup.com

Oxford is a registered trademark of Oxford University Press

Library of Congress Cataloging-in-Publication Data
Beeson, Lillian L.
   Persuasion : theory and applications / Lillian L. Beeson,
University of Pittsburg, Greensburg.
      pages cm
   Includes index.
   ISBN 978-0-19-973235-7
   1. Persuasion (Psychology) I. Title.
   BF637.P4.B344   2014
   153.8'52--dc23

                                        2013006471

BRIEF CONTENTS

CONTENTS

CHAPTER **4** **Language: The Code of Persuasion** *74*

CHAPTER **5** **Messages: Verbal and Nonverbal Support** *104*

PART II APPLICATION OF PERSUASION IN THE CONTEXT OF POLITICS, LAW, RELIGION, ART AND CINEMA, ADVERTISING, AND PUBLIC RELATIONS *133*

CHAPTER **6** **Political Communication: Mediated Constructions** *135*

PREFACE

Back in the early 1970s Hugh Rank warned that the public schools were not preparing students to discern between persuasion and propaganda, and he feared that students would fall prey to unethical speakers who would have great influence over these vulnerable minds. The fears of the Cold War era have been replaced by a messy blend of global politics and a national identity crisis. Today we have an avalanche of information emanating from every corner of the globe. If ever educators needed to be vigilant and to sharpen the skills of discernment between the songs of the Harpies to beguile students and credible speakers who carry messages of importance the time is now. This textbook was written with those intentions in mind, to educate students to understand the complexities of all forms of speech, but most specifically to arm them with the tools to recognize deceitful or fallacious messages, to familiarize them with the perspectives on rhetorical address through time, and to introduce social science research that has contributed to our understanding of sources, messages, and receivers in different contexts and through different applications. Why have such flatulent phrases as "kicking the can down the road," "pushing granny off the cliff," or choosing "Wall Street over Main Street" become the lexicon of congressmen and congresswomen this election season? What energy is ignited that lifts such phraseology into everyday discourse? How does such talk influence voters, media, and everyday citizens? We need to seriously address the discourse that leads us into wars, sells nonnutritious foods to our children, or even seduces adults into embracing a utopian vision that ends in a revolutionary act of mass suicide. The text *Persuasion: theory and applications* is dedicated to enabling students to understand persuasion theory and how practitioners use it in politics, law, religion, art, advertising, and public relations.

For professors who are searching for a comprehensive textbook for an undergraduate class in persuasion theory and practices, this is the book that includes both rhetorical and social science scholars. Many complain that they require three or more books to teach such a class, but this text covers the theory from both perspectives and includes many innovations as well. Part I of the book includes the rationale for studying persuasion theory, definitions and functions of persuasion, rhetorical theories from the Sophists of ancient Greece through contemporary scholars like Michael McGee, and social science theories from Carl Hovland through Petty and Cacioppo's Elaboration Likelihood Model and others. Language as the building block of persuasion is analyzed with rich examples from scholars like George Lakoff and his work on metaphors as well as David Crystal's insights into English as an evolving language. School violence and recent assassinations are offered as case studies regarding the poisonous climate that hateful discourse creates and which raises ethical questions about such crimes as the shooting of Gabrielle Gifford and others in Tucson, Arizona, where advocates from both the political left and right pointed fingers at each other for the strident tone of current political rhetoric that they said caused this horrific crime. Messages are analyzed for structure, speaker credibility, fallacies in reasoning, and nonverbal components that influence persuasion. Part I offers foundational definitions and theories that prepare the student for Part II, which applies the theories of persuasion to the fields of politics, law, religion, the arts, advertising, and public relations. The second portion of the text uses case studies and historical movements and events to illustrate the strategies and tactics used by speakers in political campaigns, in the courtroom, in religious and other movements like the civil rights movement, in art and music videos that make statements, in advertising, and in public relations or image-restoration efforts.

Visual rhetoric is analyzed using Sonja Foss's work to emphasize the power of the visual world to win political campaigns or to make arguments about social issues such as homosexuality, mental illness, and commemorating the dead. With the rise in new media and the visual images that accompany the Internet, this territory offers a gold mine for the rhetorical critic or scholar. The book offers ethical icons to mark passages or cases that have been offered throughout the book that address ethical considerations such as the links between language use and violence; how informative speech, persuasion, and propaganda differ as messages; and how speakers should address their audiences in an ethical manner. Examples that violate normative ethics include Jonestown and the Branch Davidians to illustrate followers exposed to apocalyptic rhetoric by their corrupt leaders. The analyses include not only how advertising and public relations should work, but also offer cases and circumstances that raise serious ethical challenges, such as advertising to children, portrayals of the elderly in ads, or the use of subliminal messages in both political and product campaigns.

PEDAGOGICAL TOOLS

The book is written in a very accessible style for undergraduate students with a wealth of examples to support each concept or theory. Each chapter offers key words at the beginning of the chapter, which will be shown in bold type in the text with definitions. Each chapter offers a preview and a review with suggested exercises or assignments. The book contains a glossary with terms defined for easy reference, and an index is included to enable the user to find either scholars or concepts easily in the text. The ethics icons will flag important cases or events that raise awareness of the importance of ethics in communication of all types, especially in persuasion, where receivers are urged to vote, to buy, to act, or to embrace belief systems and various leaders. Ethical arguments are presented throughout the book rather than having just one chapter devoted to that important component of communication. PowerPoint slides are provided for each chapter with notes as well, which will support instructors who are new to the classroom as well as veteran teachers. Test banks are provided for each chapter that allow the user to select from essay, multiple choice, or true and false types of questions or to combine them for chapter examinations or major tests. The text reflects the complexity of persuasion efforts in a world that is connected 24/7 with both old and new media where the old editors are missing and information has unbridled power to access the receiver, to influence the receiver, and to deceive the receiver—unless he or she is educated to the effect that the information revolution has upon their most private and public life. The material introduces controversy, which reviewers have seen as a strength to embolden discussion and to create interest in the subject matter.

The text includes the classical views of rhetoric as well as the impact of mass media and new media platforms, especially in the area of visual rhetoric. The text is comprehensive and integrates suggestions from reviewers from universities and colleges across the country, especially in the chapters on rhetorical scholars and language usage. The author's experience and insights from decades in the classroom are reflected in this textbook's approach to the study of persuasion and the everyday applications that demonstrate both the theoretical foundation of the subject matter and the professional fields in which such strategies and tactics are practiced. Students who complete a course using this text will be more prepared to understand, analyze, and appreciate the complexity of persuasive discourse, and at the same time they will be inoculated against the more strident propagandists who occupy the stage in public life and invade their private mental space. Instructors are given the tools to conduct a thorough and exciting course in the theories of persuasion which invites a multidimensional approach to the whole enterprise.

REFERENCES

Anderson, R. D. (2004). *Religion and spirituality in the public school curriculum*. New York: Peter Lang Publishing.

Brummett, B. (1991). *Contemporary apocalyptic rhetoric*. Praeger Series in Political Communication. New York: Praeger.

Burke, K. (1970). *The rhetoric of religion: Studies in logology*. Berkeley: University of California Press.

Cary, M. S. (January–April 2002). Ad strategy and the Stone Age brain. *Journal of Advertising Research, 40*(1/2), 103–107.

Clark, T. (2006). *Lipstick on a Pig: Winning in the no-spin era by someone who knows the game*. New York: Free Press.

Crystal, D. (2007). *The fight for English: How language pundits ate, shot, and left*. New York: Oxford University Press Inc.

Korzybski, A. (1933). *Science and sanity: An introduction to non-Aristotelian systems and general semantics*. Lancaster, PA: Science Press Printing Co.

Lakoff, G. (1999). The system of metaphors for mind and the conceptual system of analytic philosophy: A study of the metaphorical constraints on philosophical discourse. In B. D. Fox, D. Jurafsky, & L.A. Michaelis. *Cognition and function in language*. Stanford, CA: Center for the Study of Language and Information.

McCroskey, J. C. (1997). *An introduction to rhetorical communication.* Boston: Allyn and Bacon.

Petty, R. E., & Cacioppo, J. T. (1986). *Communication and persuasion: Central and peripheral routes to attitude change.* New York: Springer-Verlag.

Schultze, W. J. (2003). *Christianity and the mass media in America: Toward a democratic accommodation.* East Lansing, MI: Michigan State University Press.

Schwartz, T. (1973). *The responsive chord.* New York: Anchor Books/Doubleday.

Shaw, M. (March 22, 2007). Advertising posing as PR: Why they want to be like us (and what to do about it). *Bulldog Reporter's Daily Dog.* Sirius Information, Inc. Retrieved July 9, 2007, from: http://wf2la4.webfeat.org/Jux7111 51/url=http://web.lexis-nexis.com/universe/printdoc.

Taylor, E. (April 1, 2001). What's in a work? School violence. School Violence Program. Retrieved May 20, 2008, from: http://www.hemisphonics.com/progressive/papers/Semantic_distortion .html.

ACKNOWLEDGMENTS

Jeffrey Bellows, Emerson College

Sheena M. Carey, Marquette University

Jo Anna Grant, California State University, San Bernardino

Bonnie Kay, California State University, Sacramento

Geoffrey D. Klinger, DePauw University

Jerome Mahaffey, Indiana University

INTRODUCTION

According to Greek mythology, Prometheus, one of the Titans, stole fire from the Vulcan's island of Lemnos and gave it to humans as a gift; in anger, Zeus chained him to a rock in the Caucasus. Every day an eagle gnawed at Prometheus's liver, but being unable to die, he was destined to suffer his fate anew every day. Like Prometheus, we are submerged in the technological mess that we have created for ourselves, having accepted the gifts of fire, industry, and information at the speed of light. We cannot disconnect our lives from the technology of the Information Age, where the conflicts from around the world are brought into our living rooms or offices with powerful effects. The current information explosion is similar to that of fifth-century Greece, when democracy was instituted and a tidal wave of verbiage hit the city-states. That was the oral age when the most gifted orators were also the leaders in government and in commerce. The Print Age arrived with the Gutenberg printing press in 1456, which printed the first Bibles. Gutenberg ushered in a new age of ideas and attitudes that would challenge both the church's dogma and the state's powers to censure and to control ideas. Later, the Industrial Age gave us mass-produced media and an infrastructure to deliver it to a population that became increasingly literate. The Electronic Age created media that brought voices, images, and ongoing commercial appeals into every household in America. This onslaught of powerful messages began to erode the traditional institutions like family, schools, and religious groups. Various scholars began to examine the power and influence of these mass messages upon individuals and their belief systems. The Information Age arrived with the creation of computers and the neural network that connected us to every continent, and we were catapulted into another explosion of conflicting ideas. The French sociologist Jacques Ellul wrote of *la technique*, which was the constant propaganda machine of industrialized society that indoctrinated the masses. The current age can be described as being subjected to *la technique* on steroids. The information flow from mass media and intimate sources through new technology is overwhelming. We are bound like Prometheus in a sea of powerful, sometimes angry waves of ideologies. How can we free ourselves?

The Information Age has democratized the platform for citizens to have a voice where before most had only eyes and ears to see or hear others' views in newspapers or on television or radio. The deluge of news 24/7 carries politics, disasters, and entertainment in media delivered on our preferred medium—iPods, Blackberries, computers, radios, televisions, or cell phones. We are wired 24 hours a day and obsessed with the latest instant message on our cell phones, which a Harvard University study reported cause more than 200 deaths and half a million injuries each year from automobile accidents. This constant bombardment of messages has driven us to find ways to sift through the clutter to select what is meaningful to us, what is worthy of belief, and what we need to act upon to be solvent, safe, and reasonably happy. The choices that we make depend upon what resonates with us given our circumstances. We are not just informed that there was a devastating earthquake in Haiti but that we should donate $10.00 by texting "Haiti: to 90999" according to First Lady Michelle Obama, who used the White House as an elegant stage to make her plea. Church organizations urge us to adopt orphans or to support the Red Cross. Both the Democrats and Republicans exhort us to vote to break the gridlock in Washington on healthcare, taxes, energy issues, and education. On the way to work or school we are exposed to thousands of advertisements on billboards, storefronts, and the car radio. Bumper stickers announce the driver's preferred candidate or make other political statements like, "Save the Whales." This tidal wave washes over us, submerging us in a tempestuous sea of information.

How are we to understand the forces that cause the public to embrace or vocally reject a policy like national healthcare? The State of the Union message was more than an hour long in January 2010, but while President Obama's words hung in the air, Governor Bob McDonnell of Virginia was featured on television to offer a rebuttal to the speech. What are citizens to believe about bailouts, employment, energy policies, or the cost of an education? Would President Obama's vision of the nation prevail or the words of Governor McDonnell's "frugal government" win the confidence of the nation? When we try to analyze this state of affairs with controversial ideas, powerful speakers, and consequences that will influence our own welfare, we are analyzing rhetoric, the fine art of persuasion. This textbook offers theories to explain the dynamics between speakers and audiences with attention to special appeals that have a particular effect upon us.

This textbook includes both rhetorical and social science research that addresses communication theory so that students may enjoy the blend of theory and practical application. The content will satisfy the desire for a comprehensive, innovative, and scholarly approach to the study of persuasion in a medium that is accessible to students. Students often read texts and ask what relevance the material has for their future. What does this information have to do with me? Why do I need to study this theory or that model? The answer is simple in this case: you cannot avoid being a target of persuasive messages. Commercials interrupt every television program, unless you record them and zip through them, and during election cycles candidates appeal to you to vote for them to fix everything from student loan programs to withdrawing from wars in various parts of the world. Your best defense against unethical candidates, ads, or enterprises is to be an educated citizen, which means that you must know the strategies and tactics used in persuasive discourse.

The basic roadmap to the book includes two parts of the same journey. Part I, Chapters 1 through 5, investigates concepts and theories of persuasion to pave the road for the coming chapters. The first part of the text will familiarize students with the theoretical foundation for persuasive discourse from the Greeks to contemporary scholars. Part II, chapters 6 through 11, investigates the application of persuasion theory through various fields—politics, law, religion, art and entertainment, advertising, and public relations. The latter section answers the practical question: How does persuasive discourse work in everyday life?

LAYOUT AND PEDAGOGICAL AIDS

The table of contents outlines the text and the topics discussed in each chapter. The first part of the text addresses basic rhetorical theory from the ancients to contemporary scholars, including social science researchers. Feedback from communication scholars indicated that they expected both perspectives to be included as an introduction to theories of persuasion. Chapter layouts include the following:

- Key words at the head of each chapter, which will be boldfaced in the chapters
- A preview of material to be covered
- The chapter's content with keyword definitions and examples
- A summary of the chapter's content
- Applications for students to explore at the end of the chapter for research paper topics or class projects
- A reference list to document sources

At the end of the volume the reader will find a glossary of key terms for easy reference and an index to reference names and words.

PART I: THEORETICAL FOUNDATIONS

Chapter 1, "Introduction to Persuasion in Everyday Practices," explains the basic communication model and offers a rationale for why students should study persuasion. It answers two questions: What is persuasion? And, why should I study it? A brief preview is offered for persuasion in politics, law, religion, art and film, advertising, and public relations—all of which are developed further in Part II. The characteristics of persuasive discourse and how it differs from informative speech and propaganda is presented on a continuum where the three forms are not as clear-cut as one might hope, but each form merges into another. Definitions for persuasion are explored, and the role that persuasion plays in contemporary conflicts, such as international disputes, is profiled. The functions of persuasion are presented, which illustrate how important this form of communication is in everyday affairs that affect all of us. These functions include everything from names that we give to people, events, and things, to publicizing products, candidates for office, and movements that support some ideology or social change. Throughout the text we apply these functions to various cases to see how persuasion works to identify friends or define enemies, create attitudes and stimulate actions, and create a vision that will be embraced or resisted. These functions are fulfilled through the use of language, even though we sometimes feel divided into tribes or foreign territories even within our own communities or households.

Chapter 2, "Rhetorical Scholars: Perspectives on Rhetoric," discusses different views on rhetoric, which is the philosophical foundation for persuasion theory from the Greek writers like the Sophists, Plato, and Aristotle through current scholars like Kenneth Burke and Walter Fisher. Plato is presented as the philosopher who believed in ideal forms, along with Aristotle, his student, who focused more on what was probable given the evidence at hand. In rhetorical theory, Aristotle explained the classic appeals of (1) *ethos*, ethics of the speaker, (2) *logos*, logic, and (3) *pathos*, emotions. Scholars from the Middle Ages through the eighteenth century are presented, demonstrating how Christian teaching and preaching evolved beyond the elocutionary movement to focus upon evangelistic persuasion and conviction. Kenneth Burke is presented as the literary critic who defined man as the symbol-using (and symbol-misusing) animal who invented the negative with the "thou shalt nots." Fisher's narrative theory offers an alternative to Aristotelian logic, since storytelling reaches audiences where rational argumentative discourse may not, because stories capture our experience in the world and reaffirm our self-conceptions. Jacques Ellul's *la technique* demonstrates the vulnerability of a technological society that receives information secondhand and thus is exhausted by the omnipresence of propaganda that dominates the formation of attitudes. Hugh Rank's intensify/downplay schema is presented as a model to distinguish between persuasion and propaganda. Rank feared that public schools were not enabling students to engage in critical thinking during the Cold War era, thus he began to analyze propaganda practices. Any study of persuasion should include an analysis of mass consciousness and the conflict that contrasting belief systems bring to society. Michael McGee addresses how mass consciousness is created, which leads to ideology, or a body of beliefs peculiar to each national group. He explained that ideology and group identity come through language acquisition where the "Ideograph" or slogans evolve that reflect the attitudes, values, and worldview of the masses. Obviously, not all scholars can be discussed, but those offered here will give ground for contemplation and further inquiry into the foundations of persuasion from a rhetorical perspective.

Chapter 3, "Audiences: Social Scientists Address Needs, Attitudes, and Beliefs," focuses upon receivers of persuasion and the various ways that social researchers have studied subjects to find how persuasion works. In the 1920s, Edward Bernays, the father of public relations, introduced social science to audience behavior analysis by using polls, statistics, and market research to test their attitudes and beliefs. We now take demographic and psychographic research for granted in all political and product campaigns. How many polls did you read in the 2012 election? Every day a new set of figures showed either Obama or Romney in the lead—like a racehorse approaching the finish line. The persuader must understand the nature of the audience, whether it is one person, a small group, or a mass audience. Source credibility is discussed as one variable that can be analyzed before, during, and after the persuasion attempt with different effects according to William McCroskey (1997). A.H. Maslow's pyramid of needs paradigm is explained as drives that exist at different levels of potency, which motivate receivers to satisfy their needs, not only to survive physically but to belong, to be secure, and to achieve goals. Vance Packard recognized that people have hidden needs that persuaders can exploit in product, political, and ideological campaigns. For example, the boom in home freezer sales following World War II had less to do with food preservation than it did with making buyers feel secure after years of food rationing and deprivation. Leon Festinger's cognitive dissonance theory is explored in relation to attitudes, beliefs, and the desire to maintain or achieve psychic balance or harmony. Milton Rokeach's work on beliefs is discussed and how they are resistant to change—like the layers of an onion, those beliefs closer to the core are most closely guarded. Martin Fishbein and Isaac Ajzen's theory of reasoned action is included, which shows that we evaluate risks in decision making along with taking into account what our friends think of our choices. Carolyn Sherif, Muzafer Sherif, and Robert Nebergall's (1965) social judgment theory is included, which demonstrates that attitudes and beliefs exist along a continuum where noncommitment, acceptance, or rejection depend upon the receiver's anchor position or their current position on the topic. Gerald R. Miller's research on counterattitudinal persuasion is included as well. Miller pointed out that most research focused upon trying to get receivers to do something, but he asked the question of how to make receivers resistant to persuasion attempts by others, like the father who wished to dissuade his college-age son from smoking marijuana or to inoculate him from the influence of others who did. Miller's research demonstrated the complexity of the receiver's self-esteem, the source's appeal, the intellect of the subject, and other variables. Violation expectancy theory demonstrates that the unanticipated behavior that violates norms may be from language usage, nonverbal behavior, or social norms. For example, because of gender expectations, a female doctor may not use the negative messages that a male doctor can use to motivate compliance in diet change; she can only use positive messages as a nurturing source. The elaboration likelihood model (Petty & Cacioppo, 1986) is explained as a dual processing route for information along with criticism of their views. Chapter 3 focuses more upon psychological appeals based upon needs, attitudes, beliefs, and the drive to find balance or harmony between our thoughts, feelings, and behaviors. While this chapter in no way manages to introduce all the social scientists who have contributed so much to persuasion theory, it serves as a sufficient menu for an undergraduate persuasion class. The tension between the qualitative and quantitative researchers is never resolved, but this text does a good job of surveying the contributions of both camps.

Chapter 4, "Language: The Code of Persuasion," explores language, which is the essence of all communication, especially persuasive discourse. No oral or written communication between humans would be possible without the code of language wherein we attempt to bridge the gulf that separates us from each other. Later chapters will explore visual rhetoric, but it is language that defines us as rational beings. The same vehicle of thought can create havoc as we wretchedly label each other and engage in racist, sexist, and tyrannical or violent discourse, but scholars offer insights to how language creates frames of reference or terministic screens that propel us into a worldview with a compulsion to see things in a certain light. Alfred Korzybski (1933) wrote the book *Science and Sanity: An introduction to non-Aristotelian systems and general semantics,* which began the general semantics movement. Eldon Taylor (2001) studied the power of words to create semantic distortions that lead to such aberrations as school shootings and other social pathologies George Lakoff (1999) not only explored the power of metaphors to describe the social-political sphere of influence, he posits that metaphors create our reality. Kenneth Burke (1970) described the four types of words: those that describe the physical world, such as the wind and human conditions like hunger or thirst; words about the social-political realm; words about words, such as dictionaries, literary criticism, or grammar texts; and words about the supernatural, such as God and the hereafter. Emotional language surrounds us and is used to exploit attitudes toward politicians, our government, and other groups or factions in society. Rush Limbaugh is discussed as a media phenomenon who uses labels, stereotypes, either/or choices, anecdotes, or stories to reaffirm his biases with an army of "dittoheads" who follow his conservative ideology. David Crystal (2007) reminded us that no one owns the language of a country; it is dynamic, ever-changing with marked influences from every group that speaks the mother tongue. Walter Lippmann wrote about wartime rhetoric that vilifies the enemy and moves populations to hatred that distorts reality, yet we need a public philosophy based upon natural law that supports civility and a unifying force embodied in the language of a people. Chapter 4 explores the language of race and gender with examples from a speech delivered by the late Ossie Davis, an African American who declared the English language as his enemy because of all the negatives associated with the word "black." Former Secretary of State Hillary Clinton, who defies the feminine style by not using anecdotes, dependent, or powerless speech that audiences expect from a woman, is an illustration of expectancy violation theory because she uses the logical, organized, and evidence-backed arguments that her legal background required. This chapter explores the power of language to define who are the "freedom fighters" or the "assassins," so any student of persuasion must be aware of the rivers of thought that are carried in the torrential currents of language usage.

Chapter 5, "Messages: Verbal and Nonverbal Support," is a logical follow-up to the former chapters that explained how persuasion differs from other forms of speech, how persuasion theory has evolved through time from the writings of ancient teachers, contemporary scholars of rhetoric, and social science research, and how psychological needs motivate receivers to accept some messages and reject others. Finally, Chapter 5 focuses upon the message itself. This chapter explores the relationship between the speaker and the audience. We begin with Plato's ideas on the duality of man, who is divided between his passions and reason, and include Aristotle, Plato's student, who took a more scientific approach to studying human behavior. Aristotle's appeals of *ethos* (ethics of the speaker), *logos* (logic), and *pathos* (emotions) are reviewed. Wayne Brockriede's sexual metaphor of the speaker–audience relationship is explored as he explains the rapist, the seducer, and the lover, with each representing either ethical or unethical behavior in the speech transaction. The forms of supporting material or evidence in persuasive messages are discussed with narratives, examples, or stories offered with anecdotes from Bill Clinton's presidency and an international business transaction as illustrations. The nature of testimony, statistics, and analogies is examined with various fallacies in reasoning identified (ad hominem, ad populum, ad misericordiam, ad adsurdum, non sequitur, post hoc ergo propter hoc, slippery slope, and false dilemma). These ideas tie argument to persuasive address where logic is powerful as an influence upon rational and critical thinkers. Fallacies or faulty reasoning can be identified and understood as either an intentional device (lying) or unintentional faulty reasoning. The organization of the message is discussed with the primacy-recency theory explained, which states that we remember best the first and last parts of a message so that the opening and closing arguments should be powerful. Nonverbal components in all speech transactions must be noted, with psychologist Abraham Mehrabian estimating that 93 percent of a message's *meaning* is carried on the nonverbal band. The characteristics of nonverbal communication, the functions of nonverbal communication, and the various nonverbal codes are examined.

The codes that are explained are: affect displays—emotional expressions; eye behavior—eye contact or avoidance; kinesics—body language; proxemics—use of personal space; vocalics—voice properties; chronemics—time elements; olfactics—smell like body odor or familiar scents of home; and haptics—which includes intimate, social, and professional touch like a handshake. In persuasion it is frequently "not what we say, but how we say it" that matters. Remember the vice presidential debate between Paul Ryan and Joe Biden and the criticism that Biden received because he laughed or smiled frequently when Ryan was speaking? Many voters saw this as scene stealing or as Biden treating Ryan with contempt or as a lightweight. Generally the vice president's congenial manner is seen as a positive attribute but not in the TV split-screen portrayal during a serious discussion of national issues. Nonverbal elements cannot be separated from the verbal or written messages; even the written page shows spatial arrangements and creates an image. For students who have separate courses in argument and nonverbal communication, Chapter 5 will serve as a helpful review or cause them to think about message composition further and how speakers attempt to strengthen performances.

PART II: APPLICATION OF PERSUASION IN THE CONTEXT OF POLITICS, LAW, RELIGION, ART AND CINEMA, ADVERTISING, AND PUBLIC RELATIONS

Chapter 6, "Political Communication: Mediated Constructions," discusses the functions of political or deliberative communication in a democratic society and the role that mass media plays in protecting the interests of citizens to be informed. The impact of new technology upon campaigns is discussed along with the characteristics of political campaigns. Visual rhetoric is presented where images make arguments or create illusions through television coverage, photography, convention film, or posters like the Daisy Girl ad of 1964 which torpedoed Barry Goldwater's campaign. That one-time ad has been discussed in every presidential campaign since that time. Television debates that began in 1960 now have become routine and ever more frequent through the primary period and the general election in presidential campaigns. Many argue that sound bytes have replaced real issue–centered campaigns, but as Marshall McLuhan, the mass media guru, predicted, political campaigns have become more and more about images and ambiguity where the voter fills in the blanks. The Internet has given voters a voice and instant access to the sites of candidates where accuracy is checked and challenged daily. Howard Dean was the first to exploit this technology in a presidential campaign, so communication with voters has changed forever with interactive technology. In the presidential debate between Romney and Obama in October 2012, some television stations recorded the number of Tweets that audience members sent during the debate to register their responses to the ideas. Many issues evoked over 75,000 Tweets during the debate, which underscores the role that social media had taken on through the election cycle. Voters no longer wait to see what the commentators have to say about these clashes between candidates, their responses are immediate.

Entertainment sites like *JibJab Media*, where a viral video of George W. Bush and John Kerry received over 70 million hits during the 2004 election, are discussed because increasingly the campaign circuit includes regular appearances on comedy shows like *Saturday Night Live,* thus blurring the lines between news and entertainment. Who can forget Tina Fey as Sarah Palin during the 2008 election campaign or Jay Pharoah as Barack Obama in 2012? Visual rhetoric dominates political conventions with videos featuring candidates like Ronald Reagan's 18-minute promotional film and others in every contest who have followed him. Bill Clinton, the man from Hope, Arkansas, George W. Bush, the Texas cowboy where the "Sky's the Limit," and Barack Obama's biography were made into media images that all Americans could embrace and remember. Mitt Romney's promotional film in 2012 presented him as a devoted family man who embraced the free enterprise system and America as the land of opportunity. Jamieson and Campbell's *Interplay of Influence* is discussed as we understand that persuasion is an interactive process between senders and receivers. The roots of political discourse go back to the fifth-century Athenians, but the oral tradition has been subjugated to mass media. Jürgen Habermas's views on democracy and deliberation are reviewed with his explanation offered on how condescending and paternalistic media corporations frame debates with citizens cast in a passive role. Media as the "watchdog" of the people has been defanged with the adversarial relationship corrupted by the desire of journalists to have access to powerful sources. Bernard Goldberg's critique of media bias and the effect upon politics is discussed along with views on "cultural elites" who confuse their celebrity status with political expertise. The political process has absorbed new technology to give voters greater access than ever before, but the filters of careful editing have been removed so right now political campaigns are a free for all, except for the carefully packaged and managed candidate. Chapter 6 reports various perspectives on political campaigns and how they continue to evolve. Persuasion is at the heart of all political discourse, which has earning credibility, instilling conviction, and gaining the endorsement of candidates and their policies as the ultimate goal.

Chapter 7, "Legal Communication: Persuasion in Court," explores the role that persuasion plays in legal proceedings beginning with the forensic oratory of the Greek and Roman empires and continuing to media saturated trials like the O. J. Simpson verdict. The public's fascination with *Court TV* and *Judge Judy* or *Judge Joe Brown* demonstrates their voyeuristic nature, which delights in the stupidity of others who find themselves standing before a judge—or perhaps it is the drama of identifying with the victims of criminals that attracts us. The court system is an adversarial one, with defense and prosecuting attorneys arguing their case before a judge and jury where all the appeals of rhetoric are employed in the name of fair representation and justice. Aristotle's views on forensic speech are covered, and Susan Drucker's four categories of legal communication are outlined. Cameras in the courtroom or undue publicity has resulted in some cases being overturned because of the conflict between the First Amendment, which guarantees freedom of speech and the press, and the Sixth Amendment, which promises a fair and speedy trial by an impartial jury of peers in the state where the crime was committed. The influence of pretrial publicity has often been an issue in how impartial a jury could be. While all trials are a great drama, the decision is left up to the jury, which writes the conclusion to the story. As citizens and the community's conscience, ordinary people sit in judgment of the accused while professionals in jurisprudence ply their trade with the best research, organization, and delivery skills they possess. Storytelling is a skill that all good lawyers cultivate, and their success is dependent upon their ability to communicate immediately from the opening statement through the closing argument. Chapter 7 examines the process along with the most effective strategies for introducing expert witnesses or helping judges and jurors remember the facts of the case. Walter Fisher's narrative theory is discussed with examples of stories from trials. The notion that trials are theater is illustrated with such examples as Dr. Jack Kevorkian, who advocated euthanasia, and O. J. Simpson, who was accused and found innocent of murdering his wife and her friend. Nonverbal communication is as important as what is said in the courtroom, with lawyers attempting to connect with jurors and the judge through behaviors that exhibit credibility, trust, and likability. Powerful speech demonstrates that the speakers know what they are talking about, but professionals must know how to read their audience from the moment jury selection begins and continues throughout the trial. This chapter examines the ethos of the lawyer and the role of the judge in the proceedings. The ability to be persuasive in legal proceedings is paramount for the parties involved; at the heart of the process is an understanding of the motives, emotions, the character of humans and the ability to communicate them passionately and effectively within the guidelines of the profession.

Chapter 8, "Religion and Persuasion," addresses the role that religion has played in American life and the uneasy alliance between politics and religion that exists. Religious discourse is separated into two categories: utopian and apocalyptic. Puritans who expected to see the Reformation in Europe create a new covenant with God in the new land in the colonies became disappointed and turned their rhetoric to apocalyptic visions with Armageddon ushering in the millennium. Barry Brummett's (1991) views on apocalyptic rhetoric are discussed. John Woolman's Quaker faith and the right of all men to be free lead him away from signing documents that transferred the ownership of slaves to heirs. The abolition movement was mobilized by such people of conscience. Quentin J. Schultze's (2003) analysis of the five forms of rhetoric (conversion, discernment, communion, exile, and praise) used by Christian groups to attract and convert people through mass media organizations is included. R. D. Anderson's (2004) views on the conflict between orthodoxy and modernity are presented as philosophies of naturalism and postmodernism are discussed. Colonial America, with our Constitution that neither advances nor inhibits religion, is discussed along with challenges today from agnostics, non-Christians, and strict constructionists who believe that religious ideology has invaded government, business, and public schools. It is impossible to separate the role that religion has played in the development of our Judeo-Christian roots and national character. Kenneth Burke's (1970) views on the creation account and the Genesis narrative are presented along with the role that religion plays as a force in our society. Both Jimmy Carter and George W. Bush identified themselves as "born-again Christians" and laced their rhetoric with references to the ideology of an omnipotent God and belief in divine interventions. Some Americans fear this practice of comingling affairs of state and a conservative Christian ideology, which dissolves the imaginary wall between Church and state that Jefferson metaphorically constructed. While some Americans adhere to the belief that God is a God of wrath who punishes unrepentant sinners, others find pleasure and comfort in their plastic Jesus as Janis Joplin did and exploit images from religion as Madonna has in her *Pappa Don't Preach* or *Like a Virgin* videos. Jonathan Edwards's (1741) angry God is demonstrated in his sermons to the parishioners who grew weary of his condemnations as "children of the devil," so he was sent to minister to the Indian (sic) mission; but later he was appointed to the presidency of the college that would become Princeton University. Religion has been the foundation of reform movements such as the civil rights movement. Dr. Martin Luther King Jr.'s nonviolent resistance movement is discussed as he said "religion deals with both heaven and earth." King's leadership and ideology is explored through his sermons, letters, and documents. Religious diversity is examined with examples of Muslim, Jewish, and Catholic leaders who have found themselves caught between their faith and the political expediency of justifying their beliefs to the general public—for example, John F. Kennedy, a Catholic; Congressman Keith Ellison, a Muslim; Herbert Hoover, a Quaker; and recently Mitt Romney, a Mormon. Cults have taken up the banner of religion and created dangerous, even deadly, empires. Jim Jones's Christian utopia in Guyana, South America, is discussed as a cult that gained legitimacy with good works that turned deadly as 911 people were killed or committed suicide when Congressman Ryan went to investigate abuses of Americans there. The Branch Davidians, under the leadership of David Koresh, similarly perished when the U.S. government sent BATF agents to investigate abuse of children in Waco, Texas. David Koresh's sermons demonstrate the ideology of apocalyptic rhetoric; he presented himself as a messiah anointed by God to interpret the Seven Seals of the book of Revelation. The government was seen as Babylon, and Korish told followers that they were about to be slain because they were servants of God. Chapter 8 examines the ideologies of utopia and the apocalypse and how religious leaders have carried their messages of hope or doom to their followers. While the chapter cannot examine all religious doctrines or the prophets of them, clearly, religious conviction is the stuff of which persuasion is made and perpetuated. In 2008, the Rev. Jeremiah Wright controversy threatened to derail Senator Barack Obama's presidential campaign, and in the same year another sect was invaded in Texas where polygamy was practiced and children were taken from their parents for protection from sexual predators, which the appeals court later rescinded. It is difficult to find balance between those God-fearing believers who preach and teach moral living and the self-anointed who elevate themselves for personal gain and dominate the media's attention. Perhaps this chapter does too much of the sensational as well, but rhetoric is the bedfellow of the divine as well as the damned.

Chapter 9, "Art as Persuasion: Visual Rhetoric," explores the role that art forms such as cartoons, sculpture, photographs, film, and music play in the communication process, especially as they exert influence upon people's thoughts, emotions, and actions. Charles Kostelnick and Michael Haslett's rhetoric of visual conventions is discussed along with Sonja Foss's views on visual rhetoric. The power of visual representations can be seen in the recent controversy over the cartoons of the prophet Mohammed in a Denmark newspaper that resulted in death threats against the editor, which continue to this day. In Benghazi, Libya, on September 11, 2012, terrorists attacked the U.S. Embassy and killed four, including the American ambassador. According to the Obama administration, the attack was the result of a video that desecrated the Muslim prophet, but investigators have not concluded the circumstances of the tragedy, even though evidence points to a planned attack by al-Qaeda.

Many works of art create controversy, even if the outcome is not as deadly. The Vietnam War Memorial by Maya Lin is an example of a controversial work that seemed to violate expectations. It was condemned by many critics but awarded prestigious design accolades by others. A homoerotic exhibition by Robert Mapplethorpe in 1989 created a furor over the role of art in American society and who would pay for it. Chapter 9 explores his work and the various responses to it. Further, this chapter explores the impact of film upon subjects such as homosexuality, mental illness, and violence. The film *Brokeback Mountain*, for example, was viewed as an attempt to naturalize homosexuality in a love story featuring two cowboys. The role of music in campaigns, ceremonies, and youth culture is discussed using gangsta rap as a genre that has created the most criticism. The communication model of Tony Schwartz (1973) is explored as he believes that most communication theory is mistaken based upon the linear model while a resonance model is more accurate. Schwartz said we do not "get something across"; we evoke something that is already in the receiver to extract meaning. MTV has been shown to have tremendous influence upon youth fashion and musical taste. Increasingly the young get their news from MTV or comedy shows like Jon Stewart's *The Daily Show* so that the word "infotainment" has evolved. This chapter covers new ground with visual rhetoric, but the material only scratches the surface of what is open to investigation to communication scholars. Visual rhetoric is a gold mine yet to be unearthed; persuasion is powerful when the aim is subliminal, as it is in most art. This discussion is intended to raise awareness of a rich area of inquiry where irrefutable influence is being wielded.

Chapter 10, "Advertising: Integrated Marketing Communication," focuses upon advertising, or the Latin word *advetere*, "to turn," as practitioners attempt to direct our heads and minds toward their product or candidate. The various methods used to establish a unique selling position (USP) are discussed as well as the regulatory agencies that monitor products, such as the FDA, FTC, FCC, SEC, and Postal Service. Advertising strategies and tactics are explored, demonstrating why we speak of advertising campaigns. The whole communication effort must be strategically timed and organized for maximum effect. Wang and Schultz's seven-stage planning model is summarized. Celebrity endorsements are discussed as well as the risks of using individuals like Paris Hilton or Tiger Woods, both of whom have lost public approval for their bad behavior. The history of commercial speech is reviewed with some ancient examples offered to show similarities in branding a product. The impact that the printing press had upon advertising is covered, and the subsidy of advertising for newspapers with the evolution of magazines to carry targeted advertisements is reviewed. Integrated marketing communication (IMC) evolved to coordinate multiple efforts to strengthen customer relations. Channels for advertising have multiplied with the technology of the Internet, just as television and film gave advertisers the ability to embed products in shows. The criticisms that advertising is intrusive, deceptive, and unethical or demeaning are shown as the most frequent complaints against the industry. How manipulative is advertising? Can consumers be made to buy products that they do not need or want? Regulators attempt to protect consumers against the complaints just mentioned. Advertising does more than describe products; ads create images and make promises that are not readily measurable. Truth in advertising is not just a goal. Credibility is actually an asset to the company; this is evidenced by Johnson & Johnson's chairman and CEO, James Burke, who spoke immediately to the American people after some bottles of their product, Tylenol, were contaminated with cyanide in 1982 in Chicago. Sometimes the best persuasion is to simply confront a problem and to tell the truth. It took only one year for Tylenol to regain most of its market share. Chapter 10 investigates the attitudes and practices of "conspicuous consumption," as outlined by the Yale-educated Max Veblen. The Stone Age brain theory is explained as a tie to reproduction, power, speed, and survival, which are underlying motives to accept some ads. Mark S. Carey (2000) explained that during the Stone Age a woman's value to a man depended upon her reproductive value, which was evident by the features of youth—"full lips, clear, smooth skin, clear eyes, lustrous, healthy hair, good muscle tone, and high energy levels" (Cary, 2000, p. 103). While feminists cringe at sexploitation, most ads use the beauty and power of youth. Research from Carnegie Mellon and MIT is summarized, which uses brain mapping and magnetic resonance imaging to see brain activity when subjects view objects to determine immediate intentions to respond by buying a product or intervening rational decision making when the price is visible. Subliminal advertising as presented originally has been discredited, and a report from professionals in the field of advertising demonstrates that only one in 120 knew of an instance of subliminal advertising being used. This chapter discusses these findings. The latest tempest over subliminal messages comes from the field of politics, where Republicans attacked Al Gore's prescription drug plan in 2000 with a 1/30-second spot that flashed the word "RATS" on it. Alex Castellanos, producer of the ad for the Republican National Committee, denied using the subliminal embed. Demographic and psychographic research is reviewed with some examples of profiles included, for example, "Successful Singles" vs. "Low-Income Blues." Niche marketing is a growing trend with the diversification of the population. Target, Starbucks, and Apple began as narrow niches to satisfy a band of potential customers; each of these is now a household word. Age-sensitive advertising is discussed with a focus upon children and the elderly. Gender stereotypes are reviewed, as are the impacts of disasters upon some industries, such as the airline industry following 9/11. A discussion is also included of how various companies responded after 9/11 to the tragedy so fresh on consumer's minds; would it be possible to recognize Americans fears and yet position a company's product in that climate of confusion? Anheuser-Busch and The Boeing Company are used as examples of adaptation to social upheaval. Advertising budgets in the United States exceed those of any other country, and on Super Bowl Sunday the advertisements have become as important to some viewers as the football games. Advertising exists to cut through the clutter of an overcommunicated society, to arrest attention, to create a favorable impression, and to motivate buyers to purchase one product over another. A concerted effort exists to complete this complicated process based upon the selective perception of targeted audience.

As seen in Chapter 11, "Public Relations: Engineering Public Consent," Edward Bernays, Sigmund Freud's nephew, combined sociology and psychology to win adherence to his ideas and to create campaigns for his clients. He defined public relations as "engineering public consent." Public relations (PR) practitioners combine advocacy and adversarial types of communication that are both visible and invisible to publics. This chapter reviews perspectives on PR, including Professors Larissa and James Grunig's Excellence Report that attempted to establish a template for ideal types of public relations practices. They offered four models: (1) press agentry/publicity, (2) public information, (3) two-way symmetrical, and (4) two-way asymmetrical forms. Persuasion runs from the organization to the public and from the public to the organization regarding changes in attitudes and behaviors. Distinctions between advertising and public relations are discussed, although both disciplines claim that the other is invading their territory, according to Matt Shaw, vice president of the Council of Public Relations. Shaw said, "It turns out that when advertising grows up it wants to be public relations" (2007). The recommendations from a Commission on Public Relations education are offered, which lists both skills and knowledge that students of PR should have. The multiple functions of public relations are discussed. Ogilvy Public Relations Worldwide has joined JL McGregor & Company to promote the Chinese government, and between these two agencies, tremendous expertise is brought to the table on behalf of Chinese interests. Given the problems with dog food, toothpaste, and lead-painted toys, some medications, and other products, the question arises about the proper role for a PR firm. When abuses or deception exist, the PR firm can only advocate changed policies. In America, PR firms engage in public education, with one such example being Al Gore's Academy Award–winning documentary on climate change, *An Inconvenient Truth*. The role of public relations in social and political controversies is explored, ranging from managing communication for the National Hockey League to managing publicity for the American Red Cross. Part of PR's job is to engage in image restoration or to handle crises. Torie Clarke, former president of Bozell Eskew advertising and head of Hill & Knowlton and Assistant Secretary of Defense for Public Affairs wrote a book, *Lipstick on a Pig* (2006), in which she reminds us that you can put lipstick on a pig, but it is still a pig. She advised, "Deliver the bad news yourself, and when you screw up, say so—fast" (p. 1). William Benoit's theory of image restoration is offered with his explanations of the various parts that can be applied to scandals, crises, or international incidents both large and small. Public relations firms have many roles to play in managing the affairs of governments, corporations, individuals, and their campaigns or careers. As communication technology evolves and multinational companies expand, practitioners will have to employ new means to achieve their ends. Chapter 11 presents some of the trials and triumphs of such efforts.

SUMMARY

It is the goal of this text to arm students to be able to understand the underlying premises upon which both demagogues and ethical speakers base their claims. In this contentious, partisan society where various factions abrasively rub up against each other (Democrats–Republicans, young–old, Americans–global others), we need to know the basic tenets of persuasion theory and practices. Further, students must know the needs, motives, and worldview of audiences who are targeted by politicians, lawyers, religious zealots, advertisers, and public relations specialists. The Information Age has the virtual ability to channel propaganda 24 hours a day, 7 days a week, to unsuspecting subjects. We need to become discerning receivers of all messages to foil the deception, the exploitation, and the siren songs that play on our heartstrings whether we are watching our favorite news channel, attending a political rally, playing a video game, or seeing a movie with product placements embedded in them. This book equips readers to recognize strategies and tactics that overtly and covertly influence our thoughts, attitudes, and behaviors. To quote President Obama upon signing the much-contested Health Care Reform Bill, "This is what change looks like." Persuasion requires an interplay between speakers and receivers that involves a thought process that changes attitudes, which leads to action.

While Prometheus was the mythical figure damned to eternal suffering who stood between the Gods and man's ability to survive the elements with the comfort and destructive potential of fire, we embraced his gift with gratitude. We used his fire to forge our civilization and to multiply the forbidden fruit of knowledge to the point of enslavement to the information avalanche that could bury all of us. The ability to push back the tidal waves of spin and enjoy the sweet fruit of credible persuasive discourse is a worthy goal, one that this textbook embraces as a way to alleviate the suffering not of Titans bound to a rock somewhere in this universe but of students transfixed before computer screens, textbooks, media broadcasts, and cell phones who are drowning in information. Their deliverance is in understanding the currents of thought that give ideas such tempestuous power and enabling them to discern how to use the gifts offered by long-suffering Titans rather than the siren songs of Harpies. These sirens seduce us with beautiful images or messages but rob us of the sustenance of either knowledge or virtue. This book is intended to enable students to recognize seduction with ears and eyes wide open to the melodies of deceit.

REFERENCES

Anderson, R. D. (2004). *Religion and spirituality in the public school curriculum.* New York: Peter Long Publishing.

Brummett, B. (1991). *Contemporary apocalyptic rhetoric.* Praeger Series in Political Communication. New York: Praeger.

Burke, K. (1970). *The rhetoric of religion: Studies in logology.* Berkeley: University of California Press.

Cary, M. S. (2000). Ad strategy and the Stone Age brain. *Journal of Advertising Research, 40*(1/2), 103–107.

Clarke, T. (2006). *Lipstick on a pig: Winning in the no-spin era by someone who knows the game.* New York: Free Press.

Crystal, D. (2007). *The fight for English: How language pundits ate, shot, and left.* New York: Oxford University Press.

Dozier, D. M., Grunig, L. A., & Grunig, J. E. (1995). *Manager's guide to excellence in public relations and communication management.* Mahwah, NJ: Lawrence Erlbaum Associates, Inc., Publishers.

Korzybski, A. (1933). *Science and sanity: An introduction to non-aristotelian systems and general semantics.* Lancaster, PA: Science Press Printing Co.

Lakoff, G. (1999). *The system of metaphors for mind and the conceptual system of analytic philosophy: A study of the metaphorical constraints on philosophical discourse.* In B. D. Fox, D. Jurafsky, & L. A. Michaelis (Eds.). Stanford, CA: Center for the Study of Language and Information.

McCroskey, J. C. (1997). *An introduction to rhetorical communication.* Boston: Allyn & Bacon.

McLuhan, M., & Powers, B. R. (1989). *The global village: Transformations in world life and media in the 21st century.* New York: Oxford University Press.

Petty, R. E., & Cacioppo, J. T. (1986). *Communication and persuasion: Central and peripheral routes to attitude change.* New York: Springer-Verlag.

Schultze, Q. J. (2003). *Christianity and the mass media in America: Toward a democratic accommodation.* East Lansing: Michigan University Press.

Schwartz, T. (1973). *The responsive chord.* New York: Anchor Books/Doubleday.

Shaw, M. (March 22, 2007). Advertising posing as PR: Why they want to be like us (and what to do about it). *Bulldog Reporter's Daily Dog.* Sirius Information, Inc. Retrieved July 9, 2007, from: http://wf2la4.webfeat.org/Jux711151/url=http://web.lexisnexis.com/universe/printdoc.

Sherif, C. W., Sherif, M., & Nebergall, R. E. (1965) *Attitude and attitude change: The social judgment-involvement approach.* Philadelphia, PA: W.B. Sanders.

Taylor, E. (April 1, 2001). What's in a word? School violence. School Violence Program. Retrieved May 20, 2008, from: http://www.hemisphonics.com/progressive/papers/Semantic-distortion.html.

PART

1

THEORETICAL FOUNDATIONS

CHAPTER 1

INTRODUCTION TO PERSUASION IN EVERYDAY PRACTICES

KEY WORDS

a priori	encode	propaganda
channel	feedback	public relations
charisma	feedback loop	receiver
communication context	field of experience	receiver-centered
credibility	identification	rhetor
cultivation theory	informative speech	rhetoric
decode	jargon	Socratic method
demagogue	IMC	source/speaker
effects	message	subliminal
elaboration likelihood	noise	universals of communication
model	persuasion	vocalics

PREVIEW

The goals for this chapter are simple. After reading it, students should be familiar with the basic communication model, be able to define and apply the terms listed at the beginning of the chapter, and be able to differentiate between speech to inform, speech to persuade, and propaganda. Further, students should be familiar with the functions that persuasion performs in society. As students read the chapter, they should be able to reflect upon their own communication transactions and how the concepts offered here are similar to or different from their own experiences or how they apply to their interactions at school, in the workplace, or among family and friends.

Before we begin our analysis of what persuasion is and why we should study it, we need to understand the basic nuts and bolts of the communication process, which is a complex transaction with interdependent dimensions. When communication studies began, the laboratory approach was used by engineers for AT&T, Westinghouse, and RCA, who were accustomed to dealing with electronic equipment such as the telegraph, telephones, and radios.

The neutral terminology, such as *source, receiver,* and *noise,* came from these experiments with "things" rather than "people." While persuasion is often dependent upon technology to spread the word, it is a very human activity.

JOSEPH DEVITO'S COMMUNICATION MODEL

Joseph DeVito (1982) offered a fairly coherent model for communication in his book *Communicology: An Introduction to the Study of Communication* in what he called the **universals of communication**. The term "universals" indicates that, regardless of the language one speaks, these interdependent parts will be present in any communication transaction. We begin with the basics, because before we can analyze particular types of communication, we need to understand the interacting variables of the process. While we are applying DeVito's model, the interpretation belongs to the author.

According to DeVito, all communication occurs in some **communication context**, which has four parts: the time, place, and social and psychological aspects of the event. For instance, our communication style differs if we are in church, where meditation is part of the service, or if we are attending a football game, waving the Pittsburgh Steelers' "terrible towel," or supporting our favorite team with body paint, tailgate parties, and other wacky antics. The rules of engagement are very different if we are in a formal setting, such as a conference, or just hanging out with friends. These rules of etiquette or propriety deal with the social norms that are often not written but certainly enforced through the shunning of certain types of people in public or at work. The psychological mood depends on how friendly or hostile the setting appears, which can be read by the formality of the people or the room and other signs. If your boss requests that you meet with him or her at 8:30 in the morning, you would not refuse the request by saying, "No, let's make it 1:00 p.m. since

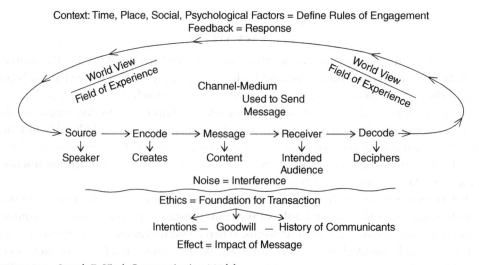

FIGURE 1.1 Joseph DeVito's Communication Model.

I am not a morning person." We understand that a hierarchy exists at work and certain people have the right to make demands on our time and efforts. So we understand that superiors, such as our bosses or professors, can set deadlines and set standards for our work that is compensated with either monetary rewards at work or grades at school. We also have an understanding of the difference between interacting with subordinates and equals. Among friends and equals, our language may be a bit more informal or sprinkled with street references that would change immediately if a child were present or if Grandma just walked into the room. Further, the element of time and timing is part of all transactions. It is impolite to call people after 9:00 p.m. or at mealtime, unless it is an emergency or you have their permission to do so. In addition, we calculate how much time we should allocate to a conversation depending on our relationship with the other, the task before us, and sometimes the patience of the communicants involved. The communication context interacts with every other part of the model so that if one thing shifts, it affects all other parts of the model.

The **source**, also known as the speaker, is the person who **encodes** or creates the **message**, which consists of the ideas or thoughts that they hope to send to the **receiver**, who is the intended audience. Being able to either encode or decode messages requires language competence. According to DeVito:

> Essential to an understanding of encoding-decoding are the concepts of language competence and performance and of communicative competence and performance. Let us focus first on language competence and performance. Consider the "simple" act of speaking. Verbal messages are formed with no real problems; we open our mouths and certain things are said without any difficulty. At times we make an error and perhaps say what we did not want to say, but for the most part the vocal mechanism seems obedient. Similarly, when we listen to the words of others, we usually have no difficulty understanding them. (DeVito, 1982, p. 9)

DeVito included the **field of experience,** which showed his sensitivity to communication as a human endeavor, because the more common ground the source and the receiver have, the more probable they will like and understand one another. Much of what we see in the news or in political discourse today consists of attacks on philosophies or policies that emanate from speakers (e.g., Barack Obama, George W. Bush, John F. Kerry, or Rush Limbaugh) who see the world in starkly different ways from one another. From such people we have heard speeches that vary from the ridiculous to the sublime. So when the source and the receiver share similar philosophies, lifestyles, and communication styles (e.g., political conservatives like Bush and Limbaugh or liberals like Obama and Kerry), they will more likely "get" the message that was intended for them when they talk with a kindred spirit. However, to the extent that they differ in their worldviews, they may not even take time to hear what the other has to say. The problem may be with the speaker, the message, or the receiver, but taken together with all the complexity of human nature, the words spoken, and the relationship of those involved, we can begin to appreciate the importance of studying **rhetoric**, which is the theory and practice of persuasive discourse.

Some speakers are masterful communicators who create visions of the world and humankind that elevate our expectations, such as Dr. Martin Luther King Jr., who in his "I Have a Dream" speech painted a new picture of race relations in America. Any time someone **encodes** a **message**, he or she performs a complicated act of putting thoughts into symbols that must be **decoded**, in other words, interpreted or deciphered by the **receiver** or intended audience. The language code embodies symbols that can easily be misunderstood because of abstract references, ambiguous use, or different levels of difficulty. As the semanticists reminded us, "the map is not the territory." To say this another way, the word is a representation of an idea, not the thing itself.

The **channel** is the medium used to send the message from the source to the receiver. DeVito's model did not include the channel, but certainly the way a message is sent is significant. The most intimate way to send a message is in face-to-face conversation, because it affords immediate feedback both verbally and nonverbally to both the source and the receiver. A source should choose the channel carefully, since each form offers an advantage or disadvantage over another type. The telephone gives us speed and distance, and while the visual presence of the receiver is absent, we still have the human voice that gives us some clues to educational level, age, gender, and perhaps the ethnicity of the receiver. Letters are a medium that affords a permanent record, and e-mail gives us access to the global network. But e-mail lacks some of the immediacy of other forms of communication. Other channels are newspapers, compact discs, and instant messaging; the channel is simply the means selected to send the message. So we need to decide what we want to communicate and then decide how to send it for maximum results.

All kinds of barriers to communication exist that stand between the source and the receiver, creating **noise** or *interference* in the *transmission* or *reception* of the message. There are two types of noise: physical and psychological. *Physical noise* is easy to explain. Anyone who has worked in a factory can understand that machines can operate so loudly that no one can hear over the din of the workplace. In such instances, people become very adept at sign language or nonverbal communication. Actual hearing loss is common in engineers or those who have worked in industrial plants, and rock concert aficionados who sit in front of blaring speakers that exceed the decibels for safe levels of sound are at risk. Another form of noise is *psychological noise,*

 which refers to those values, attitudes, and beliefs that have taught us to hate or fear other types of people. Sometimes these barriers are very conscious and embraced with rigor—a close-minded approach—and other times these prejudices are so deeply engrained through our upbringing that we are not even aware that we have become dogmatic and unfair in our treatment of other people and their ideas. Anything that interferes with the transmission or reception of a message, then, can be referred to as **noise**. Some sources or speakers have speech impediments, such as stuttering, that prevent them from communicating effectively; others in a specialized field such as medicine or science misread their audience and use **jargon** that only their colleagues understand. We have all been inundated with "geekspeak," which most often comes from someone overly impressed with himself who is talking to hear himself rather than to communicate with listeners.

Problems in communication can come from either end of the transaction; the source may lack language skills, have attitudinal abrasiveness, or exhibit behavioral mannerisms that impede her ability to communicate. The receiver may have decided up front that he did not like the source, the message, or anything about either, so the message was not even heard because of selective inattention. Further, the receiver may have been so busy counterarguing with the speaker that she missed the actual message altogether, or psychological barriers build a wall between the person who is speaking and us that is so impenetrable that nothing gets through. So how do we know that actual communication has occurred or that the receiver got the message? **Feedback** is the response given to the message that informs the source that the idea was transmitted successfully and interpreted and understood by the receiver. The response may be positive or negative, but if a response occurs, this assures that the message did get through and the **feedback loop** was completed. While DeVito's model did not include the word "feedback", it showed the arrows going from the source to the sender, which indicated that a response did occur. The **feedback loop** means simply that the message went from the speaker to the receiver and back again. Feedback is essential in all relationships if they are to be successful. Students want their graded tests back the day after they take the examination. When your boyfriend leaves a message, he expects you to call back as soon as you get it. Children need their parents to pay attention to what they have to tell them, and they want an immediate response. This principle of feedback is essential in families, at work, and in wider circles such as government. Many jobs are botched and millions in revenue lost because instructions were misunderstood; relationships are ruined and families disintegrate simply because questions were not asked, answers were not given, or attention was not paid.

The final concept in DeVito's model was **effects**. While we use that term loosely all the time when we speak of "effective communication," the actual definition of effects is hard to nail down. The effect of the message can be defined—as Edwin Black, a rhetorical critic, did many years ago—as the impact the message had immediately and through time (Black, 1965). Sometimes we do not respond to a message—whether it be a book we have read, a film we have seen, or a lecture we have attended—until years later when it floods back into our consciousness because something else evoked the idea as relevant and the meaning has expanded or taken on new significance. Sometimes there is no *discernible* effect of a speech, but this does not mean that there was none. A candidate measures the effect of a campaign by the number of votes she received and whether or not she won the election. Advertisers measure the success of their campaigns by the number of products sold, but how does one measure the effect that an idea has had on another's thought process? This effect is far more complicated to evaluate. DeVito went on to add an ethical dimension to communication effect. He said:

> To the degree that communication has an effect, it also has an ethical dimension. Because communication has consequences, there is a rightness–wrongness aspect to any communication act. Unlike principles of effective communication, principles of ethical communication are difficult if not impossible to formulate. Often we can observe the effect of communication and on the basis of the observations formulate principles of effective communication. But we cannot observe the rightness or wrongness of a communication act. The ethical dimension of communication is further complicated by the fact that it is so interwoven with one's personal philosophy of life that it is difficult to propose universal guidelines. (DeVito, 1982, p. 15)

Ethical considerations are at the center of any discussion of persuasion theory. DeVito identified this as the rightness–wrongness of any communication act. Throughout this book we discuss how people's moral compass has steered them into social justice and reform movements like civil rights or exposed them as liars or crooks that used others. Both the moral leader and the confidence man use persuasion to move people.

While DeVito wrote of universals, he was keenly aware of the specificity of any given communication transaction. We can think of right and wrong communication practices, but we know that the context in which the communication occurs imposes certain rules of correct conduct. Ultimately, judgments about ethics are unique to individuals as they decide how to conduct themselves as either speakers or receivers of messages. Just because a strategy is extremely effective does not mean that it is ethical. Look at the 2012 U.S. presidential election and the attack ads that ran in both the Democrats' and Republicans' campaigns. The ads were strategically useful, but should they have been used? While they were immediately effective in turning voters away from the targeted candidate, what were the long-term effects on the political process in this country? Cynicism seems to be a likely response to such rhetorical tactics. The effect of a message depends on a complex interplay between the source, message, and receiver based on similarity of attitudes, values, and beliefs held by the people involved.

The DeVito model implies even more than we have discussed here; for instance, we can interject that the history of the communicants is a significant factor in their ability to communicate with one another. We know that communication is dynamic, ongoing, and reflective of what went before. Ethics is the backdrop against which all human interaction must be weighed; we can always ask what would have happened ideally rather than what transpired. In persuasion, particularly where the intention is to move people to action, we must be mindful of what is right or wrong, what is the greatest good for the greatest number of people, and whose ends are being served by the speaker. These are ideals in rhetoric, but in practice such ideals are often violated.

RATIONALE: WHY STUDY PERSUASION?

Persuasion is a human activity that is as basic to a democratic society and the welfare of the people in it as the Constitution that guarantees U.S. citizens the freedom of speech, press, and religion, the right to assemble, and the right to petition our government for redress of grievance. In other words, persuasion and the First Amendment are counterparts of the same ideology, which posits that all people have the right to speak their minds and to be given a fair hearing. Any student who envisions a career in law, teaching, politics, journalism, medicine, ministry, counseling, diplomacy, or any other public endeavor will need to understand the dynamics of persuasion. On an interpersonal level, we practice persuasion every day as we negotiate with loved ones about how we will spend our money and our leisure time or continue our partnerships.

While the first books on rhetoric came from the Golden Age of Greece and the fifth century BC, humans develop some understanding of persuasion as they develop language skills, even before they have the ability to read. Therefore, it would be a fallacy to believe that

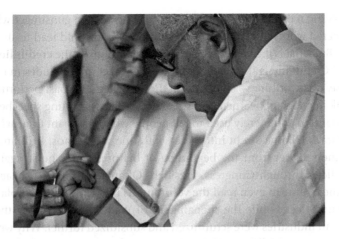

Medical professionals understand part of their capacity to get patients to comply with their directives depends upon their ability to persuade patients of their credibility and goodwill toward the patient.

persuasion began in the fifth century BC, since words and deeds intended to sway others existed from the beginning of human interaction. The creation story tells how Eve tempted Adam to eat of the forbidden fruit of knowledge and thus caused the fall from grace. We know that Julius Caesar had publicists, in the vein of contemporary press secretaries, who wrote of his great victories to rally support for his war efforts, and we know that ancient orators spoke convincingly of the virtues and vices of their rulers. Today we see both theories of persuasion and the practical applications of them used in every facet of American society. Frequently there is a struggle to see who will have the last word and whose words will strike the heart and imagination of the masses, but one of the measures of leadership is to communicate policies effectively to followers so that support can be maintained and resistance avoided. Words can create a communal bond that ties a nation together, or words can be used as weapons thrown at an enemy to injure their reputation, contain their power, or enlist others to march against them. Living in a post-9/11 world, we have become mindful of how words construct the social reality in which we live.

RHETORIC IN POLITICS

Rhetoric is to politics what oxygen is to the human organism—an essential energy force. No politician can exist without communicating programs, past achievements, and future policies with constituents and the mass audience. Beginning with the president, rhetoric establishes the political climate in which major decisions are made and fulfilled. We see this struggle played out in the Iraq war. In various speeches, former President George W. Bush attempted to establish the semantics of the "war on terror" while Donald Rumsfeld, then his secretary of defense, called it a "global struggle against the enemies of freedom, the enemies of civilization" (Holmes, 2005). When President Bush declared that Osama Bin Laden was wanted "dead or alive," many said that his rhetoric represented the Wild West language of the gunslinger when we needed measured, tempered words to lead us through a morass that could lead to the destruction of our civilization. But what is the value of words if the intentions or the **credibility** of the speaker is questionable? Credibility is the reputation of the speaker and includes many components such as expertise, trustworthiness, similarity to the audience, and past performances. It is impressive to speak in coherent, learned phrases, but what if these lilting speeches are as hollow as a Halloween lantern and merely used to tell people what they want to hear?

President Barack Obama swept into office with one of the most brilliant political campaigns ever witnessed, yet from the beginning of his presidency he struggled with words to usher his policies through Congress. President Obama's stimulus package was urgently embraced—without time to even read the voluminous bill, Congress complained—to bring recovery to "Main Street" while the shenanigans of Wall Street involving the banking and mortgage and loan industries were scrutinized and subsidized further. Why were those words selected—Main Street vs. Wall Street? What is going to happen to America's oldest general— General Motors? What is the tipping point between recovery of a sagging economy and a socialist agenda with government ownership where the free enterprise system used to negotiate supply and demand and quality control? Right now no one has the answers to these questions, but one unmistaken principle will determine the outcome of the ideological battle. The president's success is dependent upon his administration's ability to explain their actions, to persuade Congress and the American people that their policies are workable and right, and to convince the majority that this is "change we can believe in." President Obama has been masterful in communicating his ideas to the American people, but he will succeed or fail based on his ability to communicate his vision to this country and abroad in the coming years. The 2012 election cycle was a contentious one marked with language that was

The slogan *Forward* from Barak Obama's 2012 presidential campaign was a sharp contrast to the themes of *Hope* and *Change* from his 2008 campaign.

more common to barroom brawls than to statesmanlike discourse. As students of persuasion, we must have the tools to analyze the complex dynamic that exists between the speaker, words, values, and outcomes. This book is intended to supply the tools necessary to observe, analyze, comprehend, use, and evaluate competing messages that fill the marketplace of ideas.

We must understand that effective persuasion is a multifaceted endeavor that cavorts as readily with the angels as it does with Faustian bargains with the devil. Political rhetoric is a growing field within the discipline of rhetoric and public address.

Discussions about the relationship of rhetoric to events and assigning meaning to them are uniquely pertinent to political rhetoric. The presidency offers what Theodore Roosevelt called a "bully pulpit" from which to speak to the nation. FDR used the new medium of radio to console a nation enduring the Great Depression and approaching World War II when he delivered more than 40 fireside chats to U.S. audiences, telling Americans that they had nothing to fear but fear itself. Part of his rhetorical strategy was to invite the public into his homey office by the fireplace to discuss affairs of state; he was trying to display security in an intimate setting when there were great threats to our nation. Persuasive discourse is part of leadership and goes back to the times of Julius Caesar.

Aristotle (330 BCE/1954) defined **rhetoric** as "the faculty of observing in any given case the available means of persuasion" (p. 24). Further, he noted that unlike geometry or medicine, rhetoric does not have its own subject matter; it involves ideas about any field of inquiry. Therefore, persuasion uses every discipline, and since it requires advocacy of a position or perspective, it can be used for evil as well as for good purposes. Throughout history, examples of rhetorical movements that have led people into dangerous territory are legendary. McCarthyism reflects such abuses of power when blacklists and witch-hunts existed because of the ranting of one man and his cohorts in government against communist spies and infiltrators.

During the 1950s and the Cold War, Senator Joseph McCarthy had the power to ruin careers by accusing leaders of being communists or "Reds." He always carried a briefcase, which he claimed contained files on enemies of the state; hence, he was called the briefcase demagogue. A **demagogue** is one who tries to stir up the people to achieve his own selfish ends, generally power and wealth. In retrospect, we ask why anyone would believe Senator McCarthy since he was unveiled as a great liar. During the 1950s, the political climate of fear of growing Soviet power created a fertile ground for McCarthy to plant the seeds of mistrust and suspicion. Surprisingly, it was the media that helped bring him to power, and it was the televised congressional hearings that would bring him down. Where there is fear and distrust, like that following 9/11, the ground is fertile for demagogues to spread rumors and to play upon the worst instincts of people.

After 9/11 and during the Iraq War, some speakers were accused of going too far in criticizing the war and former President Bush, while others said ethical lapses, such as the Abu Ghraib prison abuses, occurred because someone did not speak out sooner in favor of moral principles or constitutional freedoms. The naming of initiatives coming out of the Bush White House clearly illustrated rhetorical efforts to win support for policies such as the Patriot Act, which entitled the government to step up surveillance efforts through interception of communication between suspected members of al Qaeda and individuals within the United States. Private data that could be reviewed or accessed included library records, financial records, and other material generally protected through privacy rights. But critics felt that trying to speak critically about the Patriot Act made them appear unpatriotic and made it easier for the Bush administration to question their support for the protection of the American people from another attack. The president framed the argument and terms of the act so that any criticism was seen as "unpatriotic."

An important function of rhetoric is naming or labeling things and people. In a climate of fear and demonization of the enemy, people are more likely to endorse repression than to embrace the First Amendment and the rights guaranteed for free speech and a robust press. Scholars of persuasion are concerned not only with content and messages but also with the person who is sending the message. The character and goodwill of the individual are as important as what they have to say.

What is central to all measures of discourse is truth, with an ethical climate that will choose the interest of the people over the vested interest of the opportunist, the racist, the sexist, or the CEO who has jettisoned the welfare of the workers for his golden parachute to retirement with multiple homes, yachts, and wealth. Look at the recent investment, banking, and mortgage scandals and imagine what went wrong with those organizations.

Aristotle said a **rhetor,** which is a public speaker, should be a man of good character speaking well. Neither of these requirements—virtue of character and communication skills—is simple, but Aristotle believed that through good habits of living, where goodness is a habit of choice, both attributes are possible.

RHETORIC IN LAW

Persuasion is central to the judicial system and the people who have chosen professions in jurisprudence. While judges and attorneys must be experts in the law, they must also know how to communicate what they know convincingly. Court proceedings are dramatic, sometimes with all the tension or comic relief of good theater. Accused felons are coached by the defense attorney on how to testify before the jury so that their version of the truth is more palatable than that offered by the prosecutor. Even the most brutal offenders of social order will be dressed in a clean-cut manner, prepared to make consistent arguments, and coached to present their version of events to win the confidence and sympathy of the jury. Attractive people receive lower sentences and fines, and those who use "powerful speech," that is, without hedges, qualifiers, and hesitancies in their voices, are seen as more credible. Nonverbal factors such as clothing, vocal qualities, posture, and facial expression are all part of the message. Anyone who hopes to practice law must be an effective communicator and an effective persuader since they use all forms of appeals to win their cases, including personal power. These nonverbal attributes, found in appearance and **vocalics,** which are vocal qualities such as rate, pitch, inflection, and dialect, are persuasive because they communicate control, power, and status.

Lawyers like Clarence Darrow and William Jennings Bryan have argued great issues through time, such as the controversy between creationism and evolution in the Scopes

Monkey Trial in Tennessee in 1921, where John Scopes, a young biology teacher, was teaching evolution in his classes. Scopes was prosecuted and fined for his transgressions against the state law that forbade teaching anything but divine creation, but later evolution would be declared the scientific theory that educators should adopt for their curriculum. Scientific theories can be either facilitated or obstructed by rhetorical advocates or opponents, as with the current disagreements over climate change, its causes, and its remedies. Further, great moral issues such as abortion and the death penalty are argued in many tribunals before they reach the court of last resort—the U.S. Supreme Court.

The **Socratic method** employs leading questions to enable jurors, students, and other audiences to discover the truth. Lawyers are skilled in controlling the chain of logic that leads to an inexorable conclusion about their client's innocence or the adversary's guilt. A trial is built on a coherent picture that integrates witnesses, evidence, artifacts, and a convincing narrative, which the lawyer constructs. The ability to communicate these facts effectively and persuasively is a matter of life and death in many cases.

RHETORIC IN RELIGION

We know that rhetoric is central to the life of any politician, but it is essential in the life of holy men and women as well. Religious leaders from all denominations are dependent upon their communication skills to carry the message of their faith to the congregations whom they serve. One minister, Rick Warren, wrote a best-selling book titled *"The Purpose Driven Life—What on Earth Am I Here for?,"* which resonated with a national audience (Warren, 2002). As pastor of the Saddleback Church in Lake Forest, California, some say that his work has created not just a book but a social movement. His work gained further recognition when a young widow, Ashley Smith, was being held captive in Georgia by a man who had just shot a judge in a courtroom along with three other people in a two-day killing spree. During the 24 hours that Brian Nichols held Smith in her apartment, she pleaded with him not to kill her because her husband had been murdered four years earlier and she had a little girl to raise. She read to Nichols a passage from Warren's book that dealt with the purpose that each individual has in life. While millions had read the book, perhaps none experienced the same dramatic effect that it had on her and the man whom she tried to convince to turn himself in to authorities and allow her to live. The next day he permitted her to walk out of her apartment, and then she reported his location to police officers, who removed him without further bloodshed (A. Smith, personal communication).

Despite the fact that the secular and the profane exist alongside the sacred dimensions of society, there is a search for spirituality that those in the ministry fulfill. It is obvious that messages that have powerful effects on some listeners can be rejected by others because they hold different beliefs or ideologies. Ashley Smith talked to Brian Nichols as a Christian; she quoted scriptures to him and told him that he came to her for a purpose—to turn himself in to authorities and to end the wanton murders that began in the courtroom. Religious leaders use persuasion daily as they exhort followers of their faith to embrace the sacred teachings of their denominations, and they fulfill multiple roles as scholars, teachers, administrators, and role models for the flock.

Ashley Smith was able to persuade Brian Nichols, who had already murdered four people, to allow her to walk out of her apartment where he had held her at gunpoint.

RHETORIC IN ART AND FILM

The role of persuasion in politics, religion, law, advertising, and public relations are obvious, but there are more subtle means of influencing others that are below the level of consciousness, or covert. Much of what passes for entertainment is quite persuasive. Art, literature, and drama popularize powerful positions regarding all manner of taboo subject matter. *Brokeback Mountain*, a movie nominated for multiple awards in 2006, was criticized by many as an attempt by the film industry to make homosexuality acceptable by presenting two virile cowboys who led deceitful lives by marrying and having children with women but finally realized that they were living a charade. The two lover's lives were tormented by their separation and the appearances they tried to maintain because of the fear of discovery and reprisals. Many saw the film as a love story with a tragic ending, while others saw it as another indicator of the culture war against traditional family values. Another persuasive movie was *Rain Man* (1988), starring Dustin Hoffman, which depicted the life of an autistic person and brought a hidden form of mental illness to the public's awareness at a time when mental illness was a taboo subject. The film *Shawshank Redemption* portrayed the brutality of prison life with a corrupt warden and guards who exploited all the prisoners, including one who was innocent. John Singleton's movie *Boys N' the Hood* opened with a scene showing African

American prisoners reaching out of the bars with a voice-over saying, "A mind is a terrible thing to waste." The movie proceeded to portray families in South Central Los Angeles, where gang activity and drive-by shootings were regular occurrences. Only two of the young people escaped the neighborhood to attend college, while many died in gang violence. The message was heavy-handed, but it was memorable. The overriding message was that a strong, loving father figure could save and separate youth from gangs, which offered identity, affection, and protection but ultimately only death and violence to the young men who joined them. As audiences came out of the theaters after attending these thought-provoking movies, discussions continued and reflection occurred about what they had just experienced. In other words, persuasion occurred as attitudes were being examined and perhaps changed through the power of narrative and emotional involvement.

Art exhibits, sculptures, and other works of art evoke powerful responses in receivers. George Gerbner (1994) created the **cultivation theory** to explain that heavy viewers of television believed the world to be a "mean" place because of the violence they saw regularly. He said this "mean world syndrome" was evident in heavy television viewers. Gerbner believed that the ideas that individuals are exposed to, especially children, cultivate their views of the world. Further, he stated that if you knew the stories that a society tells its children, then you could understand the values and beliefs of that culture. He called television the "electronic storyteller" (Jhally, 1997). While we are enjoying the entertainment medium, we are being influenced by messages that are both **subliminal,** or below the conscious level, and others that are very propagandistic, or slanted in such a way as to lead you to a foregone conclusion. The **elaboration likelihood model** (ELM) can be useful in explaining why entertainment does far more than amuse us.

> Thus, the ELM posits that for the sake of simplicity, persuasion can be thought of as following one of two routes to persuasion: central and peripheral. More specifically, in their pure form the two routes to attitude change correspond to anchoring points on an elaboration continuum. The central route entails attitude change that requires much effort and thought to reach a decision. For example carefully scrutinizing the merits of the substantive information in a message and integrating one's thoughts into a coherent position are prototypical actions based on the central route on persuasion. The second route, the peripheral route, entails attitude change that occurs primarily when elaboration is low, and it can involve thought processes that are quantitatively or qualitatively different from the high elaboration central route. For example, a low elaboration processor might carefully scrutinize only the first argument or two rather than all of them (quantitative differences in processing) or might process all of the arguments by counting them rather than scrutinizing them for merit (qualitative differences). (Petty et al., 2004, p. 67)

This idea is explored and applied more fully in later chapters, but we know that when our defenses are down, as in entertainment situations where we are distracted, the peripheral pathways to our brains are being used rather than our central processing units, which utilize our critical faculties. Art is a very powerful medium of persuasion with artists, playwrights, and poets revealing truths to us often before the rest of the population comprehends it.

RHETORIC IN ADVERTISING AND PUBLIC RELATIONS

Advertising and public relations are recognized fields where persuasion is essential to successful campaigns. Advertising focuses on products, whereas public relations is a management function that focuses on the total image, communication network, and educational component of the organization. **Integrated marketing communication (IMC)** is an approach that includes all facets of communicating with consumers in a world cluttered with consumer goods and advertising intended to gain customer loyalty. More money is spent on advertising in the United States than in any other country. On Super Bowl Sunday, many viewers tune in to watch the commercials rather than the football game. The Budweiser frogs and the Clydesdale horses that pull the beer wagon will be remembered long after certain players are traded to other teams or retire from football. Babies talking about E*TRADE and other advertisements arrest our attention briefly before we channel-surf or stop at the sexy Axe commercial. These images are intended to get us to remember a brand, to like it, and to buy it. Media-savvy consumers need to understand these appeals and why they work.

Public relations firms enlist professionals who are expert in strategies for creating, maintaining, or repairing the image of government agencies, corporations, or individuals. Edward Bernays, sometimes called the father of public relations, defined public relations as the "engineering of consent" through the rights given in the First Amendment to practitioners and to mass media (Bernays, 1952, p. 159). Although he established the framework for his practices in the early part of the twentieth century, his ideas still have validity. Bernays spoke of

how American businesses spent "fabulous sums of money" to sell "the American way of life" (Bernays, 1952, p. 336). He was one of the first to use polls, to understand that businesses sold dreams as well as products, and to use scientific research in his work. He said:

> I think that the ideal public relations man should, first of all, be a man of character and integrity, who has acquired a sense of judgment and logic without having lost the ability to think creatively and imaginatively. He should be truthful and discreet; he should be objective, yet possessed of a deep interest in the solution of problems. From his broad cultural background, he should have developed considerably intellectual curiosity; and he should have effective powers of analysis and synthesis along with the rare quality of intuition. And with all these characteristics, he should be trained in the social sciences and in the mechanics of public relations. (Bernays, 1952, p. 126)

Bernays said that salesmanship was a basic principle in the free enterprise system, so he approached the analysis of customers as a social scientist enquiring into the nature of attitudes. He said customers can be approached in three ways: first, we can intensify an existing attitude; second, negate an unfavorable attitude; and third, convert a passive attitude into an active one (Bernays, 1952, p. 216). The advice that he gave throughout his writings dealt with how to be a better persuader through the understanding of human nature, through the study of the situation, product, or intended task, and needs that were invisible.

Persuasion uses symbols to define our social reality, to set goals for our nation, and to explain what we ought to be doing to achieve a more just society; therefore, to study persuasion, one must also study semantics, the code of discourse. One must be a scholar of human nature who can analyze the character of the speaker as well as the audience that they hope to influence. Many of the most corrupt and evil persons in history presented themselves as reformers or creators of a utopian vision for their followers. In order to understand why people are convinced that one leader, a particular religion, or one product is better than another, we need to know human motivation. For example, why did young voters like and identify with Howard Dean when many older voters thought he was an unstable man on the edge of sanity as he gave his enthusiastic primal scream about what the Democrats were going to do in the 2004 election? Similarly, in 2008, an army of young people rushed to support Barack Obama, granting him "rock star" status, according to media commentators, as they elected him president of the United States. His messages of "hope" and "change we can believe in" resonated with their passions for a different vision for this country.

As the foregoing discussion of applied persuasion indicates, persuasion can be seen in both obvious and more covert ways. Each field introduced here is explained more fully in coming chapters, but whether we are aware of it or not, persuasive discourse saturates our everyday life. The bumper stickers that we saw at the stoplight on the way to work, the billboards along the highway, and the T-shirt the student behind you in class was wearing with his favorite band imprinted on it all sent messages that you did not choose to view, but most likely you responded to them anyway. Some of these messages may have evoked laughter, anger, or a nod of approval from you. Our response depends on our unique characteristics as a receiver and the view of the world that we carry around in our heads.

RECEIVER-FOCUSED COMMUNICATION

The simplest communication model is source–message–receiver. A critic or scholar of communication could focus on any aspect of this simple model, but persuasion focuses on the receiver and is dependent upon his or her consent to be successful. Many communication studies focus on the speaker or source of a message, especially great orators such as

The Internet's "global village" was envisioned and named by Marshall McLuhan as the electronic age was extending human consciousness into the Information Age.

Abraham Lincoln or Martin Luther King Jr. Others analyze the channels of communication, or the medium by which the message is sent, such as radio and television; as Marshall McLuhan said: "The medium is the message" (McLuhan & Powers, 1989). The Internet with blogs, websites, Twitter, and other communication capabilities has changed the political landscape, the nature of education, commerce, and even recruitment for hate groups. We shift through the new technologies to understand what 24-hour newscasts have done to the political process or to public discourse on matters of national importance. Following the presidential debates, pollsters report how the audience responded to the candidates, their message, and their images. But rhetorical discourse is a **receiver-centered** form of communication, meaning that the outcome depends on what the audience thinks about the speaker, not what the speaker thinks about himself or herself.

Cultural myths and allegories are also part of persuasion, with people waiting for a candidate to save them from economic doom, the enemy, or a corrupt society. Like theater, many personas are portrayed, with some favorites being the war hero, the astute businessman, the outsider who has not been corrupted by power and remains close to the people, the patriot who will stand up to any threat with courage, and the closer, like President Lyndon Johnson, who bragged that before he went to Capitol Hill he always had his ducks lined up in a row. In other words, persuaders attempt to find out what moves an audience and then tap into that energy source or source of power to win followers.

Audiences have to sift through "mere rhetoric" or mass media's "spin" to decipher the truth, and at the very heart of their decision is their opinion of the speaker, the logic of the message, and their perceptions of how each of these appeals to their own needs, wants, and belief system. The complex dynamic between a speaker and members of the audience is difficult to comprehend because the response to messages, campaigns, or appeals is so individualized. Each of us decides whether to support a given candidate, donate to a particular cause, or support artists by buying their movies or CDs or going to their concerts. Why would some people follow a fanatical, self-styled prophet even unto their own death when other folks, even family members, tell them that the cause is insane? If we understood all of this, we could easily explain how Jim Jones caused 913 people to die in Jonestown, Guyana, how David Koresh won the loyalty of the Branch Davidians who died in Waco, Texas, and how Charles Manson convinced his "family" to commit murder in the desert. Clearly, when persuasion goes awry and becomes propaganda or indoctrination, which demands the opposite of thoughtful decision making, all manner of excess is possible. How does one distinguish between a worthy cause and a cult that demands absolute obedience and commitment to the leader? Clearly, one should beware of any leader, cause, or community that demands that you deny your own morality and intellect to become a member.

DISTINCTIONS BETWEEN INFORMATIVE SPEECH, PERSUASION, AND PROPAGANDA

If you can imagine a continuum that has three stations, none of which is wholly distinct from another as one type merges into another, we can begin to focus on the similarities and differences between persuasion and other forms of speech. First, there is **informative speech**, which instructs us about ideas, people, and events. Simple math can demonstrate this principle: we know that two plus two equals four, and that April 1 is known as April Fool's Day. These are facts that can be verified; the focus is on the transmission and comprehension of knowledge. Second, there is **persuasion,** which not only transmits information, as in the first instance, but also aims to convince or influence others to believe certain ideas, adopt a defined attitude toward others, or engage in a certain action or behavior. Persuasion uses many strategies to influence people and move them to action, so it is a **receiver-centered** form of communication. Persuasive campaigns aim to deter people from drinking and driving, having sex without protection, or eating Big Macs, which contribute to the epidemic of obesity. In this realm, people still have choices, and this form of communication exists between rational discourse and the extreme on the other end of the spectrum, propaganda. Jowett and O'Donnell (2006) define **propaganda** as "the deliberate, systematic attempt to shape perceptions, manipulate cognitions, and direct behavior to achieve a response that furthers the desired intent of the propagandist" (p. 7). In Latin *propaganda* means simply "to propagate" or "to sow." The origin of the term can be found in the Catholic Church:

> In 1622, the Vatican established the *Sacra Congregatio de Propaganda Fide*, meaning the sacred congregation for propagating the faith of the Roman Catholic Church. Because the propaganda of the Roman Catholic Church had as its intent spreading the faith to the New World, as well as opposing Protestantism, the word *propaganda* lost its neutrality, and subsequent usage has rendered the term pejorative. To identify a message as propaganda is to suggest something negative and dishonest. Words frequently used as synonyms for *propaganda* are *lies, distortion, deceit, manipulation, mind control, psychological warfare, brainwashing, and palaver.* (Jowett & O'Donnell, 2006, p. 2)

Propaganda is a form of indoctrination that has extended persuasion beyond the realm of ethics into the arena of objectifying people to be used for questionable ends. Propaganda uses informative speech, persuasive tactics, as well as the more unethical means outlined earlier. Propaganda has as its goals those similar to persuasion, except that the objectives have been determined **a priori**, or from the beginning. Propaganda functions to direct perception, cognition, behavior, and maybe all three of these to achieve goals that have been predetermined by the propagandist. Frequently the propagandist will be a charismatic individual who promises a utopian society but who actually is interested only in domination or power. Adolf Hitler would be a prime example of this form of leader. He convinced Germans that if only they could rid the country of Jews, then all the economic, social, and personal problems of the German people would be solved. As his power and ambition grew, the Holocaust was actualized with the death of over 6 million Jews, including women and children. Prison camps existed in Poland, Germany, and France. A veteran of World War II recounted the story of when the Americans marched into France and entered a prison camp where bodies were piled as high as the ceiling of an average room with two of the people still breathing. Before the soldiers could separate them from those who had already died, the last two prisoners died also. Revisionist historians are minimizing the record or denying it altogether. It will be a rhetorical task to determine whose view of history will be adopted and preserved in the coming centuries, especially since those who survived and participated in that war are becoming fewer. Their truths will die with them in some instances, since no one recorded them. Propaganda is treated more fully in coming chapters in relation to Jacques Ellul's warnings about how the technological society conditions people, especially intellectuals, to believe propaganda through *la technique* because it is not a discontinuous thing but immerses the whole society with loudspeakers, radio, television, newspapers, and magazines (Ellul, 1968, p. 9). Ellul wrote before the Internet was created, so the influence of media now is global without the checks and balances that editors or censors used to exercise.

The source of some leaders' power is not easily identified. **Charisma** is a term that comes from the Greeks, who believed that the magic that some leaders had that caused others to follow them with great devotion was a divine gift from the gods. When we look at historical figures, it is difficult to imagine why millions would support and die for tyrants. Not all charismatic figures are tyrannical, though; some transcend everyday leaders through their goodness, like Mother Theresa, the nun who served the poor in India until her death, or Sir Winston Churchill, who distinguished himself for his courage and leadership of the English people through World War II as their cities were being bombed by the Axis powers.

Informative speech transmits facts; persuasive speech changes attitudes, beliefs and behavior; and propaganda uses deceit to carry people to a predetermined end, which serves the goals of the propagandist over the welfare of the people. They can be summarized as follows:

Informative Speech	Persuasion	Propaganda
message-centered	receiver-centered	receiver-centered
cognition	beliefs, attitude,	deception common
critical thinking	and behavior	coercion or obedience
comprehension of ideas	critical thinking with choice	one-sided, distortion
	advocacy of a position	

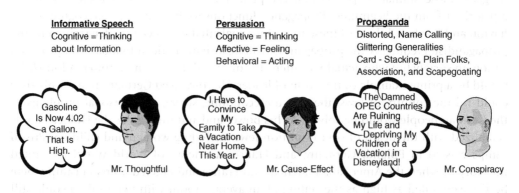

FIGURE 1.2   Informative speech, persuasion, and propaganda.

DEFINITION OF PERSUASION

I define persuasion in the following manner: *Persuasion is a form of communication that employs both verbal and nonverbal symbols that intend to influence receivers to voluntarily change attitudes, values, beliefs, and behaviors to agree with those supported by the advocate of the message.* Inherent in this definition is the notion that there is an interplay of influence between the source or speaker and the audience or receiver. The code or language that is used is primary in that it furnishes the structure, meaning, and feel of the message. The psychological, social, and political ground that each participant occupies becomes definitive as well. To the extent that the source can influence the receiver to share his version of truth as legitimate and desirable, they will probably be successful in the persuasion attempt, but to the extent that each continues to occupy different positions or ground there will be no consent or agreement. Kenneth Burke called this state of consonance *identification,* wherein the receiver's ideas were in alignment with those of the source (Burke, 1969, p. 55). Persuasive discourse aims at creating a state of consonance or harmony between the speaker and the audience so that the receivers are willing to accept the message, adopt the necessary beliefs or attitudes, and ultimately act on the basis of this agreement. Whether a state of harmony is created or not depends on what positions the receivers already possessed. Often the speaker only alienates the audience members further if they are already resistant to the idea being espoused because of deeply held values such as the sanctity of life. The debates on abortion illustrate this polarization, with fixed positions that are resistant to argument or evidence. Abortion is such a pivotal issue that it defeats candidates, obstructs larger congressional bills such as the national health proposal, and individually torments some who seek choice but confront denial of communion in their church because of it.

RHETORICAL EFFORTS IN INTERNATIONAL DISPUTES

The truth is never simple, but if fear, power relations, and bad blood from the past contaminate the rhetorical climate, there is little hope for resolution and respect for differences. The stakes are too high to dismiss our responsibility to know as much about persuasion as we can. For example, the former president of Iran, Mahmoud Ahmadinejad, talked about wiping Israel off the map and stated that the Holocaust never actually happened. Further, he ignored attempts to stop any development of nuclear power and potentially nuclear weapons in Iran. While the United States, Germany, France, and Britain are trying to get Russia and China to find some common ground to go to the International Atomic Energy Agency's board of governors, there are Arab nations that love the position that Iran has placed Israel's friends in politically. So rhetoric separates friends from enemies and defines courses of action that are intended to win the support of various factions. We can imagine the internal dialog from the Arab nations that say, "We only want to be able to defend ourselves from invasion and occupation from the superpowers." Friends of Israel might say, "How could anyone trust nations who distort the history of the world in this manner? Their goal is not autonomy, but dominance in the region, which would include driving Israel into the sea." Former Secretary of State Hillary Clinton spoke about international sanctions and isolating Iran, but clearly two different worldviews are in conflict.

DAS VOLK WÄHLT LISTE 1

NATIONALSOZIALISTEN

This poster was used to announce the political campaign for the Nazi party in Germany indicating that they were number one with the swastika as a foundation and throngs of people entering the symbol to vote for the National Socialists.

Our very survival may depend on exposing the propagandist who uses words as Hitler did in his campaigns to create what he called the "fifth column." He used leaflets, speeches, and broadcasts to demoralize neighboring countries so that they believed that they would be defeated before the German army arrived. Propaganda was used to prepare the way for armed conflict. Persuasion enlists rational decision making, appeals to moral purposes, and offers choices where propaganda extends to subversion and coercion.

THE FUNCTIONS OF PERSUASION

One way to examine persuasion is to see what it does or how it functions. The list presented here includes some of the primary applications of persuasion:

- names or defines people, ideas, and things
- creates a social reality by focusing on some dimensions and ignoring others
- establishes a code of conduct or ethics by which to judge people, actions, and programs
- offers an historical context for a culture that describes a past, present, and future vision
- exhorts receivers to change beliefs, attitudes, behaviors, and values
- unifies the group by reinforcing common ground and divides them from enemies who compete for power
- offers products for consumption, candidates for office, and movements to support some ideology or social change
- employs ways and means to achieve goals

Throughout the text, we apply these functions to various cases to see how persuasion works to identify friends or define enemies, create attitudes and stimulate actions, and create a vision that will be embraced or resisted. These functions are fulfilled through the use of language, even though we sometimes feel divided into tribes or foreign territories even within our own communities or households.

SUMMARY

This chapter explained the DeVito communication model and discussed each part of what he called the universals of communication. The role that persuasion plays in the fields of politics, law, religion, art and film, advertising, and public relations was introduced. Persuasion was defined with an emphasis on both verbal and nonverbal properties that are intended to influence receivers, therefore; persuasion is a receiver-centered form of communication. The definition of persuasion was given: *Persuasion is a form of communication that employs both verbal and nonverbal symbols that intend to influence receivers to voluntarily change attitudes, values, beliefs, and behaviors to agree with those supported by the advocate of the message.* Persuasion was distinguished from informative speech and propaganda on a continuum, with the characteristics of each form discussed. The functions of persuasion were outlined and demonstrated with examples that included international affairs. The rationale for studying persuasion was shown because it overshadows every field of endeavor, and those who understand the dynamics of rhetoric will be better positioned in their personal, professional, and social life.

In the next chapter, research from scholars who have written widely in the field of rhetoric is discussed. This will enable us to understand various positions on persuasion and how it has changed through the years. Each of the fields introduced in this chapter is examined more thoroughly in the text as we look more closely at how persuasion is applied in various disciplines. As this introduction shows, persuasion is a significant form of communication that affects us at an interpersonal level, in our professional life, and in the national and international arenas.

APPLICATIONS

1. How successful are you in influencing people to listen to what you have to say? What skills do you have to win agreement in debates at school or at work? Are you more convinced by rational arguments based on logic or emotional arguments that make you feel sympathy or anger toward the subject?
2. Choose a successful leader on either the national or local scene and analyze his or her appeal. Why do you believe that he or she has credibility? Do you know other leaders who lack credibility? How could they have changed this public perception?
3. Using the DeVito model and other variables discussed in this chapter, analyze a controversy or debate that was resolved or one that remains troublesome. Apply the following terms: *communication context, source, encode, message, channel, receiver, decode, noise, feedback, effect, ethics,* and *field of experience.* Try to identify in your case study what was effective or ineffective communication in that instance.
4. What role do you believe persuasion will play in your future profession?

5. When did "propaganda" become a pejorative term? Is "rhetoric" also a negative term?

6. Read news accounts about the Ashley Smith/Brian Nichols story. Identify all the means of persuasion that she used to convince him to let her go. Why was she successful? Was it something that she did, or was he already looking for a way out of his situation? What common bonds did they share?

7. Think of a recent movie that you have seen and do a rhetorical critique of it based on what the lead character was trying to communicate. What lessons could be taken from the story line? What attitudes did the various characters represent? Did you feel differently about the subject matter after you viewed the movie? Did it reinforce your existing attitudes, or did it make you feel more negative or more positive toward the matter? Discuss the movie with a group in class or with friends. Did it affect them the same way that it did you? Why or why not?

REFERENCES

Aristotle. (1954). *Rhetoric* (W. R. Roberts, Trans.). New York: The Modern Library. (Original work 330 BCE)

Bernays, E. L. (1952). *Public relations*. Norman: University of Oklahoma Press.

Black, E. (1965). *Rhetorical criticism: A study in method*. New York: The MacMillan Company.

Burke, K. (1969). *A rhetoric of motives*. Berkeley and Los Angeles: University of California Press.

DeVito, J. (1982). *Communicology: An introduction to the study of communication* (2nd ed.). New York: Harper & Row.

Ellul, J. (1968). *Propaganda: The formation of men's attitudes* (K. Kellen & J. Lerner, Trans.). New York: Knopf.

Gerbner, G. (1994). Reclaiming our cultural mythology: The ecology of justice. *In Context: A Quarterly of Humane Sustainable Culture, 38* (Spring), 40. Retrieved April 3, 2006, from http:www .context.org/ICLIB/IC38/Gerbner.htm.

Holmes, D. R. (2005, August 4). *Renaming the war: It's not just semantics*. Retrieved August 10, 2006, from http://www.foxnews.com.

Jhally, Sut, director. (1997). *The electronic storyteller: Television and the cultivation of values*. In the series *George Gerbner on media and culture*. Northampton, MA: Media Education Foundation.

Jowett, G. S., & O'Donnell, V. (2006). *Propaganda and persuasion* (4th ed.). Thousand Oaks, CA: Sage.

McLuhan, M., & Powers, B. R. (1989). *The global village: Transformations in world life and media in the 21st century*. New York: Oxford University Press.

Petty, R. E., Rucker, D. D., Bizer, G. Y., & Cacioppo, J. T. (2004). The elaboration likelihood model of persuasion. In J. S. Seiter & R. H. Gass (Eds.), *Perspectives on persuasion, social influence and compliance gaining* (pp. 65–89). Boston: Pearson/AB.

Warren, R. (2002). *The purpose driven life*. Grand Rapids, MI: Zondervan.

CHAPTER 2

RHETORICAL SCHOLARS:
PERSPECTIVES ON RHETORIC

KEY WORDS

allegory of the cave	hermaneutics	narrative theory
artistic proofs	homiletics	paradigm
coherence	identification	*pathos*
common ground	Ideograph	political rhetoric
credibility	inartistic proofs	Rank Model
epideictic rhetoric	inoculate	Sophists
ethos	*la technique*	*topos*
fidelity	*logos*	
forensic rhetoric	myth	

PREVIEW

This chapter offers perspectives in rhetoric from the Greek Sophists and their critics, Plato and Aristotle, to Cicero and Quintilian from the Roman empire, through some current writers like Kenneth Burke and Walter Fisher. Since this book is not a history of rhetoric, the chronological record is by necessity incomplete, jumping from the roots of rhetoric to more modern writers. After students read this chapter, they will be familiar with the key words herein and the theories that apply them. The **Sophists** began the tradition of teaching rhetoric and were paid to teach pupils to use persuasion to succeed in Athens. Plato wrote of the nature of knowledge and the realm of ideas, while Aristotle, his pupil, wrote of how we apply reasoning to arrive at knowledge. Cicero classified the skills necessary for speech making, and Quintilian became the best known rhetorician in the Classical period. Christian teaching and preaching emerged between the classical period and the eighteenth century, and various perspectives are presented to represent their ideas. Kenneth Burke focused on how we use or misuse symbols to align or identify our views with others. Walter Fisher viewed humans as storytellers who understood the world through experience more readily than through expert proofs or rules of logic. Jacques Ellul offered *la technique*, the use of propaganda to achieve the goals of a technological society to integrate the public and to immerse them in a mindset that would create conformity and beliefs that would galvanize them to action. Hugh Rank offered a model to analyze persuasion and propaganda through intensification and downplay schema that employed various communication strategies that will be discussed. Michael Calvin McGee explained how mass consciousness or ideology is created through an analysis of how language cultivates "Ideographs," which exert control or adherence to the cultural imperatives of a society. Although all of these scholars differ in their approaches to understanding the communication process and rhetoric, they share an interest in analyzing how human beings conceive their world and share it with others.

THE SOPHISTS: THE FIRST RHETORICIANS

In the fifth century BCE the Athenians and Spartans had expelled the Persians and were experiencing an era of affluence, exuberance, and creativity. They had instituted democracy, and average citizens were serving as legislators, executives, bureaucrats, and soldiers. This widespread participation in government by amateurs brought a "verbal explosion" in which "men argued, debated, soliloquized, declaimed, contradicted, orated" (Jarrett, 1969, p. 3). The man most gifted with words became the victor. With this explosion of verbiage the need for teachers arose, and the Sophists, the first professional teachers in Greece, were there to instruct the children of the wealthy—who wanted them to fill political, diplomatic, or economic leadership roles. Their educational philosophies would influence the next thousand years of teaching. They derived their name from *sophia*, meaning wisdom, cleverness, or skill. They claimed to teach wisdom and virtue for a fee, while their critics, like Isocrates and Plato, claimed that their motives were mostly the fees and that only philosophers could teach truth or virtue. Their ascendancy occurred during a time of change in Greece where religion, science, and power were being challenged, and as teachers they taught their pupils to confront conventions without remorse of conscience. They used the theories of science, language, and religion to make their arguments convincing. Greece was an oral culture, and many of the

 books written by leading Sophists like Protagoras were lost. Later writers like Plato and Aristotle included the Sophists' ideas in their works, which have survived. The Sophists used "antilogic," or arguments that used contradictory propositions. Students argued both sides of the issue, which led critics to claim that they had no interest in truth, only money and display. When the Sophists came to Athens, they created great excitement. They tried to explain human affairs without reference to the gods, which irritated and excited the Greeks at the same time (Rankin, 1983, p. 29).

The Sophist movement is important to rhetoric and is entangled with the skills of prosecution and defense. Many tributaries of thought arrived at Greece around 466 BCE, when democracy was established, and numerous court cases required speakers to overthrow unconstitutional laws (Rankin, 1983, p. 24). Many attribute the discovery of rhetoric to Corax, who focused on forensic speech, which he taught exclusively for courts of law. A question arose concerning whether Corax should be paid if his student lost a case because many Greeks were contemptuous of the fees the Sophists charged. (If every teacher were held accountable for every one of their students' success, many of us would be bankrupt.)

Protagoras was a friend of Pericles and one of the best known Sophists. He was charged in 444 BCE by the Athenians with creating a constitution for the colony of Thurii in Italy (Rankin, 1983, p. 27). He is most quoted for writing, "Man is the measure of all things," which means that he believed that humans are the only valid measure of reality (Rankin, 1983, p. 33). Even though perceptions vary, they cannot be called false because Protagoras believed in the social virtue that each individual possessed. He was an agnostic, meaning that he did not deny the existence of the gods, but rather was a skeptic regarding them. He said he could not establish their existence, their appearance, or anything else because of the shortness of life and the obscurity of the subject (Rankin, 1983, p. 33). This skepticism earned him the wrath of the Athenians. Protagoras maintained that it was impossible to know the existence of the gods and that, even if they did exist, he lacked the ability to communicate their nature accurately.

Gorgias was an influential Sophist who was born in Sicily about 480 BCE and came to Athens in 427 BCE as an ambassador seeking an alliance against the Syracusans. He was famous enough to be satirized by Aristophanes in *The Wasps* and in *The Birds*. He was a great orator whose techniques would influence Greek and Roman teaching for a century (Rankin, 1983, p. 36). Gorgias urged Greeks to unite against the Persians and to stop the Peloponnesian Wars. His funeral oration for the dead was pan-Hellenic. His best student, Isocrates (436–338 BCE), continued Gorgias's call for unity between Athens and Sparta. Some accounts say Gorgias lived to be a hundred years old. He was aware of the distortion between the word for a thing and the thing itself. In that respect he predated the semanticists by over 2000 years in his analysis of language use and abuse.

ISOCRATES: PLATO'S COMPETITOR

Although Isocrates was Gorgias's best student, he became a strong critic of the Sophists' greed. Isocrates was slightly older than Plato and was his competitor as a teacher in Athens.

The Academy of Athens, Greece has sculptures of Plato on the left and Socrates on the right.

Isocrates was not a great orator because he had a weak voice and was timid in nature. Isocrates was very critical of the Sophists, whom he compared to jugglers because they drew large crowds but only entertained the "empty-minded," he said, with their tricks instead of dealing with the substantive ideas of life (Jarrett, 1969, p. 229). He claimed that the Sophists did not teach either virtue or political discourse but rather became "professors of meddlesomeness and greed" (Jarrett, 1969, p. 218). Isocrates taught that the nature of man was composed of two parts—the body and the mind. The body had to be exercised to be strong, and the mind similarly had to be nurtured to be intelligent. One had to submit to training and master the subject matter of their given profession. The master or teacher has the ability to impart knowledge, but the pupil has to follow the master's instruction. Individuals who were born with natural talent in oratory still had to be schooled in substance, because speaking without truth or knowledge was a gymnastic exercise. He believed that the man who had the power of speech would be rewarded if he approached the "art of discourse with love of wisdom and love of honour" (Jarrett, 1969, p. 231). Isocrates believed that the Sophists were not concerned with truth or honor but that their prime motivation was to make money. Even though Isocrates was the student of the famous Sophist Gorgias, the first treatise that he wrote for his new school was entitled *Against the Sophists* (De Romilly, 1992, p. 53). These criticisms would be similar to those found in Plato's dialogues where the arguments of various Sophists were refuted by Socrates.

PLATO'S DIALOGUES

During the Golden Age of Greece, in his dialogue *The Republic* Plato attempted to define the difference between opinion and knowledge by dividing the world between those things seen and thought, distinguishing between the world of "the light and power of the sun" and the "world of Good—the world of the mind" (Plato, Book VI 508E–510A). He placed knowledge in a hierarchy, having four stations with the exercise of reason as the highest, understanding second, belief third, and conjecture last (Plato, Book VI 510–511E). In the **allegory of the cave**, Plato depicted people as prisoners chained to a cave wall where their world consisted of shadows cast by others passing before a fire which was the only light in the cave. This shadowy existence represented the world of sense perception and how distorted our knowledge about the world of Good really is. The Good world is one of ideal forms of knowledge, justice, and truth. In the allegory, one prisoner escaped from the cave by climbing up where he saw the world of ideas or ideals that represented true knowledge, but when he went back to tell the other cave dwellers of this radically different world, they killed him. Plato's view of knowledge and truth was that there is only one truth; there was no room for relativistic ethics or judgments, which was his primary criticism of the Sophists. He believed that knowledge and truth were powerful and transformative, but he did not trust common people whose intellect he thought was limited. His utopian society should be ruled by a philosopher king.

In the Platonic dialog *Gorgias*, Plato compared rhetoric to cookery or mere flattery that had no subject matter of its own, unlike science, medicine, or politics. He concluded by having Socrates tell Callicles that it is better to be wronged than to commit a wrong, so Callicles' attack on Socrates' inability to defend himself in a court of law ended with Socrates

In the artist's depiction of Plato's Allegory of the Cave, we see a representation of Plato's views on knowledge based upon the senses, which he compared to distorted shadowy figures on a cave wall, and the nature of true knowledge that is revealed in the world of Light or intellectual discovery.

demonstrating that it was better to enter the afterlife a virtuous and just man with a soul that is in the best of health than to win applause in this world (Bizzell & Herzberg, 1990, p. 112). Plato's dialogs are devoted to drawing distinctions between universal truth and relativistic possibilities that come from the world of the senses, and he attacked the Sophists' teaching as superficial and self-serving.

ARISTOTLE

Aristotle was Plato's student, but his approach to discovering truth differed greatly from that of his teacher. Aristotle wrote *The Rhetoric*, the foundational book on rhetoric that is the art of persuasion. He, unlike Plato, his teacher at the Academy, addressed the practical application of ethics, reasoning, and communicating in everyday life in a methodical way to discover what was probably true. Aristotle claimed that we arrive at truth through logical examination of the facts. He pursued the establishment of truth through both inductive and deductive reasoning. He taught that we live in the world of the probable, which is why the rhetorician was so significant, because those who possess the power to persuade will eventually have the power to establish what is believed and acted upon by others.

Aristotle (330 BCE/1954) defined rhetoric as "the faculty of observing in any given case the available means of persuasion" (p. 24). Rhetoric encompasses all fields of learning, but he distinguished between artistic and nonartistic proofs. **Artistic proofs** are those invented by the orator's knowledge, creativity, and appraisal of what is appropriate in a given situation. He referred to five "nontechnical" means of persuasion—laws, witnesses, contracts, tortures, and oaths. These would be **inartistic** means of persuasion, which he said had to be merely used but not invented. He wrote of the speaker's moral character, how the audience had to be put into a certain frame of mind, the message itself, and the proofs that the speaker used to convince audiences. Today we would recognize his description as the simplest model for communication: source–message–receiver. This depiction of communication is linear and assumes that the speaker has to transmit a message to an audience where breakdowns can occur at any step, but it begins with the speaker, which Aristotle believed to be the most important component in the process of persuasion.

Aristotle (330 BCE/1954) divided rhetoric into three categories: **political, forensic,** and **epideictic** forms of speech. **Political** speech was deliberative and focused on five subjects: ways and means, war and peace, national defense, imports and exports, and legislation. Congressional hearings and presidential debates are examples of political rhetoric. Surprisingly, even though Aristotle wrote in the fifth century BCE, his work still informs us of the field of communication that has as its goal persuading others on matters of national importance. **Forensic** communication focused on the legal system, where prosecution and defense of individuals occur. The word derives from the Latin *forensis,* meaning public or of the marketplace, suitable for public debate (*Webster's,* 1959). Every day in courts across the United States, rhetorical strategies are employed as prosecutors and defense attorneys argue their cases before judges, who preside over proceedings to either exonerate the accused or sentence them for their crimes. Many remember Johnnie Cochran's defense of O. J. Simpson and the slogans he improvised for the jury. In court, Simpson seemed to struggle to pull on the leather glove found at the murder scene where the bodies of his wife, Nicole Brown Simpson, and her friend, Ron Goldman, were discovered; Cochran said, "If it does not fit, you must acquit." Apparently, the jury bought it as an effective bit of theater; Simpson was acquitted.

Epideictic speech is largely ceremonial in nature, offering eulogies or tributes to the deceased or offering accolades to the living. In 2006 Coretta Scott King, widow of the civil rights leader Dr. Martin Luther King Jr., was eulogized by four living U.S. presidents and various other celebrities, some of whom used her funeral as a platform for political speeches, while others, notably Bill Clinton, reminded mourners that the service was to eulogize a woman who was made of flesh and blood. He said that during her lifetime she had shown great courage in returning to the site of her husband's murder to support the garbage workers who were on strike in Memphis, Tennessee, where Dr. King had been assassinated.

These examples demonstrate that Aristotle's three types of speech are still used: political, which involves deliberation on state matters; forensic, which involves prosecution and defense of citizens; and epideictic, which involves public eulogies or ceremonial address. Other matters that he might have considered are commercial communication, which occupies much of corporate budgets today through advertising, but he cannot be faulted for not anticipating the technology that dominates the marketplace today. In those days the shoemaker simply hung his sandals out for inspection, and the winemaker put out the wine skins for citizens to buy. Perhaps a return to the day when the product spoke for itself would be an improvement over the billions that are spent each year on advertising campaigns that enlist lizards to sell insurance, beautiful people to model clothes, or anti-wrinkle creams that guarantee eternal youth if you can be persuaded to buy the product.

Aristotle wrote of the three classic appeals in rhetoric—*ethos*, **logos**, and **pathos**. Appeals are ways that can get the audience to be moved or motivated to accept or reject a message. *Ethos* can be described as the character of the speaker, which would be equivalent to the image of the speaker today; Aristotle believed that this appeal was the most persuasive of the three that he offered because it relied upon ethics. The **credibility** of the speaker was primary in his view in persuading the audience, since any action on the receiver's behalf rested on the believability of the speaker. There are three things that inspire confidence in an orator's character, according to Aristotle—good sense, good moral character, and goodwill (1954, p. 91). *Logos* simply meant the logic of the arguments created by the speaker. Aristotle offered advice on the quality of reasoning that would lead to correct conclusions. *Pathos* is the emotion, or appeals to passion, a speaker uses. Rhetoric offered sound reasoning or proofs to support an argument. Further, the audience had to choose freely through their own powers rather than comply through coerced methods. Aristotle spoke of oaths and how truths that are gleaned through torture have no value because an individual would say anything to relieve his suffering. This whole debate was reawakened with the Abu Ghraib prison scandal that arose during the Iraq War as experts testified to the value of information extracted from prisoners who were mistreated there. The general consensus was, as Aristotle found centuries ago, that information gathered under duress was unreliable.

Topos, or place, Aristotle thought of as a metaphor similar to a place where the hunter would go to find game, with each animal having its own haunt that it occupied and where it could be found. Similarly, he regarded *topos* as a pigeonhole in the mind of the speaker where whole lines of argument could be found to present to the audience, maybe a whole realm of science (Aristotle, 330 BCE/1932). If the speaker has such spaces in his mind, certainly the audience members would have such mental spaces as well. Aristotle believed that speakers could be successful with audiences if they could establish **common ground** with them. How often have we said, "I know where you are coming from," or "I know where you stand on this issue"? We trust and like people who "speak our language." When the speaker connects with the listeners in the audience, there is a shared meaning, and successful communication occurs. Later, Kenneth Burke would refer to this phenomenon as **identification**.

Aristotle's work has remained relevant because he connected rhetorical address with ethics, reasoned deliberations, and emotional dimensions of humans, who are receivers that actively accept or reject messages. He believed that individuals should be as able to defend themselves in an argument with their intellect as with their muscles. He said, "It is absurd to hold that a man ought to be ashamed of being unable to defend himself with his limbs, but not of being unable to defend himself with speech and reason, when the use of rational speech is more distinctive of a human being than the use of his limbs" (Aristotle, 330 BCE/1954, p. 23). In other words, Aristotle believed that it was our mental capacity to reason that defined us rather than our physical prowess, and if we possessed the skills inherent in the art of persuasion, along with the attributes of good moral character, then we should possess happiness and success. Aristotle's approach was fairly direct. He stated:

In making a speech one must study three points: first, the means of producing persuasion; second, the style, or language, to be used; third, the proper arrangement of the various parts of the speech. We have already specified the sources of persuasion. We have shown that these are three: for we have shown that persuasion must in every case be affected (1) by working on the emotions of the judges themselves, (2) by giving them the right impression of the speakers' character, or (3) by proving the truth of the statements made. (Aristotle, 330 BCE/ 1954, p. 164)

Most scholars in the field of persuasion reflect the influences of Aristotle's early work. Aristotle's work has stood the test of time and furnished the foundation for many communication teachers to follow.

THE RHETORIC OF CICERO

Rome, which was originally an oligarchic city–state, began to emerge as a power on the edge of the Hellenistic world. In the first century BCE, Cicero struggled to prevent Mark Antony, Julius Caesar's nephew, from assuming power after Caesar was assassinated in 44 BCE. Cicero is seen as the next great rhetorician after Aristotle in the classical tradition. Cicero's work *De invention* (84 BCE) summarized the categories for rhetorical study at that time. There were five steps to creating a speech: one, invention, or creating the arguments; two, arrangement, that is, placing the speech in order; three, style, or choosing the best words; four, memorizing the speech; and five, delivery, that is, using the voice, gestures, and costumes to effectively present the speech. These five steps were called the canons of rhetoric (Bizzell & Herzberg, 1990, pp. 31–32).

Cicero was a potent political force as well as an eloquent orator. He taught that the orator should alter his style depending on the effect he wanted on the audience. Plain style was for exposition, middle style to get attention, and high style to arouse emotions. He was a prolific writer who produced seven treatises on rhetoric. Cicero believed that natural ability was the greatest gift for an orator but that these gifts needed to be honed by constant practice and learning in history, literature, and law. Isocrates wrote that the Athenians had corrupt orators because the audience responded only to base appeals, but Cicero believed that the audience took their moral tone from the orators who presented noble models for the audience to emulate. Cicero's five canons—invention, organization, style, memorization, and delivery— are still applicable to good public speaking.

THE RHETORIC OF QUINTILIAN

Quintilian, who lived between 35 and 96 CE, studied in both Rome and Spain, but returned in 68 CE to Rome, where he had great success as a teacher of rhetoric. In the years following Cicero's time, Rome deprived rhetoric of political importance because of censorship, but rhetorical training continued with a return to the Sophistic tradition. This era, known as the Second Sophistic, was evident from the first century CE to about 410 CE. The focus was more on literary style, which Quintilian resisted. He began his career as a lawyer, but he became famous in politics and established a school subsidized by the emperor Vespasian (Bizzell & Herzberg, 1990, p. 293).

Rather than engage his students in idle declamation, Quintilian urged them to read the great works of both Greek and Latin scholars. He may not have added to rhetorical theory, but he was an effective teacher who understood that education was a lengthy process influenced by the student's environment and development. Quintilian wanted to educate the child from infancy to bring out natural gifts but to continue learning into old age to produce the ideal orator—a "good man speaking well," which combined Plato's love of virtue, Aristotle's focus on ethos, and Cicero's power of public speaking (Bizzell & Herzberg, 1990, p. 35).

Quintilian wrote the *Institutes,*which combined the views of numerous Greek and Latin authors, but his focus was on the pedagogical process necessary to produce an orator who was both effective and virtuous. He would become an important resource for Christian rhetoricians in the early Middle Ages. Quintilian's *Institutes* were composed of 12 books, with each one addressing a particular aspect of oratory. The study of moral philosophy, literature, law, and poetry was necessary, he believed. Quintilian's work focused attention on the *ethos*, or character of the orator (Bizzell & Herzberg, 1990, pp. 295–296).

THE MIDDLE AGES: EMERGENCE OF CHRISTIAN RHETORIC

During the period between the fall of Rome and the Renaissance, much Greco-Roman learning was lost as the empire split into the Greek-speaking East and the Latin-speaking West. When Constantine became Emperor of Byzantium in 306 CE, he changed the name of the capitol to Constantinople and legalized the Christian religion in 313 CE (Bizzell & Herzberg, 1990, p. 367). After Constantine endorsed Christianity, Talmudic textual commentary emerged with the practices of letter writing and preaching. The fourth century CE began a tradition of study that included Greco-Roman philosophy and rhetoric as well as the Bible. Constantinople continued this scholarly tradition until it was conquered by the Turks in 1453. Attic Greek was the language of instruction in these Christian schools, while the Latin-speaking Romans became more corrupt and salacious in their literature.

Augustine (354–430 CE) converted to Christianity and recognized that classical learning was a great source for Christian education. He had taught the classics until his conversion, and when ordained Bishop of Hippo in 396, he began to instruct pastors in Biblical **hermeneutics** (explanation and interpretation of scripture) and **homiletics** (the art of writing and preaching sermons), which used classical rhetoric as an important teaching tool (Bizzell & Herzberg, 1990, p. 369). He believed that Christian sermons had to be persuasive because the people's understanding of the doctrine was imperfect. Augustine legitimized the use of classical learning in Latin and preserved much from the teaching from earlier scholars. Germanic tribes raided and besieged Christian towns and monasteries several times, and Augustine died in an attack in 430 CE. The Christian Church maintained an organizational structure outside of the local cities in Europe, and the Bishop in Rome assumed the title of Pope as a way to maintain order during these pagan invasions.

Benedict founded the monastery in Monte Cassino in Italy in 539 CE on the former site of an old temple of Apollo, and he replaced the secular texts the monks were reading with the sacred texts of Christianity. This model would influence monastic life in western Europe for a few centuries. Curriculum was devised that focused on mostly the rhetorical art of letter writing in the later Middle Ages (Bizzell & Herzberg, 1990, pp. 370–371).

St. Augustine converted to Christianity and was ordained Bishop of Hippo in 396 CE.

Political turmoil reigned in Europe as Islam spread from Palestine and Africa into Spain. Charlemagne formed alliances that subdued pagan rulers in both Italy and Germany and pushed the Moslems back over the Pyrenees to establish order in western Europe. He then founded a school for his family and noblemen and brought teachers from all over Europe. An English monk came to France and encouraged Charlemagne to encourage literacy when most noblemen were illiterate. These schools would supplement the resources of the monasteries and influence later schools in Europe. Beginning in the eleventh century there was a renaissance of Greco-Roman classical learning with Cicero, Aristotle, Augustine, and others in the curriculum.

After the fall of Charlemagne's empire in 814 CE, the Roman Catholic Church was created in western Europe and the Greek Orthodox Church in Palestine, Asia Minor, the Balkans, and Russia (Bizzell & Herzberg, 1990, p. 373). Aristotle's philosophy and works on logic became integral to the scholarship in Europe.

The role that rhetoric played in the education and political arenas from the time of the Sophists through the Middle Ages depended on the rulers of the various states, who were besieged by competing ideologies and tribes. Pagan priests came to compete with Christian priests, and monasteries were converted along with the texts they used to proselytize. The monasteries were vulnerable to Germanic tribes as well as to Muslims, but the Roman Catholic Church exercised great influence, emerging as a political, intellectual, and religious authority at the time of the Renaissance, existing between the fourteenth and seventeenth centuries. The Age of Enlightenment occupied the seventeenth through the nineteenth centuries, with democracy firmly in place but with restrictions from the church and the state.

RHETORIC AND BELLES LETTRES

By the seventeenth century there was a focus on both psychology and science, so that the works of Aristotle, Cicero, and Quintilian enjoyed attention because they reflected authorities not only on oratory but on human nature as well. Writers were reclassifying mental faculties into those of reason or understanding and the will. Semantics and linguistics would become areas of interest as well as a fetish for correct diction and pronunciation in the Elocutionary Movement, where dialects were seen as the vulgar speech of the uneducated lower classes. Language standards were monopolized by the ruling class so that dictionaries and books on elocution abounded. These ideas would be challenged by later academicians who stressed preaching as a way to reach audiences using acceptable standards for that time and place.

GEORGE CAMPBELL AND HIS *PHILOSOPHY OF RHETORIC*

George Campbell (1719–1796) was a Scottish clergyman who created a philosophical study group to improve pulpit eloquence, elocution, and the connection of rhetoric with literature and criticism. He believed that preaching had to inform and convince. "Campbell argues that persuasion is the culmination of the sequence just outlined: informing, convincing, pleasing, moving, and then persuading" (Bizzell & Herzberg, 1990, p. 655). He rejected the notion of a universal grammar and stated that the only correct usage was the "reputable, national, and present" grammar that was acceptable to the time and place (p. 656). Logic alone would not persuade audiences, but rhetoric combined appeals to all the faculties that would use ideas and images along with emotional messages to move the will of the people, Campbell believed. Campbell's *Philosophy of Rhetoric* was reprinted over 20 times during the eighteenth and nineteenth centuries, but Hugh Blair's *Lectures on Rhetoric and Belles Lettres* (1783) was the most popular rhetoric book of the times. Blair separated conviction and persuasion as Campbell did, but he thought that conviction came from reason and argument while persuasion came from evoked feelings and moving the will of audiences. Blair discussed delivery not as ornamentation but as a way to extend persuasion, and he included nonverbal expression that would be compatible with twentieth-century textbooks (Bizzell & Herzberg, 1990, p. 657).

RICHARD WHATELY'S ADVICE TO PREACHERS

Richard Whately, who was Archbishop of Dublin, wrote *Elements of Rhetoric* (1828) primarily for his divinity students who would confront congregations that were unlettered as well as skeptics who would oppose Christian doctrine. His work attempted to move sermons away from the rhetoric of belles letters and elocution because the first was concerned more with literary criticism and the latter with formalized gestures and voice rather than content (Ehninger, 1963/2010, pp. xxiv–xxvi) Whately stated that for conviction, which is an essential part of persuasion, the object must be desirable and the means of attainment reasonable (Whately, 1828, p. 175). Persuasion depends first on argument and second on exhortation, which appeals to the passions. Whately distinguished between merely practicing the art of rhetoric and offering ideas that were worth the audience's time.

> Universally, a writer or speaker should endeavour to maintain the appearance of expressing himself, not, as if he wanted to say something, but as if he had something to say: i.e. not as if he had a subject set him, and was anxious to compose the best essay or declamation on it that he could; but as if he had some ideas to which he was anxious to give utterance;—not as if he wanted to compose (for instance) a sermon, and was desirous of performing that task satisfactorily; but as if there was something in his mind which he was desirous of communicating to his hearers. (Whately, 1828, p. 329)

Whately recommended speaking naturally as though the words were the speaker's own when delivering biblical texts rather than focusing on the voice and body, as the elocutionists did. Whately saw rhetoric as argumentative composition and as an offshoot of logic (Whately, 1828, p. 4). He was familiar with the works of the ancient Greeks as well as the criticism of English writers like Swift, Addison, Hume, and Chesterfield, who acknowledged "the low state to which pulpit delivery had fallen, particularly among the Anglican clergy" (Ehninger, 1963/2010, p. xxiv). Modern speakers could learn from Whately that it is more important to have something worthwhile to say than simply to engage in the exercise of expressing oneself. Whately was not concerned with the discovery of the truth about Christianity but rather with proving to congregations what he already knew to be true (Einhorn, 1981, p. 96). The Age of Enlightenment combined rationalism, empiricism, and psychology to understand communication. The twentieth century expanded the marriage of art and science, and criticism began to analyze the effect that literature had on people. Social science research would emerge as a twin to the quest for truth and understanding of human nature. Kenneth Burke saw all great literature as rhetoric.

KENNETH BURKE: A LITERARY CRITIC'S VIEW OF RHETORIC

Kenneth Burke was born in Pittsburgh in 1897, attended Ohio State and Columbia Universities briefly, and then joined a group of writers in Greenwich Village. Burke began his scholarly career as a literary critic; later he turned to linguistic analysis and finally to rhetorical analysis in all forms. He believed that all effective literature was rhetorical. Burke defined persuasion in this manner: "Here is perhaps the simplest case of persuasion. You persuade a man only insofar as you can talk his language by speech, gesture, tonality, order, image, attitude, idea, *identifying* your ways with his" (Burke, 1969b, p. 55). Burke's work was inter-disciplinary and cut across boundaries to describe speech as symbolic action.

Burke gave the following empirical definition of man so that the reader might conceive of how he viewed us:

Man is

(1) The symbol-using animal
(2) Inventor of the negative
(3) Separated from his natural condition by instruments of his own making
(4) And goaded by the spirit of hierarchy. (Burke, 1970, p. 40)

Notice that Burke defines man as a symbol-using animal, not a rational animal, and he would make much of man's being a symbol-*misusing* animal as well. It was man's creation of the negative as a mark of linguistic genius that allowed distinctions between "thou shalt" and "thou shalt not," which enabled us to distinguish between what is and what *ought* to be, or between good and evil. His ideas appear in various chapters throughout this text, be-cause he was a prolific writer who addressed every form of interaction from purification from guilt to blatant marketplace pitches. His starting point was that "rhetoric is concerned with the state of Babel after the Fall" (Burke, 1969b, p. 23). We are familiar with the state of confusion and alienation that occurred when the people of Noah were divided by for-eign languages and scattered across the earth with no vehicle for common understanding. According to the Genesis version of how man became divided into tribes unable to under-stand each other, it was because of their ambition to build a tower designed to satisfy the spirit of man, not God.

> Now the whole earth had one language and few words. And as men migrated from the east, they found a plain in the land of Shinar and settled there. And they said to one another, "Come, let us make bricks, and burn them thoroughly." And they had brick for stone, and bitumen for mortar. Then they said, "Come, let us build ourselves a city, and a tower with its top in the heavens, and let us make a name for ourselves, lest we be scattered abroad upon the face of the whole earth." And the LORD came down to see the city and the tower, which the sons of men had built. And the LORD said, "Behold, they are one people, and they have all one language; and this is only the beginning of what they will do; and nothing that they propose to do will now be impossible for them. Come, let us go down, and there confuse their language, that they may not understand one another's speech." So the LORD scattered them abroad from there over the face of all the earth, and they left off building the city." Therefore its name was called Babel, because there the LORD confused the language of all the earth; and from there the LORD scattered them abroad over the face of all the earth (Genesis 11:1–9). (Dolphin, 2000, Para. 4)

According to Lambert Dolphin, "Babel" means "the gate of god" ("baa" means "gate" and "el" means "god"). A related Hebrew word, *balal*, means "confusion" (Dolphin, 2000). The problem with the great tower that the Babylonians intended to reach into the heavens was that they built it to achieve a name for themselves. Thus, their vanity resulted in their

The Tower of Babel represents the intrusion of divisions or foreigners as God punished man for building this structure to glorify their own power.

separation by language from each other, which caused a state of confusion that could only be mended by an eternal search for words that resonated with those who heard them not as foreigners but as those who could embrace a common meaning. This metaphor explains how people have been both divided and unified by words. This unity and alienation would be a major theme in Burke's work, and it remains a major theme in rhetoric as well.

Rhetoric attempts to reach across all the barriers that separate us from one another in interpersonal relationships, separate groups within our culture, and separate groups across nations. Even when our aspirations intend to reach into the heavens with something grand to express the human spirit, the Babel account can enlighten us about the difficulty of finding a common bond when language and our vision of the heavens and earth divide us. We have seen the horrible severance of all that was good through designs to elevate one ruler or nation above all others. *Mein Kampf*, or *My Struggle*, by Adolf Hitler, offered a blueprint for the destruction of a whole people, the Jews in Germany, whom he redefined as vermin and lice to be exterminated.

Dr. Abdul Mawgoud Dardery noted that the world has been defined in terms of Judeo-Christian **paradigms**, but he added that the Arab nations gave the world the alphabet, geometry, Arabic numbers, and many other primary ideas. He said we need a paradigm shift, meaning that we need a new model for viewing the world that includes the contributions of Islamic nations (Dardery, 2005). A **paradigm** is the accepted view of an idea or a thing. So how do we negotiate the turbulent waters of words where a scholar describes his people as great thinkers who gave the world arithmetic systems but others refer to his tribe or group as "terrorists"? One version focuses on history and the world of math and science, while the other version focuses on the current political struggle for power to define land, religion, and national character.

The power to define all things in this world relies on the skills of the rhetorician, not because the rhetorician captures reality all the time, but because they capture the convictions of the listeners who empower them to define social reality. Words alone do not create the reality of war or peace, but they are instrumental in forging the images that comprise our view of the world and how we should conduct the business of nationhood, commerce, and even religious traditions.

It is the human capacity to use and misuse language that separates us from other animals, according to Kenneth Burke. We persuade others by identifying our ways with theirs. This may be the city slicker lawyer who introduces himself to the jurors as "just a plain old country boy" or the Harvard candidate for president who won every televised debate, according to polls, but somehow managed to lose the election. We tend to like and trust others whom we perceive to be similar to ourselves, who share our values and lifestyles.

Burke said that *The Rhetoric* dealt with classifications in its partisan aspects and showed how individuals are at odds with one another, or how one identified with a group that was at odds with another group. He explained the paradox of people being identified with one another and acting cooperatively to enact the greatest of human divisions—war. He stated that it required many constructive acts of cooperation before each act of destruction could be committed in the blasts of war. Burke explained that if men were not divided against each other, there would be no need for the rhetorician to proclaim their unity or to seek to bring them together:

> If men were wholly and truly of one substance, absolute communication would be of man's very essence. It would not be an ideal, as it now is, partly embodied in material conditions and partly frustrated by these same conditions; rather, it would be as natural, spontaneous, and total as with those ideal prototypes of communication, the theologian's angels, or "messengers." (Burke, 1969b, p. 22)

Because men are divided by all manner of differences, then rhetoric must lead us through the "Wrangle of the Market Place . . . and the flare-ups of the Barnyard," Burke said (1969, p. 23). He noted that rhetoric as used by Aristotle meant "[t]he manipulation of men's beliefs for political ends" (Burke, 1969, p. 41). Burke said that, unlike the conjuring of primitive magic, if you are in trouble, you use human speech in a very realistic way. You cannot call your utterances "science" because they are not impersonal or offered in a descriptive way. Rather, he said that your call for help was to *move people*. Burke continued:

> As for the relation between "identification" and "persuasion": we might well keep it in mind that a speaker persuades an audience by the use of stylistic identifications; his act of persuasion may be for the purpose of causing the audience to identify itself with the speaker's interests; and the speaker draws on identification of interests to establish rapport between himself and his audience. (Burke, 1969b, p. 46)

Kenneth Burke shows the influence of Aristotle as he explained how both unity and division were possible through persuasion, which involved the speaker attempting to use the unifying principles of identification, which Aristotle called common ground between the speaker and the audience.

In *A Grammar of Motives* (1969a), Burke offered the Dramatistic Pentad, which broke events into five parts: act, scene, agent, agency, and purpose. The act named what took place, and the scene was the background or setting of the act or where it occurred. The agent analyzed the person or the kind of persons who committed the act, and the agency looked at the instruments used to commit the act. The purpose answered the question of why the action occurred or the motive for the action. This model from drama offers a way of analyzing complex events in terms that we are accustomed to using every day. Walter Fisher's **narrative theory** is akin to Burke's dramatistic metaphor, since he endorsed storytelling as a form of proof.

WALTER FISHER'S NARRATIVE THEORY

Walter Fisher (1984) created the narrative paradigm, which "synthesizes two strands in rhetorical theory: the argumentative, persuasive theme and the literary, aesthetic theme" (p. 1). His work is based on the conception of man as *homo narrans*, that is, storytellers. Literature has both a cognitive as well as an aesthetic dimension. For example, *Death of a Salesman* and *The Great Gatsby* give us good reasons to distrust the materialist myth of the American Dream, Fisher noted. He went on to define narration:

> By "narration," I do not mean a fictive composition whose propositions may be true or false and have no necessary relationship to the message of that composition. By "narration" I refer to a theory of symbolic actions—words and/or deeds—that have sequencer and meaning for those who live, create, or interpret them. The narrative perspective, therefore, has relevance to real as well as fictive worlds, to stories of living and to stories of the imagination. (Fisher, 1984, p. 2)

Fisher offered the narrative paradigm, or model, as an alternative to the rational, argumentative one that could only be judged by experts. He said:

> The narrative paradigm insists that human communication should be viewed as historical as well as situational, as stories competing with other stories constituted by good reasons, as being rational when they satisfy the demands of narrative probability and narrative fidelity, and as inevitably moral inducements. The narrative paradigm challenges the notions that human communication—if it is to be considered rhetorical—must be an argumentative form, that reason is to be attributed only to discourse marked by clearly identifiable modes of inference and/or implication, and that the norms for evaluation of rhetorical communication must be rational standards taken essentially from informal or formal logic. The narrative paradigm does not deny reason and rationality; it reconstitutes them, making them amenable to all forms of human communication. (Fisher, 1984, p. 2)

Storytelling is all-inclusive, since we learn to tell and interpret stories through socialization. We do not need experts to establish the rules or to use technical jargon that excludes the "public," whom some would claim are "ignorant," as Edward Teller did in the nuclear arms debate when he said: "The American public is ignorant, even of the general ideas on which they (nuclear weapons) are based" (in Fisher, 1984, p. 13). For the narrative to have validity, it must have **fidelity** and **coherence**; that is, the story must ring true and hang together to have the power to explain a truth or serve as a moral precept. Fisher wrote:

> Any story, any form of rhetorical communication, not only says something about the world it also implies an audience, persons who conceive of themselves in very specific ways. If a story denies a person's self-conception, it does not matter what it says about the world. In the instance of protest, the rival factions' stories deny each other in respect to self-conceptions and the world. The only way to bridge this gap, if it can be bridged through discourse, is by telling stories that do not negate the self-conceptions people hold of themselves. (Fisher, 1984, p. 14)

Fisher said that narratives are a form of discourse that is more universal than argument for nontechnical communication. Narrative rationality can be applied to specific stories; for example, Hitler's *Mein Kampf* was a bad story because although it had formal coherence in structure, it lacked fidelity to "the truths that humanity shares in regard to reason, justice, veracity, and peaceful ways to resolve social-political differences. On the other hand, one may cite the cosmological myths of Lao-tse, Buddha, Zoroaster, Christ, and Mohammed which satisfy both narrative probability and narrative fidelity for those cultures for whom they were intended" (Fisher, 1984, p. 15).

Fisher's narrative theory gives us another way to analyze public discourse that does not fit the model of formal evidence, yet storytelling is how history came to us before the technology of paper, pen, ink, and printing presses and other mass media. Most great speakers were also great storytellers. The narratives of a culture contain the essence of the people and their history. Fisher's work supports storytelling as the communal discourse that excludes no one.

JACQUES ELLUL'S *LA TECHNIQUE*: A SOCIOLOGICAL PERSPECTIVE ON PROPAGANDA

Ellul differs in his approach to persuasion in that he does not treat it as a campaign or some message that is aimed at an individual; rather, he sees *la technique* as an inseparable part of the technological society that totally immerses the individual continuously. He wrote of propaganda in the same vein that some would write of socialization or education. Ellul stated in the preface of his book *Propaganda: The Formation of Men's Attitudes* that propaganda embraced four areas:

Psychological action: The propagandist seeks to modify opinions by purely psychological means; most often he pursues a semi-educative objective and addresses himself to his fellow citizens.

Psychological warfare: Here the propagandist is dealing with a foreign adversary whose morale he seeks to destroy by psychological means so that the opponent begins to doubt the validity of his beliefs and actions.

Re-education and brainwashing: Complex methods of transforming an adversary into an ally, which can be used only on prisoners.

Public and human relations: These must necessarily be included in propaganda. This statement may shock some readers, but we shall show that these activities are propaganda because they seek to adapt the individual to a society, to a living standard, to an activity. They serve to make him conform, which is the aim of all propaganda. (Ellul, 1965, p. xiii)

Ellul spoke of a *pre-propaganda* phase and an *active propaganda* phase. To create the pre-propaganda phase, the two routes of conditioned reflex and myth are used as the organization-established attitudes and involvement that dealt with the psychology of the masses. "By **myth** we mean an all encompassing activating image" (Ellul, 1965, p. 31). Such myths would include the myth of race, the proletariat, and the Fuhrer; myths had to be constantly rejuvenated or reworked to avoid atrophy. Myths prepared the masses for the action phase of propaganda, but this was not a campaign—it was a way of life. Ellul said the United States preferred to use the myth while the Soviet Union preferred the reflex of conditioning (Ellul, 1965, p. 32).

Ellul dispelled the fallacy that propaganda was a series of "tall stories, a tissue of lies, and that lies are necessary for effective propaganda" (Ellul, 1965, p. 52). Hitler said the bigger the lie, the more likely it is to be believed, but this had two effects on the people, which was to **inoculate** or make them immune to lies and to have them believe that anything the enemy said was untrue. Goebbels, Hitler's propaganda minister, insisted that facts be disseminated to the masses. Facts pay off, Ellul said, but it is the intentions and interpretations that are essential for propaganda analysis.

Ellul posited that five conditions were essential for the evolution of *la technique*: the Industrial Revolution, population expansion, the economic milieu, the plasticity of the social milieu, and a clear technical intention that combined all of the foregoing elements. He wrote of the incubation phase of technology where science came forward with a powerful combination of theories and practices that gave rise to the Industrial Revolution that goes beyond the machine to the technique that engulfs man. The population explosion gave rise to research and technical growth by creating favorable markets and materials. The economy must be at the same time stable and in flux, Ellul said, to absorb the new inventions. The next condition of the social milieu involved two factors—the disappearance of both social taboos and natural social groups. The taboos were from Christianity and sociological norms (Ellul, 1976, p. 49). He explained that Christian beliefs hardened into prejudices and ideology and then became a social institution wherein these moral positions created genuine taboos. Alongside that process came sociological taboos that supported a social hierarchy, placing the king, nobility, and clergy above the people, who had no power to question them or their actions. This organization stood in the way of *la technique* because of the natural organization of these groups. Families, guilds, universities, Parliament, and other groups were organized according to their collective interests. But these group obstacles disappeared at the time of the French Revolution, according to Ellul. During the revolution there was an attack on all natural groups under the guise of the defense of the rights of the individual. With the removal of natural groups, the individual in an atomized society left only the influence of the state, which gave technical phenomena the most favorable condition in history.

Ellul stated:

> The propagandist tried to create myths by which man will live, which respond to his sense of the sacred. By "myth" we mean an all-encompassing, activating image: a sort of vision of desirable objectives that have lost their material, practical character and have become strongly colored, overwhelming, all-encompassing, and which displace from the conscious all that is not related to it. Such an image pushes man to action precisely because it includes all that he feels is good, just, and true. (Ellul, 1965, p. 31)

Ellul distinguished between *political propaganda* and *sociological propaganda*. Political propaganda involves techniques by the government to change the behavior of the public, and it can be either strategic or tactical. The strategy is the message or line they hope to embed, and the tactics are the means of spreading the word, such as leaflets, loudspeakers, or other means to an end. Sociological propaganda was "the penetration of an ideology by means of its sociological context" (Ellul, 1965, p. 63). Unlike traditional views of propaganda, where a campaign attempts to spread an ideology, or set of beliefs, sociological propaganda allows the ideology to penetrate the masses through the economic and political system. It springs up spontaneously through advertising, the movies, in education, and in social services. Ellul said some people hesitate to call this propaganda, but they use the same media as propaganda, are directed by those who make propaganda, and have identical purposes. The society really advertises itself by advertising its way of life.

Ellul also defined *agitation propaganda* and *integration propaganda*. Agitation propaganda gets all the attention because it confronts the present system and has the stamp of opposition. The ends are rebellion or war. This type was used by Lenin, Hitler, and in communist China by Mao. Integration propaganda aims to stabilize the social body by unifying it and reinforcing it. Ellul said that integrative propaganda works slowly, gradually, and imperceptibly, whereas agitation propaganda was spectacular. Much of what Ellul calls propaganda, especially integrative propaganda, we have studied as part of the education and socialization process where the individual takes roles based on what he perceives a good citizen should do or be. His approach is a sociological one that analyzes every facet of society to understand the effect of the educational, political, economic, and religious institutions and the role that mass media plays in the ideology of the individual.

HUGH RANK'S INTENSIFY/DOWNPLAY MODEL OF PERSUASION

Like Jacques Ellul, who wrote of the social myths across cultures and how technology had totally immersed humans in propaganda through *la technique*, Hugh Rank joined a group of concerned educators in the 1930s to identify and analyze propaganda. Rank noted that we live in a "doublespeak" world where much communication is intended to mislead and to propagandize rather than to elevate discourse, and he believed that the school system in the United States was ill-equipped to prepare students to analyze these communication strategies to mislead rather than inform.

Rank offered his intensify/downplay schema to supplement the work that the Institute for Propaganda Analysis (IPA) performed identifying the strategies used in propaganda blitzes like those that Adolf Hitler used in his Nazi campaigns. The IPA identified these techniques as glittering generalities, name-calling, card stacking, transfer or association, bandwagon (the most people), plain folks (the common people), and testimonies (the best people or admired people) (Rank, 1976, p. 4). Rank believed that although these devices are still relevant as a way of categorizing propaganda, they are insufficient to capture the sophistication of modern persuasion with technological aids and media bombardment. He asked, "Who trains the citizen?" He noted that the schools were not even addressing this deficit in communication, and he believed that a systematic method should be developed within the schools to inoculate students or immunize them against the dangers of organized public persuasion or "doublespeak" (p. 5). While the intensify/downplay model that Rank offered is now 35 years old, it still is applicable to analyze communication, persuasion, and propaganda techniques.

Rank said the three most common ways to intensify communication are through *repetition, association,* and *composition.* We know that we love the familiar and listen again and again to our favorite songs, stories, or books, and commercial advertisers recognize the effectiveness of repetition by playing commercials over and over again. Association works when we link an idea, person, or product with something already loved and desired or something hated or feared by the intended audience. Visuals images of children or aural stimuli like musical scores that accompany television commercials are memorable when associated with products like i-phones, E*TRADE, or other unrelated items. Composition intensifies communication through word choices, logic, nonverbal patterns such as color, size, and shape, CAPITALS, or underlining. The most common ways to downplay communication are through *omission, diversion,* and *confusion.* It is harder to detect the techniques to downplay communication than those that intensify it, but omission through withholding or hiding information is one way to cover up or manage news, especially bad news; this technique is used by politicians, CEOs, and everyday folks to downplay their bad qualities or performances. Diversion is a tactic that draws attention away from significant negative issues and may be accomplished by addressing a side issue referred to as a "red herring" or a "straw man" argument or using humor and entertainment to divert attention from more serious matters. Confusion can also be used to downplay a situation by giving information overload, commonly called "boring them to tears," or using jargon, equivocation, and just general chaos to obstruct understanding.

Hugh Rank's intensify/downplay model of persuasion can be applied across many situations from running for student government president to a job interview. For example, college students through the years have complained that after graduation they are confronted with interviewers focusing upon their inexperience, despite their outstanding college performance. This Catch-22 situation means that they are not hired because of their inexperience, and they cannot gain experience unless they are hired. The strategies that Rank recommended persuaders use are repetition, association, and composition to emphasize their good points and omission, diversion, and confusion to downplay their bad points. Placed in the interview situation where their lack of experience becomes an issue, students could talk about their time-management skills in college, which demanded that they complete all

FIGURE 2.1 Hugh Rank, created an intensify/downplay schema that explained how unethical speakers might intensify their good qualities through the use of repetition, association, and composition and downplay their bad qualities through the communication strategies of omission, diversion, and confusion.

classes with high grades while they worked late hours as a bartender or waitperson at a local lounge, which is not at all uncommon. They could associate this idea with the work ethic that employers expect from their employees, and they could detail the interpersonal skills that their part-time job required. Further, they could use repetition by highlighting relevant material from their resume such as a high QPA, any scholarships or recognition they received while in college, and describing leadership positions that they held. They could point to special skills such as computer languages, technology-based projects like web pages, or fluency in a foreign language or international travel experiences. Often students neglect to recognize the talents or skills they have acquired because they have not thought about how to present them in a job interview. That situation is all about persuasion, and students could implement the Rank model by downplaying their inexperience while focusing upon the skills they do possess. Internships in college frequently lead to jobs for students who perform well. To downplay their inexperience, they can divert attention from that weakness by stating that they are quick learners and that they recognize when to seek direction, although they are quite capable of autonomous work.

The Rank model of persuasion is easily applied and supports the logic that we put our best foot forward when we wish to create a favorable impression, and we try to manage the back stage so that the rough edges of our performance does not show. Attack ads in political campaigns are superlative examples of intensification of the opponent's bad traits, while the virtues of the challenger are intensified through glowing portrayals and media images. Equipped with Rank's method for analysis, all forms of communication can be analyzed, from political messages, commercials, and Internet blogs to community campaigns to raise utility rates. Rank worried that students were being poorly prepared to recognize these techniques in government, mass media, and interpersonal relationships. He summarized by saying that people do manipulate communication by (1) intensifying their own "good"; (2) intensifying others' "bad"; (3) downplaying their own "bad"; and (4) downplaying others' "good" (Rank, 1976, p. 15). He noted that all people in all eras and in all countries use these techniques as part of human activity.

MICHAEL CALVIN MCGEE: THE IDEOGRAPH

Michael Calvin McGee, a rhetorical critic, offered an eclectic view that claimed that scholars who studied mass consciousness from a dramatistic perspective as well as those who studied ideology from a power perspective both have legitimacy. Further, he noted that underlying both those camps was the rudimentary fact that indoctrination or a commitment to a worldview came with language acquisition. In an article published in 1980 in the *Quarterly Journal of Speech*, McGee analyzed the formation of mass consciousness or how ideology is formed from two perspectives. First he addressed the "symbolic" or "dramatistic" tradition of Kenneth Burke, John Dewey, George Herbert Mead, and Walter Lippmann, and then he examined the perspective of Karl Marx and Karl Mannheim, which focused upon dogma or doctrine used collectively by political organizations. The first group believed that people voluntarily agreed and participated in the "myth" of the masses, while the second group believed that the "lies" or system of beliefs are foisted upon the masses by the ruling class.

McGee believed that there is no error in either position, but the error exists when we conceive of "myth" and "ideology" to be opposites or incompatible concepts. Marx believed that a person immersed in ideology was victimized and exploited by the ruling class. Marx was concerned with the elites' power to control the political, economic, and military sectors of the state. McGee reconciled the two perspectives by stating: "The falsity of an ideology is specifically rhetorical, for the illusion of truth and falsity with regard to normative commitments is the product of persuasion" (Ferrell, 1998, p. 87). McGee said ideology, and the persuasion that validates it, is accessible through discourse used to produce it with enough force to control public belief and behavior, and this discourse is characterized by slogans or "Ideographs" that are easily mistaken for the technical terminology of political philosophy" (Ferrell, 1998, p. 87).

Ideographs reveal a structure of public motives that have the power to influence, or maybe determine, the shape of each individual's reality (p. 88). McGee offered the following hypothetical characteristics of Ideographs:

- Social control is a learned predisposition over human agents to comply or disobey that is conditioned by rhetorical faculties.
- A vocabulary of concepts (like liberty, law, or tyranny) function as guides, warrants, reasons, or excuses for beliefs and behaviors.
- A rhetoric of control exists in a system of persuasion that produces some degree of conformity in behavior and beliefs (for example, to wage war or head for Canada).
- Such structural terms as "property," "religion," "right of privacy," and "liberty" are building blocks of ideology and can be thought of as "Ideographs" that signify or contain an ideological commitment (p. 88).

- Ideographs become "God" or "Ultimate" terms with unquestioned logic that exist in real discourse functioning as "agents of political consciousness" (p. 89).
- Language has coercive power that socializes us to a society through a vocabulary that consists of ideographs that unify us collectively and separates us from others with different mother tongues.
- Ideographs have a cultural imperative that obstructs "pure thought"; therefore, they cannot be used to test truth or the pure thought of philosophy (p. 92).
- Ideographs must be historically examined or judged by precedent (p. 92).
- Ideographs may clash with one another, i.e., rule of law vs. confidentiality or national security, so they must be considered horizontally as rhetorical forces (p. 94), i.e., R. M. Nixon and the Watergate investigations, where he claimed executive privilege and confidentiality to avoid yielding to the subpoenas for documents.
- Ideographs may be reprioritized in relationship for consonance and unity in social and political arguments (p. 95).

You can see where any one of these characteristics could be mined to do critiques of various situations, for example, the idea that these "ultimate" terms engender a commitment from us to resist breaking the social contract such as committing a crime, or refusing to uphold our patriotic duty to go to war, or simply being conditioned to think of these abstract terms such as liberty, rule of law, or justice in specific ways that separate us from the Russians or Iranians who use the same terms, but with different meaning. Rather than focus upon the power of the elites as Marx did, or focus upon the motivation that arises from myth or dramatism, McGee nails the power of mass consciousness or identity on language and persuasion itself as contained in these powerful ideographs.

McGee identified the weaknesses in the critiques of Burke, Dewey, and Cassirer as getting mired in poetic metaphors and their never conceiving of their work as relevant to mass consciousness. The Marxist critique with the focus upon power, especially the power of the elite to oppress the proletariat, ignores the fact that even the elite cannot avoid the social control or influence of Ideographs. These slogans come to everyone as they acquire the mother tongue, which contains the ultimate terms of persuasion that instill social consciousness or a commitment to impulse control or choices. Each individual is conditioned, socialized, and linguistically predisposed through Ideographs to embrace these concepts that dominate our consciousness.

McGee is eclectic in his critique, and his work supports the power of linguistic determinism and the social construction of reality through persuasion. Critics claim that he ignores the power equation that elites have over those who are marginalized or lack a voice in the social discourse that supports the status quo, but he would remind them that even the elite are not immune from the power of language that engineers our thoughts and commitments to conformity or social rules.

McGee's focus upon how language, more than any other factor, predisposes the masses to think, act, and behave in predictable ways combines many of the ideas that we have covered in this chapter. For example, he discussed "God" or "Ultimate" terms, which we identify with Kenneth Burke, and we can include Jacques Ellul's myths perpetuated by *la technique* or the propaganda devices that the IPA identified. Certainly Ideographs could involve the power of metaphors that George Lakoff analyzed, the public philosophy of Walter Lippmann, and the social interaction of George Herbert Mead, which will be discussed in Chapter 4.

SUMMARY

These teachers, theologians, literary critics, sociologists, and rhetoricians have some common ideas, but their frames of reference for studying persuasion are very different. The introductory material in this chapter has only scratched the surface in each case, but these theories will be useful as we explore practical applications in later chapters. Many of the ideas on the nature of persuasion, emotional appeals, and human psychology moved into the laboratories of major universities during the twentieth century. The next chapter addresses the theories and research that were added to communication theory from those studies. Since persuasion is a receiver-centered form of communication, we need to understand the needs and motives of audiences.

APPLICATIONS

1. How has technology changed from the time Aristotle's citizens spoke in the Assembly and now that mass media spreads messages internationally?
2. Contrast Aristotle's view of rhetoric, which was the discovery of all available means of persuasion, and Whately's view that Christianity was the truth and the communicator was merely to find the most logical arguments and persuasive style to communicate to their congregations.
3. Use the dramatistic pentad of Kenneth Burke, to analyze the attack of September 11, 2001, on the Twin Towers in New York rhetorically.

REFERENCES

Aristotle. (1932). *The rhetoric of Aristotle* (L. Cooper, Trans.). New York: Appleton-Century-Crofts. (Original work 330 BCE)

Aristotle. (1954). *Rhetoric*, translated by W. R. Roberts. New York: Modern Library. (Original work 330 BCE)

Bizzell, P., & Herzberg, B. (eds.). (1990). *The rhetorical tradition: Readings from classical times to the present.* Boston: Bedford Books.

Burke, K. (1969a). *A grammar of motives.* Berkeley and Los Angeles: University of California Press.

Burke, K. (1969b). *A rhetoric of motives.* Berkeley and Los Angeles: University of California Press.

Burke, K. (1970). *The rhetoric of religion: Studies in logology.* Berkeley and Los Angeles, CA: University of California Press, Ltd.

Dardery, A. M. (2005). Islam and interfaith dialogue. Fulbright Scholar Lecture presented at University of Pittsburgh at Greensburg, Academic Village Presentation, March 3.

De Romilly, J. (1992). *The great Sophists in Periclean Athens* (J. Lloyd, Trans.). Oxford, UK: Clarendon Press.

Dolphin, L. (April 16, 2000). The tower of Babel and the confusion of languages. Retrieved January 29, 2006, from http://www.idolphin.org/babel.html.

Ehninger, D. (2010). Editor's introduction. In Richard Whately, *Elements of rhetoric: Comprising an analysis of the laws of moral evidence and of persuasion, with rules for argumentative composition and elocution.* Landmarks in Rhetoric and Public Address. Carbondale: Southern Illinois University Press. (Original work published 1963)

Einhorn, L. J. (1981). Consistency in Richard Whately: The scope of his rhetoric. *Philosophy of Rhetoric, 14*(2), 89–99.

Ellul, J. (1965). *Propaganda: The formation of men's attitudes* (K. Kellen & J. Lerner, Trans.). New York: Alfred A. Knopf.

Ellul, J. (1976). *The technological society* (J. Wilkinson, Trans.). New York: Alfred A. Knopf.

Fisher, W. R. (1984). Narration as a human communication paradigm: The case of public moral argument. *Communication Monographs, 51,* 1–22.

Jarrett, J. L. (1969). Isocrates "Against the Sophists" and "Antidosis." In J. L. Jarrett (Ed.), *The educational theories of the Sophists* (pp. 212–231). New York: Teachers College Press.

Jowett, G. S., & O'Donnell, V. (2006). *Propaganda and persuasion* (4th ed.). Thousand Oaks, CA: Sage Publications.

McGee, M. C. (1998). The "Ideograph": A link between rhetoric and ideology. In T. B. Ferrell (Ed.), *Landmark essays on contemporary rhetoric* (pp. 85–101). Mahwah, NJ: Lawrence Erlbaum.

Plato. (1956). The republic. In E. H. Warmington & P. G. Rouse (Eds.), *Great dialogues of Plato.* (W. H. D. Rouse, Trans.). New York: The New American Library.

Rank, H. (1976). Teaching about public persuasion: Rationale and a schema. In D. Dieterich (Ed.), *Teaching about doublespeak* (pp. 3–19). Urbana, Illinois: National Council of Teachers of English.

Rankin, H. D. (1983). *Sophists, Socratics and cynics.* Totowa, NJ: Barnes & Noble Books.

Webster's New World Dictionary of the American Language. (1959). Cleveland and New York: The World Publishing Company.

Whately, R. (1828). *Elements of rhetoric: Comprising an analysis of the laws of moral evidence and of persuasion, with rules for argumentative composition and elocution.* Landmarks in Rhetoric and Public Address. Carbondale: Southern Illinois University Press.

CHAPTER 3

AUDIENCES: SOCIAL SCIENTISTS ADDRESS NEEDS, ATTITUDES, AND BELIEFS

KEY WORDS

attitude
cognitive dissonance
  theory
    free-choice paradigm
    belief-disconfirmation
      paradigm
    effort-justification
      paradigm
    induced-compliance
      paradigm
credibility

demographics
eight hidden needs
elaboration likelihood
  model (ELM)
ethos—initial, derived,
  terminal
expectancy violation theory
  (EVT)
hypodermic needle theory
mere exposure theory (MET)
psychographics

pyramid of needs (deficit/
  being)
role-playing/
  counterattitudinal
  advocacy
selective exposure
social judgment theory
theory of reasoned action
  (TRA)

PREVIEW

Beginning in the 1920s, people like Edward Bernays, the father of public relations, and the Women's Anti-Saloon League began to use the social science methods of polls, statistics, and market research to test audience attitudes and beliefs before political, ideological, or product campaigns were launched. Social scientists became interested in what people think, how we make decisions, and why we behave as we do. This chapter examines some of the theories from the last 75 years that attempt to explain audience responses in relation to persuasion. A number of these theories are included to explain how audiences make judgments that either facilitate or obstruct persuasion, how they handle doubts about their own decisions, how inconsistencies create psychological angst in people, and why folks sometimes appear to be totally illogical in their responses to persuasion attempts.

After reading this chapter, students should be familiar with leading social science theories regarding audience characteristics, motivation based on needs or psychological premises, and attitudes, values, and beliefs that influence audience choices.

AUDIENCE DEMOGRAPHICS AND PSYCHOGRAPHICS

The general characteristics of an audience are referred to as audience **demographics.** Persuaders attempt to learn as much about their audiences as they can before they create a message or deliver it. The age, gender, education level, income, political and religious affiliations, geographic location, ethnic group, and position on the intended topic are all significant factors to consider. Much research is conducted to define an audience's characteristics and attitudes before a campaign is waged or a speech is delivered to a national audience. The nature of the audience is of primary concern before the speaker begins to create the message.

Psychographics are audience profiles that aim to reveal the lifestyles and mindsets of the intended audience, for example, veterans, baby boomers, generation Xers, or generation nexters. According to profiles found in "Commitment" (2006):

> Veterans are those born from 1922–1943. The Great Depression, World War II, and Patriotism are the defining events of their life. They value hard work, law and order and respect for authority.
>
> The Baby Boomers are those born between 1943–1960. Defining events include Television, the Civil Rights Movement, and prosperity. They value health and wellness, personal growth, and involvement.
>
> Generation Xers are those born between 1960–1980. Watergate, MTV, and the Fall of the Berlin Wall are defining events for this generation. They value diversity, global thinking, and pragmatism.
>
> Generation Nexters are those born after 1980. Defining events include school violence, multiculturalism, and TV talk shows. They value civic duty, achievement and diversity. ("Commitment," 2006, pp. 1–2)

It is always dangerous to generalize or stereotype, but psychographics reflect trends and commonalities. Baby boomers are frequently analyzed in terms of their voting habits, purchasing power, and the consequences of their aging on social services like Social Security and healthcare. Because the experiences of the generations differ, they have different perspectives on work, play, religion, and relationships. In other words, their needs are different. Marketing researchers attempt to define niche markets for products, and political pollsters attempt to research and clarify political positions for candidates. Whole industries revolve around audience analysis for mass media, including Nielsen ratings, Arbitron, and others. So audience analysis has been going on since the philosophical writings of the ancient Greeks, but in the twentieth century the social scientists began to devise methods for analyzing those needs, attitudes, and beliefs that were seen to be inextricably tied to human behavior, thus joining philosophy, psychology, sociology, and communication in this search for understanding and predictability.

The receivers of messages are referred to as audiences; an audience may be one person, a small group, or a mass audience, but the success of any persuasion attempt hinges on the source and the message connecting with the receiver of the message. In this chapter we will discuss how audience needs, attitudes, and beliefs either open them up to persuasion attempts or put up barriers against them. It is a common opinion that "there's a sucker born every minute," which supports the powerful effects of stimulus–response conditioning—also called the **hypodermic needle theory**, because the message is thought to enter the body in a well-targeted and effective manner like a shot with no defense. Many people believe that gullible audience members can be led to buy products that they neither need nor really want, to vote for the slickest politician, and to follow leaders with blind obedience. A second view of human nature supports the selective nature of audiences who respond very positively to some messages while they ignore others entirely. The first view of people sees them as herd animals, like sheep, that are easily led or misled; the second integrates the knowledge that people are unique in their preferences and that they exercise discretion in their voting

Flash mob events reflect the herd mentality of following the leader or mass conformity to suggested behavior.

behavior, buying power, and willingness to be influenced by another based on their own worldview, which allows them to make enlightened decisions based on the gratification of needs that they recognize.

PERSUASION IN INTERPERSONAL EXCHANGES, SMALL GROUPS, AND MASS AUDIENCES

In interpersonal communication, where two people are talking face-to-face, there is the possibility for instant feedback both verbally and nonverbally. The speaker sends the message to the receiver, who interprets it and gives a response, and the exchange continues with each individual taking turns speaking and listening. Facial expressions can be read as well as body movements that signal agreement or hostility in such an exchange; further, the message is direct, timely, and probably more intimate in nature.

In small group communication there must be at least three members to compose a group and generally no more than 25; some theorists say only up to 15. We know that with the addition of every member of a group or audience the possibility for miscommunication multiplies geometrically as each member's personality, role, communication skills, and personal style feed into the dynamic of sending and receiving the message. Most business meetings and everyday discourse, including family decisions, occur in small groups. James Anderson (1989) wrote in *Speaking to Groups: Eyeball to Eyeball*:

> Nevertheless, in modern organizations today, to get your ideas across and get things done, you often have to speak—to individuals and groups, in public and private—eyeball to eyeball.
>
> Lee Iacocca, for instance, in his autobiography recalls engineers with "terrific ideas" who were unable to explain them to anyone else. To Iacocca, "It's always a shame when a guy with great talent can't tell the board or a committee what's in his head."
>
> In their landmark study, *In Search of Excellence,* Thomas Peters and Robert Waterman suggest that a vital reason for success in the best-run American companies is an "intensity of communications." The best companies (IBM, Walt Disney, McDonald's, 3M, and others) keep a bias against detached bureaucracy in favor of person-to-person contact. At Hewlett-Packard, this attitude was captured by the phrase, "MBWA"—"management by walking around." (Anderson, 1989, p. 16)

To extrapolate some of the general themes in this quote, we know that communication exists on every level, but great persuaders know that being bright is not enough. A skilled communicator knows how to speak to individuals, groups, or mass audiences, and they are not detached but very involved in the process by knowing the work environment and its problems as well as the people who contribute to the company.

Mass audiences are very different from two persons talking in a **dyad**—that is, two people face-to-face—or a small group of three or more. Generally, mass audiences are reached through the media, which means that there are layers of organization between the speaker or writer and the receiver or audience. It is unusual to have a live audience of 250,000 members like Dr. Martin Luther King Jr. had at the Lincoln Memorial when he delivered the "I Have a

Dream" speech, but even in such instances, the speaker is removed from most of the crowd and amplification equipment is essential, with projection screens to carry the speaker's image as well as security forces to ensure order. "Mass media" means that the message is mediated as it passes through different layers of the organization, whether it is a newspaper with editors or a radio or television broadcast with various specialists. We can define a mass audience as large in number—hundreds or millions; heterogeneous, that is, including all the demographic elements mentioned earlier—education, income, ethnicity, political and religious affiliation, geographic location, and special interests; anonymous to each other; and, with the exception of electronic messaging, incapable of giving instant feedback.

Published works like books, newspapers, and magazines, radio and television broadcasts, and more recently the new media of computer blogs, websites, and networks qualify as mass media. Political campaigns, product campaigns, and social movements are dependent upon these sources for success. Certainly, the channel of the communicated message will affect the manner in which the audience receives and responds to it. Since 1960 the presidential debates have been a tradition in the United States, with a great national audience numbering in the millions, but the question of how to best persuade either a mass of voters or a single individual remains a question for communication specialists to research. The field of social psychology grew out of the efforts of such researchers as Carl Hovland, A. H. Maslow, Milton Rokeach, Gerald Miller, and Leon Festinger, all of whom studied attitudes, values, and beliefs and how humans processed information or changed their cognitive, affective, or behavioral responses to messages.

Psychology has its roots in philosophy, which attempted to answer some of the issues raised by the ancient philosophers, beginning with Aristotle. Carl Hovland's research at Yale University on attitude change has much in common with Aristotle and Cicero, since all three considered the content of communication, the nature of the communicator, the audiences' predispositions, and their responses to messages. According to Portolano and Evans (2005, p. 133), the Roman orator Cicero listed areas of knowledge that an orator must possess to be successful, which included:

> Complete knowledge of the subject matter addressed.
>> Appropriate convention (or style) of communication for that discipline.
>> Arrangement of communication in appropriate and effective order.
>> Extensive knowledge of human emotions: "All the mental emotions, with which nature has endowed the human race, are to be intimately understood, because it is in calming or kindling the feelings of the audience that the full power and science of oratory are thought to be brought into play." (Cicero, 55 BCE, I.v.17–19, cited in Portolano and Evans, 2005, p. 133)

Cicero, like Plato before him, used characters in dialog form to explore the nature of such skills. Aristotle wrote *The Rhetoric* and *Nichomachean Ethics*, which recorded his views on both communication and the nature of moral conduct separating him from the Sophists of Greece (see Chapter 2), who taught students to argue all sides of issues regardless of the integrity of that position. In the 1950s Hovland brought these philosophical issues into the laboratories at Yale and applied social science methods to testing the hypotheses of the ancient writers; so while their methods of inquiry differed, all three addressed the same issues concerning speakers and audiences and how their attitudes, beliefs, and behaviors could be analyzed (Portolano & Evans, 2005). One consistent finding in all communication theory and philosophy of communication is that the perceived credibility of the communicator is at the foundation of audience behavior.

SOURCE CREDIBILITY

When Aristotle wrote of the three classical appeals in rhetoric, he explained how *ethos*, *logos*, and *pathos* combined to build the best case of persuasion; however, of the three, he identified *ethos* as the most important among them. The *ethos*, or character of the speaker, was believed to be most powerful in convincing audiences that an argument was true. While *logos*, or logical proofs, were also important, and *pathos*, or emotional appeals, were also a means to gaining support for ideas and actions, the appeal of the speaker was the most influential means of winning adherence to the message, Aristotle believed.

Credibility, which is the believability of the speaker, is composed of many attributes, among them intelligence, expertise, trustworthiness, similarity, likability, and attractiveness. However, expertise is more important to persuasion than the effect of trustworthiness, attractiveness, or similarity. Many studies have attempted to identify the effect that source credibility has on message reception, but it is a complicated dynamic to understand. The **elaboration likelihood model (ELM)** of persuasion, which is explained more fully later in this chapter, states that particularly when listeners are not very informed or able to elaborate cognitively on the idea, they are more likely to be most heavily influenced by the person speaking—the source of the message.

If the listener is motivated and able to elaborate on the arguments, then the source credibility may be inconsequential. Where the listener is able to elaborate only to a moderate degree, then the source credibility may cause people to decide that the message is important and that they should pay attention to it. The image or reputation of the speaker may be considered (1) before they begin addressing the audience, which is called **initial ethos** based on reputation or credentials, or (2) during the presentation when listeners may change their attitudes either for or against the speaker, which is **derived ethos**, or, finally, (3) after the presentation, when listeners evaluate the performance, which is **terminal ethos**.

Initial ethos is the reputation or status that the speaker has when they are presented to the audience. James McCroskey reviewed studies done on ethos and attitude change in audiences by Kelman and Hovland that showed that initial ethos based on the background and personal characteristics of bogus sources in experiments was significant in their ability to persuade subjects. Subjects were told the source was a juvenile court judge, an audience member chosen at random, and a juvenile delinquent. The studies showed that the source had a significant effect on acceptance of the message. The higher-status speakers produced the most attitude change (McCroskey, 1997). **Derived ethos** is the impression that the speaker earns while addressing the audience, regardless of their initial image. Aristotle spoke of rhetorical choices that the source chooses to support arguments; among these are finding common ground with the audience, supporting positive attitudes in the audience, giving evidence to support assertions, and having effective delivery of the message to gain respect. McCroskey stated that sincerity is another component of derived ethos. Speakers whom audiences perceive to be sincere are significantly more effective than those perceived to be insincere. **Terminal ethos** "is the product of the interaction between initial ethos and derived ethos" (McCroskey, 1997, p. 99). Ethos is not static, but a dynamic impression that the audience derives of the speaker that can and does change over time. A high-ethos source will lose standing over time, while a low-ethos source may gain in credibility. The 1960 televised debate between Richard M. Nixon and John F. Kennedy demonstrates an ethos-centered rhetorical situation, which is common in speeches made by candidates for public office, McCroskey said. Following the debate in 1960 those who only heard the debate on radio more often thought that Nixon had won it, but those who saw the debate on television believed that Kennedy had won. This would lead us to believe that JFK's youthful appearance and good looks certainly helped his cause, since Nixon was a seasoned debater in college and had considerable experience in government as Eisenhower's vice president. Kennedy's image was more charismatic than Nixon's, although Kennedy had less experience, had to win the confidence of Protestant voters, and had to demonstrate that he was knowledgeable on international affairs, where Nixon was well versed. Mitt Romney was in a similar situation in the 2012 presidential debates against President Obama. Romney, the first Mormon to be nominated in a presidential election, needed to demonstrate that he was knowledgeable on foreign affairs and was credible, whereas the president already had four years of experience in that arena and was known as an effective communicator.

In 1960 John F. Kennedy was thought to have won the debate against Richard M. Nixon by those who saw it on television, but voters who heard the debate on radio thought that Nixon won.

Source credibility is a worthy topic for research and discussion, which would command many books on its own; however, for our purposes, we need to remember that the speaker or source of the message cannot be separated from it and is a powerful agent in attitude change and persuasion. Perhaps before we discuss how audience members parse and mull over messages individually, we should look at the human need to discern those common qualities that we share that make us susceptible to persuasion or the influence of others.

A. H. MASLOW: THE PYRAMID OF NEEDS

A. H. Maslow, who was Chair of the Psychology Department at Brandeis University from 1951 to 1969, conducted many experiments and wrote widely on human personality, motivation, and needs. He began to observe in animal experiments that there was an order to behavior to satisfy basic needs, with some taking precedence over others. Humans share this ordering with other animals; for example, if you are hungry or thirsty, you would tend to satisfy those needs before you became engaged in anything else. Through the years Maslow developed the pyramid of needs that began with basic needs, or what he called **deficit needs**, and moved up the pyramid to **being needs** (Maslow, 1987, pp. 18–31):

A. H. Maslow's Pyramid of Needs
(Being Needs)
Self-Actualization Needs
Esteem Needs
Belonging Needs
Safety Needs: Shelter, Order
Physiological Needs: Air, Food, Water, Sex
(Deficit Needs)

On the first level of the pyramid are *physiological needs* such as oxygen, water, food, the need to eliminate wastes, and the need to have sex. The second layer consists of *safety needs*, which deal with finding safe circumstances, stability, and structure or order in life. The third level consists of *love and belonging needs*, which include friends, lovers, and children—a social network that enable humans to be accepted, loved, and nurtured. The fourth level consists of *esteem needs*, which Maslow divided into two types, lower and higher. At the lower level he placed the need for respect from others, the need for status, fame, reputation, dignity, and even dominance. The higher forms of esteem involved self-respect, which included feelings of competence, confidence, achievement, and freedom that do not depend on what others think of you. When an individual lacks self-esteem and self-respect, they suffer from inferiority complexes or great difficulties accepting themselves. Maslow agreed with Adler, his colleague, that these negative feelings were the roots of many psychological problems. These first four levels of needs Maslow called **deficit needs**, or **D-Needs** (Boeree, 2006). Maslow used the term *homeostasis* to describe how these needs work; almost like a thermostat, they serve a regulatory function. The first four levels address needs that are essential to maintain physical and mental well-being. Maslow called them "instinctoid," or instinct-like needs (Boeree, 2006). The final level, or fifth state, involved *self-actualization*, which, unlike the deficit needs discussed earlier, was called **being needs.** The other four levels require satisfaction, but this final stage is concerned with your becoming the most satisfied, complete, and fulfilled person that you can become. Maslow wrote, "Musicians must make music, artists must paint, poets must write if they are to be ultimately at peace with themselves. What humans can be, they must be. They must be true to their own nature. This need we may call self-actualization" (1987, p. 22). Early on Maslow spoke of the self-actualizing experience, but later works supported this peak as an ongoing project or a continuous work in progress.

Maslow's pyramid of needs illustrates drives that humans have that must be satisfied beginning at the lowest level before they can advance to the next state; however, these basic needs are potent at all times until they are satisfied. That is not to say that one must have sex every day to survive, but in order to sustain the species there must be reproduction. Safety needs are perhaps better understood by Americans following September 11, 2001, whereas citizens of many other countries placed a high priority on their security before this date because they had experienced warfare and internal strife in the past. Although many major American cities manifest great threats with gangs and underground activities, sociological studies indicate that gangs often exist for safety needs and belonging needs when the general family foundation is lacking. William Foote Whyte's book *Street Corner Society* (1957) analyzes gangs' secret communication codes, dress, and colors in the early 1950s, long before the Crips, Bloods, or MS-13 were well known. Maslow's pyramid of needs can be used to analyze many persuasion attempts ranging from the most rational political candidate to underarm deodorant ads that promise to banish your social insecurities and win admiration and beautiful partners. Maslow began a revolution in psychology with his humanistic approach to therapy, education, work, and social interaction. In the afterword to Maslow's *Motivation and Personality* (1987), Ruth Cox cited a Maslow journal entry written four months before he died:

> I had thought that I'm at the peak of my powers and usefulness now, so whenever I die it will be like chopping down a tree, leaving a whole crop of apples yet to be harvested. That would be sad. And yet acceptable. Because if life has been so rich, then hanging on to it would be greedy and ungrateful. (Cox, 1987, p. 245)

Maslow's work on human motivation, needs, and values informs us of why humans pursue certain goals and activities that allow them to gain recognition or leadership roles while others are happy to live just to create art, to write, or to satisfy their inner souls. Persuaders tap into this need structure to sell products, present political candidates, or start reform movements. Others have written of human needs that offer insights into subconscious desires. Vance Packard was one of the first to explore the marriage between social science research and the marketplace.

VANCE PACKARD: EIGHT HIDDEN NEEDS

Vance Packard wrote a book in 1957 called the *The Hidden Persuaders*, which attempted to explain the underlying needs and desires of people who engaged in "conspicuous consumption," that is, a vulgar materialism that had little to do with basic needs, but rather showed a motivation to achieve other intangibles like power, status, and immortality. By 1974 the book was in its 44th printing—Packard's revelations of how social science, or the in-depth explorations of the human psyche, was being applied to political, product, and ideological campaigns was a great exposé. His research and findings focused mostly on consumers and their behavior, but the idea of subconscious urges and needs was anchored in what he called **"eight hidden needs"** (Packard, 1957, pp. 61–70):

Emotional Security

Reassurance of Worth

Ego Gratification

Creative Outlets

Love Objects

Sense of Power

Sense of Roots

Immortality

According to Packard, *emotional security* is at the root of any number of commodities generally sold for economic benefit or convenience. Packard reported on a psychiatric pilot study that found that home freezers became popular following World War II, during which uncertainties and deprivation were common in American lives. Having food in the house represented warmth, security, and safety. The same agency found that air conditioners allowed citizens to lock down windows and keep the threatening world outside, while others felt claustrophobic by being shut off from nature.

Reassurance of worth is tied to common products like soap, which had been marketed to keep a house or our bodies clean; however, when advertisers realized that many women saw household chores as drudgery, they connected the product to their feelings of worth and self-esteem so that the products promised to smell good and help women to have lovely hands or to make their husbands and children appreciate them.

Ego gratification involves users feeling good about themselves. One instance that Packard explained was that of a steam shovel company whose sales were lagging; a study revealed that the operators resented the ads, which pictured the mighty machines doing all the miraculous work without any mention of the skill and expertise of the operators. Subsequently, the ads showed the operators at the controls of the huge machines, which reduced the hostility they felt toward the corporation's representation of them and their work.

Creative outlets are essential for people who suddenly find themselves in need of a redefinition of their life's work. Most of us have some hobby or pastime that relaxes or gratifies our creative urges. Some engage in musical endeavors such as garage bands, church choirs, or just solo playing. Flower or vegetable gardens are a substantial way to commune with nature and seek inner peace after hectic schedules elsewhere. We all know the CPA who also constructs violins, dulcimers, or other carved, constructed, or painted things as a diversion from the minutiae of daily life. Sewing, cake decorating, and gourmet cooking are other common outlets.

Love objects are people, pets, or activities that become objects of affection and gratification. Many viewers embrace television personalities as though they were family members: Oprah, Dr. Phil, Judge Judy—the list is endless. We have a need to belong to or with others and to shower affection on people whom we admire. A member of a support group used to bring a tiny dog to sessions that she dressed in miniature outfits, including hats and elaborately decorated jackets. Perhaps the dog needed her own therapy session following this display, but it demonstrated devotion to the ritual of costuming the little pet as a kind of fulfillment.

A *sense of power* is easily seen as an obsession in American life and in our relationships with our automobiles. This urge to extend our own personal boundaries and to control the road can be seen at any stoplight as some motorists rev up their engines and invite like-minded drivers to race out of the space, demonstrating the surge of freedom and dominance. Everyday products like vacuum cleaners reflect our devotion to powerful tools and toys. Surely quieter machines could be manufactured than those that threaten to suck up the dog and half the furniture in the family room as the vacuuming ritual begins. The word "power" has been incorporated into everyday activities such as walking, napping, and boating, even though a "power nap" seems to be a contradiction in terms.

A *sense of roots* has been demonstrated to be a very strong need in humans. Packard notes that a relatively unknown brand of wine became popular when advertisers began to tie it to nostalgic family gatherings and family practices including wine making. Themes of home, motherhood, and warm embraces of relatives are effective evocative themes. With the mobility required by twenty-first-century job demands and the division of families that has accompanied this shift, there is a hunger for family stories, traditions, and bonds. This need to cling to our roots has been exploited by advertisers, politicians, and other persuaders in the arts for a long time; one example is Alex Haley's 1977 made-for-television miniseries *Roots*, which brought record-breaking audiences to witness the black experience from the slave ships to new struggles in a new country. Following that broadcast there was a surge in genealogical research to trace family trees, and now computer software exists to enable users to trace family histories with ease.

Our search for immortality leads men and women to seek Botox treatments, hair implants, plastic surgery, and other techniques to assure a youthful appearance.

Immortality is a hidden desire that humans have to guarantee that their place in history does not dissolve when they die. Life insurance agencies struggled to determine the best way to sell life insurance without offending the "breadwinner," who might feel that he or she had simply been obliterated through death—companies focused on a perspective that the worker continued to exercise economic influence and control over their family's life even after death. On a smaller scale, anyone walking through a cosmetic department will be inundated with anti-aging products that boast mysterious scientific ingredients that defy wrinkles and laugh lines and keep skin young and beautiful. The pursuit of youth goes back to antiquity; it is ironic that Juan Ponce de León was seeking the Fountain of Youth when he discovered Florida, a state now boasting the greatest aged population in the United States. Only the famous or infamous have the luxury of immortality, unless you leave behind a work of art or writing that represents a piece of your mind or talent, but most of us are blessed with another promise to continue life through the lives of our children and grandchildren.

Packard's hidden persuaders tap into human needs that we all share that make us vulnerable to appeals that promise to meet these needs. While this discussion has addressed products more than political or ideological campaigns, humans are also moved to pursue leaders and actions that preserve their dignity. The black power movement of the 1960s, the women's movement of the 1970s, and continuing political struggles revolve around the notion that dignity does not come with exploitation or servitude but with the power to define who we are and how we should live.

The needs that Maslow and Packard outlined complement and overlap each other, but both writers offer insights into the human condition that help explain how audiences hear messages, take them to heart, and act on them. Beyond these needs, humans also strive to find a harmonious view of the world where our beliefs and attitudes are synchronized or are at least not in discord with those around us. That is, we seek to find consistency in the world in regard to what we believe to be true about ideas, people, and things. Many theories have evolved to cast light on how people handle mental turmoil that requires tough decisions and attitude adjustments to find contentment. The next section addresses some of these findings.

AUDIENCE ATTITUDES AND BELIEFS: CONSISTENCY THEORIES

Many studies have been conducted to understand how people think, feel, and ultimately respond to messages that differ from their current attitudes and beliefs. Much of the conflict that we experience in communities today is attributable to clashing attitudes and beliefs about the nature of social problems like illegal immigration, drug abuse, unemployment, and homelessness. While various theories are useful in explaining some cases of persuasion, none of them paints the whole picture.

Modern persuasion theory is rooted in the study of attitudes and the work of Carl Hovland, the founder of the Yale Attitude Research Program. An **attitude** is "a learned predisposition to respond in a consistently favorable or unfavorable manner with respect to a given object" (Fishbein & Ajzen, 1975, p. 6). According to the tri-componential viewpoint on attitudes, they have three parts—the affective component, the behavioral component, and the cognitive component. That is, attitudes are composed of feelings, actions, and thoughts about a single entity (Oskamp & Schultz, 2005). According to Fishbein and Ajzen's (1975) definition, *beliefs* are a person's subjective thoughts that an object has a particular characteristic and that they assert a relationship between an object and a characteristic, such as: "This book is informative" (Oskamp & Schultz, 2005, p. 13). Milton Rokeach has studied beliefs extensively and posited that there are four positions within a belief system that determine the importance of a belief to the individual based on its connections to other parts of the whole. One's belief system may be compared to the layers of an onion with the middle or inner core being more central and more strongly embraced than the outer layers.

1. Beliefs about one's self, one's existence and identity, are much more central than other beliefs.
2. Shared beliefs about one's existence and self-identity are more central than unshared beliefs (ones held only by oneself).
3. Beliefs that are derived from other beliefs (rather than from contact with the object or belief) are less central than underived beliefs.
4. Beliefs concerning matters of taste are less central than other beliefs. They are usually seen by the holder to be arbitrary in nature, and thus they are relatively inconsequential in their impact on other beliefs. (Oskamp & Shultz, 2005, p. 93)

It is obvious that a belief that is a core belief, about who someone is and what kind of person they are, is more resistant to change than those that are on the outer layer of the system. For instance, we may change the style of our clothing, but we would not change our religion or spouse as readily because we perceive ourselves to be moral, devoted believers or partners. The intensity of the belief is how strongly the person holds it and how sure they are that it is true. *Primitive beliefs* are most resistant to change because they are based on direct contact with the object ("I am a moral person" or "My mother loves me"). These primitive beliefs concern both objects and people and require a consistency or harmony in one's belief system. Beliefs that are derived come from authority figures like parents, priests, or teachers. Rokeach believed that it would be inconceivable that countless beliefs would be unorganized and chaotic in our minds. He said:

> Rather it must be assumed that man's beliefs—like the astronomer's moons and planets and suns, like the geneticist's chromosomes and genes—become somehow organized into architectural systems having describable and measurable structural properties which, in turn, have observable behavioral consequences. (Rokeach, 1970, p. 1)

He noted that a change in a central belief will bring forth changes in the whole belief system. These central beliefs deal with self-identity and character and are more resistant to change than beliefs about sin, birth control, fascism, and communism because they are so taken for granted and either "shared by virtually everyone or because they are not at all dependent on social consensus" (Rokeach, 1970, p. 57).

Opinion is closely related to attitudes and is sometimes used synonymously with belief, but often opinions are evaluative beliefs expressed on a subject, such as "Pizza is a health food." If one were to say, "I love pizza," that would be an attitude statement describing one's feelings about it. *Values* are defined as an end rather than a means to an end, so that they are societal conditions or life goals. Values are inextricably tied to attitudes, because individuals will hold strong feelings toward those things that they value (Oskamp & Schultz, 2005). Persuasion is communication that targets attitudes, beliefs, and values because the speaker or source hopes to win adherence to their message, which may be acceptable or repulsive to the hearer of it. *Habits*, which are frequently repeated activities or patterns of behavior, are broader behavioral patterns that also contribute to an individual's persuasibility.

We learn through the socialization process in our families, among our friends, and in our neighborhoods to value or to disdain certain things and people. As a song from the musical *South Pacific* says, "You have to be taught to be afraid of people whose eyes are strangely made, you have to be carefully taught." Attitudes are learned or acquired, not innate. Generally, we are not aware of some of our attitudes until we are separated from our families or our home turf, when interactions with others who have very different views are unavoidable in our lives. Have you ever had someone say to you, "You talk funny," or "Why do you say 'pop' instead of 'soda' or 'Coke'?" Often these observations that you are different, even in small ways, are accompanied with an evaluation that these differences are somehow negative or threatening. When we leave home, we discover that not everyone values the same things that we do, nor do they have our perspective on how time, money, or energy should be spent. Much of our first year in college is a study in attitude adjustment as roommates learn how to negotiate dorm life. What happens when one roommate's attitude toward classes is that they are optional and that the dorm room is a place to bring all of your friends to party until three in the morning while the other roommate is an honor student who requires an ordered life with quiet time for study? Conflict is often the manifestation of opposing attitudes toward work, play, and others' rights and responsibilities.

Attitudes are important to persuasion because they are believed to predict behavior. This A–B relationship is the subject of much research that has tested just how well attitudes correlate with behavior. Studies that are concerned with compliance gaining, that is, getting people to do what you want them to do, are not as concerned with attitudes as they are with behavioral conformity.

COGNITIVE DISSONANCE THEORY (CDT)

Consistency theories are based on the assumption that individuals desire to have consistency or agreement in beliefs, attitudes, and behaviors. When there is dissonance, an inconsistency, there is psychological discomfort, which drives the individual to restore a feeling of balance. For example, an individual who considers himself to be an ethical person may have seen a copy of a test from a roommate who had taken the examination earlier and, upon receiving an A on the test, felt guilty because he knew that he had an advantage that none of the other students did. So the view of this person's being an ethical individual is not in agreement with the act of having cheated on an examination. Consistency theory states that this individual will seek to bring alignment between his held self-image and the action he took. He may rationalize the situation by saying that the teacher should have changed the test, thus displacing the blame, or he may generalize by saying "everyone does it." Consistency was thought originally to be a drive reduction theory, but more recently it has been seen as an effort to manage one's self-image. Perhaps the best known consistency theory is **cognitive dissonance theory** (CDT), which was developed by Leon Festinger (1957).

CDT, which was developed in the 1950s, fell out of favor in the 1970s and 1980s but has had a revival as researchers have extended the original theory. Dissonance occurs in varying degrees depending on the importance of the decision or action. There is far less regret for having worn the wrong suit for an interview than for having married the wrong partner, because the consequences are far more serious and longer lasting.

Persuasion can be used to either increase dissonance or decrease it. The message may aim to make individuals uncomfortable with their current product, candidate, or belief so that they will perhaps change their commitment to them. Daily advertisements come in the mail to have you change your car insurance, medical providers, or household products. On the other hand, the persuader may seek to reduce the ambivalence that individuals feels about choices that they have made. High school seniors who have made a selection for college will receive follow-up information on a fairly regular schedule informing them of their acceptance, announcing events that include scheduling classes for the fall, dates and events for freshman orientation, assigning living space, and reinforcing the value of the education they will receive at the chosen university or college. Each step toward completion of these provisions connects the freshmen more firmly to their chosen university and generates loyalty to it. Students experience tension when they have accepted one college and then receive an acceptance letter from another one where possibly the sports teams are better or their best friend or girlfriend will be attending.

Four paradigms are used to study cognitive dissonance: the free-choice paradigm, the belief-disconfirmation paradigm, the effort-justification paradigm, and the induced-compliance paradigm. The **free-choice paradigm** deals with the psychological doubts that a person feels after making a decision. They worry about whether or not they have bought the right car or house; in sales this is referred to as "buyer's remorse." The person tries to justify his or her decision to reduce the tension that they feel. Generally they have a period of two to three days to rescind the contract they have signed, and knowing this, great ambivalence may be present during this trial time.

The second paradigm deals with **belief disconfirmation,** wherein people are confronted with information inconsistent with their held beliefs. They may have had an investor change their portfolio to heavily invest in the real estate market, then later have seen, read, and heard information everywhere that the real estate bubble has burst and that values are falling precipitously, endangering their investments. The theory states that the individuals will avoid, reject, or distort such information by engaging in **selective exposure** and seeking information that is consistent with the choice that they have made. They will seek sources that buttress or support their investment decision. This paradigm also addresses religious beliefs and how true believers reconcile challenges to their faith. Eddie Harmon-Jones (1999) related a number of experiments where devout Christians were presented with external information that contradicted their belief. One experiment involved a contradiction in the belief that God was a benevolent God who protected innocent children and answered prayers. The suffering of innocent people is the hardest condition to integrate into a religion that teaches that God is benevolent. The situation presented to subjects was an incident covered in the newspaper where an infant boy was shot to death in his grandmother's arms while she and the infant's father prayed for protection. Participants were presented with the discrepancy between their belief that God protects the innocent and answers prayers and this incident that was covered in the newspaper. They had to read the account, which concluded, "some people would think that the grandfather's continued belief and trust in a good God is naive and misguided" (Harmon-Jones, 1999, p. 89). The experimenters hypothesized that if participants were exposed to belief-discrepant stories and were allowed to reconcile this dissonant information with a superordinate principle—transcendence—they would experience less turmoil or negative effects (p. 89). The experiment supported their hypothesis. We know that people reduce dissonance by finding ways to bolster their beliefs or to explain the challenges to their faith by using the superordinate principle that their loved one is at peace or in a better place—heaven.

Perhaps the most studied of the four types is the **induced-compliance paradigm**, also called the **forced-choice paradigm**. Researchers have found that when individuals are induced to engage in an action that is contrary to their attitudes or self-image, they find it easier to accept than if they were handsomely rewarded for it or chose the action of their own free will. For example, if an attorney represented some unsavory character, such as a pedophile who killed an innocent child, the attorney can choose to do the work pro bono (without charge, as a court-appointed attorney) rather than gain thousands of dollars for mounting such a defense.

The fourth paradigm is the **effort-justification paradigm**, which holds that if a person has to earn something, he or she appreciates it more. For example, basic training in the

U.S. Defense Secretary Robert Gates is met by Air Force officials at Manas Air Base in Bishkek, Kyrgyzstan where the GIs reflect the discipline of the military, which is an excellent example of the effort justification paradigm.

military not only prepares troops for their battles, it also builds esprit de corps. The initiations of "hell week" in fraternities where hazing occurs, sometimes ending with serious injuries or even death, were based on the premise that easy entry would not contribute to loyal pledges who felt great affinity to the group. Gang rituals that require members to "jump in," involving violent assignments such as seriously injuring or even killing someone, are common so that all members are cemented to the violent code that gang activities require to maintain drug territories, repel advances by rival gangs, and seal the veil of silence against other members so their misdeeds remain group secrets.

GERALD MILLER'S COUNTERATTITUDINAL ADVOCACY AND ROLE-PLAYING

Gerald Miller used the behavioral approach to analyze the impact of persuasion on audiences. He isolated variables and assigned values to them in an attempt to establish laws that emerged from the controlled studies. He did not oversimplify the task, but took into account the power or attractiveness of the persuader and the characteristics of the persuadee, such as intellect, self-esteem, and the effort expended at the task. Miller wrote:

> The scientific student of speech communication sees his primary task as the development of behavioral laws regarding the process. He seeks to discover a regularity in events that will enable him to make explanatory and predictive statements concerning those phenomena that are of importance to speech communication. That is, the task of the scientist is to arrive at statements concerning the ways in which specified objects (e.g. sources and receivers of communication) will behave or respond in specified communication environments. In pursuing this objective, he relies on the scientific method; unlike the humanist, he does stress such factors as controlled observation, manipulation, statistical analysis and replication. (Miller, 1966, p. 26)

Miller stated that persuasion involves a conscious attempt to influence the persuadee, and most persuasive communication aims to reinforce convictions already held by, say, Methodists or Democrats rather than converting them to these ideologies. He wrote:

> The value of persuasion as an inhibitor of change is undeniable. Nevertheless, in examining the writings in the field from antiquity to the present, we find relatively few pages devoted to persuasive techniques that seek to increase resistance as a facilitator of change: *persuasion is almost synonymous with changes in overt behavior or attitudinal valence.* (Miller & Burgoon, 1973, p. 5)

Miller looked at the persuasion process in a different light and investigated different techniques in altering attitudes including **role-playing** and **counterattitudinal advocacy**. These techniques involved taking a role in a real or hypothetical situation and creating the appropriate script for the situation or, in counterattitudinal advocacy, presenting a message that was contrary to the subject's beliefs. Suppose that a father wished to dissuade his college-bound son from smoking marijuana. He might ask the son to imagine that he were arrested and had to call home from the police station: What would he say? Rather than lecture the son, the father allows the son to write the script in the hypothetical situation.

This example uses the role-play technique. Psychotherapists use this technique wherein clients take the role of another or verbalize their feelings in a given situation. Another technique involves counterattitudinal advocacy, which requests that the target of the persuasion attempt to publically present a message that is at odds with his or her current beliefs. The father might ask his son to prepare and deliver an anti-marijuana message for a youth group in the community. The son would experience dissonance between his beliefs as a pot smoker and the message he composed and delivered, if he followed through. According to cognitive dissonance theory, he should seek a way to reduce the dissonance between how he actually feels about pot and the anti-drug message he has delivered to others. The father's hope would be that through the process of looking for good arguments against marijuana use the son would be able to create a good counterattitudinal message that would lead to self-persuasion. If the father offered an incentive, such as reasonable payment or other rewards, the positive outcome would be more likely. "The greater the justification, the greater the reluctant self-persuasion" (Miller & Burgoon, 1973, p. 70). While insufficient research exists to explain all the ways in which attitudes can change, we do know that mere exposure to stimuli can cause messages to gain acceptance.

MERE EXPOSURE THEORY (MET)

Mere exposure theory, also called **mere exposure effect,** states that repeated exposure to an unfamiliar stimulus can have a positive effect toward the stimulus, even in the absence of any reinforcement, which is necessary in classical conditioning like the Pavlov dog experiments. This phenomenon is present across different cultures. One explanation is "fluency," or the proficiency with which subjects recognize the stimulus, correlating this recognition with positive affect or liking.

Robert Bornstein and Paul D'Agostino (1992) reported over 200 published experiments on the exposure-effect relationship that involve a variety of stimuli such as polygons, drawings, photographs, nonsense words, and ideographs. They stated that these studies reflect robust and reliable findings that mere exposure effects can be demonstrated by stimuli that are "neither recalled nor recognized by subjects" and that those below the level of awareness seem to be more memorable (They stated: "Thus, if laboratory studies confirm that stimuli perceived without awareness produce significantly stronger mere exposure effects than do stimuli that are clearly recognized, extant models of the exposure effect may need to be revised or replaced" (1992, p. 545). They noted that a meta-analysis of research on exposure effects verifies that the effects of stimuli that are not recognized are substantially larger that those effects produced by clearly recognized stimuli. Their work has great implications for subliminal stimuli and persuasion.

Based on the positive effects of MET, whether conscious or subliminal in nature, we can understand how entertainers have gained a foothold in politics based not on expertise of any kind but merely on name recognition; examples include former President Ronald Reagan, governors Arnold Schwarzenegger of California and Jesse Ventura of Minnesota, Congressperson Sonny Bono, and Senator Al Franken. Some have done a decent job while others have not. Ventura was a wrestler; Reagan and Schwarzenegger were actors; Bono was a singer, once married to Cher; and Franken was a comedian—hardly internships for important political positions. Each man will be judged upon the merit of his performance, and some of them have won the admiration of millions—like President Reagan who is quoted by both Republicans and Democrats alike when it fits their rhetorical needs. Certainly, name recognition or exposure would give them an advantage on the ballot, but that does not mean that they had the essential skills to be effective in office once they were elected. Some research indicates that the law of diminishing returns occurs with MET, with a leveling-off or drop-off in effectiveness after about 10 to 20 exposures (Zajonc et al., 1972; Stang & O'Connell, 1974). However, it is evident that exposure in political campaigns is a great advantage for the candidate unless the exposure is of a negative nature, such as scandal or corruption. Those political bumper stickers, campaign buttons, and lawn signs do pay off, and so do the commercials and graphic images that marketers use to help you remember and select their brand when you shop.

THEORY OF REASONED ACTION (TRA)

The **theory of reasoned action** has great application in persuasion because it addresses the deliberative process that an individual engages in while analyzing messages, evaluating information, and weighing the benefits and risks of complying to the message. This theory was developed by Martin Fishbein and Isaac Ajzen in the late 1970s and focused on the individual's behavioral intention, which is not always what that person will ultimately do but is a good indicator.

Two factors are present in the theory of reasoned action. The first involves the individual's attitude toward the behavior, which is the evaluation of the *risks and benefits* associated with the decision, and the second is *subjective norms*. If the benefits are obvious, then the individual will use approach behavior, but if the risks are perceived to be great, then they will use avoidance behavior. For example, if you believe that your car will be damaged or stolen if you drive it to school, then you will likely take public transit even if it is inconvenient. However, if you believe that you will have greater freedom and greater convenience, or if public transit is not available, then you will choose to drive to school, but perhaps you will take precautions like parking in lighted places and using additional security systems. The second factor, *subjective norms*, means that a person's normative beliefs about what significant others think and the motivation to comply with those others' opinions are very influential. For example, the foregoing student would be more likely to drive to school, despite any risks of vandalism, if his friends all commuted to classes from their apartments or homes and he believed that having a car on campus was a status symbol. So receivers attend to messages that they believe will benefit them in some way and that will be comparable with their reference group's values.

Later studies have asked if the theory of reasoned action applies to moral decisions such as cheating in sports or confronting the umpire on an unfair call, and results show that both personal (attitudinal) and social (or normative) components do play a significant role in moral behavior (Vallerand et al., 1992). Both personal attitudes and social or normative components influence our behavioral and moral decisions. That is to say, the main determinants of our attitudes and moral inclinations may be heavily dependent upon our social environment.

SOCIAL JUDGMENT THEORY (SJT)

Social judgment theory, created by Muzafer Sharif, Carolyn Sharif, and Robert Nebergall (1965), addresses how persuasive messages are evaluated by receivers and whether or not persuasion occurs. Positions exist along a continuum with an anchor point, which is the person's most preferred position. Some positions may stretch this anchor position somewhat but still be in the latitude of acceptance. On the left of that point is the area of rejection, or latitude of rejection. The person may feel ambivalent about some messages and strongly opposed to others.

Latitude of Rejection		Latitude of Acceptance	
Strong Opposition	Ambivalence	Anchor point	Acceptance

<————————————————————————— X ——————————>

For example, a person may be an ovo-vegetarian who consents to eating eggs because they reason that the hen would continue to lay them even if we did not eat them. However, those who practice veganism would never eat animal flesh or eggs. The vegan avoids meat, diary, eggs, honey, or any other animal product, so you can see that within a belief system there are degrees of commitment or revulsion.

The person's anchor position is the one from which he or she evaluates all positions on the subject. It is difficult to persuade a person whose anchor point is too disparate from the one being advocated. A person who is opposed to abortion totally on ethical grounds would be opposed to any form of it, including the "morning-after pill." Another person may support abortion rights but be opposed to partial-birth abortions. Generally, persuaders will be more successful if they advocate a message that falls within the area of noncommitment or ambivalence rather than a message that falls within the latitude of rejection.

The positions on the gun controversy cluster in either the strongly opposed to regulation or strongly accepting further action groups, which indicate deep divisions between citizens on this issue with little common ground for compromise measures.

EXPECTANCY VIOLATIONS THEORY

Expectancy violations theory addresses three areas in communication: *language expectancy theory* (Burgoon, 1995), the *nonverbal expectancy violations model* (Burgoon, 1994), and *reinforcement expectancy theory* (Klingle, 1996). These variations on the same notion state that people have expectations of what normal behavior is, and when someone violates it, say with obscene language or inappropriate nonverbal behavior, or acts outside gender roles or social norms, then the receiver's attention turns to the source of the message. How the receiver responds depends on what they think of the sender of the message. If the source is very attractive to them, they may respond positively. For instance, the sexy waitress who violates the nonverbal rules of proxemics, that is, personal space expectations, and touches the patron gently on the arm may receive a better tip. However, if the touch is perceived as inappropriate, then the opposite would be true.

The members of the audience dictate what is appropriate both in language use and behavior. For example, a student completed a rhetorical analysis of the comedy *South Park* for her Senior Capstone course, which was fine until the day that she gave her final presentation and an older student brought his nine-year-old son to the class. The obscenities and misbehavior of the fourth-graders in *South Park*, which she included in her analysis, seemed particularly inappropriate with this unexpected young addition to the class. Her analysis had not been written for a fourth-grade audience but for the professor and the college class, where most members were at least 21.

Reinforcement expectancy theory posits that because of social norms some people have a narrow range of acceptable behavior. For example, when students have internships in business environments, they are expected to dress appropriately, not as they would if they were going to a nightclub. These are visual signs of conformity. Gender roles are another form of expectations. When women use powerful speech that is lacking in the general qualities of nurturing and self-disclosing anecdotes, they are punished. Hillary Clinton has routinely

South Park is a perfect example of expectancy violations theory with a gaggle of foul mouthed kids who are irreverent, politically astute, and satirize powerful institutions.

violated social expectations based on 'gender assignments because she exercised power like a man. She used facts, engaged in confrontational arguments, and challenged male-dominated institutions like Congress, presidential platforms, and social policies (we discuss this phenomenon further with regard to Clinton's rhetoric in Chapter 5). Social expectancy theory can work for or against the persuader depending on how he or she is perceived by the audience.

ELABORATION LIKELIHOOD MODEL (ELM)

The **elaboration likelihood model** attributed to Richard Petty and John Cacioppo (1986) analyzed the manner in which receivers or audiences process messages. We have already introduced this theory in relation to source credibility and how listeners who lack the ability to cognitively elaborate on an idea are more influenced by the sources' attributes. Petty and Cacioppo postulate that there are two basic routes to persuasion. The first is the *central processing route*, which is accompanied by cognitive elaboration and reflective thought on the content of the message. The second route is the *peripheral route*, which relies on shortcut forms of processing, which may consist of the source's attractiveness or the quantity of the arguments rather than their quality or logic (Petty, Cacioppo, & Goldman, 1981, p. 847). Critics have stated that both routes can be used simultaneously rather than making it an either/or choice. Petty and Cacioppo agree with this possibility, but critics say they should have made this point more central to the theory. The ELM theory helps explain some of the contradictions of former theories on whether the source, the message, or the receiver's predispositions account for the influence of a message and attitude change. Their research takes into account what the audience already knows and whether or not they take the short route to make a decision—such as source attractiveness—or even how actively engaged the listener is or how motivated they are to be discerning and participatory. The theory deals not only with the message but also with information processing routes or levels of consciousness. ELM explains how subliminal or unconscious cues aid persuasion because the receiver, who uses the peripheral route, is disarmed or beguiled by the message or by the source. The better informed listener will use the central processing route because they have the capacity to critically examine the message through cognitive elaboration or details.

SUMMARY

Audience analysis is complicated, because audiences may consist of one person, a small group of individuals with a common goal, or a multitude of people with nothing in common beyond their humanity. We know that persuasion can be found in either the sources of the message and their credibility, the message that they construct to connect to their target audience, or the hidden needs and desires of the audience members themselves. The attitudes, beliefs, and values of the audience can either facilitate persuasion attempts or thwart them. Primitive beliefs that are held deeply within a person and are central to his or her self-concept and self-esteem are very resistant to change, even without the consensus of another person. Derived or authority beliefs are handed down by parents, teachers, and trusted others who have socialized and nurtured us. Inconsequential beliefs dealing with personal tastes are easily changed because the consequences are not as harsh or long-lasting as are the core beliefs about our identity, our devotion to ideology, or our desired destiny. Persuaders use consistency needs to create dissonance or uncertainty in attitudes and beliefs in order to restructure them. Various strategies, such as repeated exposure to the desired idea, product, or candidate, are used, and in-depth analysis of audience needs, habits, and desires are used to persuade. Despite the work of ancient writers and modern research methods, much mystery still exists about what actually occurs when an individual allows another to change his or her thoughts, feelings, or behavior.

APPLICATIONS

1. Why have drug prevention programs failed to change attitudes toward drug use in the United States?
2. Do you think that mere exposure theory accounts for the cult of personality that entertainers such as Tom Cruise, Brad Pitt, Jennifer Lopez, Brittney Spears, and Angela Jolie have? How about Oprah or Dr. Phil? What is the audience appeal of these entertainers?
3. How would you apply the elaboration likelihood model to most advertisements that you have seen in the last week? How would you apply it to the presidential debates between Mitt Romney and Barack Obama?

REFERENCES

Anderson, J. B. (1989). *Speaking to groups: Eyeball to eyeball*. Vienna, VA: Wyndmoor Press.

Boeree, C. G. (2006). Personality theories: Abraham Maslow. Retrieved June 26, 2006, from http://www.ship.edu/~cgboeree/maslow.html.

Bornstein, R. F. (1989). Exposure and Effect: Overview and Meta-Analysis of Research, 1968–1987. *Psychological Bulletin, 106*, 265–289.

Bornstein, R. F., & D'Agostino. (1992). Stimulus recognition and the mere exposure effect. *Journal of Personality and Social Psychology, 63*, 4, 545–552. Retrieved July 5, 2012 from: https://sremote.pitt.edu/ids70,DanaInfo=csaweb115v.csa.com+display_fulltext_html.php?S.

Burgoon, J. K. (1994). Nonverbal signals. In M. L. Knapp & G. R. Miller (Eds.), *Handbook of interpersonal communication* (2d ed., pp. 229–285). Thousand Oaks, CA: Sage Publications.

Burgoon, M. (1995). Language expectancy theory: Elaboration, explication, and extension. In C. R. Berger & M. Burgoon (Eds.), *Communication and social influence processes* (pp. 29–51). East Lansing: Michigan State University Press.

Commitment: How Veterans, Baby Boomers, Generation Xers and Generation Nexters Can All Get Along in the Workplace. Retrieved July 5, 2006, from http://www.committment.com/getalong.html.

Cox, R. (1987). Afterword: The rich harvest of Abraham Maslow. In A. H. Maslow (Ed.), *Motivation and personality* (3rd ed., pp. 245–271). New York: Harper & Row.

Festinger, L. (1957). *A theory of cognitive dissonance*. Stanford, CA: Stanford University Press.

Fishbein, M., & Ajzen, I. (1975). *Belief, attitude, intention, and behavior: An introduction to theory and research*. Reading, MA: Addison-Wesley.

Harmon-Jones, E. (1999). Toward an understanding of the motivation underlying dissonance effects: Is the production of aversive consequences necessary? In E. Harmon-Jones & J. Mills (Eds.), *Cognitive dissonance: Progress on a pivotal theory in social psychology* (pp. 71–99). Washington, DC: American Psychological Association.

Klingle, R. S. (1996). Physician communication as a motivational tool for long-term patient compliance: reinforcement expectancy theory. *Communication Studies, 47*, 206–217.

Maslow, A. H. (1987). *Motivation and personality* (3rd ed.). New York: Harper & Row.

McCroskey, J. C. (1997). *An introduction to rhetorical communication*. Boston: Allyn and Bacon.

Miller, G. R. (1966). *Speech communication: A behavioral approach*. New York: Bobbs-Merrill.

Miller, G. R., & Burgoon, M. (1973). *New techniques of persuasion*. New York: Harper & Row.

Moreland, R. L., & Zajonc, R. B. (1977). Is stimulus recognition a necessary condition for the occurrence of exposure effects? *Journal of Personality and Social Psychology, 35*, 191–199.

Oskamp, S., & Schultz, P. W. (2005). *Attitudes and opinions* (3rd ed.). Mahwah, NJ: Lawrence Erlbaum.

Packard, V. (1957). *The hidden persuaders*. New York: David McKay Company.

Petty, R. E., & Cacioppo, J. T. (1986). *Communication and persuasion: Central and peripheral routes to attitude change*. New York: Springer-Verlag.

Petty, R. E., Cacioppo, J. T., & Goldman, R. (1981). Personal involvement as a determinant of argument-based persuasion. *Journal of Personality and Social Psychology, 41*(5), 847–855.

Portolano, M., & Evans, R. B. (2005). The experimental psychology of attitude change and the tradition of classical rhetoric. *American Journal of Psychology, 118*(1), 123–140.

Rokeach, M. (1970). *Beliefs, attitudes and values: A theory of organization and change*. San Francisco: Jossey-Bass.

Sherif, C. W., Sherif, M., & Nebengall, R. E. (1965). *Attitude and attitude change: The social judgment approach*. Philadelphia: W. B. Saunders.

Stang, D. J., & O'Donnell, E. J. (1974). The computer as experiment in social psychology research. *Behavior Research Methods and Instrumentation, 6*, 223–231.

Vallerand, R. J., et al. (1992). Ajzen and Fishbein's Theory of Reasoned Action as applied to moral behavior: A confirmatory analysis. *Journal of Personality and Social Psychology, 62*(1), 98–109.

Whyte, W. F. (1957). *Street corner society: The social structure of an italian slum*. Chicago: University of Chicago Press.

Zajonc, R. B., et al. (1972). Exposure, satiation, and stimulus discriminability. *Journal of Personality and Social Psychology, 21*, 270–280.

CHAPTER 4

LANGUAGE: THE CODE OF PERSUASION

KEY WORDS

black power movement
co-cultures
connotation
David Crystal
denotation
devil-terms
double bind
The Feminine Mystique

functional meanings
gender styles
general semantics
god-terms
S. I. Hayakawa
idiosyncratic
Alfred Korzybski
George Lakoff

"Letter from Birmingham Jail"
metaphors
paradigm shift
pejorative
public philosophy
stereotype

PREVIEW

School shootings have become a national nightmare, and one fact that surfaces in the profiles of the shooters is that they have been bullied at school and publically humiliated by words. They have been the object of ridicule and labeled as different or inferior. Eldon Taylor has analyzed the impact that words have on school violence and how semantic distortions create tragedies. He wrote:

> Further, there exists today a direct linear relationship between the development of semantic distortions and the ever-increasing mental disorders in our modern society, particularly among the youth. The sheer numbers of disturbed young people carrying out the most violent of acts is especially frightening." (Taylor, 2001, p. 1)

His essay, "What's in a Word? School Violence," explains his ideas further and demonstrates the power that words have to trigger action. Taylor (2001) wrote:

> It's easy to note the fear of many when it comes to words of rejection, words that make fun of people or are excessively and inappropriately critical, words that condemn, words that are negative labels such as ugly, stupid, loser, failure, and so forth. Words, however, have still

other emotional domains that they either anchor, or that are like search words in a web browser, when inputted they trigger a host of related sites stored deep in one's memory. Indeed, due largely to our educational system and culture, most words can be said to have values. Think about it, even so called innocuous descriptors such as color have value attached. Some colors are preferred over others, some colors are simply obnoxious, and for some, an emotional disturbance or trauma can be connected to a color. (p. 4)

Words are used as weapons to entrap an enemy, and words can create historical change in a body politic. Some of today's best wordsmiths remind us of landmark words. Barack Obama in a political speech stated:

Don't tell me words don't matter. "I have a dream." Just words? "We hold these truths to be self-evident, that all men are created equal." Just words? "We have nothing to fear but fear itself"—just words? Just speeches? (Shafer, 2008)

ETHICAL SPEECH OR LETHAL WORDS?

On Saturday, January 8, 2011, 22-year-old Jared Lee Loughner was arrested and accused of opening fire upon a crowd of people who had come to a supermarket in Tucson, Arizona, to hear their local congresswoman, Gabrielle Giffords, address their concerns. Loughner is being held for murdering 6 people and injuring 13 more that morning. Among the dead was a 9-year-old girl who was interested in public service and wanted to see Gabby, as the town folks called her, hold a town hall meeting called "Congress on Your Corner." Judge John Roll, chief judge for Arizona federal courts, was also killed along with two of Giffords' aides. Congresswoman Giffords was shot at short range through the head, but she miraculously survived and days later seemed responsive to doctors and her husband's requests to acknowledge commands by eye movement or hand movements. A volunteer, Daniel Hernandez, who had only been working with her staff for five days rushed to her side and put pressure on the wound, preventing her from bleeding to death before the ambulance arrived (Pettersson, 2011). Loughner had been characterized as "creepy" and mentally unstable by both professors and students at the community college where he attended classes.

President Obama eulogized the victims of that shooting spree and set a tone of reverence at the memorial service at Tucson that resembled a political or football rally before he embarked upon the serious notes that would mark the lives of the 6 victims. He said:

Already we've seen a national conversation commence, not only about the motivations behind these killings, but about everything from the merits of gun safety laws to the adequacy of our mental health systems. Much of this process, of debating what might be done to prevent such tragedies in the future, is an essential ingredient in our exercise of self-government.

But at a time when our discourse has become so sharply polarized—it is a time when we are too eager to lay the blame for all that ails the world at the feet of those who think differently than we do—it's important for us to pause for a moment and make sure that we are talking with each other in a way that heals, not a way that wounds. (Obama, January 11, 2011)

Immediately after the shootings, a fierce debate erupted over the volatile rhetoric from the Tea Party and conservative talk show hosts during the recent midterm elections. Sarah Palin was targeted with accusations of feeding the frenzy of unbalanced individuals. "You cannot flippantly talk about 'reloading' and putting people on your TARGET list and not expect some nut to take you literally," read one typical comment posted to Palin's Facebook page. "This is on you partially whether you like it or not" (Goldberg, January 8, 2011).

Conservatives answered these charges from liberals by stating that they cannot be held accountable for some mentally unbalanced person, and Palin stated that she and her husband offered their prayers to the families that they would find peace and justice. Jonah Goldberg wrote on the *National Review* website:

I've been reading the instant reaction on Twitter and on the Web and I've been trying to filter out the urge to vent my rage at those who immediately shoehorned these awful crimes into their ideological prism. There have been some truly disgusting displays of opportunism out there. (Goldberg, January 8, 2011)

The question is: what comprises ethical speech? When does graphic speech or violent imagery fuel hatred or discontent enough to motivate action? Where does the First Amendment right to freedom of speech and press end and incitement to riot or to take up arms begin? Does it

Congress woman Gabrielle Giffords' shooting renewed the debate about inflammatory language, guns, and violence.

endanger our public officials when they are referred to as "enemies," "Nazis," "socialists," or "communists"? These inappropriate terms have been used by politicians on both the right and left of the political spectrum

When does discourse cross the line between right and wrong and begin to dehumanize us, to poison our political climate, and to escalate divisions between parties, ethnic groups, and everyday citizens?

A controversy arose when Obama's political opponent in the 2008 election, Hillary Clinton, accused him of plagiarizing Deval Patrick, a Democratic congressman and friend to Obama. Patrick had used the same words in a former setting, but he stated that he gave Obama permission to use them in his campaign. So who owns words? We recognize those in Obama's aforementioned speech as first belonging to Dr. Martin Luther King Jr., to the Declaration of Independence, and to FDR, a wartime president who consoled his citizens, and in this series of quotations we have a minister, a state document, and a presidential speech. Therefore, we can surmise that no one owns words; we merely use them to inform, to persuade, to exhort, and to inspire others who have the liberty to interpret them as they see fit. We do protect other's intellectual property through copyrights, but words are not the possession of any one person, class, or nation. Words are the vehicles that move thought from one person to another through the communicative acts of speaking and writing.

In this chapter we focus on the role that language plays in the persuasion process. General semantics are discussed using Hayakawa's definition, and examples are offered of how language affects race, gender, politics, and our conceptions of the "supernatural," to use Burke's term. By the supernatural, we mean awesome, beyond common experience, such as God, angels, and heaven. Even though none of us have ever seen any of these things, we can talk about them because they have been given an existence through language. George Lakoff's analysis of **metaphors** and how they frame an argument or establish the grounds for action are discussed. Words allow us to transmit meaning between senders and receivers both humble and grandiose. The function of words is reviewed as they affect imparting ideas, conjuring feelings and attitudes, and moving us to action. Political movements that have challenged names, existing stereotypes, or labels are illustrated from the **black power movement,** the women's movement, and some current political struggles or wars. No study of persuasion would be complete without focusing on the code of communication, which is the words that we choose to use, and the effect that they have on others. There could be no "encode" or "decode" without the code itself.

GENERAL SEMANTICS

Words are the embodiment of our past history, our future dreams, and our present condition. Words weave the fabric of human thoughts, create epics, lyrics to songs, and political discourse. Words carry meaning that must be interpreted, digested, and accepted or rejected by the hearer. While there is a physical world beyond our words, we are the creators of the social-political sphere where language is the necessary medium of exchange.

John Condon (1966) wrote in *Semantics and Communication:*

> The study of language leads us to an apparent dilemma. On the one hand, we seem to have the freedom to describe the world in many ways; and yet on the other hand, no matter how we describe the world we will be distorting it through our words. We have *abstracted from* and *projected to* that which we wish to describe. *Whatever* we say a thing *is,* it is not *that.* (p. 67)

Words are mere symbols which stand for whatever "that" is. While words do not compose the material world, words do assign meaning to people, events, and ideas in the world. Words can be either weapons that wound or tools that heal the human spirit. We are talking about **general semantics,** which S. I. Hayakawa defined as follows: "General semantics is the study of the relations between language, thought, and behavior: between *how we talk,* therefore *how we think,* and therefore *how we act*" (Hayakawa, 1962, p. vii). Semanticists are concerned not with how eloquently we are speaking or our pronunciation but with whether our language is specific or general, descriptive, inferential, or judgmental. Further, they are concerned with our attitudes toward our own language whether we are open-minded or dogmatic (Hayakawa, 1962, p. vii).

Alfred Korzybski (1879–1950) started the semanticist movement when he wrote *Science and Sanity: An Introduction to Non-Aristotelian Systems and General Semantics* (1933), in which he stated that if people used language to solve social and personal problems the way we approach science, then problems deemed insoluble would be soluble. While many did not agree with his conclusions, he did introduce a new area of inquiry into human behavior that focused on the role that language played in thought and action. The quote most associated with Korzybski is, "The map is not the territory" (Rapoport, 1962, p. 20). This means that the word that we assign to a thing is not the thing itself. The comedian Stephen Wright used to say, "I have a map of the United States, actual size." Well, even if he did, it certainly would not *be* the United States but a poor representation of it. The map would be flat, foldable, made of paper or some other perishable thing, and it would contain nothing of the nation that it represented. Like Wright's map, words are poor representations of the things they attempt to communicate to you, but they are a map *to* the territory.

The problem with semantics and people is that people respond as if the word were the thing itself. One assignment that my students complete is to write the words "man" and "woman" and under each generic word, they write all the other words that they know that refer to men and women. At first they are very proper and cautious because they already know the power of words to insult or to flatter, and furthermore, in a class setting, they do not want others to know that they are conversant with some of the terms. Pretty soon they get to the more visceral language of studs, foxes, bitches, hutchies, and whores. This exercise introduces the idea of propriety or political correctness and how we must adapt to the intended audience for language usage. When talk show hosts refer to feminists as Femi-Nazis, they have told us more about themselves and their attitudes toward feminists than we know about the individuals to whom they refer. Any other pejorative label has the same quality of stereotyping a person or group, such as "wetbacks," "queers," "towel-heads," and others too despicable to list here. A **stereotype** is a prejudicial characterization or mold that does not allow for any individuality and when applied to people the image is generally negative. The problem is that people respond to these labels as though they were real, so the word causes physical reactions such as anger, embarrassment, or hatred. Words can affect our well-being by causing our autonomic nervous system to produce an adrenaline rush with rapid heart rate, heavy breathing, sweating palms, and a will to fight or take flight. Words affect our thoughts, feelings, and behaviors.

COGNITIVE, AFFECTIVE, AND BEHAVIORAL FUNCTIONS OF WORDS

Words have three dimensions—cognitive, affective, and behavioral components. That means that words transmit cognition, or thoughts and ideas; affect, that is they evoke feelings and attitudes toward the subjects; and behavior in that they induce people to act upon what they have heard or read. We have already established the functions of persuasion, and at the head of the list was naming things, people, and events. One of the most popular names for baby girls in 2010 was Nevaeh, that is "Heaven" spelled backwards. Imagine such a woman at age 18; she may be seen as divine or as a "space cadet" who wishes her parents had used better judgment. Children's names have often been the cause of schoolyard brawls; parents should consider carefully what label they hang on their offspring. The language that we use to describe people influences how we think about them, feel about them, and treat them. John Condon (1966) wrote:

As children we learned to chant that sticks and stones may break our bones but words can never hurt us. Sophisticated philosophers have said very much the same thing. Ludwig Wittgenstein, for one, said that the world is independent of our will—in our terms, the world is what it is regardless of what we call it. And so it is, the semanticist agrees, with some of this world but not with all of it. The division between natural science and social science might be the distinction between worlds unaffected by language and those that are very much changed by language. The brick may not care in the least whether it is called *a brick*, or *structural material*; but the bricklayer may behave differently if he is called *laborer* or *artisan* or *Construction engineer*. In the world of people, of conversation and argument, personal adjustment and insanity, words exert a tremendous influence. (p. 51)

Words are the building blocks of thought and the expression of our thoughts. Try to think of an idea without using words. You can produce images in the mind's eye, or even feelings or sensations, but try to think about how to share this experience with another person. We are all symbol users with varying degrees of skill at capturing ideas, experiences, or creative endeavors.

Kenneth Burke (1970) in *The Rhetoric of Religion* drew distinctions between "words" and "the Word," as in "In the beginning was the Word" (John 1:1, NIV). He offered four realms to which words may refer. First there are words for the natural, such as material things like trees, the wind, and clouds; animality, such as dogs or bears; and physiological conditions, such as hunger or thirst. These things or conditions would exist whether we talked about them or not. Second, there is the socio-political realm with words for right and wrong, American, property rights, and matrimony. Third, there are "words about words," which he called "logology." In this category we find dictionaries, literary criticism, grammar, discussions such as this chapter, and rhetoric. The final realm is words for the "supernatural." We borrow words from the other three realms to discuss that which is "ineffable" or too overwhelming to be expressed, as God's name or the hereafter (Burke, 1970, pp. 14–15). Words, as symbols, transcend the things that they name by becoming representative of all such types of things. For example, the word "tree" may mean a mighty oak or a willow that blows in the wind, but we can conceive of the idea of a tree regardless of the specific nature of it. Words give us the ability to talk of the past, the present, and the future.

Some form of communication preceded drawings on caves, alphabets, ink, paper, and printing presses, but all of these developments would standardize language after periods of confusion among territories and make a permanent record possible. One appropriate metaphor for the ability to produce "talk" would be to see the brain as the hardware of communication and to think of language as the software. To further our computer metaphor, every language brings a logic, or grammar, of its own which offers a particular program to complete tasks. The language that we use brings with it a worldview with normative prescriptions of how things ought to work, what people ought to do, and a value system that prioritizes everything into some kind of a hierarchy. Some scholars believe that through symbolic interaction we actually define ourselves. George Herbert Mead's lectures supported this view.

GEORGE HERBERT MEAD'S SYMBOLIC INTERACTION THEORY

George Herbert Mead, who taught at the University of Chicago, published very little during his lifetime, but his student, Herbert Blumer, coined the phrase "symbolic interaction" based on Mead's theoretical work. After Mead died, a group of his students published a book titled *Mind, Self, and Society* (1934) taken from his lectures. Mead believed that the concept of "self" was constructed through the symbolic interaction of individuals in society. Contained within the self are two interacting parts of an individual, composed of the "I" and the "me." The "me" is composed of social attitudes that are reflected in the mirror image that others project upon the individual, but the "I" asserts how much control the community will have and "thus makes for novelty, social change, and reconstruction. "Taken together, the 'I' and 'me' as phases of the self, they constitute a personality" (Pfuetze, 1954, p. 89). The notion of a "looking glass self" originated from the idea that we come to know ourselves from the reflection of another's gaze (Thomas, 2004). While this idea may appear abstract, a humorous example may help illustrate the point of the impact that stereotypes have on people's self-image or images others try to project on them. Mead considered friends, family, and work colleagues as "particular others," while society as a whole or groups were "generalized others" (Thomas, 2004). Through social interaction, we feel the power of rejection or pride, but some self-assured individuals, like Frank Zappa, exercised the power of the "I" to set things straight. The following story has circulated about Frank Zappa for years. A radio talk show host who was known for his vitriolic personality, which some claim came from his disability and having a prosthetic leg, had an exchange with Frank Zappa, a musician, composer, and producer who was wearing long hair in the 1960s when it was not the prevailing style and was seen as a political statement. The interviewer said, "So Frank, you have long hair. Does that make you a woman?" Zappa replied, "You have a wooden leg. Does that make you a table?" This succinct exchange demonstrates how social norms tend to stigmatize anyone who does not conform, unless, like Zappa, the "I" position allows us to cut

Frank Zappa promised that his music would not send listeners to hell's fire, which he believed was reserved for televangelists.

through the hypocrisy or stereotypes that threaten to define us. Zappa's response focused on the fallacy of taking one attribute and making it the defining principle for an individual.

LANGUAGE IN POLITICS

Language defines our worldview by defining our attitudes, beliefs, and values more clearly than anything else we might use. In a book titled *What's Language Got to Do with It?* (2005), the editors, Keith Walters and Michael Brody, answered the question their title posed by saying, "Everything." They wrote:

> If most folks think about language at all, they assume it works like a window—a clear pane of glass—beyond which we see reality as it truly is. . . . We'll take a very different perspective, assuming that something as mundane as word choice makes an argument, often a powerful one.
>
> Kenneth Burke (1897–1993), a scholar of literature, rhetoric, and religion, suggests that words and phrases act as terministic screens, encouraging or even forcing us to see reality in particular ways, ruling out alternatives. As Burke points out, words don't just reflect particular views of reality; they actually complete arguments. If, for example, someone refers to a fetus as an "unborn child," it's logical for that person to believe that abortion should be banned because in his or her eyes, it is the murder of a child. If someone else thinks of abortion as a "right" that women should have in order to have control over their own bodies, that person probably doesn't even use the term "unborn child." Similarly, men who perceive that to be just who they are would not likely use such a term like "disease" to talk about homosexuality. In all these cases, the arguments complete themselves: by choosing language like "unborn child," "right," "disease," or "who I am," you set up chains of propositions leading inevitably (or nearly so) to a particular conclusion. (Walters & Brody, 2005, p. 2)

The metaphors that we use to describe an event colors the entire truth that we create concerning the narrative. Common types of metaphors come from the language of war, sports, and the animal kingdom. For example, we speak of winners and losers, victory and defeat, someone who plays hardball, or a dark horse who wins an election.

Clyde Haberman discussed an incident in which the Israeli Army fired missiles at the Hamas offices on the West Bank, killing eight Palestinians, but regrettably two small boys who were playing in the vicinity were also killed. While the United States and other countries condemned the attack, Israel defended their actions by saying that they were protecting their own people. Haberman described the language of war from both sides in this way:

> Easy, Palestinian officials said. It was a cold-blooded assassination. But just as one person's terrorist has long been another's freedom fighter, one side's "assassination" is the other's "active self-defense," a term favored by some Israeli officials.
>
> Foreign Minister Shimon Peres became practically apoplectic when an Israeli television interviewer used the A-word. Israel does not assassinate people, Mr. Peres said angrily. It goes after leaders who dispatch young men to blow themselves up in the midst of Israelis. "Suicide bombers cannot be threatened by death," he said. "The only way to stop them is to intercept those who send them."

All this goes beyond mere political spin, though each side in this near-war is out to persuade the world that it is the true victim. The use of language touches the psychology of the conflict, not only how Palestinians and Israelis view each other but also how they judge themselves. No way, for example, is Israel about to pronounce itself an assassin state, no matter how much the wisdom and morality of its strategy is questioned abroad. (Haberman, 2005, p. 4)

It depends on who is reporting the event as to who is the "martyr" or the "terrorist." Haberman stated that in earlier times there was more hopeful rhetoric; in 1993 at the Oslo peace agreement, Yitzhak Rabin and Yasser Arafat shook hands to seal the deal, and they were called "peace partners" as they spoke of the "peace process." Despite the lack of progress there, both countries share a word from Hebrew, "salom," and Arabic, "salaam," which means peace, a state that both yearn to achieve (Haberman, 2005, p. 7).

The wars in Iraq and Afghanistan are discussed in news stories with some journalists writing of the bravery, sacrifices, and liberation the U.S. military brought to the people. But other journalists report that atrocities occur with deaths of innocent women and children, and they define the role of the United States as an occupation of Arab countries. Do you think these descriptions influence American resolve in the war? Do you think that the language of war influences foreign policy? Do you think that reporters, commentators, and everyday citizens should weigh their words well when discussing the war, the nature of the enemy, and how America should respond to terrorism? The answer to all these questions is a resounding yes, because the manner in which the arguments are framed will create the reality of the situation and dictate policy that our young soldiers will have to live and die to support. Further, the language of war will determine what kind of peace is possible. So are U.S. troops occupiers or liberators? Was it a just cause? What does democracy mean in the Middle East? Democracy is a word with a high level of abstraction. In order to capture reality or truth, one must deal with facts that are described in words. In an essay titled "Language and Truth," Weller Embler wrote:

> Anyone who has the temerity to speak of "truth" usually finds that he is performing verbal dances around the *word* truth, rather than letting truth perform for itself. The truth is as hard to talk about as it is to tell, though it is not, I think, so hard to find as people say, nor so ready with a dusty answer. If there is one thing certain, the truth will not be caught *once and for all* in a net of words alone, nor does it like to be imprisoned in a theory; it is much too fond of its liberty. At the outset of any inquiry into the nature of truth, one has, in my opinion, to begin with "facts," that is, with things themselves. (Embler, 1962, p. 230)

Any truth that will be told must be clothed in words that will give it both form and substance. Since speech is purposeful, we must look to the motivations of the speaker or writer of those words. As in any communication transaction, you would be well armed to "consider the source" of the message and analyze any hidden agenda or special word use that might be designed to have you respond in a knee-jerk way rather than to rationally examine the message before you. Some scholars have written on how perceptual frames both restrain and liberate thought. George Lakoff offered insight into the nature of metaphors and how they create perceptual frames of thought.

GEORGE LAKOFF'S ANALYSIS OF METAPHORS

George Lakoff (1999b) examined metaphors used for the mind and how the conceptual system of thought influences philosophical discourse. Lakoff and Mark Johnson have studied the conceptual structure of philosophical systems evident in Plato, Aristotle, Descartes, and Kant. Lakoff offered essential metaphors that describe the act of thinking and explained how these metaphor systems for the mind provide common places for philosophical theories. For example, the "thinking is moving" metaphor includes the premises that the mind is a body, thinking is moving, and ideas are in locations. Examples of this metaphor include such expressions as "My mind was racing," or someone goes off "on flights of fancy," or another "reached a conclusion" after having "arrived at a crucial point in the argument" (p. 160). Another metaphor includes "thinking as perceiving," which integrates the idea that most knowledge comes through vision. How many cartoons have you seen with a light bulb representing a moment of insight? Here are the premises of knowledge acquired through vision as outlined by Lakoff:

The Mind Is a Body
- Thinking is perceiving.
- Ideas are things perceived.
- Knowing is seeing.
- Communicating is showing.
- Attempting to gain knowledge is searching.
- Becoming aware is noticing.
- An aid to knowing is a light source.
- Being able to know is being able to see.
- Being ignorant is being unable to see.
- Impediments to knowledge are impediments to vision.
- Deception is purposefully impeding vision.
- Knowing from a "perspective" is seeing from a point of view.
- Explaining in detail is drawing a picture.
- Directing attention is looking at.
- Being perceptive is hearing.
- Taking seriously is listening.
- Sensing is smelling.
- Emotional reaction is feeling.
- Personal preference is taste. (Lakoff, 1999b, p. 162)

Some of the idioms that arise from this metaphorical structure are, "I see what you are saying," . . . deception in communication is "trying to pull the wool over [someone's] eyes," . . . and an ignorant person is kept "in the dark" while some have "blinders on" and can only see "what's in front of [their] nose" (p. 162). Since this metaphorical view of the mind includes all the senses, we can include the person who turns a "deaf ear" to another or senses that "something doesn't smell quite right here," which indicates that mentally we suspect that something is not as it should be (p. 163). Another structure that Lakoff analyzed was The "thought as language" metaphor, which has the following elements:

- Thinking is linguistic activity (speaking or writing).
- Simple ideas are words.
- Complex ideas are sentences.
- Fully communicating a sequence of thought is spelling.
- Memory is writing. (Lakoff, 1999b, p. 167)

Phrases that arise from this structural frame are taking "mental notes," "reading someone like a book," or "misreading someone's intentions," while others can" hardly hear themselves think" while trying to "read between the lines" (p. 167). Lakoff offered many metaphors for the mind or the thought process including the mind as a mathematical computation where reasoning is adding and inferences are sums. The "mind as machine" metaphor views ideas as products and the normal operation of the machine is thoughts, but the inability to think is seen as a malfunction of the machine. The "mind as computer" metaphor has become commonplace, where knowledge is the database and understanding is successful computation. Lakoff demonstrates that metaphors form a frame of reference from which a logic flows with appropriate words or images that arise from them. On the one hand, this form of metaphorical thought is facilitative, moving us from the known to the unknown, but on the other hand, such thought processes are a restraining force with parameters drawn around the model. Lakoff is important because he applies his analysis to contemporary social and political conditions. In one such analysis he presented the metaphor of the nation-as-the-family in his book *Whose Freedom? The Battle Over America's Most Important Idea* (2006). He wrote:

> In monarchies, the royal family is the government; the king is the father. We know about monarchies and other patriarchal forms of government, which means we know about how parents can also be rulers. In the Catholic church—God's Kingdom on Earth—the ruler of the church is called the Holy Father. And countries around the world are called by names such as Mother India, Mother Russia, and the Fatherland.
>
> It should not be a shock that we Americans also conceptualize our nation metaphorically as a family. We have Founding Fathers. We send "our sons and daughters" to war. We have organizations like the Daughters of the American Revolution. Groups in the military think of themselves as "bands of brothers." In America, we have "homeland security," where the nation's landmass is seen as "home" to the nation seen as a "family." And conservatives are clear about the centrality to their politics of "family values." (Lakoff, 2006, p. 66)

These metaphors influence our worldview about our purpose on earth, the relationship that we have with the cosmos, and any deity, if one is a believer. Lakoff believes that metaphors offer models which frame arguments, attitudes, and beliefs. He noted that these frames of reference have emotional as well as intellectual content and that they shape the political and social ideologies of our time. Lakoff stated that language reframes a situation, and those who successfully frame the argument will win the debate. He used the Bush administration's language of the war in Iraq as an example:

The Bush administration first framed the Iraq War as "regime change," as though the country would remain intact except for who ran the government. Saddam Hussein would "fall"—symbolized by his statue falling, an image played over and over on American TV—and a new democratic government would immediately replace the old tyranny. As the insurgency began to emerge, it became clear that the old frame was inoperative and a reframing took place: Iraq became "the main front in the war on terror." (Lakoff, 2006, p. 12)

With news channels like FOX News using the words "War on Terror" any time they showed pictures of the insurgency, by the time the 2004 election occurred three of four Bush supporters believed that Saddam Hussein had given substantial support to al-Qaeda terrorists. The language of war with the ability to reframe the perceptions about the war was highly successful for the Bush administration (Lakoff, 2006, p. 12). Words not only reflect and report reality, as Lakoff demonstrated, words can create a whole new social and political situation. He believes that the political right in America has taken possession of the most sacred words in our vocabulary like "freedom" and twisted them to represent the exact opposite of what our Constitution guarantees to all citizens. We do not just utter or write words; we "feel" them too.

EMOTIONAL LANGUAGE

Words have the capacity to fire off emotional responses that may be positive or negative depending on the hearer's experience. For example, the word "quagmire" still resonates with the Vietnam generation as an irresolvable mess or failure with images of "blood baths," "Agent Orange" defoliates, and kaleidoscopic pictures of burned victims or massacres. That word strikes a responsive chord with those who lived through that era, and it was resurrected by journalists to describe the war in Iraq with the intentions to draw parallels that would lead one to conclude that the outcome would be a dismal failure. The word "quagmire" has a predisposition to create a negative attitude that will, through association, lead one to conclude that Iraq is a lost cause. If one buys into the basic premise that the two wars are indeed comparable, the syllogism would state: (Major premise): The Vietnam War was a quagmire that ended with the fall of Saigon and a bloodbath. (Minor Premise): The war in Iraq is a quagmire like Vietnam. Conclusion: Therefore, the war in Iraq will see the fall of Baghdad and a bloodbath. Logically, one could argue that no parallels exist since the countries have different histories and different political possibilities, but clearly some commentators use the word "quagmire" as a buzzword that brings all the negative cargo of history with it. There is a tendency recently to use historical terms such as Nazi, gulag, and Eichmann to create negative associations with fairly mundane affairs, which distorts the horror of these historical people or events. As students of persuasion, we need to become sensitized to the power of language to represent reality or to distort and manipulate it. If you listen to talk radio and political commentators, you will easily observe their use of labels, emotional language, and various vehicles to win your support.

RUSH LIMBAUGH'S USE OF EMOTIONAL LANGUAGE

Rush Limbaugh is the number one talk show host in the country for conservatives, with millions of loyal listeners. He is flamboyant in his use of language, and he frequently labels his opponents or gives them nicknames, such as "John F'n Kerry," which denigrates his target but entertains his audience members. The problem with such "entertainment" is that it also persuades mass audiences, who assume that they are immune to the influences of such rhetoric, which they will concede does impact other people. This is referred to as the "third person effect" in mass media—the idea that while we are immune to such appeals, less intelligent others are certainly affected by it. In an article, "The Red Flags of Persuasion," Don Jacobs admonished that persuasion is often cloaked in anecdotes, stories, and metaphors that disarm the listener (Jacobs, 1995). We already discussed Fisher's narrative theory, which posits that humans were storytellers before anyone was literate, and thus stories are a communal activity that teaches, preaches, and influences others. Another persuasive strategy is what Jacobs called the "**double bind**," where two alternatives are offered but both lead to the desired objective. He quoted Rush Limbaugh, who said, "I don't know who is worse, the environmental wackos or the feminazis!" (Jacobs, 1995, p. 378). Clearly, Limbaugh's intentions were to put both groups into a category of dangerous types. A third strategy is to establish rapport with the audience by calling them "my friends" or "folks" and showing respect for their good sense. Jacobs continued:

> Speaking the language of the listener also creates rapport. This, of course, includes speaking the same national language as the listener, although a trained person can develop

Rush Limbaugh claims to have more sense with half his brain tied behind his back than the best of the liberals whom he taunts.

rapport with body language during a one to one encounter. Essentially, though, this means identifying with the person or people the speaker wants to persuade. Anything that accomplishes this, such as using the local vernacular, will suffice. Even the rate of speaking can help a speaker identify with an audience. For example, the average high school-educated audience prefers a speaker who talks around 170 words per minute. (Incidentally, Limbaugh speaks an average of around 177, based on a sampling of three TV broadcasts.) (Jacobs, 1995, p. 381)

Jacobs noted that a fourth strategy Limbaugh uses is to establish his authority by referring to great thinkers throughout his broadcasts or saying, "See, I told you so," and referring to other issues on which his predictions were proven correct. Further, Limbaugh uses humor to make fun of politicians or their policies, and he uses rhetorical questions to set up his conclusions. Jacobs identified emotional words that Limbaugh uses repeatedly in his broadcasts. The following are used to promote affirmative feelings and responses:

hot	**compassion**	**American**
enormous	great	hope
phenomenal	proud	freedom
hottest	flawless	free enterprise
positive future	excellence	our country
power	righteous	democracy
winning	right	
truth	baby	humanity

(Jacobs, 1995, pp. 384–385)

Negative words that Limbaugh uses to invoke cynical feelings are:

hot air	**frenzied**	**tyranny**
dead wrong	liar	insincere
enslave	communism	radical
doomsday	soaking the rich	terror
horrendous	gut-wrenching	dread
staggering	astronomical	manipulate

(Jacobs, 1995, p. 385)

Limbaugh manipulates his audience through the use of his conservative ideology and loaded language to produce the effect that he desires in his radio listeners. He has been very effective in demonizing liberal politicians and their positions on national issues. He refers to Hillary Clinton as "Billary," a combination of Bill and Hillary, and he refers to Barack Obama as Barry, a name that his grandmother used to call him. These manufactured names that Limbaugh uses become labels that injure the target of his satire or attacks. As Jacobs noted, Limbaugh uses anecdotes, stories, and metaphors; double bind choices of either/or; and rapport, authority, and rhetorical questions; but his language usage unifies conservatives and labels liberals by dividing them into good and evil camps.

ENGLISH: AN ONGOING PROJECT

David Crystal, in *The Fight for English: How Language Pundits Ate, Shot, and Left* (2007), traced the evolution of the English language from Latin through the Anglo-Saxon era when French was introduced, until the One Hundred Years War made French less inviting, and then the English language continued to reflect the dialects of both the north and south with animosities embedded in those rivalries. Crystal noted that this change did not mean that the language was harmed, only that each sectarian influence was to be found in it. He wrote:

> All languages borrow from each other. It is one of the linguistic facts of life. We know of no "pure" language—that is, one which has a homogeneous linguistic character, displaying no influence from the contact its speakers have had with other languages. To adopt an analogy from the American political domain, the linguistic world has many of the characteristics of a melting pot, rather than a salad bowl. But there is a long-standing salad-bowl attitude, which is found in several countries, that it is a good thing to keep languages free from foreign influences. (Crystal, 2007, p. 13)

Generally, the controversy is not about the language at all but about who has the power to define how political power will be exercised and by whom. Crystal wrote:

> In a nutshell: we need to know what we are doing. We need to be in control of our language, and not have it control us. As Lewis Carroll's Humpty Dumpty once said, referring to the way he changed word meanings at will: "the question is: which is to be master—that's all." We have to be masters of language. (Crystal, 2007, p. 211)

Within the United States there are enclaves with **co-cultures,** that is, a different culture co-existing alongside the dominant one. According to the U.S. Census Bureau in 2000, among the 262.4 million people aged five and over, 47.0 million (18 percent) spoke a language other than English at home. In 1990, the Census Bureau reflected that 14 percent spoke a second language at home, so in 10 years there was a 4 percent increase. After English the second most frequently spoken language was Spanish, with Chinese second and French third (Shin & Bruno, 2005, p. 181). In "Language Use in the United States: 2011" written by Camille Ryan (August 2013), the U.S. Census Bureau reported that of the 291.5 million people aged 5 and over, 60.6 million people (21 percent of this population) spoke a language other than English at home. (p. 2) Those who spoke Spanish grew from 12.0 percent in 2005 to 12.9 percent in 2011 (p. 4). Since 1980 the largest numeric increase for languages other than English spoken in the home was for Spanish speakers who grew by 25.9 million between 1980 and 2010. Conversely, because of aging populations or dwindling migration some language groups showed declines, like Italian with a net decline in language use of about 900,000 speakers (55 percent decline) (p. 6). Other languages that have declined in the U.S. include Polish, Yiddish, German, and Greek. Two influences will determine the language use trend and that is immigration and population aging, which means if immigrants remain in the U.S. they will acquire English skills. These figures show an increasing non-English speaking population that will complicate the political landscape.

What does this mean for our educational and political institutions? It depends on how these new arrivals choose to define themselves. Will they assimilate, as the Germans, the Irish, and the Chinese of the last century did? Recent demonstrations challenging the immigration proposals in Congress call assimilation into question. As our population becomes more diverse and more segmented, how can public discourse aid in finding unity rather than divisions? This will be the rhetorical challenge of the twenty-first century. There are major disagreements about how the new arrivals describe themselves even, with some, for example, preferring the generic term of *Hispanics* while others prefer to be called *Latinos.* The immigration debate is a heated one, with one major issue being legislation that requires newcomers to speak English to be accepted, because to succeed in this country one must be able to speak the dominant language. The political question is whether the United States is going to become bilingual, like Canada, or address the language issue now to avoid the same conflicts regarding how to conduct the economy, government, education, medical services, and the socialization of citizens. A common language is essential to participating fully in our representative democracy. Underlying the foundation that holds this nation together is the public philosophy of civility, which includes respect for the laws and traditions of this nation.

Walter Lippmann wrote a book called the *Public Philosophy* (1955), which was a critique of Western democracies and the decay of civility in them. He wrote of the effects of war propaganda during World War I and II:

> When the world wars came, the people of the liberal democracies could not be aroused to the exertions and the sacrifices of the struggle until they had been frightened by the opening disasters, had been incited to passionate hatred, and had become intoxicated with unlimited hope. To overcome this inertia the enemy had to be portrayed as evil incarnate, as absolute and congenital wickedness. The people wanted to be told that when this particular enemy had been forced to unconditional surrender, they would re-enter the golden age. This unique

Hispanics are the fastest growing co-culture in the U.S. which will influence all major institutions.

war would end all wars. This last war would make the world safe for democracy. This crusade would make the whole world a democracy. (Lippmann, 1955, p. 21)

The effects of such "envenomed" and "impassioned nonsense," according to Lippmann, was that the people would not allow a workable peace. He noted that it was impossible to wage war without "inciting the people to paroxysms of hatred and to utopian dreams" (p. 23). Lippmann noted that there was a malady in the democratic nations that would only be healed through a public philosophy that he described in this manner:

> . . . I believe there is a public philosophy. Indeed there is such a thing as the public philosophy of civility. It does not have to be discovered or invented. It is known. But it does have to be revived and renewed.
>
> The public philosophy is known as *natural law*, a name which, alas, causes great semantic confusion. This philosophy is the premise of the institutions of the Western society, and they are, I believe, unworkable in Communities that do not adhere to it. Except on the premises of this philosophy, it is impossible to reach intelligible and workable conceptions of the popular election, majority rule, representative assemblies, free speech, loyalty, property, corporations and voluntary associations. The founders of these institutions, which the recently enfranchised democracies have inherited, were all of them adherents of some one of the various schools of natural law. (Lippmann, 1955, p. 101)

Lippmann noted that people are increasingly alienated from the inner principles of their institutions, and he asked if this rupture in the traditions of civility can be repaired. The principles have not been abandoned because they are antiquated but because they are not being taught (1955, p. 102). He wrote of the limits of accommodation where the schisms and sects become so irreconcilable that the principle of toleration is unable to cope with the diversity of beliefs. The solution would be to find "agreement beneath the differences" (p. 172). Lippmann called for rational discussion to rearm all of those who are concerned with our society and "its progressive barbarization, and with its descent into violence and tyranny" (p. 180). The drift in social unity that Lippmann wrote about in 1955 has only widened in the twenty-first century as our social institutions have been challenged directly both from within and from competing ideologies or belief systems outside our borders. This breach can only be healed through some common ground or adherence to communal rituals and beliefs that bind our nation together in what Lippmann called the "**public philosophy**" that embraces civility and natural laws that place our welfare above the demands of the individual. A common language in the United States is only the beginning to reconciling differences of culture, political thinking, and policies that will serve all of us or divide us further.

The ability to create this vision of unity and claim actions that uphold it is a rhetorical task that conjures the magic of the "word merchants," to use St. Augustine's term (Burke, 1970, p. 117). The Sophists of Ancient Greece taught citizens to argue both sides of any issue, and they were compensated well for their craft. Today there are many professionals who are paid to offer *Accounts, Excuses, and Apologies*, which is the title of William Benoit's book, to create a credible image, restore credibility, or explain away some disaster. Even more compelling than the use of press secretaries to tailor words for any challenging occasion, we need

"True Believers," which Eric Hoffer described, to uphold the public philosophy. If words are to work their magic, there must be receivers who embrace them as truth for all of us as a community, not just a few special interests. Even if we speak the same language, this does not ensure that we derive the same meaning from the words used because words function in different ways on different levels.

Language is directly related to culture and community with ties that unite or divide people. Unless there is a common ideology and value system to hold a nation together, the social contract becomes corrupted with special factions that fracture the body politic. America is struggling with finding a public philosophy that rings true for everyone within our borders; much of the dissent is born of language barriers and shared visions of what it means to be a responsible citizen.

DENOTATIVE, CONNOTATIVE, AND FUNCTIONAL AXIS OF WORDS

Denotative meaning is that which you can find in the dictionary, the one that is commonly accepted. For example, "patriot" is defined as "fellow countryman"; or "a person who loves and loyally or zealously supports his own country" (*Webster's*, 1959, p. 1073). Beyond this dictionary definition there is a thematic meaning that is called **connotative**, which refers to the images or feelings that the word conjures up in the receiver. Students of history may think of Paul Revere when they hear the word "patriot," or they may think of the Patriot Act that has received much attention in the last few years. Denotative meanings are those with general acceptance, while connotative meanings are **idiosyncratic** or highly individual interpretations of the same term. The connotation of a word depends on the experience of the receiver and the meaning they attach to it. An 18-year-old student would not interpret the word "quagmire" as their grandfather would, because Vietnam is only an historical reference, not a lived experience for the student. Further, words have **functional meanings** that they fulfill in grammar so that a noun is the name of a person, place, or thing. Verbs are action words that inform us of what the subject of the sentence is doing or being, and conjunctions join words or phrases. All of this is elementary for those who have studied speech and writing. It sounds simple enough, but to have the ability to name or describe individuals, groups, or nations is to possess the power to create the image or essence of them. Leaders in the black power movement in the United States during the 1960s and 1970s noted that the power to define one's self in a culture was the power to decide who would be the master and who would be the slave, according to Stokely Carmichael, a more radical voice during the 1960s.

LANGUAGE AND RACE

The black power movement in the United States during the late 1960s and 1970s was an effort to remove the negative connotation of the word "black" for all persons who considered themselves any shade of black or brown. Ossie Davis, an African American actor, delivered a speech called "Racism in American Life—Broad Perspectives of the Problem," or "The English Language Is My Enemy." He stated both titles during the speech, but what he said in essence is that the English language teaches black children to hate themselves because of the

pejorative terms linked to blackness. A pejorative term is one that creates a negative image or characterization of the subject such as name calling or labeling a person with a racist, homophobic, or ethnic slur. Davis said there are 134 synonyms for whiteness, and 44 of them are favorable, such as "purity," "cleanliness," "innocent," and "trustworthy"; but the word "blackness" has 120 synonyms, of which 60 are unfavorable, such as "blot," "dingy," "sinister," "unclean," and "foul." He listed 28 such words, but he said he omitted 20 of the worst words among these in *Roget's Thesaurus of the English Language* because they were related directly to race, and he then included "Negro," "Negress," "nigger," "darkey," and "blackamoor" as labels that were most offensive. He said:

> When you understand and contemplate the small difference between the meaning of one word supposedly representing one fact, you will understand the power, good or evil, associated with the English language. You will understand also why there is a tremendous fight among the Negro people to stop using the word "Negro" altogether and substitute "African-American."
>
> You will understand, even further, how men like Stokely Carmichael and Floyd McKissick can get us in such serious trouble by using two words together: Black Power. If Mr. McKissick and Mr. Carmichael had thought a moment, and said Colored Power, there would have been no problem.
>
> I submit that racism is inherent in the English language because the language is an historic expression of the experience of a people; that racism, which is the belief that one group is superior to the other and has the right to set the standards for the other, is still one of the main spiritual policies of our country as expressed in the educational process. (Davis, 1969, pp. 75–77)

Ossie Davis's speech demonstrated the power of naming, which could create a stereotype in which you dumped all of a race of people together, and they, being a minority group, felt powerless to change their characterization. That was the goal of the black power movement: to redefine what it meant to be a person of color. Davis's analysis of the problem confronting African Americans in the 1960s was heightened by his semantic analysis of the labels applied to his race.

While Ossie Davis analyzed the semantics of social discourse, Dr. Martin Luther King Jr. mobilized a movement to resist everyday discrimination against African Americans. Dr. King (1963/1975) used many forms of appeal in his rhetoric, but his persuasion was action based. In his **"Letter from Birmingham Jail"** he answered the criticism of eight fellow clergymen from Alabama who believed that the demonstrations of the civil rights leader were harming their cause and were untimely. Dr. King wrote a letter to the clergy explaining that attempts to negotiate with city fathers in Birmingham, Alabama, had failed; he decided to take direct action, which meant marches, sit-ins, and mass demonstrations. Even though he was a man of action, he was also a master with words. He wrote:

> As in so many past experiences, our hopes had been blasted, and the shadow of deep disappointment settled upon us. We had no alternative except to prepare for direct action, whereby

we would present our very bodies as means of laying our case before the conscience of the local and the national community. Mindful of the difficulties involved, we decided to undertake a process of self-purification. We began a series of workshops on nonviolence, and we repeatedly asked ourselves: "Are you able to accept blows without retaliating?" "Are you able to endure the ordeal of jail?" We decided to schedule our direct-action program for the Easter season, realizing that except for Christmas, this is the main shopping period of the year. Knowing that a strong economic-withdrawal program would be the by-product of direct action, we felt that this would be the best time to bring pressure to bear on the merchants for the needed change. (King, 1963/1975, pp. 356–357)

Dr. King said that his direct action campaign was intended to create so much tension that it would bring forth negotiations so that the Southland could no longer engage in only monologue but dialogue as well. He wrote:

Just as Socrates felt that it was necessary to create a tension in the mind so that individuals could rise from the bondage of myths and half-truths to the unfettered realm of creative analysis and objective appraisal, so must we see the need for nonviolent gadflies to create the kind of tension in society that will help men rise from the dark depths of prejudice and racism to the majestic heights of understanding and brotherhood. (King, 1963/1975, p. 357)

Dr. King chided his critics for looking only at the effect, the civil disobedience, without ever giving any analysis to the causes, the oppression of black people. He did an analysis of time, noting that waiting for the white leaders to do the right thing had brought no progress. He said, "We have waited for more than 340 years for our constitutional and God-given rights" (p. 358). He said that "wait" had come to mean "never." He quoted St. Augustine, saying, "an unjust law is no law at all" (p. 360).

When we analyze the words of Dr. Martin Luther King Jr., we see power in the images that he painted, including one of the 72-year-old woman who said, "My feets is tired, but my

Dr. Martin Luther King Jr.'s "I Have A Dream" speech created a new vision for America.

soul is at rest." His long letter included references to the most learned philosophers and theologians and the most ignoble tyrants like Hitler, so we know that he was an educated man. His choice of words and the cadence of his language were poetic as he closed the long letter with this vision:

> Let us all hope that the dark clouds of racial prejudice will soon pass away and the deep fog of misunderstanding will be lifted from our fear-drenched communities, and in some not too distant tomorrow the radiant stars of love and brotherhood will shine over our great nation with all their scintillating beauty. (King, 1965/1973, p. 371)

Dr. King was able to exhort others to conduct the Montgomery bus boycott, to march through the most racist of cities, conduct sit-ins at segregated lunch counters, and to travel to Washington, D.C., where over 250,000 people heard the famous "I Have a Dream" speech (Sylvester, 1998). His words struck the heart and imagination of African Americans and other Americans with whom his soaring rhetoric resonated as a message delivered from the mountaintop from which he spoke to lift up the most lowly and to move the most mighty to deliver on the promise of freedom so long denied. Many would judge King as the greatest orator of the twentieth century. Clearly, his words had the power to transform intransigent bodies in government, but more compelling were his moral and ethical challenges to the establishment to look past the color of one's skin to contemplate the content of their character. He was assassinated on April 4, 1968, in Memphis, Tennessee, where he had gone to support the garbage workers who were on strike, but his legacy lives on in the words that he used to liberate his people from the political and economic chains that had characterized their past history. Dr. King was a master not only with words, but with "The Word" as a minister who quoted the scriptures as easily as he cited philosophers. Professor Melvin Sylvester wrote this tribute to Dr. King:

> Black Americans needed a Martin Luther King, but above all *America* needed him. The significant qualities of this special man cannot be underestimated nor taken for granted. Within a span of 13 years from 1955 to his death in 1968 he was able to expound, expose, and extricate America from many wrongs. His tactics of protest involved non-violent passive resistance to racial injustice. It was the right prescription for our country, and it was right on time. Hope in America was waning on the part of many Black Americans, but Martin Luther King, Jr. provided a candle along with a light. He also provided this nation with a road map so that all people could locate and share together in the abundance of this great democracy. (Sylvester, 1998, p. 1)

In the "Letter from Birmingham Jail," Dr. King took exception to the clergy who called him an "extremist," and he explained how he preached nonviolent resistance: "Love your enemies, bless them that curse you, do good to them that hate you, and pray for them which despitefully use you, and persecute you." But at the same time he demanded justice, quoting Amos from the Bible: "Let justice roll down like waters and righteousness like an ever-flowing stream" (King, 1963/1975, p. 365).

King's life was short, but his shadow was long as he stood in the light to raise his voice against the injustices that his people had endured. He was eloquent, but he did not speak for admiration—he spoke with high purpose. Dr. King raised a mighty voice with words that galvanized a young president, John F. Kennedy, and many who would follow him to address the wrongs that King was willing to die to have righted. Any student of rhetoric should read his work for inspiration and insight into the civil rights movement of the 1950s and 1960s in this nation and to savor the words of a man who was a master craftsman.

LANGUAGE AND GENDER

Following the civil rights movement of the 1960s, the women's movement attempted to change the stereotypical views of women as well. Women have spoken since the beginning of history, but they did not have a public voice until the middle of the nineteenth century in America, when the abolitionist movement began. In 1850, Elizabeth Cady Stanton spoke at the Seneca Falls Convention, which many historians cite as the beginning of the women's rights movement in the United States. Her husband, abolitionist Henry B. Stanton, said that if she spoke he would leave town because she intended to propose voting rights for women. Elizabeth spoke even though she knew it compromised her "modesty, purity, and virtue" because in her time, a woman was supposed to "noiselessly" follow her husband (Borisoff & Merrill, 1998, p. 8). Henry Stanton did leave town while his wife Elizabeth said:

> . . . Were I not nerved by a sense of right and duty, did I not feel the time had fully come for the question of women's wrongs to be laid before the public, did I not believe that woman herself must do this work; for woman alone can understand the height, the depth, the length, or the breadth of her own degradation, man cannot speak for her. (Borisoff & Merrill, 1998, p. 8)

It was believed at that time that women were biologically unfit to engage in intellectual pursuits because it could affect their reproductive abilities (Borisoff & Merrill, 1998, p. 1). The masculine communication model is one of "direct, confrontative, forceful, and logical" speech, while the feminine model for speech is the opposite of these traits (Borisoff & Merrill, 1998, p. 12). Just as the women's movement, which would ultimately give women the vote 70-some years later, began fomenting at the time of the abolitionist movement, a resurgence would follow the black power movement in the United States.

During the 1960s women began to examine language that they believed characterized women in a negative way. One approach to instigating change was to examine the labels that they believed stereotyped women. The designation of Ms. became more common, replacing the Miss or Mrs. to signify marital status. Women believed that a neutral term was more desirable than the one that had no counterpart with men, since a Mr. could be married or not, but the title Mrs. tended to put marital status above any other attribute that women might have such as expertise, ambition, or competence. The stereotype of women as dependent, clinging, and living only through their spouses was one that many wanted to see redefined. Not everyone was happy with this social change, though; some wives felt that the change in traditional salutation devalued the role of the housewife or the relationship of husbands, wives, and children as a family.

While marital status and the title to it was only one aspect of the women's movement, the definition of what constitutes a family has changed significantly since Betty Friedan first wrote *The Feminine Mystique* (1963), which was the touchstone book for a renewed feminist movement, demanding not just voting power but parity in corporations and in sexual politics as well. Friedan gave the "problem with no name" an identifying marker so that women could diagnose their discontent with household chores that were unending, which demanded that they somehow had to live through their husbands or children, forgetting that they had worked in labs, written critical papers, and had fulfilling jobs out of college before marriage. Educated women were at the forefront of this political movement to call into question how they were defined, what they were called, and what possibilities were envisioned for them in life. Friedan quoted a *Newsweek* article on American women (March 7, 1960):

> She is dissatisfied with a lot that women of other lands can only dream of. Her discontent is deep, pervasive, and impervious to the superficial remedies which are offered at every hand. . . . An army of professional explorers have already charted the major sources of trouble. . . . From the beginning of time, the female cycle has defined and confined woman's role. As Freud was credited with saying: "Anatomy is destiny." Though no group of women have ever pushed these natural restrictions as far as the American wife, it seems that she still cannot accept them with good grace. . . . A young mother with a beautiful family, charm, talent and brains is apt to dismiss her role apologetically. "What do I do?" you hear her say. "Why nothing. I'm just a housewife." A good education, it seems has given this paragon among women an understanding of the value of everything except her own worth. (Friedan, 1963, p. 20)

Critics claimed that women across the world would die for the position that American women enjoyed with modern conveniences, lovely homes, plenty of food, and leisure time to pursue interests, but many women felt unfulfilled with the role that placed their lives in the shadow of their husbands. The women's movement would call into question employment, legal, and sexual practices that placed them in passive or subordinate roles. Landmark legislation such as affirmative action, legalized abortion, birth control, and equal status in government grew out of their campaigns. Hillary Rodham Clinton was one of the representative types that emerged from this cohort of aggressive, successful, professional women, and she used her platform as first lady to address important issues. Since she was a standard-bearer, as well as a first in many endeavors, she has confronted resistance from not only the establishment but from women themselves, because sometimes they believed that she did not represent their interests or those of women overall.

THE RHETORIC OF HILLARY CLINTON

Hillary Rodham Clinton is one of the highest profile women in America today. Senator Clinton mobilized a campaign for the presidency in 2008, but she was defeated by Barack Obama, who named her his secretary of state. During her tenure as first lady, Hillary made many speeches, but generally she was seen arguing as a lawyer—using legalese, marshaling evidence, and making claims based on these proofs, but lacking in the feminine style that would endear her to women. **Gender styles** in rhetoric stereotype women with speech that is characterized by hedges, self-disclosing anecdotes, and tenuous statements, while men are supposed to use logic, evidence, and powerful speech. Mandy Manning addressed this paradox by writing:

> In an analysis of Hillary Rodham Clinton's rhetorical style during her term as First Lady, Karlyn Kohrs Campbell (1998) asserts that Rodham Clinton "symbolizes the problems of public women writ large" (p. 15). She suggests that women who have training in a professional field, and fail to enact their expected femininity, instead asserting their professional training, will inevitably encounter hostility from the general public. Campbell concludes that it is not only Rodham Clinton's inability to feminize her rhetorical style that prevents her from gaining favor with the voting public, but also society's adherence to traditional perceptions of a woman's role. She states, "Her (Hillary Clinton's) limited ability to feminize her rhetorical style, to perform a culturally defined feminine role publically, is clearly a disadvantage. At the same time, our failure to appreciate the highly developed argumentative skills of an expert advocate when that advocate is a female, reveals our deficiencies, not hers." (Manning, 2006, p. 15)

So what is the problem? Hillary Clinton does not exude the gender-specific characteristics identified, but certainly not prescribed, by Borisoff and Merrill of being "soft-spoken, self-effacing, and compliant. Considered more emotional than logical, she (the typical woman) is prone to be seen as disorganized and subjective" (1998, p. 9). Hillary does not fit the mold at all. Clinton uses power skillfully in arenas generally dominated by men by exhibiting expertise, making logical arguments without supporting anecdotes or heartwarming stories, and challenging the hegemony of male-dominated governmental bodies and international norms regarding women's rights. Manning wrote:

> For the purposes of this analysis feminism shall be defined according to feminist theorist Cheris Kramarae, as "the practice of challenging the linguistic system as well as the structures and institutions it produces, including education, politics, religion, and the economic system" (Foss, Foss, & Griffin, 1999). Ultimately, Kramarae focuses on "restructuring" and "rethinking" the current systems that maintain men as the dominant being in our society. According to Kramarae (1981) the language, words and syntax we use, give structure to the world in which we live, as well as, how people, act and interpret their experiences. "If we discover the principles of language usage . . . we will at the same time discover principles of social relations." (Manning, 2006, p. 112)

Karlyn Kohrs Campbell (1998) characterized Hillary Clinton's style as impersonal, presented like a lawyer's brief, with no self-disclosing examples but only those told to her secondhand. Again Campbell reminded us that the fault was not in Hillary's rhetoric but in the receiver's expectations that she would use conventional devices to deliver her messages. Campbell wrote:

> In what I have written, it may seem that I am identifying deficiencies in Hillary Rodham Clinton's performance as a rhetor. Judged purely in terms of achieving her goals, whether seen as approval ratings or the passage of the health care reform initiative, her limited ability to feminize her rhetorical style, to perform a culturally defined feminine role publicly, is

clearly a disadvantage. At the same time, our failure to appreciate the highly developed argumentative skills of an expert advocate, when that advocate is a female, reveals our deficiencies, not hers. Legislation attendant on the second wave of feminism opened doors for able women who seek to exercise skills in all areas of life, including the formation of public policy. If we reject all those who lack the feminizing skills of an Elizabeth Hanford Dole, we shall deprive ourselves of a vast array of talent. (Campbell, 1998, p. 15)

Going back to general semantics and mass media theory, the issue is who says what to whom with what effect? On such important issues as women's rights, including the right not to be subjected to violence, we need an advocate who is "aggressive, confrontational, and ambitious," like Hillary Clinton (Manning, 2006, p. 118). In those instances where the former first lady spoke for the rights of women at the United Nations Fourth World Conference on Women Plenary Session, and more currently in her roles as secretary of state and challenger for the presidency, it would be counterproductive and unprofessional for Hillary to emulate the feminine style, even when traditionalists do not support her in the polls, because that is not *her* style. A **paradigm shift** must occur that allows for competent, educated, and powerful women to speak for our concerns without feigning palpitations or insecurities.

The media was far more critical of Hillary Clinton during the 2008 campaign than of Barack Obama, using such words as "obituaries" for her campaign, even after her wins in Ohio, Pennsylvania, and West Virginia, and party leaders like Howard Dean called for her to drop out of the race. CBS reported on May 7, 2008, that "Hillary Clinton's chances of winning the Democratic nomination have become slim to none—and slim looks to be leaving town" (Ververs & Montopoli, 2008). Other sources stated that she would do almost anything to win, including taking positions that she had been adverse to earlier, which painted a Lady Macbeth-like character whose defining characteristic was blind ambition. During the campaign her opponent, Barack Obama, was called a "rock star" and enjoyed all the positive

Hillary Clinton violates the stereotype of feminine style of argumentation by using logical, organized, and evidence-based arguments.

press of an entertainer rather than a politician, and with his miniscule record in public office, who could attack his credibility on issues? Meanwhile the press referred to Hillary's "coronation," her pantsuits, hairstyles, and emotional "meltdowns," none of which shed any light on her positions on policies. Occasionally a report would characterize her as a "policy wonk," but her opponent enjoyed unfettered popularity until Reverend Jeremiah Wright gained the media's attention. A new label gained currency in the media with "black liberation theology" being intertwined with charges of racism, which was supposed to sink Obama's campaign by associating him with Reverend Wright's rants. Wright labeled America as the "U.S. of K.K.K.A" and the country that created the AIDS virus to kill black men, and he attacked Israel as a terrorist state. Peter Wehner wrote:

> The words of Jeremiah Wright are acedic—both in their own right and in what they are doing to the Barack Obama's presidential campaign. For his next sermon Reverend Wright might consider meditating on the words of James: "the tongue can no man tame; it is an unruly evil, full of deadly poison." To these words Senator Obama may simply say, Amen. (Wehner, 2008)

Powerful words are not the possessions of any gender, but social expectations and biases persist. Hillary Clinton's rhetoric is a classic example of social expectancy violation, she does not argue like a woman, and those who hope to conserve the power equation that exists judge her negatively. It is very telling that a woman who had been in the public spotlight for 30-some years as a prominent lawyer, first lady of the state of Arkansas, first lady of the White House, U.S. senator, then candidate for the president of the United States reported only in 2008 to have found her voice on the campaign trail. One has to wonder where her words were all that time or whose script she had been speaking. Hillary Clinton has always understood the power of words, and now we are hearing less about her pantsuits and more about her negotiating on the international scene. Most political pundits see Hillary Clinton preparing for a presidential campaign in 2016, which would require her to become invisible in the Obama Administration's second term so that she can redefine herself to become the first woman to win the presidency.

SUMMARY

We know that the children's rhyme that "sticks and stones may break my bones, but words can never hurt me" is a myth that denies the power of words to hurt people by capturing them in a stereotype that destroys their humanity. Further, we know that words create the social-political realm of human interaction by creating the reality of our everyday existence. Words are the vessels that carry our thoughts through symbols that are poor representations for the ideas, events, and people that we try to present to others. Some political movements have as their charge the redefinition of a whole class of people, like the black power movement, the women's movement, and more recently the gay rights movement. Words have three dimensions: first, cognitive, involving thoughts; second, affect, which involves attitudes and feelings; and finally, behavior, which involves action that is taken or halted because of messages. So, as the general semanticists noted, words are about what we think, how we feel, and how we act. The language that we share as a nation contains our culture, our past stories, and our future dreams. Words offer communal bonds to join us in a public philosophy that will strengthen the social contract so that we can fully participate in the promises of a democratic society through commerce, participatory government, and personal fulfillment regardless of race, gender, or socioeconomic status. Emotional words may contain **god-terms** or **devil-terms** that produce a powerful effect that is a conditioned response rather than a logical response to the message. Words are the tools of the tyrant as handily as they are of the most inspired and ethical leader; therefore, we should be mindful of the language use and abuse that is all around us. To understand the persuasion process, one must acknowledge the power of language and be aware of how words frame our conceptions of the world.

APPLICATIONS

1. Choose one of Dr. King's speeches and analyze the following: Who was the intended audience? What appeals did he use? Read a newspaper account from that time and see what reporters said about the speech or event. Some thought he was too "radical" while others called him an "Uncle Tom." Why would they call him that name?

2. Do you think that the salutation "Mrs." made any difference in the way women were perceived in the workplace? Was "Ms." an improvement? Why or why not? What was the "feminine mystique" that Betty Friedan expressed in her book?

3. Find a speech by Hillary Clinton and decide for yourself how effective she was in presenting her ideas. Are her language style and methods of presenting arguments "masculine"? What does that mean? What is the "feminine" style of address? Discuss language barriers in general—street language, jargon, uneducated speech, standard English, African American, Mexican American, etc.

4. Find an editorial message that uses loaded language and analyze the words used by the writer. Why did he or she choose those words? What impact do you think the article had on the reading audience?

5. Take an inventory of your class lectures today. Evaluate the language each professor used in presenting the topics assigned. Were some subjects more neutral in language compared to others that included more emotional cases or situations? Which classes? Why? Was it the material, the lecturer, or something that affected you personally that made the language more emotional?

6. Read the front page of your local newspaper and analyze the news stories. Were the "facts" presented objectively, or did you detect bias through the language used to report the daily news? Go to the editorial page and compare the language there to the front-page stories.

7. Select a speech from a special interest group spokesperson and analyze his or her language. Topics such as abortion, gay rights, capital punishment, violence in media, pedophilia, and immigration reform are emotional topics that would afford rich texts for language analysis from either the pro or con position.

REFERENCES

Beckerman, G. (January 8, 2008). Bill Clinton: Media critic—Is Hillary getting a "raw deal"? *Columbia Journalism Review.* Retrieved May 15, 2008, from http://www.cjr.org/campaign_desk/bill_clinton_media_critic.php?page=all&print=true

Borisoff, D., & Merrill, L. (1998). *The power to communicate: Gender differences as barriers* (3rd ed.). Prospect Heights, IL: Waveland Press.

Burke, K. (1970). *The rhetoric of religion.* Berkeley: University of California Press.

Campbell, K. (1998). Discursive performance of femininity; hating Hillary. *Rhetoric & Public Affairs, 1*(1), 1–19.

Condon, J. D. (1966). *Semantics and communication.* New York: Macmillan.

Crystal, D. (2007). *The fight for English: How language pundits ate, shot, and left.* New York: Oxford University Press, Inc.

Davis, O. (1969). The language of racism: The English language is my enemy. In N. Postman, C. Weingartner, & T. P. Moran (Eds.), *Language in America: A report on our deteriorating semantic environment* (pp. 73–79). New York: The Bobbs-Merrill Company.

Embler, W. (1962). Language and truth. In S. I. Hayakawa (Ed.), *The use and misuse of language* (pp. 219–34). Greenwich, CT: A Fawcett Premier Book.

Foss, K. A., Foss, S. J., & Griffin, C. L. (1999). Feminist rhetorical *theories.* Thousand Oaks, CA: Sage Publications.

Friedan, B. (1963). *The feminine mystique.* New York: Dell Publishing Co.

Goldberg, J. (January 8, 2011). The horror of the day. The corner. *National Review Online.* Retrieved July 10, 2012, from http://www.nationalreview.com/blogs/print/256671

Haberman, C. (2005). In the Mideast this year, even words shoot to kill. In K. Walters & M. Brody (Eds.), *What's language got to do with it?* (pp. 4–8). New York: W. W. Norton & Company.

Hayakawa, S. I. (Ed.). (1962). *The use and misuse of language.* Greenwich, CT: Fawcett Publications.

Jacobs, D. T. (1995). The red flags of persuasion. *Et Cetera: A Review of General Semantics, 52*(4), 375–392.

King, M. L., Jr. (1978). Letter from Birmingham Jail. In F. D. Burt & E. C. Want (Eds.), *Invention & design: A rhetorical reader* (2nd ed., pp. 354–374). New York: Random House. (Original work published 1963.)

Korzybski, A. (1933). *Science and sanity: An introduction to non-Aristotelian systems and general semantics.* Lancaster, PA: Science Press Printing Co.

Kramarae, C. (1981). *Women and men speaking: Frameworks for analysis.* Rowley, MA: Newbury.

Lakoff, G. (1999a). Metaphors, morality, and politics: Or, why conservatives have left liberals in the dust. In R. S. Wheeler (Ed.), *The workings of language: From prescriptions to perspectives.* Westport, CT: Praeger.

Lakoff, G. (1999b). The system of metaphors for mind and the conceptual system of analytic philosophy: A study of the metaphorical constraints on philosophical discourse. In B. A. Fox, D. Jurafsky, & L. A. Michaelis (Eds.), *Cognition and function in language* (pp. 159–180). Stanford, CA: Center for the Study of Language and Information.

Lakoff, G. (2006). *Whose freedom? The battle over America's most important idea.* New York: Farrar, Straus and Giroux.

Lippmann, W. (1955). The public philosophy: On the decline and revival of the western society. Boston: Little, Brown and Company in Association with The Atlantic Monthly Press.

Manning, M. R. (2006). "The Rhetoric of Equality: Hillary Rodham Clinton's Redefinition of the Female Politician." *Texas Speech Communication Journal, 30,* 2, 109–120.

Mead, G. H. (1934). *Mind, self, and society.* Chicago: University of Chicago Press.

Obama, B. (January 12, 2011). Text of President Obama's Tucson memorial speech. Retrieved July 10, 2012, from: http://www.cbsnews.com/2012-503544_162-20028366.html?tag=contentMain; contentBody.

Pettersson, E.and Flick A. J. (January 20, 2011). Loughner Indicted by U.S. Grand Jury in Shooting of Arizona Congresswoman. *Bloomberg Businessweek.* Retrieved September 9, 2013 from http://www.bloomberg.com/news/print/2011-01-20/jared-loughner-indicted-by-federal-gran.

Pfuetze, P. E. (1954). *The social self*. Library of Current Philosophy and Religion. New York: Book-man Associates.

Rapoport, A. (1962). What is semantics? In S. I. Hayakawa (Ed.), *The use and misuse of language* (pp. 11–15). Greenwich, CT: Fawcett Publications.

Ryan, C. (August 2013). *Language use in the United States: 2011. ACS-22.* American community survey reports. United States Census Bureau: U.S. Department of Commerce. Economics and Statistics Administration. Census.gov.

Shafer, J. (2008). Don't call it plagiarism: Obama's sound bite, considered. Retrieved May 18, 2008, from http://www.slate.com/id/2184070/.

Shin, B., & Bruno, R. (2005). Census 2000: Language use and English-speaking ability in the USA. In K. Walters & M. Brody (Eds.), *What's language got to do with it?* (pp. 181–196). New York: W. W. Norton & Company.

Sylvester, M. (1998). *A tribute to Dr. Martin Luther King, Jr.* Long Island University, C. W. Post Campus, Library Homepage. Retrieved November 6, 2010 from http://www2.liu.edu/cwis/cwp/library/mlking.htm.

Taylor, E. (April 1, 2001). What's in a word? School violence. School Violence Program. Retrieved November 6, 2010, from http://www.innertalk.com/progressive/papers/Semantics_distortion.html.

Thomas, R. (2004). Symbolic interaction theory. In R. West & L. H. Turner (Eds.), *Introducing communication theory: Analysis and application* (2nd ed., pp. 83–98). Boston: McGraw-Hill.

Ververs, V., & Montopoli, B. (2008). Clinton's path to victory slipping away. *CBS News.* Retrieved May 7, 2008, from http://www.cbsnews.com/stories/2008/05/07/politics/main4078586.shtml.

Walters, K., & Brody, M. (Eds.). (2005). Foreword. In *What's language got to do with it?* New York: W. W. Norton & Company.

Webster's New World Dictionary of the American Language, College Edition. (1959). Cleveland and New York: The World Publishing Company.

Wehner, P. (2008). The Wright questions for Obama. *CBS News* (Reprinted with permission from the *National Review Online*). Retrieved May 21, 2008, from http://www.cbsnews.com/stories/2008/03/17/opinion/main3944215.shtml.

Websites

http://www.cbsnews.com—to examine language through the news of the day and contemporary controversies. Candidates' speeches are examined, often with commentary. See March 18, 2008, for the transcript of Barack Obama's speech on race, a brilliant speech on his experience of race relations as the child of a black man from Kenya and a white woman from Kansas, as well as his examination of Reverend Wright's rhetoric. Most critics deemed Obama's speech unprecedented, since no presidential candidate has ever confronted race relations in America in such a direct manner.

http://www.hemisphonics.com—to access articles by Eldon Taylor, who has researched the impact of language on human behavior and self-perception. He received the International Peace Prize in 2005 for his teaching of self-responsibility. He has studied school violence extensively.

http://www.cjr.org—to review the *Columbia Journalism Review*. See Tuesday, January 8, 2008, Gal Beckerman, for commentary on Bill Clinton's appraisal of how his wife was treated by the media in the 2008 campaign—"Bill Clinton: Media Critic—Is Hillary getting a 'raw deal'?"

http://www.rushmoredrive.com—a search engine aimed at African Americans and owned by Barry Diller, who also owns Ask.com. Barry Taylor, CEO, stated that Rushmore Drive was created after focus groups requested a site that was specific to black Internet users who wanted a "Google-plus" service that would serve their interests. Topics such as the Rev. Jeremiah Wright Jr. and recipes from their childhood are contenders. Such "geo-biasing" in search engines may evolve to address other special interests, such as women, gays, Latinos, etc., according to *Newsweek* (May 19, 2008).

http://www.clinton.senate.gov/~clinton/speeches/2005125A05.html—for Senator Clinton's 2005 speech on *Roe* v. *Wade.*

CHAPTER 5

MESSAGES: VERBAL
AND NONVERBAL SUPPORT

KEY WORDS

ad hominem

ad populum

argumentum ad absurdum

argumentum ad
  miseracordiam

claim

enthymeme

evidence
  analogies
    examples (real vs.
      hypothetical)

narratives

statistics

testimony

fallacies

false dilemma

Freedom of Information Act
  (FOIA)

indices of credibility

inductive

nonverbal codes (affect
  displays, chronemics, eye

behavior, haptics,
olfactics, proxemics,
territoriality, and vocalics)

non sequitur

phaedrus

post hoc ergo propter hoc

primacy–recency effect

rapist–seducer–lover
  relationship

reluctant testimony

slippery slope

PREVIEW

The content of any communication transaction, whether it is an intimate conversation, a public speech, or a mass media telecast, is called a message. When audiences receive a message, there is more to it than the mere words they interpret. Sometimes receivers are so focused on the sender of the message that they do not actually hear what was said. Nonverbal communication is a powerful component of the overall message, and it includes the speakers' appearance, how they move, and their vocal characteristics.

    In this chapter we discuss how speakers support their messages with both rational and emotional appeals, how they structure their message to persuade audiences who may be hostile to their ideas, and finally how nonverbal codes are used in communication overall. You have heard, "It was not what you said, but how you said it," which means that sometimes nonverbal messages contradict the actual words, but they can reinforce, complement, or substitute verbal messages. In the first portion of this chapter we look at the various kinds of logical proofs or evidence that can be used to strengthen messages and to persuade audiences. We also look at emotional appeals and how they affect audiences. The organization of the message is an important factor as well in persuasion, including how the introduction, body, and conclusion of the message are constructed or invented. Finally, we focus on nonverbal codes, which are inseparable from any message where the speaker is visible or audible and part of the transaction. Edward Hall called nonverbal communication the "silent language" and the "hidden dimension" (see Hall, 1959, 1966), which he said is not written anywhere but is understood by everyone. He was talking about those unwritten codes, about how close to stand to someone when you are talking with them and whether or not it is appropriate to touch another person while speaking. This chapter gives names to those dimensions of communication that are so influential in personal and professional interactions but that are often violated and give offense to others without our even knowing it. So messages are analyzed by the actual words used (semantics); the order of the ideas conveyed (organization); the evidence used to support claims (proofs); emotional appeals used to arouse passion in audiences and involve them (affect displays); and nonverbal components, which are sometimes obvious and other times subliminal (vocal quality, facial expressions, body movement, clothing, distances from audience members, and artifacts like flags, uniforms, or presidential seals).

First, let us examine verbal messages and distinguish between content that appeals to our sense of reason and that which appeals to our emotions. There has always been a question about whether logical proofs or emotional appeals are more ethical or effective in persuasion. The answer to that question would depend on the subject matter and the actual circumstances of the argument. Some subject matter is emotionally laden because it involves ethical dimensions of such importance that core values are in conflict such as the abortion debate, capital punishment, or euthanasia. We can begin exploring the issue of logical and emotional appeals by reviewing what the ancient writers said about reason and passion in communication.

PLATO'S VISION OF REASON AND PASSION

Plato (431–351 BCE), who lived to be 81, had been greatly influenced by Socrates with whom he discussed ethical issues from about age 18 to 21; these discussions would become the themes of the Socratic dialogues that he wrote to explore philosophical issues. Plato was too ill to attend the execution of Socrates, who was sentenced to death for corrupting the youth of Athens. Plato then withdrew from political life in Athens and founded the Academy—the first European University, which was devoted to the study of philosophy and mathematics. (Edman, 1956, pp. xi–xv).

THE *PHAEDRUS*, A DIALOGUE ABOUT THE DUALITY OF MAN

Plato represented the divided nature of man by offering an allegory of two winged horses and a charioteer. One horse is noble and of noble breed, white and beautiful, characterized by reason and restraint, while the other is an ignoble breed, black, with bloodshot eyes and great strength, thus giving the charioteer a struggle steering the two who are constantly at war for direction and control of the soul (Edman, 1956, pp. 286–289). The allegory represents the duality of humans who can be winged and rational, elevated above this world with love, justice, knowledge, and goodness to commune with the gods from whom true knowledge is given, according to Plato. The other side of man, represented by the dark horse, portrays appetite and is fed by excess, evil, and foulness that causes his wings to waste and fall away, depriving him of any vision of heaven or goodness. Plato tells us that sight is the "most piercing of our bodily senses" but not the source of wisdom (Edman, 1956, p. 292). Humans must transcend the world of their senses to rejoin that vision of the good or the divine which exists on a higher plane or realm. Plato believed that the philosopher could attain this transformative knowledge and truth, which was absolute, but most others were corrupted by the world and their "brutish beast" that is not ashamed or constrained from its wantonness (Edman, 1956, p. 292).

ARISTOTLE'S VIEW OF EMOTIONS

Aristotle, who was born in 384 BCE the son of a physician, studied under Plato at the Academy and remained to teach there for 20 years, but he left upon Plato's death, perhaps disappointed that he was not named to lead the school. Aristotle became interested in scientific studies and the scientific method of exploring the physical world (Sinclair, 1962, p. 9). His search for truth was based on factual exploration and probability. He understood the interaction between the speaker, the message, and the audience.

In Book II of *The Rhetoric of Aristotle* he stated that there are three things that gain our belief in the speaker—"intelligence, character, and good will" (Cooper, 1932, p. 92). In order to tailor the message to fit the occasion and the audience, one needed to know the psychology of the human mind, which includes emotions. Aristotle defined emotions as those states that are attended by pain and pleasure such as anger, pity, and fear, which make a difference in our judgments. Anger is an impulse attended by pain because of an insult or slight one has suffered, but also anger brings pleasure at the expectation of revenge. Love and hatred both are strong emotions found at opposite ends of the scale. Aristotle wrote:

> A man will like (love) the friends of his friends, and people who like those whom he likes; will like those who are liked by those whom he likes; and will like those who have the same enemies as he has, who hate the people he hates, and who are hated by the people by whom he is hated; for all these consider the same things good as he does, and therefore wish such things as are good to him—and this, we saw is the definition of a friend. (Cooper, 1932, p. 103)

Another strong emotion that distorts judgment is fear, which Aristotle said generally comes about because of the power that another has over us to have us at their mercy. Similarly, shame is an emotion arising out of a "mental image of discredit" or ignomity (Cooper, 1932, p. 114). Pity is an emotion that he described as "pain at what we take to be (what vividly strikes us as) an evil of a destructive or painful kind, which befalls one who does not deserve it, which we think we ourselves or some one allied to us might likewise suffer . . ." (Cooper, 1932, p. 120). Aristotle explained indignation, envy, emulation, and contempt to demonstrate how these emotions could be called forth to enrage or placate an audience.

He went on to analyze types of characters through a description of the stages of life. He wrote of the passions of youth:

> Young men have strong desires, and whatever they desire they are prone to do. Of the bodily desires the one they let govern them most is the sexual; here they lack self-control. They are shifting and unsteady in their desires, which are vehement for a time, but soon relinquished; for the longings of youth are keen rather than deep—are like sick people's fits of hunger and thirst. The young are passionate, quick to anger, and apt to give way to it. And their angry passions get the better of them; for, since they wish to be honored, young men cannot put up with a slight; they are resentful if they only imagine that they are unfairly treated. Fond of honor, they are even fonder of victory, for youth likes to be superior, and winning evinces superiority. They love both honor and victory more than they love money. (Cooper, 1932, p. 132)

By contrast, Aristotle characterized the elderly as the opposite of the young:

> The old have lived long, have been often deceived, have made many mistakes of their own; they see that more often than not the affairs of men turn out badly. And so they are positive about nothing; in all things they err by an extreme moderation. They "think"—they never "know" and in discussing any matter they always subjoin "perhaps"—"possibly." Everything they say is put thus doubtfully—nothing with firmness. They think evil (are cynical); that is, they are disposed to put the worse construction on everything. Further, they are suspicious because they are distrustful, and distrustful from sad experience. As a result, they have no strong likings or hates; rather, illustrating the precept of Bias, they love as men ready some day to hate, and hate as ready to love. They are mean-souled (small-minded) because they have been humbled by life. Thus they aspire to nothing great or exalted, but crave the mere necessities and comforts of existence. (Cooper, 1932, p. 134)

Aristotle portrayed men in their prime as exempt from the excesses of the young or the old, but measured between the two extremes, thus being both confident and cautious. They judge arguments based on facts, and rule neither on honor alone nor expediency. He said they are in the prime of life between 30 and 35, while the prime of the soul is 49 (Cooper, 1932, pp. 136–137). Aristotle noted that knowing emotions and the character of the audience allows the speaker to color the speech to arouse the desired feelings in the audiences or to allay them. Clearly, the construction of the message would depend on many possibilities, which included the ethos of the speaker, the effect that the speaker hoped to have on the perceived audience, knowledge of the audience itself, and whether the content of the message would enlist rational or emotional arguments, or both of these. Aristotle noted that animals have a voice and can express pain or pleasure, but only man has speech, which serves to address that which is useful or harmful, right and wrong, evil and good, just and unjust (Sinclair, 1962, pp. 28–29). So Aristotle recognized that people are both rational and passionate beings, but his prescriptions for speaking always called for the highest order of ethical behavior.

Both Plato and Aristotle wrote of the passions of humans, which could be aroused with emotional speech. Aristotle called these emotional appeals *pathos*, which he believed to be one of three ways of persuading an audience. The other two were *logos*, which is logical arguments, and *ethos*, the character of the speaker. Aristotle, as stated earlier, believed that ethos was the most persuasive of the three appeals. Wayne Brockriede wrote an article that depicted the relationship between an arguer or speaker and the audience as one of three types—a rapist, a seducer, or a lover. His relationship model is worthy of review; even though some object to the sexual metaphor, Brockriede explored the power relationship in communication transactions in a novel way.

BROCKRIEDE'S ANALYSIS OF SPEAKER–AUDIENCE RELATIONSHIPS

Since a receiver must be convinced that the persuader is credible, it is appropriate that we analyze the motives and the ethics of the speaker. Persuaders make arguments to win our consent by establishing a relationship with us. Wayne Brockriede (1972) created the relationship model of arguers as either a rapist, a seducer, or a lover. This relationship metaphor demonstrated that arguers are **rapists,** who see their relationship with the audience as a unilateral one allowing them to objectify the audience, manipulate them, and put them down. Brockriede claimed, "The rapist wants to gain or to maintain a position of superiority—on the intellectual front of making his case prevail or on the interpersonal front of putting the other person down" (Brockreide, 1972, p. 3). The communicator who acts as **seducer** wins covertly through charm or deceit, and we frequently see seducers in both politics and advertising According to Brockriede:

> The second stance may be characterized by the word seduction. Whereas the rapist conquers by force of argument, the seducer operates through charm or deceit. The seducer's attitude toward co-arguers is similar to that of the rapist. He, too, sees the relationship as unilateral. Although he may not be contemptuous of his prey, he is indifferent to the identity and integrity of the other person. Whereas the intent of the rapist is to force assent, the seducer tries to charm or trick his victim into assent. (Brockreide, 1972, p. 4)

 The preferred relationship between the communicator and audience is that of the **lover,** who does not wish to vanquish the receiver but to empower them through argument and to enlighten them so that they have significant choices. There is no degradation or injury to the other. This discussion of the relationship between the speaker and the receiver falls under ethics, which forbids deception, telling half-truths, fabricating evidence, or fooling the audience. Since all messages have both a relationship and content dimension, it is noteworthy to consider how the speaker views the audience, and what they choose to tell them. The relationship between sender and receiver is a significant variable in the communication process because it involves issues of emotional bonds, trust, power, and respect. The content of the message involves organization, truth, meaning, consistency, logic, and clarity.

EVIDENCE IN PERSUASIVE MESSAGES

Messages that intend to persuade receivers are everywhere—televised political speeches, sermons in houses of worship, bumper stickers for social movements, and advertisements for products. In persuasive speaking, the source is an advocate for a given position that puts forth a **claim** or assertion that needs to be proven or supported somehow to convince the audience that they should believe the message and respond to it appropriately by perhaps endorsing the candidate, living a better life, protecting the environment, or buying Dial soap. These messages are supported or illustrated by what we call **evidence,** or proofs, which generally consists of one of the following forms of material—**narratives**, or stories, examples, statistics, testimony, analogies, or artifacts that are offered to win the adherence of the listeners.

NARRATIVES OR STORIES

We discussed Fisher's narrative theory earlier, and we know that storytelling is a powerful part of our lives. The oral tradition preceded any written historical record. Stories have characters, dialog, action, and a resolution. A story can have a dramatic effect and be a great source of persuasion. Here is the narrative that former President Clinton wrote in his book *Bill Clinton: My Life* (2004) about the peace agreement between Yitzhak Rabin and Yasser Arafat during Clinton's administration:

> Just before the ceremony, all three delegations gathered in the large oval Blue Room on the main floor of the White House. The Israelis and the Palestinians still weren't talking to each other in public, so the Americans went back and forth between the two groups as they moved around the rim of the room. We looked like a bunch of awkward kids riding a slow-moving carousel.
>
> Mercifully, it was over before long, and we walked downstairs to start the ceremony. Everyone else walked out on cue, leaving Arafat, Rabin, and me alone for a moment. Arafat said hello to Rabin and held out his hand. Yitzhak's hands were firmly grasped behind his back. He said tersely, "outside." Arafat just smiled and nodded his understanding. Then Rabin said, "You know, we are going to have to work very hard to make this work." Arafat replied, "I know, and I am prepared to do my part."
>
> We walked out into the bright sunshine of a late-summer day. I opened the ceremony with a brief welcome and words of thanks, support, and encouragement for the leaders and their determination to achieve a "peace for the brave." Peres and Abbas followed me with brief speeches, then sat down to sign the agreement. Warren Christopher and Andrei Kozyrev witnessed it while Rabin, Arafat, and I stood behind and to the right. When the signing was completed, all eyes shifted to the leaders, Arafat stood on my left and Rabin to my right. I shook hands with Arafat, with the blocking maneuver I had practiced. I then turned and shook hands with Rabin, after which I stepped back out of the space between them and spread my arms to bring them together. Arafat lifted his hand toward a still reluctant Rabin. When Rabin extended his hand, the crowd let out an audible gasp, followed by a thunderous applause, as they completed the kissless handshake. All the world was cheering, except for diehard protesters in the Middle East who were inciting violence, and demonstrators in front of the White House claiming we were endangering Israel's security. (Clinton, 2004, p. 544)

President Clinton wanted to record this dramatic and hopeful moment in history as well as to mark his role as peace broker, an elevated moment in his administration. He painted the characters with details so that we could sense the tension and the triumph in the meeting.

President Bill Clinton delivered a rousing endorsement for President Barack Obama at the 2012 Democratic Convention, where he called for cooperation to prevail as the dominating value in government.

President Bill Clinton is a charismatic speaker who has worked with the elder President George H. Bush and many others to address issues in recent years, and he was effective as President in bringing dissidents together. In 2012, he delivered a speech at the Democratic National Convention to coalesce alienated factions to support President Barack Obama for four more years, and Clinton's endorsement was a powerful motivational force for delegates as he played the role of teacher who refutted the "arithmetic" of Obama's opponents. He concluded that the Republican's program just did not add up, and cooperation works better than conflict "because nobody is right all the time, and a broken clock is right twice a day." (Bill Clinton, September 5, 2012)

EXAMPLES

Another common form of evidence is **examples,** which may be real historical events, like the one just narrated, or hypothetical constructs to make a point. The following excerpt from a chapter on values and credibility in business illustrates how examples can be used to reach conclusions:

> It is only 3:00 p.m. on a typical Wednesday, and Henry Kenton, the owner of a retail business, is making his third major argument of the day. He started with a meeting at his bank where he was seeking a loan, then he went to a hotel where the representative of a sportswear firm talked about the need for a rush order of specially dyed material. Now Mr. Kenton is waiting his turn at the State Industrial Commission office to argue against a former employee's claim for unemployment compensation and money damages.
>
> In another part of town, Rhonda McIntyre, President and Chief Executive Officer of a mid-size manufacturing firm, has spent the entire day in and out of meetings with Japanese executives trying to work out the details of a contract in which McIntyre's company is to supply a major component of the Japanese product. The arguments center on price, quantity, quality, and schedule. Both of these people are engaging in business argumentation, and

in each instance their arguments will rely heavily on support generated through credibility and values. (Rieke & Sillars, 2001, p. 237)

Examples may be detailed, as this one, or undetailed and merely mention a well-known name or incident, such as the Enron scandal, where the audience can fill in the details from familiarity with the referenced event or person. Such an example, where the audience fills in the essential details to reach a conclusion, is called an **enthymeme.**

TESTIMONY

Testimony is information from experts in the field who offer insight or relevant facts on the topic. Persuaders should use field-specific testimony, since the different disciplines use language in different contexts. The field of law uses precedent or former cases and existing codes, such as the Constitution of the United States and the Amendments. Science and medicine use the scientific method of research and inquiry to prove hypotheses or to conduct studies. Religious inquiry depends on ancient writings and belief in the precepts of one's faith. The worldview of the audience is a significant factor in how they perceive the message. For example, a scientist would not likely be persuaded by an argument on global warming if one were quoting the Bible as a proof on air quality; similarly, the theologian would not be persuaded by the atmospheric readings of the weather service to contradict the concept of hell and eternal damnation in the hereafter.

Some issues cut across different fields of specialization, such as law, ethics, and human rights. In the following excerpt a librarian, Ann Okerson, from Yale University raised timely questions that new technologies have prompted concerning intellectual property:

> Many works are being created through extensive electronic communities or collaborations—who owns and benefits from these? Questions about how to apply current copyright law to new formats and media abound: To what extent are works on the newer—let alone not yet created—electronic media protected by law? . . . How do we efficiently compensate information owners when their work can be sold by the word, phrase or even musical note? What are the liabilities of Internet access providers, who may be unaware of copyright violation over their facilities? Should we dispense with copyright as we have known it entirely and seek new paradigms, as the Office of Technology Assessment advocated in 1986? (Okerson, 1998, p. 344)

This expert in information transfer, a librarian, raised more questions than she answered, but experts on copyright laws and the courts have spoken. Copyright has been extended to owners who have been compensated for transgressions against their works through illegal copy, distribution, and sales of them. The Napster controversy over downloading music and making copies settled that score. Apparently, the old laws were sufficient for copyright and contract law attorneys to persuade the courts that ownership rights were superior to any challenges brought on by easy access through the World Wide Web and Internet interfaces.

Jodi was tried and convicted for the murder of her boyfriend Travis Alexander because she and her expert's testimony lacked credibility.

As situations change, like the technology that permits easy access and downloading, the arguments and evidence that persuaders use must change as well.

ANALOGIES

Analogies are merely comparisons that link a new idea to something with which we are familiar to show similarities between the known and the unknown idea or object. You have heard it said, "You are comparing apples and oranges," meaning that no real similarity exists and that the analogy is not logical. However, analogies have great applicability in persuasion since if something worked in one state or circumstances, it should work again someplace else. For example, Megan's Law has been adopted in most states in the United States to protect children from predators by forcing states to keep a data bank of known pedophiles, listing their place of residence, mandating sentences for crimes to prevent judges from giving lenient sentences to offenders, and other measures to contain child molestation and murder. States that have mandated Megan's laws can be compared to states that have not adopted such measures to see if such stringent tracking and sentencing guidelines do protect the welfare of minor children who are targets of predators. The state of California has a Megan's Law website, which reports the following:

> As a result of a new law, this site will provide you with access to information on more than 63,000 persons required to register in California as sex offenders. Specific home addresses are displayed on more than 33,500 offenders in the California communities; as to these persons, the site displays the last registered address reported by the offender. An additional 30,500 offenders are included on the site with listing by ZIP code, city, and county. Information on approximately 22,000 other offenders is not included on this site, but is known to law enforcement personnel. (Megan's Law, 2006, p. 1)

By comparison, it could be argued that all states should be vigilant and protect their children from such predators by knowing where they reside, what their offenses were, and how to share or access the data.

STATISTICS

Another form of evidence is **statistics,** which are numerical representations for many entities studied. Statistics are seductive in that they seem hard and factual with concrete numbers. However, someone said, "Figures do not lie, but liars figure." Thus one can prove many lies with statistical computations by simply manipulating the number of cases studied, the baseline for beginning the analysis, and selectively including some cases and excluding others. The following **inductive** statements, which are "statements whose truth can be assessed by collecting and analyzing data, could be proven or disproven through the use of statistics:

- My golfing partner says, "Keep your left arm straight and you will hit straighter." I try it a few times and conclude that he is right.
- I look at the sky and listen to the radio in an attempt to decide whether it might rain tomorrow.
- I decide to use Crest toothpaste because it is said to be more effective than a nonfluoridated brand.
- I choose to fly because I believe air travel is safer than driving.
- The Surgeon General says that smoking cigarettes causes cancer.
- I believe that in basketball, the home team has an advantage, but I wonder how big that advantage is.
- I believe that most beer drinkers can't distinguish between Miller and Bud; that is, most "preference" is really the result of advertising hype.
- I think the ozone layer is deteriorating. (Hurlburt, 2006, pp. 2–3)

The foregoing statements can best be analyzed using statistical procedures. Some messages lend themselves to statistical computations better than others. In election years, we are inundated with polls from Gallup and others that tell us which candidate is ahead or lagging, what the views on the economy are, and how many favor the war effort or oppose it, and these findings are persuasive since some voters simply believe that the majority must know more than they do. There are many different forms of proofs to support claims or to present arguments to audiences, but many claims are not worthy of belief because they mislead, use false information, or present inconsistent or incoherent data. Audiences should be able to identify and reject such fallacies in reasoning.

FALLACIES IN REASONING

Fallacies are errors in reasoning that lead to incorrect conclusions. According to Inch and Warnick (1998), "A fallacy is an argument that is flawed by irrelevant or inadequate evidence, erroneous reasoning, or improper expression—In other words, a fallacy is an incorrect argument" (p. 82). There are many different fallacies, depending on which expert you read on the topic, but some of the most common ones are those that misdirect the audience's attention. There are a series of *ad* fallacies, which mean arguments *to* the people. The most popular ones are discussed next.

AD HOMINEM

An **ad hominem** fallacy is one that attacks the person or source of the argument instead of responding to the ideas offered in the argument. This fallacy has also been defined as character assassination, or an attack on the character of the speaker. Consider the following exchange:

PARENT: I am really concerned about your grades this past semester. You were always such a good student in high school and now you have slipped to straight Cs. I think you need to study more and forget about seeing so much of your friends.

STUDENT: Why are you always on my back for not studying? Your grades in college were nothing to write home about! (Inch & Warnick, 1998, p. 83).

In order to qualify for an ad hominem argument, the speaker's intention must be to divert attention from the main claim being addressed, in this case, the student's performance in college.

AD POPULUM

In order to qualify as an **ad populum** fallacy, "the substance of an argument is avoided and the advocate appeals instead to popular opinion as a justification for the claim" (Inch & Warnick, 1998, p. 84). This fallacy claims that "everyone is doing it" or has it, whatever "it" is. People will cite opinion polls, or talk about all the people that they know who are voting a particular way or buying a commodity, appealing to the need for others to belong or to conform to popular opinion.

ARGUMENTUM AD MISERACORDIAM

Arguments that are intended to elicit pity are referred to as **argumentum ad miseracordiam** (Rieke & Sillars, 2001). One of the classic demonstrations of this fallacy is to argue that the young man who just murdered both his parents should not be prosecuted because he is now a poor orphan deserving the compassion of the court. In courts across the land, defense attorneys are making such pleas for their clients who have been dressed to look like any normal teenager, man, or woman, and coached on how to look compliant or victimized. The Menendez brothers in California are classic examples of this form or argument. ABC News reported:

> On August 20, 1989, 21-year-old Lyle and 18-year-old Erik burst into the family den and killed their father Jose, a successful Cuban-American business executive, and their mother, Kitty. They used shotguns they had bought days before the crime.
>
> Prosecutors said the boys' motive was pure greed—Erik and Lyle simply wanted to get their hands on the family fortune.
>
> But Erik told a rapt courtroom that he and his brother believed they were about to be murdered themselves, because their father would rather see them dead than have a shocking family secret revealed. The secret, according to the boys' testimony, was that their father had sexually abused them. Erik said he had been abused for many years. (Tammi Menendez, 2002)

The Menendez brothers, Lyle and Erik, failed in their attempt to win sympathy with the jurors by claiming sexual abuse from their father.

The first trial lasted six months and ended in a hung jury where half of the 12 jurors believed that they should be charged with manslaughter because of sexual abuse, but the other 6 thought that they killed both parents for their money and voted for first-degree murder. A second trial convicted both of the Menendez brothers of first-degree murder, and they were sentenced to two consecutive life sentences. The sympathy that the first jury felt was removed largely through evidence pointing to a spending spree they took after the murders as well as plans to purchase guns and to avoid apprehension. Both boys appealed the life in prison sentence because "dozens of his family members who witnessed the emotional and physical abuse he says he and his brother endured was excluded from the second trial," Erik Menendez said (Tammi Menendez, 2002). The appeal to pity (argumentum ad miseracordiam) is effective and often used on juries to win lighter sentences or none at all.

ARGUMENTUM AD ABSURDUM

An argument that is carried to absurd proportions is called **argumentum ad absurdum**. Good examples of this form of argument can be found in newscasts about the jilted husband who has just killed his ex-wife and their children because he knew that they could never be as happy as he could have made them. Normal people always wonder why the perpetrator would not begin with themselves if the world is so filled with misery, but their justifications are always that they are doing the victims a favor somehow by killing them.

NON SEQUITUR

In Latin **non sequitur** means literally "it does not follow" (Inch & Warnick, 1998, p. 162). The non sequitur contains an irrelevant claim or data that does not logically flow from the argument; it simply fails to support the claim that has been advanced. Orderly and tight arguments have great appeal to an audience. A claim or assertion that is supported by evidence, with subclaims identified and similarly supported with relevant data, offers an audience an orderly presentation that should be free from overgeneralizations or irrelevancies. The message that stays on track and carries the listener to a logical conclusion is one that will be more readily understood and appreciated by the audience. The non sequitur can be seen in the following hypothetical dialog:

TOM: Do you believe in capital punishment?
JIM: No, I believe in the sanctity of all life.
TOM: Where are you from?
JIM: Philadelphia.
TOM: That explains it!

When a non sequitur is committed, the argument makes an illogical turn off the path of the idea that is being presented for consideration.

POST HOC ERGO PROPTER HOC

Analysis that investigates the root causes of anything is difficult to complete, and a frequently committed fallacy is the **post hoc ergo propter hoc** fallacy, which in Latin translates to "after this therefore because of this," which posits that just because one thing preceded another in time, it caused the second event to occur. For example, we might say, "Every time I wash my car it rains." In everyday conversation we hear claims that divorce causes juvenile delinquency, but many children from broken homes are high achievers and very moral persons, so perhaps it is only coincidental that some juvenile offenders come from broken homes. In order to test such a claim or argument, statistics on children from divorced homes who commit crimes and those who do not commit crimes would have to be compared. While broken families may be a contributing factor, they are not the only cause of juvenile crimes; therefore, when a marriage ends in divorce, it is not grounds to assume that the minor children will become criminals.

FALSE DILEMMA

Another common fallacy is the forced choice of the **false dilemma** which allows only either/or choices when there are many other alternatives from which to choose. Bumper stickers announce, "Either you are part of the problem or you are part of the solution." "America, Love It or Leave It!" When someone tries to persuade an audience that there are only either/or choices, the audience should always question what else is not being presented or what else is not being recognized as part of the scenario. Since complex social-political problems are not generally cast into black-and-white terms but shades of gray, logically the audience should analyze the boundaries of the issue and any subissues that are relevant to the argument. Determinations that something is right or wrong, just or unjust, or polar opposites do not shed light on courses of action generally. Political deliberations do not work like an on–off switch with all-or-none designations.

SLIPPERY SLOPE

The **slippery slope** fallacy assumes that one event will give rise to a series of events that will lead inevitably to a bad outcome. Anti-abortion advocates argued in the early 1970s that legalized abortion would lead to promiscuity, disregard for life overall, including an easy path to euthanasia, and then death to anyone designated as undesirable. Similarly, the Liquor Control Board of Pennsylvania made the claim that selling alcohol in grocery stores where access would be easier would cause more underage drinking, more vehicle accidents, and ultimately cost the communities more in actual enforcement costs and other intangible human terms. Proponents for easier access to alcohol in superstores claim that the LCB has only the protection of a patronage political system as the motive for preserving it along with elevated prices, poor selections, and a patriarchic view of consumers.

To summarize, then, fallacies are errors in reasoning that lead to incorrect conclusions by avoiding the real issues, attacking the speaker rather than analyzing the arguments, diverting attention through emotional appeals, or selectively presenting only a partial truth. There are many more fallacies than those named specifically here, but one would need to enroll in a course of argument and debate or logic to get a more comprehensive treatment of the subject. Everyone has committed a fallacy without intentionally trying to mislead others by perhaps not being fully informed, using dated materials, or using erroneous logic, but some unscrupulous speakers are not above outright lying, quoting out of context, or manufacturing proofs that they know are false. So fallacies can be divided into those that are unintentional or unconscious lapses of reasoning and others that are intentionally designed to deceive. Persuasion is affected not only by logical reasoning but also by the organization of the ideas, the person who delivers the message, and the skill he or she possesses as a communicator.

In summary, there are many ways to support arguments to make them more clear, dramatic, memorable, and more persuasive. The content of messages has to resonate with the audience to have the ring of truth, relevance, and applicability. There are evidential tests that can be applied to supporting material by audience members to test the validity of messages. These evaluative methods concern reliability, expertise, objectivity, consistency, recency, relevance, access, and accuracy of citation (Warnick & Inch, 1994, pp. 78–85). Reliability depends on the record of the speaker or writer and how accurate they have been in the past. Relevance addresses how central the idea is to the issue at hand and whether or not the data is related to the topic. Consistency deals with how well the information matches up with other ideas in the speech or perhaps with statements made through time. Consistency means that the message is free from contradictory statements. Videotaping has enabled researchers and audience members to follow the careers of leaders and to compare their positions over time or through a campaign to see if their statements remain constant or if they "flip-flop." This does not mean that with new evidence or data one cannot change one's mind to assimilate or consider these changes, but if there are inconsistencies within a message, this is grounds to doubt the veracity of it. The recency of the data means that it is current and not out of date. Statistics on unemployment and the economy change seasonally, so the recency of the numbers is important. Perhaps most significant in credibility is the expertise of the writer or the speaker, because those who have credentials, experience, and training in the area of discussion are more informed that those without any of these.

Robert and Dale Newman (1969), in their book *Evidence*, noted that the past record of a speaker was a primary consideration in their credibility. Further, they offered **indices of credibility** (pp. 87–88) that consisted of 14 points that could be applied to test the quality of evidence. The Newmans noted that the primary sources of evidence were the government, press, pressure groups, and scholars. Each of these sources offered both advantages and disadvantages regarding evidence. For example, the government has billions of dollars for information gathering, printing, and dissemination of data, but secrecy in government means that much is unavailable to the ordinary researcher because of classified documents. However, the **Freedom of Information Act (FOIA)** was passed in 1966, making this information more accessible to scholars, journalists, and consumer groups, making it easier to gain access to government documents. The press is only as good as the journalists and editors who disseminate the news. Pressure groups exist to affect change or to advocate a given position; so while they have a high level of expertise or knowledge on the subject, there is an inherent bias toward their position. Pressure groups such as the NRA, NOW, PETA, and Greenpeace should be used as authorities with caution. According to the Newmans' book, scholars rated highest on the scale of credibility, but many scholars write from a given perspective as well, so their work should be scrutinized with the same tests for reliability, consistency, and accuracy as any other source.

PETA (People for the Ethical Treatment of Animals) use shocking tactics to persuade the public-nudity and confrontational tactics like spray painting fur coats.

EFFECTS OF EVIDENCE IN PERSUASIVE COMMUNICATION

James McCroskey (1997) offered a summary of experimental research on the effects of evidence in persuasion. Evidence was defined as "factual statements originating from a source other than the speaker, objects not created by the speaker, and opinions of persons other than the speaker that are offered in support of the speaker's claims" (McCroskey, 1997, p. 2). First, he showed that studies revealed contradictory findings regarding the effect of evidence on attitude change. Two early studies by Cathcart and Bettinghause showed statistically significant results from inclusion of evidence in a message to change attitudes. McCroskey reported that studies by Gilkinson, Paulson, and Sikkink and Ostermeier did not show statistical significance for evidence and attitude change. Further, Anderson, Costley, Dresser, Gardner, and Wagner found no significance in attitude change when high-quality evidence was offered, low-quality evidence was offered, or no evidence was offered at all (McCroskey, 1997, p. 1). Where McCroskey found that evidence made the greatest difference was when a low-credibility source used high-credibility evidence consisting of facts or opinions from experts. He pointed to other variables that could impact the power of evidence that needed further study, such as the delivery of the message, source credibility, prior knowledge of the topic, or the intelligence of the audience members and the importance of the topic to them. Several writers, Robert Newman among these, have written that reluctant testimony is the most believable; however, McCroskey found no support for that theory since his four studies found that unbiased sources were superior to biased ones and unbiased sources were also superior to reluctant sources. **Reluctant testimony** means that sources would incriminate or injure themselves by divulging these facts, so it would seem logical that they would not be eager to step forth to testify under these conditions. For example, witnesses will plead the Fifth Amendment rather than implicate themselves in a crime, but when a person offers testimony that could injure his or her reputation or result in criminal prosecution, that constitutes reluctant testimony. McCroskey's work does not support the strength of reluctant testimony. His findings from 22 studies were summarized in this manner:

1. Including good evidence has little, if any, impact on immediate audience attitude change or source credibility if the source of the message is initially perceived to be high-credible.
2. Including good evidence has little, if any, impact on immediate audience attitude change if the message is delivered poorly.
3. Including good evidence has little, if any, impact on immediate audience attitude change or source credibility if the audience is familiar with the evidence prior to exposure to the source's message.
4. Including good evidence may significantly increase immediate audience attitude change and source credibility when the source is initially perceived to be moderate-to-low-credible, when the message is well delivered, and when the audience has little or no prior familiarity with the evidence included or similar evidence.
5. Including good evidence may significantly increase sustained audience attitude change regardless of the source's initial credibility, the quality of the delivery of the message, or the medium by which the message is transmitted.
6. The medium of transmission of a message has little, if any, effect on the functioning of evidence in persuasive communication. (McCroskey, 1997, p. 6).

Given the foregoing summary, where is the greatest source of persuasion? We can go back to Aristotle's theory that the speaker is the most powerful ingredient in the whole dynamic of persuasive discourse. McCroskey noted that there are many other variables to be studied further to answer that question. But Tony Schwartz, who wrote *The Responsive Chord* (1973), stated that the response is already in the audience, not implanted by the message communicated. Schwartz wrote:

> In developing a set of useful principles for communicating, it is necessary to abandon most of the traditional rules we were taught. A resonance approach does not begin by asking, "What do I want to say?" We seek to strike a responsive chord in people, not get a message across. This involves, first, examining how stored experiences are patterned in our brain, and how previous experiences condition us to perceive new stimuli. Second, we must understand the characteristics of the new communication environment, and how people use media in their lives. Only at the final stage do we consider the content of a message, and this will be determined by the effect we want to achieve and the environment where our content will take on meaning. (Schwartz, 1973, p. 27)

It seems obvious that no one element can be separated from the others. The speaker's appearance, delivery, organization, and content will affect the audience members only so far as they allow these variables to influence them depending on their own knowledge, needs, experiences, and desires.

ORGANIZING ARGUMENTS FOR MAXIMUM EFFECT

Speakers often wonder how to order their arguments to have the maximum effect on the audience. Some frequently asked questions are: Should I begin with the claim or leave it to the audience to reach the conclusion? Should I present a two-sided view of the topic? How do I present an argument to which I know the audience is hostile or not in agreement?

To answer the first question on an explicit thesis statement or claim, researchers have generally found that explicitly stated conclusions were generally more effective than those that the audience had to discern for themselves (Inch & Warnick, 1998). Whether to use the two-sided presentation depends on four things—the nature of the topic, time to present ideas, the desire to be fair, and the nature of the audience itself. First, when two courses of action are available and recognized as such, then the speaker should present both since that shows the speaker to be knowledgeable on the topic. Second, it depends on whether there is time or space available for the two-sided argument. If time allows it, then presenting all aspects of the topic is desirable, but often one only has time to present the side that is advo- 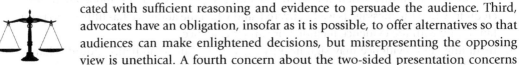 cated with sufficient reasoning and evidence to persuade the audience. Third, advocates have an obligation, insofar as it is possible, to offer alternatives so that audiences can make enlightened decisions, but misrepresenting the opposing view is unethical. A fourth concern about the two-sided presentation concerns the nature of the audience. Researchers have found that if the audience is already favorably disposed toward the topic, they do not want to hear the opposite view. Audiences who are poorly informed on the topic can become confused by complex and contradictory ideas presented to them (Inch & Warnick, 1998).

Speakers generally have a great numbers of arguments to offer to the audience, but research has shown that the stronger arguments should be presented and weaker ones omitted. Then the question arises about where to place the arguments in the speech. The **primacy-recency effect** shows that the beginning and the end of a message are the most memorable places for ideas, so the speaker should put their strongest arguments in either of these places (Inch & Warnick, 1998). If they put them in the beginning, they have the rest of the speech to explain and illustrate the ideas. If the audience is hostile to the speech or the speaker, then the beginning of the speech could be used to show listeners that the speaker does have something worthwhile to say and to show how the message relates to them. If the speaker is successful in winning some agreement, then the issues that the audience found objectionable in the beginning can be offered later in the presentation when their attention, interest, and convictions may be more readily influenced.

In summary, the message is the connective avenue between the speaker and the audience with many variables that can either facilitate or obstruct the receivers' desire or ability to accept it. Some audiences respond to logical presentations with strong evidence to back assertions made by the speakers; other audiences embrace emotional arguments that arouse their passions, igniting their beliefs in the truth and righteousness of the message. The audience's perception of the character of the speaker is always an issue in persuasion, and while we have discussed the effect of evidence, the order of the ideas offered, and some research findings on all of these, the unspoken dimension, called nonverbal communication, has not been addressed. Some scholars, like Abraham Mehrabian, claim that 93 percent of meaning in messages is dependent upon the nonverbal band, so we will now turn our attention to the "silent language" of nonverbal codes. Audiences cannot separate the message from how the message is sent and what impression the sender makes overall.

NONVERBAL COMMUNICATION

Nonverbal communication consists of body communication that includes general appearance, facial expressions, posture, the use of personal space, gestures, vocal qualities, artifactual communication such as hairstyles, make-up, jewelry, clothing, and uniforms, and personal possessions such as homes, offices, and cars, which signify status. Before speakers open their mouths, they have already sent a message regarding their gender, ethnicity, approximate age, taste in clothing, and overall appearance, which may be professional, casual, or sloppy. Before any verbal message is received, the audience has already interpreted a great deal of information about the speaker. Early researchers identified the significance of nonverbal communication. Ray Birdwhistell (1970) noted that approximately 35 percent of a message is carried by words while the rest is carried by nonverbal messages; Mehrabian (1968) more dramatically estimated that 93 percent of the total message's meaning was the result of nonverbal factors (Leathers, 1997, p. 6). In the next section we look at the common characteristics and the functions of nonverbal communication.

CHARACTERISTICS OF NONVERBAL COMMUNICATION

Joseph DeVito offered five characteristics of nonverbal communication, which began with the fact that "You cannot not communicate." This ungrammatical sentence, with a double negative, tells us that whether or not you intend to do so, your very appearance communicates something to others that creates a first impression. Attractive people get by with more transgressions because they are perceived as being more intelligent, more honest, and more likeable. So the first characteristic is that nonverbal communication operates in both subtle and overt ways. The second characteristic is that you must take nonverbal communication in the context in which it occurs to arrive at the appropriate meaning. For example, you may hear the words, "I am going to kill you," but if the person delivering that message is smiling and in a relaxed position, you know that they are just joking with a friend. If you were to hear the same message and the sender was red in the face, trembling in anger and standing in the face of the receiver of the message, you would take the threat seriously. The context of the communication transaction takes into account the people, their words and actions, and any other clues available such as motive, means, and probability. A third characteristic is that nonverbal communication is believable. DeVito offered the following formula: "Total

The GoDaddy Super Bowl ad (2013) contained a very long kiss between Bar Refaeli and Jesse Heiman, which the narrator stated symbolized the sexy side and the smart side of GoDaddy.

impact of the message = .07 verbal + .38 vocal + .55 facial" (DeVito, 1989, p. 7). The nonverbal component of a communication transaction gives the words credibility by extending the meaning through visual, vocal, and behavioral cues such as direct eye contact, body orientation, and emphatic vocalization, like shouting or whispering. A fourth characteristic is that nonverbal communication is rule governed, meaning that it is learned from social interaction. Children are socialized to know that staring, pointing, scratching, and other behaviors are inappropriate. You may touch a friend or intimate partner, but you do not touch strangers, unless you are packed into a crowded elevator and have no space—even then you constrict your space as much as possible. Finally, nonverbal communication is metacommunicational, meaning that nonverbal codes frequently comment on other messages, like someone speaking through clenched teeth or glaring threateningly at someone they dislike (DeVito, 1989, p. 8). In summary, we can say that nonverbal communication is highly communicative, contextual, socially learned and culturally bound, believable, and metacommunicational in nature.

THE FUNCTIONS AND CODES OF NONVERBAL COMMUNICATION

From the beginning, we know that nonverbal communication has many functions in the total communication transaction. According to Dale Leathers (1997) there are six major functions for nonverbal communication. The first of these is to transmit meaning, which depends on many behaviors like voice, touch, and facial expression to communicate intentions. Children read the tone of the voice before they know the words "No, don't touch!" Army recruits, dating couples, and students become very astute at deciphering nonverbal messages. We can easily tell if someone is being playful or if they mean business by these nonverbal cues.

Second, emotions and feelings are more accurately revealed with nonverbal communication than by words. We all know the expressions "keep your chin up," "down in the mouth," and "walking on air." We know what the "weight of the world" looks like on one's shoulders and how to "keep a stiff upper lip." Effective communicators are able to read emotional cues and to send them as well (Leathers, 1997, p. 6).

Third, nonverbal communication conveys meanings of honesty and trustworthiness better than words. Our bodies are more honest than our mouths. There are a few Machiavellian types who are good deceivers both verbally and nonverbally as they have practiced to manage their facial expressions, bodily communication, and vocalization, but generally we find that even practiced liars "leak" information when they deceive us with words. It may be the numbers of hesitancies in their speech, their avoidance of gaze with the eyes, or reddening of the face, but we read these miniscule cues readily, especially if we really know the other person and their normal behaviors.

Fourth, nonverbal cues serve a metacommunicational function that is necessary for quality communication (Leathers, 1997). DeVito called this one of the characteristics while Leathers considered it a function. We know that nonverbal cues can complement, reinforce, contradict, or extend the verbal message. For example, someone says, "I am so sorry for your loss," and gives you a hug. Similarly, a genuine smile radiates pleasure at another's good news, while tears shared with a friend show compassion that goes beyond words. When there is a contradiction between the verbal and the nonverbal message, we are more likely to go with the message received nonverbally. For instance, if someone is looking very agitated and angry and you ask, "What is wrong?" and they reply, "Nothing," they probably mean, "Nothing that I can tell you, or nothing that you deserve to know right now."

Fifth, nonverbal cues are much more efficient than verbal cues (Leathers, 1997). Verbal discourse is marked by redundancy, repetition, ambiguity, and abstraction, while gestures and facial expressions are a short-cut way to communicate a feeling or response. Sometimes a look is worth a thousand words; just an arch of the eyebrow can call the whole message into question.

Sixth, nonverbal cues present the greatest opportunity for suggestion or indirect expression in our society (Leathers, 1997). Nonverbal messages go a long way toward creating our images in interpersonal, business, and professional endeavors.

Generally, before we approach another person in a social situation, we have read the nonverbal cues that either tell us that we are welcome to approach or that they are engaged with something or someone else at the moment and wish to be left alone. Leathers has given us some general functions of nonverbal communication, but what are the codes and how do they influence communication overall, particularly persuasion? While only an introduction to the ideas can be offered here, nonverbal communication is both fascinating and powerful as part of the overall dynamic of relational and cognitive communication.

Ray Birdwhistell (1970) wrote a book called *Kinesics and Context*, which explored what would become known commonly as body language, but his book really focused on micro-body movement. Birdwhistell explored how good posture communicated confidence, how facial expressions along with body movement such as gait communicated anger, and how body movement overall became part of the message. Julius Fast later wrote the best-seller *Body Language* (1970), which introduced nonverbal communication to the masses. Birdwhistell was a serious scholar who set out to write an alphabet of body movements to interpret meaning, but he did not complete that task. He was instrumental in extending the field of communication to include behavior that was codified, standardized, and worthy of study. Others would break body movement into smaller units such as just facial expressions, as Ekman and Friesen (1975) did, to study what they called **affect displays**. They showed photographs to subjects across different cultures and found that there were about five facial expressions that were readily recognized interculturally, such as happiness, sadness, anger, surprise, and disgust, while others were more ambiguous or harder to read. Tiny movements such as eyelid positions, pupil dilation, or lip compression could be read as creating an expression of meaning emotionally.

Eye behavior in human communication has always been seen as a powerful component in showing honesty, confidence, and regard for the other party or audience. While staring is seen as confrontational in the United States, avoiding the gaze of another is interpreted as shyness, shame, or intimidation. Mark Knapp (1980) listed the following five functions performed by gazing: (1) regulatory, (2) monitoring, (3) reflecting cognitive activity, (4) expressing emotions, and (5) communicating relationships. First, eye contact or gaze tells the other person that you are paying attention to what they are saying or doing, so it cues them to turn-taking and signals the end of the conversation or loss of interest in it. In this manner, our eye behavior regulates the interaction by signaling when the dialog is waning or over. Second, monitoring feedback means that the responses of the receiver are being consciously integrated and accommodated in the discourse. Because face-to-face communication affords feedback such as frowning, smiling, looking puzzled, or nodding in agreement, there is the possibility of adjusting the message or reinforcing it. Third, when people are thinking they often look up as though the thought were written just above their head, or they look away from the face of the receiver to concentrate on a complex idea. These nonverbal cues tell us that the speaker is actively composing thoughts or perhaps weighing the best way to express himself or herself before speaking. In these instances eye behavior reflects cognitive activity or thought. Fourth, Gazing can express either rapt attention or indifference to another so that emotions are portrayed through eye behaviors. Finally, Relationships are communicated also through gaze, for example, if your date's eyes seem to be fixed on another woman through the evening, perhaps his interest in you has diminished as well. The intensity of a gaze constitutes either staring or glaring at another which can be read as flirtation or con-frontation. Mutual gaze between interactants signals attention and interest in the person and what they have to say. These gaze functions are read both covertly and overtly, but nonverbal signals sent through direct gaze, gaze avoidance, or the uninterrupted stare affect communi-cation transactions, show emotions, and affect relationships. All of these behaviors are cul-turally learned and socially bound so meaning must be derived in the context in which the transaction occurs. For example, a Japanese student educated in the United States returned to Japan and was being interviewed for a position; she said that she was establishing eye contact to communicate her interest in the job and confidence in her ability to perform it. She became aware that she was making her male interviewer very uncomfortable with her direct gaze, which is very American, it was seen as aggressive and inappropriate behavior culturally in Japan.

Edward Hall (1968), an anthropologist, wrote of **proxemics**, the nonverbal code that analyzes the use of personal space in communication. Hall's book offered four spatial zones that impact our communication with others and detailed what happened when someone violated another's spatial zones. The first zone was the *intimate* distance from zero (body contact) to 18 inches in the United States. The second zone is *personal*, which ranges from 18 inches to approximately 4 feet and affords a bubble of space for the individual that is approximately equivalent to extending one's arms and turning in a circle. The third zone is the *social* distance, which includes the distance between 4 and 10 feet. This distance is where most business transactions occur and affords individuals the ability to talk, move freely, and to still feel attached to the communication transactions. The last zone is the *public* one, which includes 10 feet and greater distances (Hickson & Stacks, 1993). There is such a stigma attached to inappropriate touch or encroachment on one's intimate or personal space that the idea of **territoriality** has been studied carefully. Territoriality is the idea that animals, including humans, lay claim to a given space and defend it against any threats or invasion by others. This defense can be anything from dirty looks to mortal combat. Hickson and Stacks defined this idea further by designating four territories (Hickson & Stacks, 1993). The first was public, like a street or mall, which allows individuals to access a space freely. The next area was interactional territory, where individuals may congregate informally, such as a restaurant or movie theater. The third type is home territory, where those who claim the territory may move freely and have access, but in the United States trespassing laws recognize that the home territory should be free from trespassers. The fourth spatial zone is the body territory, which is marked first by our clothing, and finally by the skin or sheath. When someone trespasses on the body territory, we have been violated, and great repercussions result from this form of invasion, such as in an assault or a rape.

The rules of conduct in each territory are socially learned and culturally enforced. Strangers are sanctioned with every measure from six-foot fences to limit trespass to incarceration for violating territories. Often we have been talking to a foreigner who does not understand our cultural definitions for space, and they keep moving into our personal space when the setting is a social one. This results in our moving back and their following because their cultural distances are very different from ours. It constitutes a strange dance of accommodation and intrusion in personal spatial use.

In the 2000 presidential debates, Al Gore was criticized when he moved across the platform to within the intimate space of George W. Bush, who appeared quite small by contrast. Some saw this spatial invasion as comical and it was panned on *Saturday Night Live* and other comedy shows, while other people perceived it as a bullying or intimidating tactic. This was an example of nonverbal violation of expected proxemic space where formal distance or public distance was expected, but Bush stood his ground and simply nodded his head in a small mock greeting to the much larger Al Gore. Audiences read nonverbal messages all the time to reach conclusions about the intentions of the speaker or their character. In the televised bipartisan congressional debates on national healthcare in February 2010, President Obama was criticized for using too much time, which would be a violation of chronemics, and further, some commentators saw his nonverbal messages as condescending toward the Republican speakers. Perhaps it was a combination of both his verbal message and nonverbal messages when he reminded Senator John McCain that the campaign was over and that he was the president, and he looked on with a bemused expression as the ideological debates progressed that day.

In the second presidential debate in 2012, Obama and Romney made viewers uneasy by "getting into each other's faces," that is, neither man stayed in his designated territory laid out on stage, but rather they approached each other with hostile charges and countercharges during the hour and half, which had been billed as a "town hall meeting" and was supposed to be a less threatening platform than the first debate. Some viewers liked the power plays of confrontation and dominance, but many others, especially women, who were interviewed after the debate were alarmed by the lack of civility, which was mostly nonverbal in nature.

Haptics is the nonverbal code that deals with touch, which is closely tied to personal space. Broadly speaking, there are four kinds of touch, beginning with functional/professional touch, which is impersonal, such as a doctor examining a patient. Next, there are social/polite touches represented by handshakes and other socially sanctioned behaviors. Then, the friendship/warmth form of touching is the most troublesome because often it is misinterpreted as having sexual intentions attached to it. Generally, this form of touching should be curtailed in social settings because sexual harassment is a real issue in business

President Obama and Senator John McCain's embrace indicates ritualized congratulations and civility between competitors.

and professional environments. Finally, the love/intimacy form of touching is most private and interpersonal with the rules mutually agreed on by the interactants (Hickson & Stacks, 1993).

Vocalics, also referred to as *paralanguage,* is the nonverbal code that deals with vocalization and the various characteristics of speech and voice production. These vocal characteristics include volume, pitch, duration of the sound, the quality of tonality, timbre, and resonance. Pronunciation and dialect are also part of this code. Often the speaker can be identified as a New Englander, a southerner, or a New Yorker by the dialect spoken. For example, President John F. Kennedy often referred to "Cuber" when he spoke of Cuba.

When we analyze vocalics, we are looking at how the message was delivered as much as the content that was offered. Annoying habits, such as *verbal fillers* like "OK," "like," "uh," "ah," and "uhn" can become distractions to any message and actually cause audience members to stop listening to the speaker. These verbal fillers are sounds that often fill the space between the last actual thought and the next one. These fillers are also called *vocal segregates.* Richmond, McCroskey, and Payne (1991) wrote:

> Although vocal segregates such as "uh-uh" and "uh-huh" function as substitutes for verbal
> utterances, we also find them in the stream of speech of persons who are thinking about what

they are going to say next. While teaching a public speaking course a few years ago, one speech professor counted sixty-seven "and-uh's" in one student's five-minute speech. In fact, the speech began with one of these vocal segregates, and each sentence ended with one. (p. 101)

Since we know that the beginning and ending of a message are the most memorable positions, such intrusive sounds would be annoying at best and at their worst an absolute turnoff for the audience. Most audiences would prefer a pause or even silence to these intrusive sounds. An appealing voice is a great asset to a speaker who has cultivated their instrument of speech.

Chronemics is the nonverbal code that deals with time and timing. In the United States we live by deadlines, calendars, and clocks, which make us very conscious of time and timing and subject us to high blood pressure and heart attacks. Our Puritan forefathers spoke of time as though it were a material substance. "Idle hands are the Devil's workshop," therefore, one should be gainfully engaged in work because slothfulness was evil. "Time is money," or time well spent should have material rewards, the social philosophy implied. Punctuality is a valued habit in this country. People who make us wait for them are sending the nonverbal message that their time is more valuable than our time or that they are worth the wait. We wait in the doctor's office or for the much-publicized speaker to take the stage, but generally we avoid people who waste our time. Time expectations are culturally defined as Dalel Khalil noted in her book, *From Veils to Thongs* (2008), on Arab culture. She noted that Arabs and African Americans are always late, probably by two hours (p. 108). While her book is written in comedic style with exaggeration, scholars have verified this trend.

In a speech situation, the speaker has to decide how long they will speak, unless the time is designated, as in a televised debate or speech. Commercial messages have been cut from one minute to 30 seconds, and now some are only 15 seconds long. Time is a precious commodity. The old adage "brevity is the soul of wit" has applications in everyday cases of persuasion. We understand that time can be sacred, which ties us to mythology or things not of this world, like eternity. Profane time is made up of "centuries, decades, years, months, weeks, days, hours, and minutes" (Hickson & Stacks, 1993, p. 177). The idea of time differs greatly if one is a space engineer measuring nanoseconds or an individual who lives by his or her own internal clock. Culturally there are great differences in expectations regarding time even within the United States. Chronemics also involves the idea of when to appropriately initiate an idea or an action. This sense of timing or momentum is a significant factor in attempts to begin a campaign, a social movement, or to introduce an idea.

Personal appearance is composed of many nonverbal factors such as attractiveness or physical attributes, such as a slender, well-defined physique, height, and age. Generally, attractive individuals have an advantage in persuasion efforts because people attribute positive qualities to them according to Malandro, Barker, and Barker (1989, pp. 30–31).

Attractive women seem to receive differential treatment when compared with their less attractive counterparts. Attractive women receive higher grades in both high school and college courses (Murphy, Nelson & Cheap, 1981; Singer & Lamb, 1966); are more successful in changing attitudes, especially when their arguments are cogent (Puckett, Petty, Cacioppo, &

Fischer, 1983); are given lighter sentences in court hearings (Landy & Sigall, 1974); and are ten times more likely to marry than unattractive females (Udry & Eckland, 1984).

Very attractive men like Tom Cruise, Mark Harmon, and Matthew Broderick reported facing professional crises in their movie careers because of others' perceptions of their attractiveness. They were often seen as "nothing more than just another gorgeous face" rather than having any talent at acting (Malandro et al., 1989, p. 31). On balance, most speakers have an advantage if they are perceived as attractive, similar to the audience, and possessing good character.

Nonverbal messages are sent with artifacts such as jewelry, makeup, clothing, and uniforms that signify teams, professions, rank in the military, or wealth. Sarah Palin has been criticized in the media for her hairstyles, clothing, and communication style, and she was furnished wardrobe items by staff when she ran for vice president in 2008. Recently, Vice President Joe Biden was shown on television on Ash Wednesday with ashes on his forehead, which caused international commentators to ask if he had a bruise on his head or what had happened to him. Christians knew the symbol and the reason that on this particular day the sign of the cross was placed on his forehead, but such religious symbols stir controversy. In France and other countries the face covering of Muslim women is being objected to as a cultural impropriety while protests of religious persecution are made against any edicts to forbid this form of dress. Artifacts not only indicate style but religion, status, and social group or cultural identity as well.

In summary, nonverbal codes are inseparable from the verbal message and may strengthen the impact that the message has on the audience. Alternatively, nonverbal codes can become a barrier to any communication attempt. There are other nonverbal codes that we did not cover here, including **olfactics,** the nonverbal code that involves smell, such as the baked goods that stimulate hunger or body odor that stigmatizes a person socially as an outcast, but those codes that are central to public performances were outlined herein.

SUMMARY

It is apparent that persuasion exists on multiple fronts, as evidenced by those variables most relevant to composing, organizing, and delivering a message to the targeted audience. It is a false dilemma to divide arguments strictly into the rational realm or the emotional realm, since most messages will have elements of both logic and passionate appeals. There are many forms of evidence or proofs that can be offered to support ideas and make them more concrete, memorable, and appealing to the audience. Fallacies in reasoning are flawed arguments that exist because the evidence lacks consistency, logic, recency, or relevance. Audiences often rely on the character of the speaker when they are less informed on the topic, and they may be influenced by the organization of the speech, the delivery of the speech, or variables other than the logic or quality of the evidence contained in the speech. It is difficult to separate the elements of a performance that appeal to an audience, but this chapter has offered some criteria to enable students of persuasion to analyze both verbal and nonverbal messages.

APPLICATIONS

1. Watch a tape of the second presidential debate between President Obama and Mitt Romney held October 18, 2012, and analyze the nonverbal messages that each candidate sent to the viewers. Pay particular attention to proxemics. Include the appearance of each candidate and research how the media covered each of them. Focus on facial expressions, gestures, and vocalics such as verbal fillers, pronunciation, and any dialect. Now focus on the verbal message, including forms of evidence used to support claims that each made. Identify emotional arguments that each used. Which candidate persuaded you to vote for them? Had you made that choice before you watched the debate?

2. Attempt to identify the profession or job of strangers on the bus or in a restaurant. Pay attention to their clothing, speech, posture, gait, and personal possessions. What messages did they send about status, educational level, and geographic area?

3. Use *Vital Speeches* in the library to find a speech by a leader and then analyze it for the claims made and the kinds of evidence used to support the claims or arguments. Can you identify any fallacies? Was the evidence consistent, relevant, timely, and from expert sources? Did they use emotional appeals to the audience? Was the message appropriate for the intended audience? How was the speech reviewed by critics or analysts?

REFERENCES

Birdwhistell, R. L. (1970). *Kinesics and context: Essays on body motion.* Philadelphia: University of Pennsylvania Press.

Brockriede, W. (1972). Arguers as lovers. *Philosophy & Rhetoric, 5*(1), 1–11.

Clinton, W. J. (2004). *Bill Clinton: My life.* New York: Alfred A. Knopf.

Clinton, W. J. (September 5, 2012). Transcript of Bill Clinton's Speech to the Democratic National Convention. Charlotte North Carolina. Retrieved September 10, 2013 from: http://www.nytimes.com/1012/09/05/us/politics/transcript-of-bill-clintons-speech-to-the-delegates.

Cooper, L. (Trans.). (1932). *The rhetoric of Aristotle.* New York: Appleton-Century-Crofts, Inc.

DeVito, J. A. (1989). *The nonverbal communication workbook.* Prospect Heights, IL: Waveland Press.

Edman, I. (Ed.). (1956). *The works of Plato.* The Jowett Translation. New York: The Modern Library by Random House.

Ekman, P., & Friesen, W. V. (1975). *Unmasking the face.* Englewood Cliffs, NJ: Prentice-Hall.

Fast, J. (1970). *Body language.* New York: M. Evans and Company.

Hall, E. T. (1959). *The silent language.* New York: Doubleday

Hall, E. T. (1966). *The hidden dimension.* New York: Doubleday

Hall, E. T. (1968). Proxemics. *Current Anthropology, 9,* 83.

Hickson, M. L., III, & Stacks, D. W. (1993). *NVC nonverbal communication: Studies and applications* (3rd ed.). Madison, WI: WCB Brown and Benchmark Publishers.

Hurlburt, R. T. (2006). *Comprehending behavioral statistics* (4th ed.). Belmont, CA: Thomson Wadsworth.

Inch, E. W., & Warnick, B. (1998). *Critical thinking and communication: The use of reason in argument* (3rd ed.). Boston: Allyn & Bacon.

Khalil, D. B. (2008). *From veils to thongs: An Arab chick's survival guide to balancing one's ethnic identity in America.* Dale L. Khalil publisher @ www.DALELKHALIL.COM

Knapp, M. L. (1980). *Essentials of nonverbal communication.* New York: Holt, Rinehart and Winston.

Landy, D., & Sigall, H. (1974). Beauty is talent: Task evaluation as a function of the performer's physical attractiveness. *Journal of Personality and Social Psychology, 29*(4), 299–304.

Leathers, D. G. (1997). *Successful nonverbal communication: Principles and applications* (3rd ed.). Boston: Allyn & Bacon.

Malandro, L. A., Barker, L., & Barker, D. A. (1989). *Nonverbal communication* (2nd ed.). New York: Random House.

McCroskey, J. C. (1997). A summary of experimental research on the effects of evidence in persuasive communication. Retrieved June 8, 2006, from http://www.jamesmccroskey.com/publications/37.htm.

Megan's Law—Information on registered sex offenders. Office of the Attorney General, State of California. Department of Justice. Retrieved August 1, 2006, from http://www.meganslaw.ca.gov/

Mehrabian, A. (1968). Communication without words. *Psychology Today, 2*, 51–52.

Murphy, M. J., Nelson, D. A., & Cheap, T. L. (1981). Rated and actual performance of high school students as a function of sex and attractiveness. *Psychological Reports, 48*, 103–106.

Newman, R. P., & Newman, D. R. (1969). *Evidence*. Boston: Houghton Mifflin Company.

Okerson, A. (1998). Who owns digital works? *Scientific American* (July). Reprinted with permission. In R. Holeton, *Composing cyberspace: Identity, community and knowledge in the electronic age.* Boston: McGraw-Hill.

Puckett, J. M., Petty, R. E., Cacioppo, J. T., & Fischer, D. L. (1983). The relative impact of age and attractiveness stereotypes on persuasion. *Journal of Gerontology, 38*(3), 340–343.

Richmond, V. P., McCroskey, J. C., & Payne, S. K. (1991). *Nonverbal behavior in interpersonal relations* (2nd ed.). Englewood Cliffs, NJ: Prentice Hall.

Rieke, R. D., & Sillars, M. O. (2001). *Argumentation and critical decision making* (5th ed.). New York: Addison Wesley Longman.

Schwartz, T. (1973). *The responsive chord.* New York: Anchor Books/Doubleday.

Sinclair, T. A. (Trans.) (1962). *Aristotle: The politics.* Baltimore, MD: Penguin Books.

Singer, J. E., & Lamb, P. F. (1966). Social concern, body size, and birth order. *Journal of Social Psychology, 68*, 143–151.

Tammi Menendez on loving Erik: What leads a woman to marry a convicted killer? (September 27, 2002). *ABC NEWS Internet Ventures.* Retrieved August 3, 2006, from http://abcnews.go.com/2020/print?id=123804.

Udry, J. R. & Eckland, B. K. (1984). Benefits of being attractive: Differential payoffs for men and women. *Psychological Reports, 54*, 47–56.

Warnick, B. & Inch, E. S. (1994). *Critical thinking and communication: The use of reason in arguments.* (2nd ed.). New York: Macmillan.

APPLICATION OF PERSUASION IN THE CONTEXT OF POLITICS, LAW, RELIGION, ART AND CINEMA, ADVERTISING, AND PUBLIC RELATIONS

CHAPTER 6

POLITICAL COMMUNICATION: MEDIATED CONSTRUCTIONS

KEY WORDS

adversarial relationship

agenda setting

biographical convention film

blogs

deliberative rhetoric

didactic narrative

entertainment function

First Amendment

fourth estate

hard news

interpretation function

linkage function

media bias

paradigm

presidential rhetoric

rhetor

surveillance function

symbiotic relationship

synecdoche

Tower of Babel

transmission of values

unilateral communication

viral video

visual rhetoric

watchdog of the people

PREVIEW

Scholars note that a political shift is occurring in America, with the two-party system becoming less compelling and a paradigm based on generational experiences becoming more influential than standard ways of persuading voters. In *Millennial Makeover: MySpace, YouTube & the Future of American Politics*, Morley Winograd and Michael D. Hais (2008) argue that the millennials (voters born after 1993) will reshape the face of American politics by interactive media, which establishes networks that bypass traditional media sources. The Democratic Party has taken the lead in the ability to use new communication technology to create the "netroots" that bypass conventional media to communicate directly with this new generation that will displace the baby boomers and the gen-X-ers, including MTV. Winograd and Hais wrote:

In 2007, survey research data, as well as the approach and tone of the announced 2008 presidential candidates, provided some clues as to who might be best positioned among the candidates to capture the hearts and minds of a new generation. Senator Obama, the youngest major party candidate, a late Baby Boomer born on the cusp of Generation X, distanced

135

himself from the rest of the candidates in a crucial way that demonstrated his awareness of generational differences and his sensitivity to the concerns and political style of the Millennial Generation. In a YouTube video prior to his announcement, Obama said the country needed "to change our politics first" and "come together around common interests and concerns as Americans," clearly signaling his awareness of the debilitating effect that the Baby Boomer Generation's continuation of the culture wars of the 1960s was having on American politics. He and Senator Clinton were the only two candidates from either party who registered significant support from 18- to 29-year-olds in a New York Times/CBS poll in June 2007. But as much fun as it is to speculate which candidate will take advantage of the technological and generational trends impacting the country's mood in order to win the ultimate prize in American politics in 2008, the complexity of current events, candidate missteps, and campaign tactics makes any such speculation a fool's errand. (2008, p. 3)

Clearly, it would be Obama that would emerge as the rock star and darling of mass media because he was a fresh new face with a new voice who did not shy away from questions of race or religion; both challenges were thrust upon him as he sidestepped the pitfalls of earlier African Americans, like Jesse Jackson, who ran for the presidency decades ago. Former president Bill Clinton noted that he had waited a lifetime to vote for either a woman or an African American candidate for president, but he had not imagined that they would both run at the same time. Both Hillary Clinton and Barack Obama ran vigorous campaigns, but Obama would emerge with the delegates necessary to catapult him into the limelight and the frontrunner status. MySpace and YouTube have smoked MTV on the Web as the door to a whole new generation of voters has opened to millennials who make their own videos in support of candidates and daily discuss the topics of the day. Obama Girl became a sensation with her video *Crush on Obama*, which was named *People Magazine* video of the year with 14,028,843 hits in 2008 (YouTube.com).

Political communication includes many forms of rhetoric, with the most commonly analyzed types being presidential rhetoric, campaign rhetoric, and, more recently, visual rhetoric. Scholars have written widely about deliberative communication, which focuses on making arguments for and against propositions to arrive at conclusions about what is probably the best course of action, the best candidate, and the most credible account of an event that a citizen can adopt. Because politics deals with the distribution and use of power, the way is often unclear, cluttered with inconsistencies and worrisome turns of events that challenge us to choose sometimes between unattractive alternatives. This chapter addresses the functions of political or deliberative communication in a democratic society and the role that mass media plays in protecting the interests of citizens to make enlightened decisions based on information from elected leaders or those who aspire to be elected. The functions and goals of political campaigns are addressed along with campaign ads that have succeeded or failed to achieve their designed goals. Visual rhetoric is introduced through selected campaign images like the 1964 Daisy Girl advertisement and autobiographical films featuring Ronald Reagan, Bill Clinton, George W. Bush, Barack Obama, and Mitt Romney to promote candidates at the national conventions. The changing role of political campaigns is analyzed by looking at Howard Dean's campaign and his use of the Internet to raise funds, to reach volunteers, and to receive and dispense ideas. The increasing role of the entertainment industry in political campaigns is reviewed as well. Political communication is being redefined in some innovative ways through new technology, which does not replace traditional media but extends and augments its use while attracting a new cohort of constituents to the process. It was Barack Obama, the son of a white Kansas mother and a Kenyan exchange student father, who would blend the ideologies of his complex lineage to capture the imagination of a new generation who responded hypnotically to his call for hope and change. Obama blended the skills of the old and new communication technology to unseat candidates that were perceived as unbeatable. The 2012 election extended the use of new media to include Twitter and popup ads on servers that featured the first lady Michele Obama, who asked, "Are you with us?" We first review conventional political communication and then move on to recent developments.

THE ROOTS OF POLITICAL COMMUNICATION

The tradition of political communication, or **deliberative rhetoric**, goes back to the writings of Aristotle. He viewed political speaking as a combination of the art of speaking and political science designed to investigate five primary subjects: "(1) ways and means; and (2) war and peace; next, (3) national defence [sic]; and (4) imports and exports; finally, (5) legislation" (Aristotle, 330 BCE/1932, p. 21). While the topics of political deliberation have not changed, the means of communicating them certainly have evolved from the ancient practice of public speaking in the Athenian Assembly to spreading the word via print or electronic media and the Internet. Mass media is an essential ingredient in the process that links candidates to their audiences, examines issues, and contributes to the marketplace of ideas in our society.

Politics concerns itself with future actions, with what is feasible and desirable, not with "accidental, compulsory, or necessary actions, but in deliberate ones" (Poulakos & Poulakos, 1999, p. 33). Deliberation means to exchange views, weigh alternatives, and exhort others to support decisions where great uncertainty or doubt may exist about either the consequences or the wisdom of the proposal. The tradition of deliberative address goes back to the Athenian Assembly where any citizen could speak to a body of perhaps 5,000, approximately a fifth of the citizenry, where each session opened with, "Who wishes to speak?" (Poulakas & Poulakas, 1999, p. 34). In the United States Congress, we have elected representatives to speak for us, unlike Athenians, who had direct participation. In the Athenian tradition the word for politician and orator became the same (*rhetor*) because the better orators dominated political discourse, even though in theory all participants were equal there. Similarly, in order to succeed in politics today, one must be an effective communicator, maintain good relationships with the media, and maintain credibility with the American people.

Our Constitution built into our system the mechanism of checks and balances through the establishment of three branches of government—the executive, legislative, and judicial branches. To ensure that these powers remained in check, the First Amendment listed five freedoms that empowered the people to guard their rights to freedom of speech and the press, to practice the religion of their choice, to peaceably assemble, and to seek redress of grievance from government infringement. These rights have been interpreted and extended through the decades, but clearly the rights to govern the citizens of this country reside in the consent of the people. Election campaigns are an important component of political communication.

Communication between leaders and their constituents is essential, and the flow must go both ways. **Unilateral communication**, which means messages that go one way to the masses, ignoring the voice of the people, makes about as much sense as driving down a two-way highway at 80 miles per hour straddling the middle line—there is bound to be a major collision with forces moving in the opposite direction. That force would be the will of the people to change the course of government. So political communication enables those who govern and the governed to understand the direction that the majority of citizens wish to travel. Political communication is by necessity rhetorical depending on the persuasive powers of leaders to win support for election, conduct the business of government, and to communicate with various constituents in the nation.

There have been dark chapters in our history when there was a breach between the reality that citizens perceived and the one that leaders presented. Political discourse can either unite or divide the country. Theodore H. White (1970) wrote about the impact that the race riots of 1968, the escalation of the Vietnam War, and the presidential race was having on the nation. The 1968 Democratic National Convention in Chicago was a case study in civil disobedience as young protesters confronted billy-club–wielding police in the streets of Mayor Daley's city. Richard M. Nixon was elected president in 1968 and reelected in 1972, claiming to have a "secret plan" to end the war in Vietnam. In 1973, the Watergate scandal would rock this country, but White seemed to see this clash coming when he wrote of the malaise that was hovering over the American people in 1968:

> Raw, dislocating change has been moving in America at such speed and with such force that in 1968 it reached the point of overpowering American understanding; and as America outran its comprehension of itself, inherited tradition and inherited knowledge could no longer master reality, "Folk-wisdom," said the late Robert Oppenheimer shortly before he died, "can cry out in pain, but it can't provide solutions."
>
> In America in 1968, folk-wisdom not only ran out of solutions, it ran out of common standards of judgment; and without such common standards, there could be no sense of order, no thongs of discipline to bind individuals to each other, to law, to moralities, to community. At the root of the matter lay a homely fact, so long buried in the past of American politics as to have all but disappeared from serious discussion: nations need dreams, goals they seek in common, within which the smaller dreams of individuals can guide their personal lives. It was as if a master hand had descended and confused the tongues of Americans, made a Babel of their words so that when one group spoke the other could not understand its language. No policeman, no new law-enforcement agency, no new laws can maintain discipline if dreams and ideas do not urge people to go the same way together, with the same civility to others that they expect for themselves. (White, 1970, p. 518)

Kenneth Burke reminded us that rhetoric became necessary when the tribes were divided by language at the **Tower of Babel**; therefore, leaders must find common threads of discourse that connect followers through identification that translates the babble of the barnyard into meaningful discourse. Political rhetoric should articulate a vision for the populace, and it should give form to the dreams and aspirations that people wish to materialize—to be free of war, to trust the credibility of leaders, to have unity and peace at home, and to have a satisfying community and personal life. The Watergate mess, as it came to be labeled, added not to the vision of America as a moral and just nation but portrayed it as a nation whose leaders were obsessed with power, secrecy, and manipulation of the masses. But in retrospect it is evident that even when there is corruption with illegal acts, our system has a self-righting principle. When two young journalists, Robert Woodward and Carl Bernstein, broke the story about the Watergate break-in and related activities, America was informed of a "cancer growing on the Presidency," to quote John Dean, legal counsel to President Nixon (Nixon, 1978, p. 578). President Nixon resigned from office rather than be impeached, and Gerald Ford, the vice president, assumed the office. The week before the House Judiciary Committee voted for impeachment, Nixon wrote in his diary: "I intend to live the next week without dying the death of a thousand cuts. This has been my philosophy throughout my political life. Cowards die a thousand deaths, brave men die only once" (Nixon, 1978, p. 636). It was an orderly transfer of government, and the function of the press to guard the people's welfare triumphed over a cabal of men who believed their sense of moral righteousness and drive to power was paramount over the ethics of truth, open accountability, and consent from the people. But the truth emerged through multiple efforts from investigative reporting, deliberation in Congress that revealed excesses in power, and exposure of these facts to the world.

Political rhetoric not only includes the deliberations that occur within a democratic society regarding the laws that will govern our citizens or the policies that will guard their welfare, but also includes campaigns to elect representatives who must win the support of the electorate. Those men and women who represent our interests in Congress and the president of the United States must be elected by the people through a process of campaigning, which includes communicating their positions on issues and their philosophy of government to mass audiences. Critics state that candidates are packaged and sold in political campaigns much like toothpaste or deodorant with little attention paid to the issues relevant to the elections, but these charges have been around for decades. Kathleen Hall Jamieson (1996), in *Packaging the Presidency: A History and Criticism of Presidential Campaign Advertising,* wrote about the major means that candidates use to communicate their messages to voters:

> Ads enable candidates to build name recognition, frame the questions they view as central to the election, expose their temperaments, talents, and agendas for the future in a favorable light, and attack what they perceive as their opponent's fatal flaws. In part because reporters are fixated with who's winning and losing instead of what the candidates are proposing, some scholars believe that ads provide the electorate with more information than network news. Still, ads more often successfully reinforce existing dispositions than create new ones. (p. 517)

While there are similarities between product advertising campaigns and political campaigns, the goals of the latter are to enable citizens to make decisions about who is better equipped to serve our national interest. The characteristics of political campaigns are as follows:

1. Political campaigns are for a short duration (until the election is over) and sponsor a candidate rather than a product.
2. Political campaigns communicate the candidate's positions to voters and present an image of the candidate that includes their past record, their future plans, and their ethos or character.
3. Political campaigns depend on multiple channels of communication to reach their target audiences and employ persuasive strategies and tactics to win the support of the voters.
4. Political campaigns utilize professional staff to plan specific initiatives to promote the candidate, including fundraising and event planning, enlisting party leaders to promote the campaign, recruiting volunteers to perform multiple roles, and maintaining media relations or news management functions.
5. Political campaigns employ both verbal and nonverbal communication to reach voters and opinion leaders.

These characteristics of political campaigns may be applied to a local mayor's race, which operates on a shoestring budget, or to the campaign for president of the United States, where the budget reaches millions of dollars for media exposure, travel, and staff support in speech writing and responding to critics or attacks from rivals

Campaign spending for the presidential election and congressional races in 2004 reached almost $4 billion, a 30 percent increase from 2000, making it the most expensive presidential election in history (Harper, 2004, p. 2). Much of the money came from special interest groups called 527s, after the tax code section that permitted their formation, like the pro-Bush Swift Boat Veterans for Truth (now called Swift Vets and POWs for Truth) and the pro-Kerry supporters at MoveOn.org; these groups collectively contributed approximately $187 million to the two candidates (Harper, 2004, p. 2). In the 2008 election, Senator Barack Obama raised $750 million from both big donors and smaller donors equally, and he was the first major candidate to refuse public financing and the spending limits imposed by those taxpayers' funds. His campaign raised more than twice as much money as Hillary Clinton's, his closest competitor for the presidency from either party, and the other candidates raised less than Clinton (Carter, Palmer, & Pilhofer, 2008). In 2012 President Obama raised $957,363,067 for the blue team and Mitt Romney raised $1,113,769,594 for the red team, but the Democrats would return to the White House and win seats in the congressional races as well (Wayne, 2012).

Increasingly, campaigns focus on impression management or images as significantly as they do verbal scripts. A relatively new field of political communication has emerged called visual rhetoric.

VISUAL RHETORIC: IMAGES, ARGUMENTS, AND ILLUSIONS

Visual communication has been defined in many different ways depending on the discipline of the writer, but in view of political discourse the primary focus has been on what kind of meaning can be extrapolated or arguments can be made through images in political advertising, conventions, and campaigns. Visual rhetoric includes graphs, charts, political cartoons, pictures, photographs, designs, layouts, even the color, fonts, and use of space on a page.

J. Anthony Blair (2004) contrasted **visual rhetoric** with verbal arguments, and he demonstrated that visual rhetoric can also make an argument through the presentation of ideas that receivers interpret as propositions, which are claims that can be proved or refuted. The tradition is that rhetoric uses verbal argument where we offer proofs or evidence for and against propositions, but the verbal argument **paradigm** does not account for all the ways that symbols may be used to change attitudes, beliefs, and actions. If instead of using the term "verbal communication" we substitute the word "'symbols" that communicate meaning, we can include the realm of unspoken and nonverbal elements—pictures, sculpture, music, cartoons, film, and all forms of presentation that have intentions to provoke a response that has meaning for receivers. Blair noted that many believe that one cannot make a visual argument because images do not offer propositions and they are vague and ambiguous. He stated that language used in verbal arguments has the same problem with vague or ambiguous meanings. He offered political cartoons as one form that can in fact make an argument.

POLITICAL CARTOONS AND PHOTOGRAPHS AS PROPOSITIONS

Blair described a pre–World War II cartoon by David Low that he offered as an example of a proposition stated through imagery:

> (A)n evidently complacent Englishman is depicted in a lawn chair reading a newspaper, sitting directly beneath a jumble of precariously balanced boulders rising steeply above him. The bottom boulder, sticking out but wedged under and holding up the rest, is marked, "Czecho." Sitting directly on it are boulders marked "Rumania" and "Poland" and together they support a large boulder labeled "French Alliances," which in turn supports a huge boulder labeled "Anglo-French Security." A thick rope is attached to the out-thrust end of the "Czech" boulder and pulled up overhead and out of sight. Clearly, a strong pull on that rope would dislodge the "Czecho" boulder, causing the rest to come crashing down on the Englishman below. The cartoon's caption reads, "What's Czechoslaviakia to me, anyway?" (Blair, 2004, p. 48)

This wordy description seems obtuse compared to the power of the cartoon to relay the message that if Czechoslovakia fell to Germany it would start a chain reaction with Rumania and Poland soon to follow, resulting in the fall of the French alliance with major consequences for the English people. Blair stated that the cartoonist expressed those two propositions which, like any verbal argument, could be either proved true or false.

By way of comparison, Blair posits that images can have truth value just as language does, as demonstrated by the preceding cartoon, but there are three advantages to visual communication. First, the impact in visual rhetoric comes from the evocative power that images have to alter attitudes, beliefs, and behavior. The emotional involvement and response of the receivers are often powerful. The images conveyed in a 30-second television commercial can present more propositions than one can present in that time verbally. Second, there is a sense of realism presented in visuals that words cannot convey. We say, "Seeing is believing," or "A picture is worth a thousand words." Finally, visual elements are more significantly rhetorical than logical or dialectical (Blair, 2004, p. 51). Unlike the action between the arguer and interlocutors who raise objections and explore the complexity of a proposition through verbal exchanges, the visual may present a *didactic narrative*, or a story that makes the point (Blair, 2004, p. 52).

During times of national upheaval, sometimes a single picture captures the essence of events that are incomprehensible in any other form. Pictures of the Twin Towers collapsing on September 11, 2001, the rubble surrounding the Murrah building in Oklahoma City in April 1995, or the salute of a little boy to his assassinated father in November 1963 all bear witness and record the power of such moments of national tragedy when it was too early yet to make sense of what had happened. These images become icons burned into our national consciousness and creating photo-memories that mark the time, place, and feelings of the moment. Janis L. Edwards wrote:

> The famous photograph of JFK, Jr.'s childish salute is probably remembered by everyone who witnessed media coverage of November, 1963, and even some who do [sic] not, due to its status as one of several visual icons of the Kennedy era. The image depicts a moment of remembrance and passage, as the presidential hearse passes by, and a child's salute stands for a national gesture of farewell. (Edwards, 2004, p. 181)

The problem with visual argument or rhetoric is that the presenter may not be that effective in relaying the desired message, the audience may not be willing to actively participate

Three-year-old John Kennedy Jr., who saluted his father as the funeral procession passed November 1963, became an iconic image that represented the grief and farewell of a nation to the era known as Camelot.

in interpretation, and finally, even if they were trying, they may be incapable of understanding the intended message. While all of these objections are relevant, the same problems exist with verbal messages. Blair stated that political cartoons, film that constructs credible narratives, and television advertising are media that are effective as examples of visual rhetoric. Because advertisers can predict the demographics of their audience with accuracy and use repetition along with visual stimuli so effectively, television is a powerful medium. Blair noted that some of the best visual arguments are political advertisements made for television, like the Daisy Girl ad used in the 1964 election when Barry Goldwater challenged Lyndon Johnson for the presidency (Blair, 2004, p. 49).

THE DAISY GIRL AD 1964

The Daisy Girl ad became a powerful reminder for the television viewers that the Cold War was ever-present and whoever was elected in 1964 should be mindful of the nuclear arms race between the Soviet Union and the United States. The controversy emerged from Barry Goldwater supporters who said that it implied that he was trigger-happy and would use nuclear weapons. Tony Schwartz created the ad for Johnson, who had completed Kennedy's term and was running to be reelected; Schwartz said the message never mentioned Goldwater. The feeling that Goldwater might actually use nuclear weapons came from the people who viewed the campaign ad. Schwartz described the ad:

> The spot shows a little girl in a field counting petals on a daisy. As her count reaches ten, the visual motion is frozen and the viewer hears a countdown. When the countdown reaches zero, we see a nuclear explosion and hear President Johnson say, "These are the stakes, to make a world in which all God's children can live, or to go into darkness. Either we must love each other or we must die." As the screen goes to black at the end, white lettering appears stating, "on November 3rd, Vote for President Johnson." (Schwartz, 1974, p. 93)

The Daisy Girl political advertisement was shown only one time, but it crushed the campaign of Republican Barry Goldwater in 1964.

Schwartz said the stimuli of the film and the sounds evoked feelings that allowed people to express their own beliefs. A *New York Times* writer claimed that the Democrats destroyed Goldwater with this one television spot, but he added something that was not in the commercial at all—the last line of his article was manufactured by Venetoulis, not Schwartz. According to Schwartz (1974, p. 96), here is how the writer described the ad:

> In 1964, the Democrats demolished Goldwater with a simple one-shot television spot. A little girl gently picking daisies moved happily across an open field. Suddenly, a mushroom cloud filled the air and the announcer asked sternly: "Whose finger do you want on the trigger?"

Ted Venetoulis
New York *Times*
May 22, 1972, p. 35

Schwartz noted that effective political ads do not communicate things *to* audiences as much as they evoke something already *in* them. There had been no mention of triggers or fingers; the audience supplied their own narrative to explain what happened when the mushroom cloud filled the screen. Electronic media is a particularly effective tool for accessing people's minds, Schwartz said. The Daisy Girl ad was shown only one time on *Monday Night at the Movies*, but it has been offered as a powerful example of visual persuasion since 1964. This is the evocative power that Blair described.

TELEVISION DEBATES

Since 1960 and the televised debate between Richard M. Nixon and John F. Kennedy, we have become increasingly aware of the power of visual images to persuade, to establish narratives, and subsequently make arguments for or against a candidate, policy, or action. Those who heard the debate on radio believed that Nixon won, but those who watched the debate on television believed that Kennedy won. Nixon was certainly the more seasoned debater with more experience and knowledge on foreign affairs, having served as vice president for Dwight David Eisenhower for two terms. Kennedy, a Catholic and junior senator from Massachusetts, offered a new look, a fresh face, and the media loved him.

We now expect television debates to be part of campaigns, since they have been used in 10 general elections and have been broadcast in about 14 American presidential elections in the primary phase. In a meta-analysis of the effects on voters of viewing U.S. presidential debates, Benoit, Hansen, and Verser (2003) found that:

> . . . General debates have several significant effects (issue, knowledge, issue salience, issue preference, agenda setting, candidate character, and vote preference), although they do not appear to influence perceptions of candidate competence. Primary debates had significant effects on the three variables with multiple studies: issue knowledge, candidate character, and vote preference (and these effects were larger than in general debates).

Debates potentially can have both direct influence (on voters who choose to watch debates) and indirect influence (on voters who learn about debates from the news). A meta-analysis (D'Alessio & Allen, 2002) confirmed Festinger's (1957) prediction that people are more likely to expose themselves to consonant than dissonant information. Thus, prior attitudes and expectations about debates could influence who watches debates and are thereby susceptible to these effects. Given the lack of media bias (D'Alessio & Allen, 2000), those influenced by a more indirect path (from news) are likely to receive a balanced report. (Benoit et al., 2003, p. 347)

Part of the effect of televised debates was attributed to the time frame of 90 minutes rather than the 30 seconds that most campaign ads last. Further, there was more time for the candidate to explain positions or to commit an error during the debates. The meta-analysis found that mass media covered the debates objectively and interpreted the outcome in an unbiased manner. Just as televised debates were an innovation that has now become a tradition, new media has entered the political communication arena.

THE INTERNET AND POLITICAL CAMPAIGNS

Recently, the Internet has become a preferred medium for political persuasion. Candidates can use the Internet to raise funds, communicate with voters, and present attacks on opponents or offer defenses for their own policies. In an article titled "How the Internet Invented Howard Dean," Gary Wolf (2004) reported in *Wired*:

It is 83 days before the Iowa caucuses, and I'm sitting at a small table on a private jet above Colorado getting a pure dose of Internet religion from Howard Dean. "The Internet community is wondering what its place in the world of politics is," Dean says. "Along comes this campaign to take back the country for ordinary human beings, and the best way you can do that is through the Net. We listen. We pay attention. If I give a speech and the blog people don't like it, next time I change the speech."

The biggest news of the political season has been the tale of this small-state governor who, with the help of Meetup.com and hundreds of bloggers, has elbowed his way into serious contention for his party's presidential nomination. As every alert citizen knows, Dean has used the Net to raise more money than any other Democratic candidate. He's also used it to organize thousands of volunteers who go door-to-door, write personal letters to likely voters, host meetings, and distribute flyers. (Wolf, 2004, p. 1)

Derek James, a blogger, noted that he would rather vote for SpongeBob Squarepants than vote for Dean back in 2004, but he was impressed with Dean's organization and the democratic way that he was running his campaign. Wolf wrote, "Bloggers are fascinated by Dean for philosophical and also parochial reasons. They feel they have a right to be proud. Dean has become the front-runner by applying their most cherished rules for attracting attention and building a social network on the internet" (Wolf, 2004, p. 1). Dean credited Meetup for his early success. Meetup is a Web tool for forming social groups that became the engine for Dean's Internet campaign. He noted that 3,000 people on the Internet can have influence that no other crowd can because of their easy access to other groups. Dean's early use of Meetup lowered the threshold for feedback and energized his campaign; in the third quarter of 2003, Dean had raised nearly $15 million a record for a Democratic candidate in a presidential race (Wolf, 2004, p. 2). A lot of disenchanted voters who were alienated from the traditional media and political process gravitated to Dean. It was the power of feedback that built Dean's momentum. Wolf stated, "The intersection of political analysis and Internet theory is a busy crossroad of cliché, where familiar rhetorical vehicles—*decentralized authority, emergent leadership, empowered grass roots*—create a ceaseless buzz. But the Dean organization has embraced this language of Web politics passionately" (Wolf, 2004, p. 2). Wolfe established five Internet axioms that explained Dean's early success in the campaign:

1. Make the network stupid.
2. Let the ants do the work.
3. Leaders are places.
4. Links attract links.
5. Allow the ends to connect.
   (Wolf, 2004, pp. 3–5)

Wolfe's axioms that he extrapolated from Howard Dean are noteworthy for the insight that they offer into the new media and political campaigns. First, the democratic nature of an Internet campaign means that there is great decentralization with little direction from headquarters where things can happen from the bottom up. Yet, if the candidate does not like an idea they can ignore it without penalty. The candidates receive all manner of suggestion, ideas, and feedback to their efforts. Second, the ant metaphor means that the swarm does the work, not the queen bee. The groundswell of workers can communicate with other networks, expanding the ranks of the candidate in many different ways, such as linking to other groups and initiating letter-writing campaigns. In the summer of 2004, polls showed Dean behind Dick Gephardt in Iowa, but 30,000 handwritten letters went out. By August Dean had caught up to Gephardt and was taking the lead (Wolf, 2004, p. 4). Third, "Leaders are places" means that whole locations are waiting to be tapped where thousands of people are members. MoveOn.org had 2 million members who ran anti-Bush ads, and while the members ran an online vote to determine the Democratic candidate, no endorsement was made. Even without the endorsement of MoveOn.org Dean was the big winner with 44 percent of the support over Dennis Kucinich, an Ohio candidate. The network that linked bloggers to MoveOn.org strengthened Dean's influence even further. Fourth, the anatomy of the Internet influences how quickly links are made to other links. Physicist Albert-Laszlo Barabasi created in *Linked: The New Science of Networks* a formal model that explained how popularity breeds more popularity and how on the Internet "links are made most quickly to Web sites that have the most links. . . . The first sites gain an early lead, and the lead tends to grow . . ." (Wolf, 2004, p. 4). Wolf goes on to explain how being first to the Web and having identifiable political positions established, for instance Dean's antiwar stance, can increase the candidate's Web advantage whether measured by "links, traffic, or Meetup numbers" (2004, p. 5). Fifth, this does not mean that messages have to flow up and down, but rather that everyone has some input. According to David Weinberger, a Dean consultant, having the ends connect means that "Democracy is supposed to be about people talking with each other about what matters to them" (Wolf, 2004, p. 5). The Internet campaign that Howard Dean ran energized constituents, who became impassioned about politics, giving energy to "Mini-rants and "hot political speeches," unlike the low style of television or radio talk shows. Dean's exploration into this new media frontier brought gold to his campaign and charted a territory that will be mined by every campaign to follow his foray in 2004; even though he lost the primary, Howard Dean will be remembered and emulated for his innovative approach to political communication. His campaign charted new territory in direct dialog with voters and opened new lines of communication with a community that had been uninvolved with traditional campaigns. Howard Dean added a new dimension to political discourse in 2004. Barack Obama capitalized on the use of Internet recruitment in 2008 even more expertly than Dean had, and he continued to exploit new media through the 2012 campaign.

Even though John Kerry, the winner of the primary war against Dean, used the Internet effectively by raising $82 million from the Internet, he spent the money by using it for old-fashioned TV ads, according to Winograd and Hais, who wrote:

> This isn't to say that television can't still be relevant, but it can be even more useful when used as a platform for Internet strategies. In late 2006, when Senator Barack Obama was making noise as a potential presidential candidate, he appeared in a short video on ESPN just before a Monday Night Football game. He began by speaking very much like he was about to announce his candidacy, but spoofed the entire ritual by declaring instead his support for his beloved Chicago Bears. The video, both funny and authentic, had a much greater shelf life than just those few minutes on ESPN. It immediately moved onto You Tube and other sites, where it became an instant hit. (2008, pp. 184–185)

Barack Obama's campaign in 2008 reflected his understanding of the transformative influence of technology, and he used it to change power in America. More than 280,000 people created accounts on his website, www.barackobama.com, and these users created over 6,500 grassroots volunteer groups. More than 15,000 policy recommendations were sent to the site, and users raised over $1.5 million with 370,000 donations, most of them under $25 (OBAMA'08, see www.barackobama.com). The Democrats saw the Web as a community that could be organized, interactive, and viral in gaining support for Obama. The Obama camp clearly won with the geeks or technologists. He had a detailed plan for implementing technology into government. While Republicans used talk radio with Rush Limbaugh, Sean Hannity, and the Drudge Report, Obama and the Democrats went directly to the people with websites that empowered them to become organizers. With the help of one of the founders of Facebook, Obama gave organizers a high-tech toolbox that enabled them to establish social networking tools and to use them as they wanted during the campaign (Dayton, 2008).

One of the most successful Internet stunts of the 2008 Obama campaign was the series of "Obama Girl" videos, which began with the "I have a crush on you" song that was independently developed for YouTube that increased Obama's popularity early in the campaign. That video was accessed millions of times during the election season. The sexy 20-something brunette elicited the inquiry from Obama's 10-year-old daughter about why her daddy had a girlfriend, but the Obama Girl ads enlivened college students' discussions about the candidate. Obama's use of networking sites like MySpace and Facebook was a unique feature of his appeal to the young voters, who supported him in record numbers. Obama learned from the mistakes of Howard Dean, who had failed to connect with the Iowa voters effectively in 2004 through his use of the Internet and his Blog for America. Dean was the first Democrat to attempt to use the Internet extensively, but Obama was expertly situated to exploit the Internet's power (Schifferes, 2008). The Republicans were far behind in their use of Internet resources in 2008.

Obama has been frustrated as president with the state of technology in the White House, and he has blamed Macon Phillips as the White House director of new media, which the president intended to enable him to communicate with citizens. For example, in February 2009, when the $787 billion economic stimulus package passed Congress, his team posted the bill on the Web at WhiteHouse.gov. They invited citizens to read the 1,071 pages and to comment on it, but to confine their "comments, thoughts, and ideas" to 500 characters, which did not fit the populace's idea of an open and transparent administration that encouraged direct communication (Vargas, 2009).

Kathleen Hall Jamieson, an expert on presidential communication from the University of Pennsylvania, said, "Obama and his team mastered the art of connecting newly involved individuals to his campaign. Now they're trying to master the process of connecting those individuals to their government. It won't happen overnight, but it will ultimately transform presidential communication" (Vargas, 2009).

The marriage between politics and entertainment began when Richard Nixon appeared on *Laugh-In* and accelerated with Bill Clinton wearing his shades and playing his saxophone on television. Today, all the politicians are stampeding to show their cute side on such comedy shows as the *Colbert Report*, *Saturday Night Live*, *Jay Leno*, or *David Letterman*, which enhances the candidate's Q score, "a Hollywood measure of a celebrity's—or politician's—audience familiarity and favorability" (Winograd & Hais, 2008, p. 64).

JIBJAB MEDIA

Further, the Internet has opened a new frontier for political entertainment which also has persuasive value. Voters remember the JibJab ads that appeared on the Internet during the 2004 election that depicted Senator John Kerry and President George W. Bush in comedic form, with Kerry's chiseled chin prominently featured and Bush in his cowboy hat singing with a Texas twang. In the skit, the Kerry character makes fun of Bush's pronunciation of "nuclear," calls him a "right-wing nut," a "dumb-ass," and reminds everyone that he, Kerry, is an intellectual who has three purple hearts, so surely the people will vote for him. The Bush character calls Kerry from "Mass-uh-chew-sits" a "liberal sissy," a "flip-flopper," with more waffles than a pancake house, while he, GW, is an antiterrorist crusader who gives tax breaks, so surely the people will vote for him (Spiridellis & Spiridellis, 2004).

JibJab Media was co-founded in 1999 by two brothers, Gregg and Evan Spiridellis, who introduced a new form of online humorists. The most famous satirical animated short, *This Land*, just described, received 70 million hits during the 2004 election. The parody was characterized as a **viral video** that spread like wildfire; the creators were invited to appear on *The Tonight Show*, where they presented a follow-up creation to *This Land* (O'Malley, 2006). The online video parodied the song by Woody Guthrie but starred the two candidates in caricatures exposing their most prominent characteristics as they danced along to the music. The video was an instant hit, and other political subjects were satirized with the same humor in the 2008 election. A new genre of political satire was born, with powerful effects. This video was an exceptional example of visual rhetoric, strengthened with auditory stimuli and the dialog of the two presidential hopefuls. The video, like television, enlisted a visual, auditory, and verbal script, none of which alone could have had the impact that this satirical presentation had because it was accessible on demand to users who quickly recommended it to friends.

Satire and humor have become common tools in campaigns to attack or discredit opponents. Such ads seem to work well for a generation that seeks entertainment value in political controversy The Bush campaign created a political ad that showed John Kerry wind-surfing with the wind blowing him first right, then left, which effectively depicted the "flip-flop" characteristic that stuck to Kerry to describe his inconsistencies on issues such as funding for the war in Iraq, about which Kerry had said, "I voted for the war before I voted against it." Actually, waffling on issues, according to Kevin McCaul, a psychologist from North Dakota State University, depends less on consistency than it does on whether the politician's position matches that of the majority of the public:

> "If you waffle on issues which people don't care about, then they don't care where you end up, they just care that you are waffling," McCaul said. But if voters are passionate about some topic—abortion, for example—then they primarily care about where a politician stands on that topic now. On issues we care about deeply, in other words, we are less interested in whether a leader's views are authentic and more interested in the bottom line—what the leader is going (to) do about the issue now.
>
> But didn't Kerry pay a price in the last presidential election for waffling on the hot-button issue of the war in Iraq? McCaul argued that Kerry lost not because he was waffling but because the country was bitterly divided over the war in 2004. Had public opinion then been as sharply critical as it is now, McCaul said voters would have ignored Kerry's waffling—or even welcomed it—because most voters would have agreed with Kerry's critical stance on the war. (Vedantam, 2007, p. A02)

With growing resistance to the war in Iraq, that flip-flop visual would play differently as President Bush's administration continued to be bogged down in Iraq and public support waned. The Democrats' victory in the 2006 midterm election reflects the changing tide of attitudes on this important issue. Senator Rick Santorum was a casualty of the 2006 switch, even though he was a rising star in the Republican Party. Santorum used an ad with his opponent, Robert P. Casey, Jr., waving to audiences until his arm fell off, portraying Casey as a man who was perpetually campaigning. All Casey had to do was keep reminding audiences that Santorum voted for President Bush's policies almost all the time. This negative associational tactic worked well for Casey, who appeared very ill-informed on issues in debates with Santorum.

Ultimately, the people decide when it is time for a change based on their perceptions of what is best for their welfare. The issues may be economics, ethics, national security, or personal—they just do not like the candidate. Their attitudes, beliefs, and values converge to determine how they process the messages they have received and finally what action they will take based on this complex web of interrelated cognitive, affective, and behavioral cues.

Visual rhetoric reinforces images already held by audiences or creates new ones to engineer consent or denial from voters. Some images stick with us, like the Kerry's flip-flop windsurfing image of 2004, or fail, like the Casey broken arm image of 2006, depending on what other realities the voters perceive to compose the entire picture—the one that will be definitive when they enter the election booth.

THE USE OF VISUAL RHETORIC IN POLITICAL CONVENTIONS

Scholars who have written about visual rhetoric wrestle with how to separate the visual from the verbal, the cognitive from the affective, or the abstract from the concrete elements of the form. In most instances these are false dichotomies because they operate together in the receiver to create a response or interpretation. Political national conventions have become the staging arena for personal videos that set the tone for the coming campaign by presenting the candidates in dramatic form. This new rhetorical genre, called the "biographical convention film," goes back to 1952 when Adali Stevenson ran against Eisenhower. In 1952 the Democrats' entire budget for television advertising was $77,000; the Republicans spent nearly $500,000 on Reagan's *The New Beginning* film in 1984, which was a mixture of news, documentary, and political advertisement (Morreale, 1991, p. 9). John F. Kennedy used newsreel footage, which introduced on-location shots, but no close-ups were used in his convention promotional black-and-white film called *The New Frontier*. After 1960 politicians would rely more on advertising and political campaign films that would grow in sophistication. Ronald Reagan's campaign film established a new benchmark for this genre of campaign work.

RONALD REAGAN: THE GREAT COMMUNICATOR

Ronald Reagan won the 1984 election by the largest margin in American history, and through his presidency he was called "The Great Communicator" or even "The Teflon President," because no charges seemed to stick to him. Reagan was the first actor elected to the office, and he brought with him an awareness of stage presence, camera angles, and how to make illusions a reality. *A New Beginning* was an 18-minute promotional film that was presented first at the Dallas convention where Republicans called it a "documentary" or "news event" (Morreale, 1991, p. 2). The major networks were divided about whether or not to carry the film, since clearly it was an attempt to manipulate them to broadcast a political advertisement that was offered as something else. NBC and CNN opted to carry it, but ABC and CBS showed only excerpts of it. The film confused them, because it was not just a documentary but included singer Lee Greenwood's "God Bless the USA" song, testimonials, interviews, news clips, archival material, and other images that allowed the film to be defined ambiguously as whatever the gatekeeper chose to call it. The "Tuesday Team," a group of advertising experts, produced the film with writer Phil Dusenberry, executive creative director of the BBD&O advertising agency, also the originator of the "Pepsi Generation" campaign. The team was allocated approximately $25 million, more than half the entire campaign budget, to create innovative political advertisements (Morreale, 1991, p. 4). Joanne Morreale, who did a frame-by-frame analysis of the 18-minute film, wrote about the reality that the Republicans hoped to establish through the ideology presented in the film:

A close examination of the text itself reveals the Republicans' use of rebirth rhetoric to communicate their ideological positions to the American public. The film is structured as a rhetorical myth; myths are ideologies in that they work to create a unified and coherent reality, and to reinforce the notion that a particular set of beliefs, values, and attitudes are right and true. The Republicans used rebirth rhetoric as a way of framing "reality." The film was structured as a mythic rebirth ritual, while its content indicated the rebirth of American myths. (Morreale, 1991, p. 6)

The Reagan convention speech brought tears to the eyes of his opponent's campaign staff, according to J. Cherie Strachan and Kathleen E. Kendall (2004, p. 138). The powerful effects of the Reagan convention film was conjured by a presentation that gathered all that is great and beautiful about America through a collage that created identification and pride in this country—wheat fields blowing in the wind, the Statue of Liberty, testimonies from hard hats, young, old, black and white citizens, images of a wedding, care-free children playing innocently, national icons like Mount Rushmore, and, most touching, the memorial service at Normandy, France, to commemorate the fiftieth anniversary of that great moment in history when Americans landed on the beach. Strachan and Kendall (2004) wrote:

Throughout the Reagan film, the audience is drawn in by a cinema-verite style, as if the shots are framed "for the absent . . . witness—the American public" (Mackey-Kallis 310–11). Unlike initial efforts in candidate films, the visual cues in Reagan's film were integral in "constructing a unified American community of adherents to mythic Main Street America and the positive values of hope and optimism" (Morreale, The Presidential campaign Film 143 [1994]). Yet the film moves beyond simply linking Reagan's character to the patriotic values portrayed. In his total commitment to American values, he is a synecdoche for America, in Burkean terms. In his humility, and courage, and perseverance in overcoming hardship, he IS America. As Mackey-Kallis claims of the Reagan film: "If we believe in the American story, we must believe in the Reagan story as well" (311). (Strachan & Kendall, 2004, p. 139)

Synecdoche is a figure of speech or a person who stands for the whole; like bread represents all food, Reagan symbolized the many faces of America and was presented to voters as a man who was given a second chance to lead this great nation. Chaotic news frames of the attempt on the president's life were included in the film, followed by Reagan's own summation that any time he had left belonged to the "man upstairs" because he had survived only through *His* providence while others were not as lucky. Year after year, college students who viewed the film testified to the emotional response that it evoked in them. It was unlike any promotional film that has been created before for a presidential convention, but now this form of autobiographical video is standard for both Democrats and Republicans at convention time. Those videos that followed would be as different as the men whose stories they told, depending on the strengths they hoped to present and the weaknesses that they hoped to hide. According to the Hugh Rank model of persuasion, the effort is to intensify the candidate's good and to intensify their opponent's bad and vice versa, to downplay the candidate's bad and downplay the opponent's good (Rank, 1976, p. 8). The autobiographical convention film offers an opportunity to dramatically forge an image of the candidate for the electorate. The Reagan film integrated the concept of America as the land of opportunity, where the invisible hand of God guided our destiny through the tribulations of World War II to the status of a triumphant nation over the evils of Nazism, communism, and nihilism.

BILL CLINTON: *THE MAN FROM HOPE*

In 1992, when Bill Clinton ran for the Presidency, his promotional film was called *The Man from Hope*, which attempted to change his image from the "Slick Willy" character assigned to him through the primary season to the triumphant optimistic man who would be elected. The film presented Clinton as a boy from a small town called Hope, Arkansas, that underscored his humble beginnings by showing his grandfather's country store, a tiny train station, and then showing a young Clinton shaking John F. Kennedy's hand in Washington, D.C., where Bill represented Boy's Nation. The film also presented him as a family man with his wife, Hillary, and his daughter, Chelsea (Strachan & Kendall, 2004, p. 141). The vision of patriotism, family, and simplicity prevailed.

GEORGE W. BUSH: *THE SKY'S THE LIMIT*

In 2000, when George W. Bush ran against Al Gore, his promotional film was called *The Sky's the Limit*, and it presented a patriotic vision of America with many close-up shots as he drove around his ranch with his dog—a descendent of the famous Millie, who belonged to his parents in the White House. Close-up shots are effective at holding viewers'

This Land featured George W. Bush and Senator John F. Kerry in a political parody that went viral.

attention and giving them a feeling that they are being included in the frame. George W. Bush did not have an identity problem, as some candidates had in the past, since he was the son of a former president and was then serving as governor of Texas. His film prominently featured his mother, Barbara; his wife, Laura; and their twin girls, who were shown as babies. The film seemed to forgo the strong American male image that many such films portray, merely mentioning his father, the former president, or G.W.'s role as governor of Texas, but appealing to women and establishing his identity as his own man (Stachan & Kendall, 2004, p. 149).

THE OBAMA BIOGRAPHY VIDEO 2008

Barack Obama's 2004 Democratic Convention speech would place him in the spotlight for the coming four years so that when he ran for the Presidency in 2008, the only question that he needed to answer was, "Who is this guy really?" In 2008, Barack Obama's biographical film would depict the multidimensional life of a biracial child who in his search for his own identity would discover the diversity and splendor of America. His opening lines were, "In no other country is this story even possible . . ." (Obama: Biography Video). Obama is the son of a Kansas white woman and a Kenyan black father, whom Barack only saw for one month, at age 10. He said there was no father in the house, but his grandparents would raise him with Middle American values of hard work, honesty, self-reliance, empathy, faith, and kindness. His grandfather was in Patton's army, and his grandmother worked on a bomber assembly line during World War II. Obama's search for identity defined him. His mother told him that he could be anything that he chose to be, and she used to wake him up at 4:30 a.m. to go over homework while she worked and attended school. She hated bullies and anyone who treated others unfairly. He described her death as the worst time in his life. He said it is a promise that we make to our children that we can make what we want of our life.

Obama's story would represent the "rock star" candidate who came from the most unlikely places—the fatherless family, displacement between the United States, Indonesia, and Hawaii, then Columbia University, and on to Congress. The myths that this biography would have to dispel were that he was Muslim, that he was trained in a radical Indonesian school, and that he identified with such radicals as Bill Ayers, a 1960s revolutionary whose group used bombing of federal buildings to protest policies, and that he took his ideology from the Reverend Jeremiah Wright, a liberation theologian who cursed America but had been Obama's mentor for over 20 years.

The video could not have been more representative of Americana—World War II patriots, college-loan–laden young couples, and civil rights activists (although the Selma, Alabama, incident that Barack recounted was not the catalyst of his parent's union, as claimed, because he was born four years before the Selma march)—but Barack's credentials as a blue-blooded American were positioned to catapult him into the White House. He represented the underclass as a Chicago political activist, an agent for change against the privileged policies of the well-heeled, like George W. Bush, who was sponsored by lobbyists, and he combined the aspirations of both white and black liberals who yearned for a "change." His eloquence was a sharp contrast to the political rhetoric of the former eight years. The biographical video represented a fresh face, a charismatic speaker, and a whole new dimension to politics that offered technology-savvy advisers who blended enough of the emergent new politics with the old tried-and-true patriotic puritan ethics sort of appeals.

MITT ROMNEY'S PROMOTIONAL FILM 2012

The central theme of Mitt Romney's convention film was his ability to turn the economy of this country around based upon his success in business, and he urged a return to the faith of our founding fathers in America's greatness. He spoke about his father, who was born in Mexico and was brought to this country as a refugee from the war. Romney's success as governor of Massachusetts was profiled, where he cut spending and repaired the deficit of $3 billion and left over $2 billion in reserves. His work with the Olympics in 2001 was used as an example of his ability to clean up economic and organizational dysfunction. His skills can save this country and turn adversity to opportunity, workers said. His narrative showed his achievement and wealth as the evidence of his hard work and ability to inspire diverse populations with serious problems to solve them. Ann, his wife, was featured as the one who kept the home together while he traveled extensively, and his son described him as "cheap" rather than frugal, a value that Romney espoused. The film was not that coherent as a media production, but clearly it was intended to portray a man of faith who has deep values, a good family, and a skill set that could heal the economic recession that the United States has seen over the previous four years. The overall impression was that Romney is a fixer, a pragmatic problem solver, and someone that you can trust. There was no clear vision for the future; his plan was just to recover what has been broken—the middle class and the economy. He came from blue-collar stock with George Romney, his father who workers called "the brick,," emerging from being a dry wall installer to becoming the president of American Motors,

Republican candidate Mitt Romney ran on a platform to fix the economy, to repeal Obamacare, and to limit the role of government.

Governor of Michigan, and competing unsuccessfully in 1968 for the Republican nomination for the presidency.

Mitt Romney's presentation needed to convince the American voters that he was not just one of the 2 percent, the wealthy elites who have lost touch with the little people who are struggling to remain afloat, but that he was the one who has the interest of the other 98 percent of this nation as his primary concern as he challenged the Obama administration. He proclaimed, "We can do better." It was more obvious what he was running against—food stamps, bailouts, unemployment, and a crippled economy—than what he was running to create.

We can see from the various convention films that they offer an opportunity for candidates to introduce their public policy agendas, to construct their images, and link their visions with American values. These biographies feed into the trend toward personalizing politics and away from the contentious wrangling over party platforms. As a matter of fact, it is difficult to discern what the parties stand for or against following these touchy-feely presentations; it is all about the candidate as a personality or image. "Films incorporate emotion-laden visual cues that simulate first-hand experiences—which enhances their ability to persuade" (Stachan & Kendall, 2004, p. 152). The audience does not always accept the images presented to them because there must be a consistency across the campaign of the impressions left by the convention film, but as we know, any subsequent action or stories can interfere with the carefully constructed image.

PRESIDENT OBAMA WINS AGAIN IN 2012

Dan Balz of the *Washington Post* wrote, "Politics and presidential elections are stories of people, ideas, and numbers" (Balz, 2012, para. 1). Clearly President Obama controlled the narrative that would prevail in the public's imagination despite Mitt Romney's attacks upon

The nomination of Barack Obama August 28, 2008, for the president of the United States was an historic moment that fulfilled a long-held dream of African Americans.

his performance and the worst economy since the Great Depression. More than anything, this election reflected the nature of the receivers of the political messages, and they represented a demographic shift in this nation that dramatically tilted toward the incumbent. The key constituents that accounted for Obama's winning coalition were African Americans, Hispanics, educated and single women, and young people. Balz wrote: "Obama offset his weak performance among white voters by winning 80 percent of the non-white electorate. He captured 93 percent of the African American vote, 71 percent of the Hispanic vote (up from 67 percent four years ago) and 73 percent of the Asian vote (up from 62 percent in 2008) (Balz, 2012, para. 8).

The social issues of women's rights, particularly reproductive rights, immigration, and growing the economy from the middle class out, were the controlling narratives that resonated with the groups outlined above. The president convinced the majority of voters that he was on the right track but that he just needed more time to get the job done. He successfully painted Romney as one of the privileged 2 percent of the wealthy who do not understand the needs of the other 98 percent of Americans, and such slogans as "Osama Bin Laden is dead, and General Motors is alive" won voters over Romney's promise to make the economy work again. Further, Romney was labeled a "pioneer in outsourcing" American jobs overseas. The impression that Obama's campaign successfully created of the Romney platform was that Republicans were too old, too white, and too reactionary with policies reminiscent of the 1920s with "trickle-down economics," social views from the 1950s, and an elitist view of the world. Romney attempted to convince voters that Obama was leading from behind and that the nation needed to move forward, reclaiming its place as the leader of the free world. Romney's attempt in the debates and on the trail to expose the inconsistencies regarding the administration's words and action in Benghazi, Libya, where four Americans were killed in a terrorist attack on the U.S. embassy, were unsuccessful because Americans are war-weary. Romney labeled the president as the "food stamp president" or the "campaigner-in-chief," who preferred to hand out doles to dependent voters rather than offer incentives for them to seek jobs.

This election cycle was extremely divisive with rhetoric that was frequently based upon class warfare or identification politics. Despite testimonials from former workers and his record as governor of Massachusetts, Romney was unable to persuade voters that he was a compassionate, strong leader who would work equally hard for all citizens in America. The polls leading up to the election showed the president and the challenger too close to call, but the battleground states like Ohio, Florida, and Pennsylvania would fall to Obama. Negative ads filled the television screens; for instance, one created by Michael Moore in collaboration with MoveOn.org in which a 97-year-old woman threatened to "burn the Mother_F---ers down if voter suppression tactics allow GOP presidential candidate Mitt Romney to win the election . . ." (Wing, 2012). Apparently she missed the riots and chaos of the 1960s, but these ads reached a new low in campaigns. Lawn signs read, "Save America, Fire Obama," and the euphemisms of former campaigns were dropped as Obama supporters accused Romney of outright lying about issues.

All this divisiveness and lack of civility does not bode well for future campaigns. A line has been crossed in political discourse, and the media has done little to clarify matters or to call for a higher standard, which is their function in a democratic society. Commentators on both the right and left joined in the fray to reflect the same partisanship that the two battling campaigns exhibited. By November 7, 2012, voters were exhausted from all the conflict, and we awaited the new year with hope that finally our government would address the real problems that had been left hanging over the campaign year—deficit spending, economic recession, unemployment, and an embattled Congress.

The 2012 election may be summarized as a drama characterized by labels, lies, and lunar tides. The Republican Convention was threatened by tropical storm Isaac, which rocked Florida during the convention in August, and one week before the national election in November Hurricane Sandy hit the East Coast and leveled areas of New Jersey and New York. President Obama earned credibility standing side by side with Governor Christie of New Jersey, a vocal critic of the president at the Republican convention, and Obama promised to send the aid that the displaced people needed to survive. This violent storm subdued criticism of a brewing investigation regarding Benghazi and the displacement of the CIA director, General David Petraeus, who resigned after he admitted to an affair with his biographer. The lunar tides were with the president as the election was over before this deluge of inconvenient events hit the investigative committees and the front pages of the newspapers. In politics, timing is to winning what location is to real estate and selling. The power of these images of two opponents, Christie and Obama, standing together to serve the people worked to diminish Romney's role in this crucial week when he had gained momentum in the polls, and the scenes of the ravaged coastline advanced Obama's standing as one who looked out for the helpless. Whether it was in the stars or not, Obama controlled the narrative, the numbers, and the people who gave him the four more years that he wanted.

Niall Ferguson wrote about the general characteristics of the former campaign in *Newsweek* November 19, 2012, in which he profiled four points of analysis that were definitive in the election:

> First, the democrats understand the new world of Internet-savvy, data-driven marketing better than the Republicans do. . . . Second, demographic trends doom any Republican campaign that appeals more to white males than to any other voter group. . . . Third, running on the economy doesn't work if people remember our own party's role in screwing it up and think improvement is in sight . . . Finally, and most important, the Democrats have figured out what European Social democrats long ago understood: the more entitlements you create, the more voters you can depend on. Let me put it very simply: given the choice between higher taxes on the 1 percent and cuts in entitlement for the 47 percent, voters went for the former. Surprise! (p. 17)

President Obama did a better job communicating with his base than Romney, and the demographics were tilted in his favor, with blacks, Hispanics, women, and the young supporting him overwhelmingly. Furthermore, he was successful in convincing voters that George Bush left the economy in such a mess that his stimulus packages and fiscal measures were essential to save the country and that the Republicans would drive us over the "fiscal cliff." Entitlements have risen from 2 percent in 1960 to 10 percent currently, with a prediction from the Congressional Budget Office of 20 percent by 2059 (Ferguson, 2012). Rush Limbaugh, conservative provocateur, observed after the election, "It's just very difficult to beat Santa Clause" (Limbaugh, 2012). In the next section we will discuss the reciprocal nature of political communication wherein meaning is established when shared experiences are given validation and voiced as legitimate.

THE INTERPLAY OF INFLUENCE: JAMIESON AND CAMPBELL'S PERSPECTIVE

In a book titled *The Interplay of Influence,* Jamieson and Campbell (2006) explain the interrelationship between the news media, advertising, politics, the Internet, government and the regulators, and the citizens or audiences who receive the messages from these various factions. In a presidential campaign, two-thirds of the campaign budget will be spent creating, testing, and broadcasting the candidate's views to the people (Jamieson & Campbell, 2006, p. 282). The premises that Jamieson and Campbell laid out are useful for our discussion of political rhetoric. First, they noted that all communication is reciprocal; that is, a transaction occurs wherein meaning and experiences are shared by the source and the audience. Second, each medium used to send a message is unique as a resource because of the ways that we receive, perceive, and interact with it. They noted that television is still the most influential mass medium, with the Internet "decisively" shaping and impacting the mediated world as well. Third, the nature of mediated messages cannot be separated from the economic and political systems within which they operate (Jamieson & Campbell, 2006, p. 2).

These principles are basic to political communication because indeed the influence flows both ways—from the government to the people, and, ideally, the voice of the people influences those in government to protect our best interests. Political campaigns enlist the resources of all forms of mass media—newspapers, magazines, television, radio, and the Internet, but the Internet has empowered people to offer immediate feedback to candidates, whereas in the past responses were delayed by lack of access.

Since the 2000 election, candidates have used the Internet to communicate directly to the people. In 2004 three quarters of U.S. adults had access to the Internet (Jamieson & Campbell, 2006, p. 29). Expanded interactivity through the Internet has changed the nature of political communication by allowing audiences to exchange views with journalists, sometimes challenging the accuracy or the slant of their stories. Further, 24-hour news has changed the quality of the telecasts with the likelihood that more inaccurate, incomplete, or false stories will be offered than when only morning and evening news were expected. Newscasters like the late Walter Cronkite, who exercised great influence on presidents as well as the viewing audience and was once voted the most trusted man in America, no longer exist. With so many hours to fill, often the networks engage us in hypothetical situations rather than reporting and interpreting actual events that have occurred. "**Hard news** is a report of an event that happened or that was disclosed within the previous twenty-four hours and treats an issue of ongoing concern. The crime story is the model for hard news" (Jamieson & Campbell, 2006, p. 41). Typically, hard news must appeal to a mass audience by being "clean, simple, and attention getting" (p. 41). Therefore, hard news has become increasingly personalized through interviews and pictures that create identification or empathy for the subject. The need to appeal to an anonymous, heterogeneous, and mass audience does not encourage journalists to feature complicated examinations of complex issues, such as the economy or foreign policy. Jamieson and Campbell wrote:

> Defining hard news as personal, about individuals, means that it is not about processes or the exploration of ideas; it is the story of a group or a movement only to the extent that a group or movement can be personified by one member's testimony. The focus on individuals simplifies and clarifies. It creates audience identification; it reflects journalistic reliance on human sources and on the interview. (2006, p. 42)

This personalization of the news means that political campaigns have become largely scripted sound bytes that candidates adhere to so that they do not go off-message in a moment of spontaneity and commit some political blunder that they cannot recover from or erase.

PRESIDENTIAL RHETORIC AS A WINDOW TO THE WORLD

When cadidates are elected, they must establish a way to fulfill campaign promises and continue to communicate with the people who believed in them and all of those who did not support them. **Presidential rhetoric** is another genre of political communication. Theodore Otto Windt Jr., who was renowned for his presidential rhetoric classes at the University of Pittsburgh, believed that rhetoricians both described and created reality. He explained deliberative rhetoric as follows:

> Though Aristotle exhorted his readers to know the various forms of government, he based his *Rhetoric* on a Greek democratic society in which rulers were subservient to laws, rules, and citizen opinion. Citizens come together in this setting to debate and deliberate on issues of state. The rules of the democratic system allow citizens to air disagreements and provide the "marketplace for competing ideas." The essence of deliberative rhetoric is that it deals with issues of probability. Every issue is open to debate. Each requires a judgment. No one possesses "truth." Persuasion is the central feature of this rhetoric. For those out of power, it means supplication to authorities to redress grievances. For those in power, it means a debate among equals about what course of action is most prudent and expedient. (Windt, 1990, p. 148)

Windt analyzed presidential rhetoric as a powerful use of discourse to communicate directly with the people through access to the media where presidents possessed authority that no representative or senator had, and further, their messages created the arena where all other politicians had to do battle. In other words, presidents were portrayed as master builders of the rhetorical climate in which all decisions of government were conducted. They set the stage for the scenes of enactment that would follow. That is not to say that they acted in isolation, since each brought his own troupe of actors with him, and they had to address all policies in both foreign and domestic settings where other powerful actors were competing for leading roles on the world stage.

APPROACHES TO PRESIDENTIAL RHETORIC

The selective screens that presidents use to explain their administrations give substance to their work, generating a political reality that lives on after their demise. John F. Kennedy was known for the "New Frontier" vision, which was realized years after his death when, as he promised, an American, Neil Armstrong, took his first step onto the moon. Lyndon B. Johnson spoke of the "Great Society" where he envisioned civil rights, embodied so eloquently in Martin Luther King Jr.'s "I Have a Dream" speech, and Johnson advanced education for working-class children in America. President Clinton spoke of a new beginning or a new covenant between government and the people. Each administration creates an image or central theme that is supposed to give wings to their plans, such as George W. Bush's "Compassionate Conservatism" that was supposed to guarantee that there would be "No Child Left Behind" in the pursuit of literacy and math skills. Barack Obama's administration has not yet defined one umbrella vision that will serve as a media trailer for these years, but he tackled universal healthcare as a flag issue. While the legitimacy of his health initiative was challenged, in 2012 the Supreme Court decided in a 4–5 split decision that the bill was legitimate because Congress does have the ability to tax citizens and the bill was a tax upon U.S. citizens. The issue was relegated to the power of the people to endorse or deny those who passed it through the elective process.

While the intricacies of funding, enacting extensive overhauls of institutions like education, healthcare, national defense, and manning the battle stations often overrun the visions of a more just society, the language that we attach to such initiatives is part of the energy that elevates or subverts social change. Different communication theories or paradigms must be used to analyze political rhetoric depending on the statesman's or rhetor's ethos, or character.

Windt addressed President Nixon's rhetoric using psychoanalysis. Looking at what psychologists had written about Nixon's childhood, analyzing what Nixon said about himself, and profiling his lifelong project of creating a public persona, Windt engaged what he called "psycho-rhetorical analysis." He concluded that the Richard Nixon that the public thought they knew was a rhetorically constructed Nixon, which came unraveled when the public heard the Watergate tapes for the first time (Windt, 1990, p. 115). Windt also analyzed the political rhetoric of protest groups, such as the 1960s antiwar activists, feminists, and ideologues who used their belief systems to unify followers and to instigate action directed toward the government and presidents. Presidents are receivers of political rhetoric as well as sources of it, and sometimes the appeals from the streets shape the rhetoric from the rose garden of the White House.

JÜRGEN HABERMAS ON DEMOCRACY AND DELIBERATION

Jürgen Habermas (2006) raised a question about whether or not true deliberation is occurring in democratic societies, and he identified certain conditions that seem to obstruct the ideal. By true deliberation he referred to Aristotle's notion of deliberation, which meant offering good arguments for or against a policy. Rhetoric is an essential part of the political process, as those in power seek to gain the support and consent of the governed in a reciprocal relationship where citizens have an obligation to be enlightened about their leaders, policies, and the effects their decisions will have on society as a whole.

THE DELIBERATIVE PARADIGM

The normative theory of democracy includes an institutional design that maximizes the three sectors that Habermas addressed: the private citizen; the political community, which includes the free and equal citizen; and the public sphere that operates as an intermediary between the state and society. First, this institutional design guarantees equal protection for all citizens through the rule of law. Second, the design assures participation through elections and inclusive suffrage between different parties through the majority principle for decisions operating in a representative body. Third, a public sphere must exist that separates the tax-based state from the market-based society that is secure to communicate and associate through a diverse and independent mass media, which requires a mass audience. Habermas described the normative values that a deliberative model is supposed to support:

> The deliberative paradigm offers as its main empirical point of reference a democratic process, which is supposed to generate legitimacy through a procedure of opinion and will formation that grants (a) publicity and transparency for the deliberative process, (b) inclusion and equal opportunity for participation, and (c) a justified presumption for reasonable outcomes (mainly in view of the impact of arguments on rational changes in preference) (Bohman, 1996; Bohman & Rehg, 1997). (Habermas, 2006, p. 3).

Habermas acknowledged how each governmental branch contributes to the institutionalized deliberation and negotiation processes, but at the periphery of the political system "The public sphere is rooted in networks for wild flows of messages—news, reports, commentaries, talks, scenes and images, and shows and movies with an informative, polemical, educational, or entertaining content" (Habermas, 2006, p. 6). These messages come from all kinds of actors, political parties, lobbyists, professionals, everyday folks, and subcultures. Without two central types of actors, the political public sphere could not work—the professionals in mass media and politicians who occupy the center of the political system.

ACTORS WHO CONTRIBUTE TO POLITICAL COMMUNICATION

Habermas went on to identify five other actors, besides politicians and media professionals, who are part of the established public sphere:

> (a) *lobbyists* who represent special interest groups; (b) *advocates* who either represent general interest groups or substitute for a lack of representation of marginalized groups that are unable to voice their interests effectively; (c) *experts* who are credited with professional or scientific knowledge in some specialized area and are invited to give advice; (d) *Moral entrepreneurs* who generate public attention for supposedly neglected issues; and, last but not least, (e) *intellectuals* who have gained, unlike advocates or moral entrepreneurs, a perceived personal reputation in some field (e.g., as writers or academics) and who engage, unlike experts and lobbyists, spontaneously in public discourse with the declared intention of promoting general interests. (Habermas, 2006, p. 6)

Oprah Winfrey drew a crowd of approximately 18,500 people in Des Moines, Iowa, when she endorsed Barack Obama for president in 2008.

With all these actors contributing to political discourse, they furnish a cleansing mechanism, Habermas said, which filters out the "muddy" elements from the process. Deliberation has three functions, then:

> To mobilize and pool relevant issues and required information, and to specify interpretations; to process such contributions discursively by means of proper arguments *for* and *against*; and to generate rationally motivated *yes* and *no* attitudes that are expected to determine the outcome of procedurally correct decisions. (Habermas, 2006, p. 7)

Habermas's discussion of the role of deliberation in a democratic society elegantly outlined the way the process is supposed to work with different "actors," as he called them, contributing to the overall production of a reasonable society. He wrote of the "unruly life of the public sphere," which indicated that he understands the role of conflict in deliberations, but the ideal cannot be reached without communication that legitimizes the interaction between the state and the civil society it is supposed to serve. He identified four categories of power: Political power, which requires legitimization; social power, which depends on the status one occupies in a stratified society; economic power, which is a dominant kind of social power because of the pressure that can be exerted on the political realm; and finally, mass media power, which is manifested through the capacity to set the political agenda through framing and priming issues. (Habermas, 2006) The major function of these "actors" is rhetorical.

MASS MEDIA'S ROLE TO FRAME DEBATE

In order for the deliberative model to work in a democratic society, the mass media sector must be vigorous and independent of the power structure. In other words, Habermas reaffirms the adversarial relationship between the press and government. Some of the problems that he revealed are that mass media organizations are dominated by economic interests rather than protecting the citizen's right to know. The trend toward candidate-centered politics, where image makers focus on traits rather than programs or issues to appeal to voters, means that the old model of political journalism is being phased out.

First, Habermas raised the possibility that mass media is not independent of the power structure at all, but rather engages in a kind of paternalism where the citizens seem to be instructed condescendingly from on high. Second, feedback from the public sphere is hampered by selective access and uneven participation by citizens. Habermas noted that access and participation in mediated communication correlate with social status and cultural background. He noted that despite recent studies that claim more involvement of citizens with politics because of the electronic media, they also have a lower level of trust and have more cynicism toward politics as a result of this relationship with radio and television. He noted that the independence that the political press won in the late eighteenth century seems to be compromised by the pressure of shareholders, which has led to displacement of one category of communication by another: issues of political discourse become assimilated into and absorbed by the modes and contents of entertainment. Habermas identified the following problems with mass media: "personalization, the dramatization of events, the simplification of complex matters, and the vivid polarization of conflicts which promote civic privatism and a mood of antipolitics" (Habermas, 2006, p. 13). Habermas, analyzing the rhetoric of former President George W. Bush, faulted the media for not providing more reliable news and alternative interpretations of events following 9/11. He wrote:

> A recent case in point is the manipulation of the American public by the White House's surprisingly successful communications management before and after the invasion of Iraq in 2003. What this case highlights is not the clever move by the president to frame the event of 9/11 as having triggered a "war on terrorism" (Entman, 2004). For the more remarkable phenomenon in this context was the absence of any effective counterframing (Artz & Kamalipour, 2005). A responsible press would have provided the popular media with more reliable news and alternative interpretations through channels of an intermedia agenda setting. (Habermas, 2006, p. 11)

Habermas reaffirmed the need for an independent, self-regulating, and vigorous media to serve the classic functions of the press whose rights are guaranteed by our Constitution. The preceding example indicates the power of political rhetoric to define a social reality in which far-reaching decisions will follow. The definition of the frame of reference will build the arena in which all other actions will follow unless there is another interpretation of that situation. What if mass media had focused on then Secretary of Defense Donald Rumsfeld's language of a "War on Culture" rather than a "War on Terror"? Would the perceptions and course of action have been different? In political, deliberative communication, there are many interconnected parties, such as national leaders, who have more power to establish the parameters of debate, but nonetheless a vigorous, independent press and an informed citizenry are all part of the process. The dialectic between the political base and mass media is essential to clear the muddy waters that Habermas referred to earlier by framing issues in a manner that identifies ideological visions that distort reality and clarifies the situation through interpretation, analysis, and thoughtful presentation.

When the media perform this function, it goes beyond "mere rhetoric" or "spin" to set the record straight.

MASS MEDIA AS WATCHDOG, OR THE FOURTH ESTATE

There are many approaches to studying media's role in society, but the role that most people know best is the "**watchdog of the people**" function, which means that media's job is to keep an eye on government for the people's welfare. Journalists are the eyes and ears of the people and report on both domestic and foreign news. The watchdog media is ever-vigilant and highly protective of citizen's right to know and to be involved in self-governance. This perspective on media's role is an **adversarial relationship** between the press and the government, with journalists investigating to expose corruption, to elevate all issues to the level of public discussion, and to enlighten citizens by reporting, interpreting, and framing public debates. Other metaphors for media include the "**fourth estate**," meaning that media stands as the fourth pillar in our society along side of the executive, legislative, and judicial branches of government. This perspective of media views its place as equal to that of the three governing branches within government. Although media organizations are supposed to be independent of the government, there is a **symbiotic relationship** between the two—each is dependent on the other for survival. Journalists who lack access to the halls of Congress and the business of government have little to add to public discourse, and similarly the politician who has a bad relationship with the media will suffer greatly in any campaign, administration, or controversy. The "fourth estate" metaphor implies that media and government are equally important, with one complementing the other in a democratic society. Media performs many functions, including **agenda setting,** which is exercising the selection and framing of public discourse that defines, interprets, and highlights some people, events, and issues while others are omitted or redefined. In this role, media practitioners are seen as agents of change who further the public agenda concerning all manner of initiatives and social problems such as crime, homelessness, illiteracy, economic concerns, and national security. Clearly, the manner in which journalists present national news will determine to a great extent public attitudes, beliefs, and actions concerning war and peace, national initiatives, and our views of ourselves as citizens of the world. Mass media has tremendous power to shape the perceptions of the public both nationally and internationally. The rhetorical visions that are generated by the media establishment are powerful in that they shape the socio-political milieu for our nation. The actors in these news stories are our president, members of Congress, and various constituents of this nation.

POLITICS AND THE FUNCTIONS MODEL OF MASS MEDIA

Harold D. Lasswell (1946) described the act of communication primarily by asking: *who,* which identifies the communicator; *says what,* which focuses upon content analysis; *in what channel,* which identifies the means of sending the message; *to whom,* the intended audience; and *with what effects,* identifying the impact of the message (Smith, Lasswell, & Casey, 1946). Lasswell identified three functions of mass media: (1) surveillance of the environment, (2) the correlation of the parts of society in responding to the environment, and (3) the transmission of the heritage from generation to generation. First, the **surveillance** function refers to the news and information role of media with about 90 percent of Americans reporting that they get their news from either the electronic media or newspapers. As stated earlier, the media's job is to keep an eye on government and keep citizens informed on matters that will affect their lives and to give warnings about matters that threaten their welfare. **Instrumental surveillance** transmits information that is useful to everyday life such as stock market prices, where to find a movie, new products, and fashion news. **Beware surveillance** warns citizens of terrorist attacks, inflation, or natural disasters.

The second function, **correlation**, explains the meaning and the significance of events that the news stories carry. The various **gatekeepers**, like editors and producers, select where to put stories, when to air them, and the slant that they will have. A dysfunction of this practice is when the news is **biased** or framed in a distorted manner to serve the ideology of the news organization rather than objectively informing citizens. Often before a presidential speech, like the State of the Union address or an important statement on a war's progress, news organizations will preview what the president is going to say to the American people and they will feature opponents of the president's policies to counterargue his ideas before the American people even hear him speak. Frequently these broadcasts project hypothetical situations and the administration's supposed response to them. Similarly, immediately following the president's address, commentators critique the material from the speech before the audience has had time to reflect upon its content.

Some analysts have extended the correlation function to **linkage.** Correlation means that media performs to connect different elements of society so that their mutual needs can be met. For example, products are linked to consumers through advertising, and legislators are linked to their constituents through news stories. Special interest groups are informed about common concerns such as health threats like the Gulf War syndrome so that political action can be taken. Recently, websites, blogs, and interactive chat rooms have permitted citizens to check the mainstream media, connect directly with candidates, and offer immediate feedback. For example, Congressman Tim Murphy (Republican, Pennsylvania) recently sent an e-mail to his constituents explaining a bill in Congress that would change the way that drugs were purchased, the impact upon prices, and changes in protocols for acquisition. He solicited feedback from his constituents regarding their positions on this proposed bill. This kind of exchange was impossible before the advent of the Internet. One of the harmful consequences of linkage is the ability of hate groups to recruit using these sites, for rumors to be passed as facts, and the standard codes of ethical conduct found in journalism to be bypassed. Citizens need to be vigilant about how much credibility they give to such sites, yet they open a new arena for useful exchanges across the political spectrum.

Transmission of values or our heritage from generation to generation is the media function that subtly informs readers, viewers, and followers, through socialization, what values and behaviors are appropriate. Generally American media is criticized for exploiting only sex and violence and producing negative effects in young consumers who emulate such behaviors. Similarly, when media covers politics they have been accused of focusing only upon sensational stories such as the Clinton–Lewinsky affair or Congressman Gary

Condit and Chandra Levy's affair, after which the young intern was found murdered in a park. On the other hand, anti-drug, safe-sex, and anti-smoking campaigns have been waged by media organizations in an attempt to tell people what is good for them. First Lady Michelle Obama has launched an anti-obesity campaign using media chats in an attempt to stem the tide of health problems for children who are overweight and at risk for many health problems.

George Gerbner noted that mass media has taken over the role of transmitting values to our youth that was, in the past, filled by parents, schools, and religious institutions. Recently,

First Lady Michelle Obama celebrated her "Let's Move" campaign by performing a dance on the Jimmy Fallon show that included hip bumps, the sprinkler, and the Dougie.

the media has exposed a series of scandals that reaffirm "family values," which have been framed by media as the monopoly of the religious right wing, as the expected standard in middle America. At the same time, the media has criticized conservative politicians for being oppressive and out of touch on such issues as stem cell research, gay marriage, and abortion. In 2012, Republican political candidate Todd Akin of Missouri claimed that a woman raped during a "legitimate rape"—an oxymoron—had physiological defense mechanisms to protect her from pregnancy, and Richard Mourdock from Indiana claimed that even under those circumstances God wanted that child to be born. Both were defeated, but their lack of capacity to identify with women under the most horrific circumstances hurt all Republican candidates, even those who condemned their statements. Social issues such as abortion are often a one-issue dealmaker which can win or lose millions of voters who use that issue as their litmus test.

Charles R. Wright (1960) reviewed Lasswell's three functions of mass media and added **entertainment** to the three that Lasswell offered in his analysis. Wright defined the entertainment function as communication intended to amuse people irrespective of any instrumental effects that it may have (p. 609).

Often the content of television shows which purport to entertain the masses is no laughing matter. In the last decade there has been a tendency toward entertainers who leave the platform of theater, music, or comedy to add their celebrity views to the political arena. They have been influential in raising issues, attacking candidates, and evaluating policies. For example, AIDS in Africa, the debacle following Hurricane Katrina, the weapons of mass destruction debate, and misinformation or news management from the White House have been frequent topics on display in comedic dialogue. *The Daily Show* with host Jon Stewart uses biting humor, which often reveals the obvious disconnect between the government and the governed. This satirical wit appeals most to those between 18 and 40 who are media savvy, are well informed, and have grown up with the credibility gap in the government that grew out of the Nixon administration and the Watergate affair in the early 1970s. Most college freshmen today were born in the 1990s and were in preschool when the Starr Report fell out of their parents' morning paper with details of the Clinton–Lewinsky affair. Therefore, scandals in government or personal indiscretions are part of the political spectrum that college students today consider the normal political agenda. They tend to separate the performance of politicians from their personal, private life, no matter how tawdry it may be. They tend to think in sound bytes reflected in the statement of a recent senior at a midwestern university: "I refuse to vote for a president who waves at Stevie Wonder." They expect politicians to know as much about the entertainment industry as that industry knows about politics.

On January 31, 2007, presidential hopeful Joseph Biden (Democrat, Delaware) appeared on *The Daily Show* with Stewart where viewers thought he might discuss the gaffe that he had made concerning Senator Barack Obama in an interview with the *New York Observer*: "I mean you got the first mainstream African-American who is articulate and bright and clean and a nice-looking guy," Biden said in the Observer. "I mean, that's a storybook, man" (Pelofsky, 2007). Jesse Jackson attributed Biden's comment to a gaffe, not a "racial pejorative statement. . . . It could be interpreted that way. But it's not what he meant" (Pelofsky, 2007).

Jon Stewart's *The Daily Show* has become a powerful plat-form for politicians to appear and for Stewart to examine major issues.

Obama replied, "African-American presidential candidates like Jesse Jackson, Shirley Chisholm, Carol Moseley Braun and Al Sharpton gave a voice to many important issues through their campaigns, and no one would call them inarticulate" (Pelofsky, 2007). Obama shrugged Biden's statement off, saying there was a war in Iraq and real issues that needed to be addressed, so he saw no value in pursuing this one. Apparently, Obama forgave any slights when he selected Biden as his vice president.

When Biden spoke with Stewart on *The Daily Show* following the remark on Obama just mentioned, he laughed at his foot-in-the-mouth gaffe by stating that he had spoken to Barack Obama, Al Sharpton, Jesse Jackson, and others. Stewart threw in Michael Jordon for comedic effect, but the whole remark was diluted through their poking fun at Biden's intended flattery that sounded like anything but a compliment for every other African American politician. But the severity of the incident was deflected when Biden chose the show as an opportunity to attack President Bush by stating, "He's abusing power." Biden supported that accusation by stating that the president did not offer background information to the Senate on his appoin-tees, that he did not use discretion matching appointees to the jobs or institutions, like his United Nations appointee, and that the president operated in secrecy. This diversionary tactic of attacking the president rather than explaining what many saw as a pejorative racial state-ment by Biden gave him a pass that many politicians would not have been granted. Yet the incident points to the power of the entertainment media to offer a forum that plays no small role in framing issues, placing praise or blame, and offering reasons for and against policies.

Newsweek carried a cartoon in the *Perspectives* section from the *Atlanta Journal-Constitution* by Luckovich (2007) that showed Biden with his foot in his mouth saying, "Furthermore . . ." while two television viewers watch and one says, "I'm voting Biden. How many candidates can get their foot stuck in their mouth and keep talking. . . ." Such political cartoons function as an enthymeme where the viewer fills in the blanks, giving the presentation all the background that is needed to make sense of it. Most would remember that this is not the first time that Biden has been forced to apologize for his public statements. Not too many years ago, he was called for plagiarizing parts of his speech that he failed to credit to the original source. This time he did take credit for the message, as negatively as it may have been viewed, but he chose to laugh it off in public, while certainly there was damage repair happening behind the scenes with apologies to key African American leaders.

Entertainment platforms have joined the ranks of media that engage in both epideictic and deliberative forms of address. Comedy has always functioned to hold up the foibles of humans for public exposure, judgment, and laughter, which is a redemptive measure to restore public order and reaffirm values through satire, unmasking, and parody. The tradition goes back to Greek theater and is being revived with new force in political communication today where the effect of such messages should not be underestimated.

MEDIA BIAS AND NATIONAL VIEWS

Bernard Goldberg (2002), who was a journalist for 28 years, wrote a critique of media elites that cost him his job, but he has continued to advocate for change. His book, *Bias: A CBS Insider Exposes How the Media Distort the News*, wrote about the liberal bias that characterized anchormen like Dan Rather, Tom Brokaw, and others who he stated had totally lost touch with the American people. He said that he lost his job because "I violated the code of omerta, the sacred code of silence that both wise guys and news guys live and die by" (Goldberg, 2002, p. 12). Comparing the cohesive professional code in journalism to that of the Mafia, Goldberg cited examples of media distortion on topics from the flat tax proposed by Steve Forbes to the depiction of the homeless in America and the AIDS epidemic, which Goldberg said misrepresented who these people were, why they were homeless or infected, and how there was no fair and balanced reporting of conservative programs in the news. Further, he stated that there was no intentional bias by the media elite, they simply did not associate with anyone who did not share their worldview. Goldberg's position is that this liberal bias distorts the way national issues are presented, the way campaigns are covered, and who gains access to media to express views, and he argued through multiple examples and expert testimony that **media bias** corrupts the deliberative process in America. He stated that the news anchors and journalists could pass a polygraph test denying that they have such an ideological view of society, but they live separate and unequal lives from the rest of us who have less trust in their reporting all the time. The profit motive, window dressing with cosmetic-type anchors rather than tough reporters, and the inability to level with audiences on race relations, disease, unemployment, and terrorist groups have all led to incomplete or distorted news. Mass media is a powerful persuader for public views and political action.

POLITICAL PERSUASION OUTSIDE THE MAINSTREAM

Anyone can use deliberative rhetoric to affect change. Jock Yablonski, a juvenile delinquent-turned-champion for dispossessed miners and their families, Ben Duskin, an 8-year-old cancer patient, and Dina Denning, who started a backpack program to feed hungry kids, have all employed deliberative address to rally support and inspire political action.

JOSEPH A. "JOCK" YABLONSKI: JUVENILE DELINQUENT, REFORMER, AND MARTYR

On December 31, 1969, three hired assassins entered Jock Yablonski's Clarksville, Pennsylvania, home and murdered him, his wife, and daughter before he could reach the shotgun that he kept by his bedside for protection. W. A. "Tony" Boyle, president of the United Mine Workers of America (UMWA) union, financed these murders in order to eliminate his challenger for the presidency of the UMWA. On the day he announced his candidacy against Boyle, Yablonski predicted that the campaign would cost him his life. Why would he risk being killed to bring down Tony Boyle? Though he had benefited from his 35-year association with the union, he said he did so with an increasingly troubled conscience. His bid for leadership of the UMWA was an ethical decision—he'd witnessed and even participated in years of corruption—but the day of reckoning had arrived.

On November 21, 1968, a mine blast in Farmington, West Virginia, left 78 miners entombed in the Consolidation Coal Company's Number 9 Mine. In the early hours of the morning, the ground rumbled, rolling smoke and flames shot 150 feet into the air, and only 21 of the 99 men who worked the cat-eye shift escaped. Boyle visited the mine shaft and spoke at length about the dangers of mining, though he had never descended into the shaft himself. He even praised the safety record of the Consolidated Coal Company's performance at the Number 9 mine—small comfort to those who lost fathers, husbands, and brothers in the disaster. Few women worked in the mines at that time, and their presence near them was regarded with superstition. This is a classic case of mistaken causation—post hoc ergo propter hoc (after this, therefore because of this)—since they were thought to bring bad luck rather than fall victim to it.

Yablonski, angered by the union's inaction in the wake of the disaster, was in a position to expose the full extent of Boyle's corruption and ineptitude. With the uneasiness that any whistle-blower experiences, Yablonski steeled himself for the attacks on his character, physical attacks on his body, and threats to his supporters. Unrest and discontent bubbled up from the bottom of the union once the miners had a champion at the top. Yablonski knew where all the secrets were buried, where the funds had gone, and who had supervised the whole charade. In response, Boyle issued the order to have Yablonski killed through a network of union leaders and associates.

When Yablonski announced his candidacy in 1969, Ralph Nader, Senator Ralph Yarborough, and Congressman Ken Heckler were already attempting to reform the corrupt miner's union, and the coalfields were rife with work stoppages caused by dissatisfied workers threatening to take their union back. On the day of his announcement, Yablonski, who had been nervous and fidgety before his speech, seemed to relax and actually lean into the performance. He began to speak:

> Today I am announcing my candidacy for the Presidency of the United Mine Workers of America.

I do so out of a deep awareness of the insufferable gap between the Union Leadership and the working miners that has bred neglect of miner's needs and aspirations and generated a climate of fear and inhibition. For thirty-five years I have been associated with the Union. I have seen this organization stand as the only bulwark against the oppression and greed of the coal operator and the insensitivity and corruption of government in the coal mining areas. I have seen the courage and determination of coal miners and coal orgaizers under the leadership of John L. Lewis against the combined power of industry and government who were determined to break the union's will and return the miners to their subterranean serfdom. Years later we participated in the establishment of the pioneering Welfare and Retirement Fund and built an unprecedented chain of hospitals and health care facilities throughout many coal mining regions. I participated in and tolerated deteriorating performance of this leadership —but with increasingly troubled conscience. I will no longer be beholden to the past. I can no longer tolerate the low state to which our union has fallen. My duty to coal miners, as I see it, is not to withdraw but to strive for leadership and to make it truly a Union of miners rather than a Union of inaccessible bureaucrats.

(J. A. Yablonski, May 29, 1969. MFD Collection, Archives of Labor History and Urban Affairs, Wayne State University. Detroit, Michigan)

Yablonski based his platform on restoring safety to the coalfields and credibility to the union halls of the United Mine Workers organization. He was not as eloquent as his predecessor John L. Lewis, who took hundreds of thousands of miners out on strikes in defiance of a wartime president with the proclamation, "No backward steps." However, Yablonski had the national stage from which to expose the graft of the Boyle machine. His challenge calls to mind Lewis's 1937 Labor Day speech, in which Lewis attacked President Franklin Delano Roosevelt for his antagonism toward mine workers. Lewis said:

Labor, like Israel, has many sorrows. Its women weep for their fallen, and they lament for the future of the children of the race. It ill behooves one who has upped at labor's table and who has been sheltered in labor's house to curse with equal impartiality both labor and its adversaries when they become locked in deadly embrace. (Lewis, 1937)

Yablonski's campaign was fraught with violence and subterfuge. Boyle, shocked that his trusted lieutenant had become his nemesis, used the full force of the UMWA to resist Yablonski's reform movement. As the incumbent, he had access to the union's machinery and resources necessary to undermine Yablonski's efforts. Boyle used the *United Mine Workers Journal* as a mouthpiece to sponsor his own campaign, calling reformers "outsiders" and "Dual Unionists," but his primary advantage was his promise to increase miners' pension by 30 percent. Yablonski and his supporters sought the Department of Labor's aid in preventing physical attacks and curbing Boyle's misuse of the *Journal* to paint Yablonski as an ex-con who had pilfered from the pension fund. Despite complaints filed by Yablonski and his lawyer, the secretary of labor, George P. Schultz, remained publicly impartial. This was his department's official position until after Yablonski was found murdered on January 5, 1970, five days after the assassins entered his home and shot all who slept there.

Though Yablonski petitioned the Department of Labor to intervene and impound all the ballots in the United Mine Workers election, the Department of Labor considered such action highly irregular. On December 24, 1969, Yablonski received the department's final response: "After such consideration the Secretary has determined that there is insufficient basis for impounding the ballots and records by the Department of Labor at this time" (Usery, 1969).

When the ballots were tallied, Boyle was declared the winner. Yablonski's campaign would have died with him, but his followers, armed with proof of the union's corruption, demanded that the Department of Labor investigate the election. In the years following the assassination, an extensive investigation revealed the full extent of Boyle's excesses. Yablonski's murder was an act of vengeance, and his sons requested that no UMW officers attend the funeral or memorial, that no work stoppages occur, and no functions be dedicated to their father, mother, and sister.

Yablonski's bid for the presidency of the United Mine Workers union began as a typical political campaign, but after his assassination the push for union reform gained steam. The resultant series of trials involved local and federal courts and relied on the cooperation of the FBI, Pennsylvania State Police, county sheriffs, and city police. The proceedings became a drama of epic proportions that exposed murder, corrupt officials, and decades of graft. Richard A. Sprague, Philadelphia's first assistant district attorney, was appointed special prosecutor in the trials. Thanks to his efforts, as well as those of the conscientious union officials and common men and women who testified against the incumbent administration, Boyle was eventually removed from office.

By January 20, 1970, the FBI had three murder suspects in custody: Paul E. Gilly, Claude Edward Vealey, and Aubran "Buddy" Martin. On January 21, Vealey confessed that he, Gilly, and Martin had been paid off by a fundamentalist preacher named David Brandenburg, who was secretary treasurer of a Tennessee UMW local (Lewis, 1975, p. 9). The money trail ultimately led to the top of the United Mine Workers union, implicating Boyle. William Jenkins Turnblazer, a member of the Tennessee Bar and former president of District 19, identified the execution team and testified that Boyle ordered Yablonski's execution on June 23, 1969 (Lewis, 1975, p. 319). Albert Pass responded that District 19 would take care of it (Lewis, 1975, pp. 303–304).

The Miners for Democracy successfully achieved the reform Yablonski sought. The secretary of labor overturned the 1969 election, and a new one was supervised by the Department of Labor. The reformers, once termed "dual unionists" by Boyle, were recognized as a legitimate group by the Supreme Court. Boyle and his cohorts were sent to prison. The murder trials, the Department of Labor investigations, and the health and safety hearings that took place in the wake of Yablonski's assassination revealed that the UMWA had indeed become an "island of tyranny" and neglect.

BEN DUSKIN'S GAME

When Ben Duskin, a young cancer patient, was approached by the Make-A-Wish Foundation to fulfill his personal wish, he decided he wanted to create a game that would help other children with cancer battle their disease. The game would take six months to create, and Ben

Ben Duskin enlisted the expertise of LucasArts to create a game to help kids
fight cancer for the Make-A-Wish Foundation.

received help from LucasArts, a company that produced *Indiana Jones*, the *Last Crusade*, *Loom*,
and *The Secret of Monkey Island*. Available free in nine different languages, the game can be
downloaded from the Make-A-Wish website.

Within two years of its launch, *Ben's Game* had been downloaded 181,920 times. Ben
Duskin's story illustrates the influence of personal power and the effect that one person can
have upon others when the cause empowers them. Duskin, who was diagnosed at age five
with acute lymphoblastic leukemia, battled the disease for three years before going into re-
mission. During this time, his mother told him to visualize the chemotherapy zapping the
cancer cells like Pac-man racing through his veins. When he was approached by the Make-
A-Wish Foundation, his parents encouraged him to choose a life-affirming celebration to
show how well he had handled his treatments (Ben's Game, http://express.howstuffowrks
.com/ep-ben-eric.htm).

Eric Johnston of LucasArts was originally drawn to the project by Duskin's desire to do
something constructive for other children with cancer. Though other organizations estimated the game's construction would take years and cost millions of dollars, Johnston
stepped forward to create this exceptional game:

> From the very beginning, Ben's enthusiasm touched all involved. LucasArts gave us permis-
> sion to use my office during off-hours, and also the recording studio. Friends at work were
> very enthusiastic about helping as well. Ellen Meijers ran the sound studio for us, and Chris
> Miles drew the character that became the icon of the game. Another friend, Brad Post, pulled
> an all-night programming shift with me to make sure that the Mac and PC versions were
> ready on the same day. This project was very unusual, and very special. (Ben's Game, http://
> express.howstuffworks.com/ep-ben-eric.htm).

Duskin's courage and compassion inspired Johnston to bring his own talents to bear on a game that alleviates the suffering of children who are undergoing cancer treatment. Though Duskin is only a child, his vision touched the hearts of many.

BACKPACKS FOR HUNGRY CHILDREN

Given the current economic crisis, food banks are stretched beyond their means, with people who used to donate to food pantries now among the needy recipients. Dina Denning, president of the Norwin Rotary, located in North Huntingdon, Pennsylvania, learned that between 25 and 135 students in her school district were without food when they left school on Fridays until they returned Monday morning when they would receive free hot lunches. She was heartbroken to learn that this situation existed. All 44 Rotary Clubs have a hunger project that funds local food banks as part of an annual program, but Denning's backpack project is still being researched to eliminate administrative fees so that every cent goes toward food for hungry kids. One concern that Denning has is identifying the impoverished child without stigmatizing them or their families. While the passion to serve is there, Frank Aiello, former Rotary district governor, said the program must be administered in an "extremely sensitive manner" (Norwin Rotary, 2010).

The proposed backpack program would furnish soups, juices, and microwavable items for the weekends. Denning received bids from the Westmoreland Food Bank for $30,000, which was later reduced to $20,000. While the Norwin Rotary provides dictionaries to third graders and scholarships to seniors, Denning believes some of the children the rotary intends to serve are not able to concentrate on their schoolwork in the first place because of hunger (Norwin Rotary, 2010).

Such local initiatives are conceived, structured, and administered because of the drive that individuals have to help the helpless, to lift up the fallen, and to address one at a time the needs of the community. College students during the holiday season adopt an "angel," a disadvantaged child, for whom they buy clothes or presents; on spring break, they board busses to inner cities or places like New Orleans following Hurricane Katrina to build or repair homes for Habitat for Humanity; or they initiate programs to feed and clothe children in programs like "Operation Bundle Up," which provides coats, boots, gloves, and scarves.

When an ordinary person steps forward to offer their imagination, time, money, or labor to improve the life of their organization, community, or unnamed neighbors, extraordinary good works can be accomplished. These individuals create a dynamic in which others are moved to action. This is persuasion through example. Jock Yablonski paid the ultimate price for his decision to address the corruption of the UMWA that had troubled his conscience. Ben Duskin's altruistic wish to alleviate the suffering of other children with cancer inspired a host of talented individuals to create a game where a superhero zapped cancer cells. Dina Denning through the Westmoreland Food Bank created a backpack program to feed children who would be hungry on weekends until they returned to their school lunch program on Monday morning. "Ethics is what we do when no one is looking" is a common expression and particularly applicable to persuasion through example. The deliberate decision to address corruption, to alleviate suffering, or to serve the needy is political power exercised in the purest sense of the word—whether your action exists on a national, state, local, or individual level.

SUMMARY

Political communication, also called deliberative communication, exists as public address that concerns itself with choosing among alternative candidates, courses of action, and ways and means. Political campaigns are part of this form of persuasion where candidates communicate their positions and programs to the people. Presidential rhetoric is also a part of this genre of communication where each leader constructs a political environment in which major decisions are made. The president's rhetoric creates both limitations and opportunities for him to exercise power, depending on the vision that he shares with the competing voices among the advocates that Habermas described as prime actors—other politicians, mass media, lobbyists, experts, intellectuals, and moral entrepreneurs who represent the public sphere, which overlaps the political arena. Freedom of speech and the press must exist for deliberative communication to be effective, because a lame press will result in muddied discourse. The media must function to assure that there is openness and accountability in government. The normative model of deliberative communication as outlined by Habermas also requires a vigilant and informed citizenry. Political discourse can become stilted or misdirected, but a concerted effort from all those involved in the process must search for clarity, purpose, and that "wild flow of messages" that Habermas described as emanating from the public sphere.

The role of media as the "fourth estate" in government or the "watchdog of the people" is essential to fulfill the functions outlined as surveillance, interpretation, linkage, transmission of values, and entertainment. Political communication is being reshaped as old channels of communication like television and newspapers are replaced or augmented by new ones like the Internet. New possibilities exist for an extended and enriched dialog with the Internet, allowing instant feedback to candidates and back to citizens. Entertainment forums have extended their influence into the political area with activist celebrities, satire, and comedy shows like *The Daily Show* with Jon Stewart and Internet videos such as the JibJab parodies all adding their messages to political discourse. Political commentaries formerly enjoyed by talk radio hosts like Al Franken, who is now a senator, and Rush Limbaugh, whom some see as the voice of the Republican Party, have competition for the audience's attention. Political communication is influenced by a convergence of the many streams of influence that were discussed throughout this chapter, including people that you have never heard of before. Jock Yablonski, the labor leader, reformed the UMWA by exposing the corruption of that mine workers' union before his death. An 8-year-old boy created a game that has been translated into many languages to help children cope with cancer, and Dina Denning has enlisted the Westmoreland County Food Bank to feed hungry children. Persuasion is at the heart of every campaign whether it exists on a national level or on your street.

APPLICATIONS

1. As a class project, view the presidential debates between President Barack Obama and Governor Romney. Assign one group to each debate to analyze (1) issues and their positions on them; (2) nonverbal components: proxemics, dress, voice, facial expressions, posture, etc.; (3) arguments made and evidence offered to support them; (4) credibility factors—trustworthiness, likeability, dynamism, and intellect; and (5) audience response to all of the above. After each group completes the analysis, compare findings across the groups, and look for similarities and differences. (Review Chapter 5 on nonverbal codes and message components.)

2. Write a paragraph describing your opinion of the candidate before you view the film, then view any of the convention films in class and analyze the appeals that were evident in the content, images, and style of presentation. What impression did the film leave upon viewers? Did you change your attitude about the candidate after viewing the film? Why or why not?

3. Go to the JibJab website (http://www.jibjab.com) and view the *This Land* parody from 2004 and later videos on the 2008 election. Discuss the videos in class and try to determine what effect it had as an example of visual rhetoric.

4. Choose a 527 group—Swift Vets and POWs for Truth (formerly Swift Boat Veterans for Truth, or SBVT) or another—and collect articles on them. Discuss their attacks or defenses during the 2004 campaign. What effect did they have on the outcome of the election?

5. Discuss the role of mass media in political discourse. Look at the five functions of media outlined in the chapter: surveillance, interpretation, linkage, transmission of values, and entertainment. Consider the benefits that each function brings to politics, and consider the dysfunctions that are evident as well. How well did media play their role in 2004 or 2008?

6. Summarize the deliberative paradigm that Habermas outlined. Consider his example of the rhetoric of "The War on Terror" and how mass media failed to reframe the debate; what did he mean? What other frame of reference might that debate have established? Why are these rhetorical frames important?

7. Choose a campaign that your campus sponsors. Identify the need that the campaign addresses and the human values that your work supports. What persuasive strategies are used to enlist students to join the effort?

8. Choose a local issue like a teachers' strike, school closing, or environmental issue. Analyze the rhetoric of the various factions involved. Who has offered better reasons for the position they take?

REFERENCES

Aristotle. (1932). *The rhetoric of Aristotle* (L. Cooper, Trans.). New York: Appleton-Century. (Original work 330 BCE)

Artz, L., & Kamalipour, Y. R. (Eds.). (2005). *Bring 'em 'on: Media and politics in the Iraq war*. New York: Rowman & Littlefield.

Balz, D. (November 7, 2012). Obama's coalition, campaign delivers a second term. Retrieved November 13, 2012, from: http://www.washingtonpost.com/politics/decision2012.

Beeson, L. L. (1978). *The rhetoric of regeneration by the Miners for Democracy*. (Unpublished doctoral dissertation). Pittsburgh, PA: University of Pittsburgh.

Benoit, W. L., Hansen, G. J., & Verser, R. M. (2003). A meta-analysis of the effects of viewing U.S. presidential debates. *Communication Monographs, 70*(4), 336–350.

Ben's Game. Retrieved December 21, 2010, from: http://express.howstuffworks.com/ep-ben-eric.html.

Blair, J. A. (2004). The rhetoric of visual arguments. In C. A. Hill & M. Helmers (Eds.), *Defining visual rhetorics* (pp. 41–61). Mahwah, NJ: Lawrence Erlbaum Associates.

Bohman, J. (1996). *Public deliberation.* Cambridge, MA: Massachusetts Institute of Technology.

Bohman, J., & Rehg, W. (Eds.). (1997). *Deliberative democracy.* Cambridge, MA: Massachusetts Institute of Technology.

Carter, S., Palmer, G., & Pilhofer, A. (2008). Campaign finance. *The New York Times,* September 20. Retrieved March 2, 2010, from: http://www.elections.nytimes.com/2008/president/campaign-finance/map.html.

D'Alessio, D., & Allen, M. (2002). Selective exposure and dissonance after decisions. *Psychological Reports, 91,* 527–532.

Dayton, S. (November 14, 2008). The Obama campaign's 'tech-savvy revolution. Retrieved March 2, 2009, from: http://pajamamedia.com/blog/the-obama-campaigns-revolution-in-using-technology/?print=1.

Edwards, J. L. (2004). Echoes of Camelot: How images construct cultural memory through rhetorical framing. In C. A. Hill & M. Helmers (Eds.), *Defining visual rhetorics* (pp. 179–194). Mahwah, NJ: Lawrence Erlbaum Associates.

Entman, R. M. (2004). *Projections of power.* Chicago: The University of Chicago Press.

Farmington mine disaster. (November 21, 1968). *Times-West Virginian.* Retrieved December 20, 2010, from: http://www.wvculture.org/history/disasters/farmington02.html.

Festinger, L. (1957). *A theory of cognitive dissonance.* Stanford, CA: Stanford University Press.

Gerguson, N. (2012). The losing habit: How long will the GOP stay in denial? *Newsweek,* November 19, p. 17.

Goldberg, B. (2002). *Bias: A CBS insider exposes how the media distort the news.* Washington, DC: Regnery Publishing.

Goldberg, M. (2012). The War on Women Backfires: Republicans Thought They Could Get Away with Endless Attacks on the Fairer Sex. They Couldn't Have Been More Wrong. *Newsweek,* November 19, pp. 56–59.

Habermas, J. (2006). Political communication in media society: Does democracy still enjoy an epistemic dimension? The impact of normative theory on empirical research. *Communication Theory, 14*(4), 411–426.

Harper, J. (2004). *The Washington Times,* October 21. Campaign spending nears $4 billion, a record level. Retrieved February 16, 2007, from: http://www.washtimes.com/national/20041021-113328-4826r.htm.

Jamieson, K. H. (1996). *Packaging the presidency: A history and criticism of presidential campaign advertising* (3rd ed.). New York: Oxford University Press.

Jamieson, K. H., & Campbell, K. K. (2006). *The interplay of influence: News, advertising, politics, and the internet* (6th ed.). Belmont, CA: Thomson Wadsworth.

Lewis, A. H. (1975). *Murder by contract: The people v. "Tough Tony" Boyle.* New York: Macmillan Publishing Co., Inc.

Lewis, J. L. (1937, September 3). Labor and the nation. United Mine Worker President's Speech. Retrieved July 23, 2012, from: http://www.american rhetoric.com/speeches/johnlewisrightsoflabor.htm.

Luckovich, M. (2007). Cartoon. *Atlanta Journal-Constitution.* Reprinted in *Newsweek,* February 12, p. 23.

Mackey-Kallis, S. (1991). Spectator desire and closure: The Reagan 18-minute film. *Southern Communication Journal, 56,* 308–314.

Mitt Romney—Full Bio. (August 30, 2012). Listitude Political Conventions Project. Retrieved November 2, 2012, from: http://www.listitude.com2012-Convention-videos.

Morreale, J. (1991). *A new beginning: A textual frame analysis of the political campaign film*. Albany, NY: State University of New York Press.

Morreale, J. (1994). American self images and the presidential campaign film, 1964–1992. In A. H. Miller & B. E. Gronbeck (Eds.), *Presidential campaigns and American self Images* (pp. 19–39). Boulder, CO: Westview Press.

Nixon, R. M. (1978). *The memoirs of Richard Nixon* (Vol. 2). New York: Warner Books.

Norwin rotary to help hunger struck students with Backpack Project. (Winter 2010). In *Norwin Community Magazine*, p. 30.

Obama: Biography Video/Convention Intro. (August 28, 2008). The National Democratic Party. Retrieved May 15, 2009, from: http://www.huffingtonpost.com/2008.08.28obamb-biography-video-at_n_122271.html.

OBAMA'08. www.barackobama.com. Barack Obama: Connecting and empowering all Americans through technology and innovation. Paid for by Obama for America. Printed in house.

O'Mally, G. (April 18, 2006). JibJab debuts stand-up social network. Retrieved January 29, 2007, from: http://publications.mediapost.com/index.cfm?fuseaction=Articles.showArticle&art_aid=42.

Pelofsky, J. (January 31, 2007). Biden starts White House run with controversy. Retrieved February 1, 2007, from: http://www.boston.com/news/nation/washington/articles/2007/02/01/biden_starts_white_ho.

Poulakos, J., & Poulakos, T. (1999). *Classical rhetorical theory*. Boston: Houghton Mifflin Company.

Schifferes, S. (June 12, 2008). Internet key to Obama victory. *BBC News*. Retrieved March 2, 2009, from: http://newsvote.bbc.co.uk/mpapps/pagetools/print/news.bbc.co.uk/1/hi/technology.

Shere, D. (November 8, 2012). Conservative media reveal their contempt for Americans who reelected Obama. Retrieved November 27, 2012, from: http://mediamatters.org/print/research/2012/11/08/.

Smith, B. L., Lasswell, H. D., & Casey, R. D. (1946). *Propaganda, communication, and the public opinion: A comprehensive reference guide*. Princeton, NJ: Princeton University Press.

Smith, R. J. (2005). The DeLay–Abramoff money trail. *Washington Post*, December 31. Retrieved February 2, 2007, from: http://www.washingtonpost.com/wp-dyn/content/article/2005/12/30/AR2005123001480_pf.

Spiridellis, E., & Spiridellis, G. (2004). *This Land: A parody of Woody Guthrie's "This Land."* Online video. Retrieved January 29, 2007, from: http://www.jibjab.com/originals/jibjab/moviedid/65.

Strachan, J. C., & Kendall, K. E. (2004). Political Candidates' Convention Films: Finding the Perfect Image—An Overview of Political Image Making. In C. A. Hill & M. Halmers (Eds.), *Defining visual rhetorics* (pp. 135–154). Mahwah, NJ: Lawrence Erlbaum Associates.

Usery, A. J., Jr. (December 21, 1969). Letter from Usery, assistant secretary of labor, to Joseph A. Yablonski, MFD Collection. American Labor Union History Archives. Detroit, MI: Wayne State University.

Vargas, J. A. (March 2, 2009). Web-savvy Obama team hits unexpected bumps. *The Washington Post*. Retrieved March 2, 2009, from http//www.washingtonpost.com/wp.dyn/content/article.2009/03/01/APR2009030101745_pf.

Vedantam, S. (2007). How deep a distaste for politicians who waffle? *The Washington Post*, January 22.

Wallace-Wells, B. (May 20, 2012). George Romney for President, 1968. Retrieved September 12, 2013 from: http://nymag.com/news/features/george-romney-2012-5/.

Wayne, L. (2012). Presidential race may be over, but not campaign finance stories. Retrieved November 19, 2012, from http://www//businessjournalism.org.

White, T. H. (1970). *The making of the president 1968*. New York: Pocket Books.

White, T. H. (1975). *Breach of faith: The fall of Richard Nixon.* New York: A Laurel Edition, Dell Publishing Co., Inc.

Windt, T. W. (1990). *Presidents and protesters: Political rhetoric in the 1960s.* Tuscaloosa: University of Alabama Press.

Wing, N. (October 30, 2012). Michael Moore's MoveOn video features elderly woman vowing to 'c**k-punch Mitt Romney (NSFW). *The Huffington Post.* Retrieved November 29, 2012, from: htttp://www.Huffingtonpost.com.

Winograd, M., & Hais, M. D. (2008). *Millennial makeover: MySpace, YouTube & the future of American politics.* New Brunswick, NJ: Rutgers University Press.

Wolf, G. (January 2004). How the internet invented Howard Dean. *Wired News,* Issue 12.01. Retrieved February 2, 2007, from: http://wired.com/wired/archive/12.01/dean_pr.html.

Wright, C. W. (Winter 1960). Functional analysis and mass communication. *The Public Opinion Quarterly, 24*(4), pp. 605–620. Retrieved February 4, 2011, from: http://www.jstor.org/stable/2746529.

Yablonski, J. A. (1969). Washington, D.C. MFD Collection, American Labor Union History Archives. Wayne State University. Detroit, Michigan.

CHAPTER 7

LEGAL COMMUNICATION: PERSUASION IN COURT

KEY WORDS

argumentum ad miseracordium	inoculation	Pygmalion effect
ATLA	*logos*	reluctant testimony
deliberative rhetoric	MOPs	self-fulfilling prophesy
epideictic rhetoric	narrative theory	*sophia*
ethos	*nomos*	territoriality
forensic rhetoric	nonartistic proofs	vocalics
	primacy-recency theory	*voir dire*

PREVIEW

In this media age, we are familiar with *Court TV* and *Judge Judy*, or the infamous trial of O. J. Simpson with his attorney Johnnie Cochran instructing jurors who watched the media-savvy O. J. struggle with the snarled glove, "If it does not fit, you must acquit." It is hard to separate such deliberations from theater, with villains and victims alike represented by some of the best legal experts in the country. Regardless of their training as lawyers, their success depends on not only their legal acumen but also on their rhetorical skills. Legal communication or preparation for forensic oratory has been tied to rhetoric since the times of classical Greece and the Roman Empire. This chapter discusses the marriage of rhetoric and the practice of law. Even though lawyers receive specialized training in jurisprudence, the rhetorical skills that they practice regularly are taught in undergraduate courses such as public speaking and argument with a focus on analysis, reasoning, evidence, organization, refutation, and delivery. In law schools these skills are enhanced in moot court proceedings in which all lawyers must participate to earn their degrees. In this chapter we review the sophistic tradition of forensic speech in Greece and move forward to the practice of law in contemporary courtrooms. The focus is on communication strategies to win the adherence of jurors, present a professional demeanor in court, and make a compelling case throughout the stages of the trial. The skills of storytelling or creating a convincing drama are reviewed

Court television, with witty judges like Judge Judy and Judge Joe Brown, is impacting the etiquette of court proceedings that legal scholars say diminishes the dignity of courts everywhere.

as appropriate legal talents. The work of the ancient philosophers is relevant to defining what courtroom oratory should accomplish as well as what the judicial process should offer in a democracy.

ARISTOTLE'S VIEW OF FORENSIC SPEECH

Aristotle wrote of the three forms of speech, in which the first form, **deliberative rhetoric**, was seen as essential to politics and government so that the practitioners should be familiar with all four forms of government—democracy, oligarchy, aristocracy, and monarchy (Aristotle, 330 BCE/1932, p. 44). **Epideictic rhetoric** was dedicated to virtue and vice, or praise and blame, so that audiences could learn from the speaker the virtues or vices of the intended subjects. The third form of rhetoric was **forensic rhetoric**, which was dedicated to accusation and defense of wrongdoing, its agents, and its victims, according to Aristotle. In this field of rhetoric, forensics, we find legal communication. Aristotle instructed his students that their arguments or syllogisms and enthymemes should contain three points: "first, the nature and number of the motives from which men do wrong; secondly, the states of mind in which they do it; and thirdly, the kinds of persons who are wronged, and their situations" (Aristotle, 1932, p. 55). The wrongdoing had to be deliberate and do harm, according to the universal laws of mankind or the laws of the state. The motives for doing wrong were dependent upon the vices or moral weaknesses of the perpetrator. The motives that Aristotle outlined would include

money, bodily pleasure, comforts, cowardice, to avoid danger, ambition, victory, revenge, lack of shame or regard for public opinion, or stupidity with the inability to distinguish right from wrong (Aristotle, 1932, p. 56). He gave seven reasons that men commit illegal acts: chance, nature, compulsion, habit, reason, passion, and desire (Aristotle, 1932, p. 59). Some people seem to think that they can engage in wrongdoing and avoid penalties because they can avoid detection. Aristotle named these people as able speakers, men of action or experience in legal matters, those who have many friends, and those who are rich (Aristotle, 1932, p. 67). Criminals think they can take advantage of their friends because friends are trusting and not on guard against abuse, and those who have judges as friends believe they will be shown favor by being acquitted or given lighter penalties (Aristotle, 1932, p. 68).

Aristotle said that the forensic branch of rhetoric used **nonartistic proofs** to persuade, which included five kinds of evidence: laws, witnesses, contracts, tortures, and the oath (p. 80). Laws were seen as either natural law, which was universal to all men, or laws of the state. Witnesses were divided into ancient witnesses and recent witnesses. Ancient witnesses were those whose judgments and views were already on the record, and these witnesses would establish precedent for contemporary judgments. Recent witnesses were useful only to establish whether an act occurred or not and were not concerned with whether the act was right or wrong, since the judges made that determination. If contracts were part of the case, the credibility of the agreement was the focus of argument with contracts being viewed as an extension of those who wrote it, signed it, and interpreted it. Aristotle defined torture as forcing a man against his will to testify, but he stated that a man may say anything to escape the ordeal and accuse others to save himself (p. 86). The last category of nonartistic proofs was oaths, which Aristotle divided into those tendered and those taken. You may take an oath to tell the truth or attempt to administer an oath to another. He went on to advise how to avoid perjury by refusing to take an oath, claiming it would be a religious affront, or one could claim that the oath was done under compulsion or trickery and was involuntary.

Aristotle's treatment of forensic speech or legal communication advises how to magnify the benefits to the side you choose and how to magnify the disadvantages to the adversary.

Forensic communication involves a combination of wisdom (*sophia*) and speech (*logos*)—with *logos* representing speech, argument, and reasoning. Philosophers like Leucippus and Democritus focused on the relationship between custom and law (*nomos*). Christopher Lyle Johnstone (2006) wrote:

> Such moral and political themes were taken up in earnest by the thinkers and teachers who resided in or were drawn to Athens in the fifth century BCE. Protagoras, Gorgias, Socrates, Antiphon, and others raised questions that were fundamentally political and moral: How should one live one's life? What are the values that should guide one's conduct? By what moral standards should our actions be judged, and how are these standards to be discovered? What legitimizes the laws that govern society? Are law and morality rooted in the nature of things, or are they merely matters of custom and convention? Such questions mark a shift in intellectual inquiry away from the sorts of naturalistic metaphysical, and ontological problems that preoccupied presocratic thinkers and toward a primary concern with matters of *praxis*, politics, and morality. (Johnstone, 2006, p. 266)

Today courts are the forum that we use to find justice for crimes committed or rights that have been denied, but the verdicts still concern the act, the motive, and the victim.

LEGAL COMMUNICATION IN THE TWENTY-FIRST CENTURY

If we were to fast-forward to the twenty-first century to attempt to define legal communication, we would find that the subject matter has not changed that much since the time of Aristotle. Certainly new technology has given us many more fields to consider in the courts, and the process has been increasingly complicated by procedural rulings, like whether or not to use cameras in the courtroom or how open the process should be to media overall. But the process still concerns wisdom and speech.

Susan J. Drucker (2005) offered four categories to define the parameters of legal communication.

1. Communication skills or communication within the legal system.
2. Communication about the legal system.
3. Rhetorical artifacts.
4. Regulation of communication. (pp. 13–14)

Drucker's first point was intrinsic to the legal system and dealt with forensic skills, which included establishing logical thinking and creating a narrative in the legal context, which would lead the opponent to accept the ending as a natural conclusion to the tale. In this category we see the most direct link to the field of rhetoric through the use of logic, instilling conviction, and the compelling organization of material to lead to the desired conclusion or verdict.

Drucker's second point, communication about the legal system, is external to the legal system and includes how the legal profession is covered in the news and entertainment industry. We think of all the court television dramas, the *Law and Order*–type shows, and contrast these perceptions with our own experiences in any legal matters. There is a vast difference between the neat resolutions that occur in the 60-minute program and actual courtroom proceedings, which may take years to resolve when court dates are changed or judgments are deferred because of one complication or another. Everyone is familiar with at least one lawyer joke, which demonstrates how typecast they are in media circles, yet every large corporation has a battalion of lawyers to protect their interests and to advise them.

Drucker's third point on law as a rhetorical artifact stated that the internal perspective of communication about the law views it as literature and rhetoric. The Constitution, the laws, judicial opinions, legal briefs, and arguments all produce rhetorical artifacts that can be studied to decipher meaning that provides understanding to human reason and decision making (p. 14).

Drucker's final point on regulation of communication dealt with the process by which legal communication "addresses rights, liabilities, privileges, duties, freedoms, and limitations on communication" (p. 14). Under this umbrella we find such issues as freedom of speech and media regulation. For example, should journalists have to give up their notes or offer up their sources? How free are you to say whatever you wish about anyone you wish to say it about? Ask Don Imus, who was suspended from his media job because of a racial remark that he made about the Rutgers women's basketball team, and you will find that there are restrictions on what one may say publicly about another, particularly if that subject is a private citizen or group and the remark appears to be malicious. Imus is back on the air, but he learned a lesson about limits on inflammatory speech.

Drucker's taxonomy of legal communication drew a distinction between skills and the substantive legal rulings, principles, and enactments within the legal field. This chapter addresses the skills that contribute to legal communication primarily and the rhetorical dimension of the practice of law.

CONFLICTING INTERESTS

The "scales of justice" must be weighed in some instances between the principle of a free press and a fair trial with the First Amendment, which states, "Congress shall make no law . . . abridging the freedom of speech, or of the press," and the Sixth Amendment, which asserts that "In all criminal prosecutions, the accused shall enjoy the right to a speedy and public trial, by an impartial jury of the State and district wherein the crime shall have been committed. . . .

Sometimes news media have inundated the public with pretrial publicity so that gag rules have to be imposed upon lawyers and other parties or the trial has to be moved to find a jury that has not been contaminated by constant coverage of the case, such as the Scott Peterson trial in California and the Casey Anthony trial in Florida. Through the years, various measures have been enacted to control the press, such as banning cameras from the courtroom, making journalists watch the trial from another room through closed-circuit television, or putting them in a designated space. Following the trial involving Charles Lindbergh's baby's kidnapping and murder, which was described as a media circus in 1935, many observers believed that the accused, Richard Bruno Hauptmann, did not receive a fair trial. The American Bar Association adopted a rule, Judicial Canon 35, in 1937 that prohibited radio broadcasting of trials and courtroom cameras. In 1965, the Supreme Court ruled that the case of Billie Sol Estes, on trial for fraud in Texas, was affected negatively by coverage of the preliminary hearings on television that probably prejudiced jurors. While their ruling did not ban television from the courtroom, it did have a chilling effect on such coverage for years. Federal courts have remained closed to cameras since 1946, but in state courts there is a high burden to show that proceedings should be closed. In 1981, the Supreme Court determined in *Chandler* v. *Florida* that cameras in the courtroom do not necessarily preclude a fair trial. Forty-eight states allow judges the discretion to determine whether or not cameras can be permitted to cover cases (*Chandler* v. *Florida* 449 Y,S, 560 (1980)). This debate on whether or not cameras motivate judges or lawyers to be theatrical at the expense of rational, professional behavior in the courtroom is regularly renewed by such trials as the Nicole Simpson and Laci Peterson cases or, more recently, the Anna Nicole Smith hearing where the judge wept openly as he appealed to the parties to consider their infant daughter's welfare.

The laws of the land are a work in progress, with new rulings adding to the details as cases move through the lower courts to appellate courts and finally to the Supreme Court, where landmark cases such as *Brown* v. *Board of Education* (1954) or *Roe* v. *Wade* (1973)

The publicity that surrounded the prosecution of Casey Anthony for the murder of her daughter did not deprive Anthony of a fair and impartial trial since she was found not guilty.

occur. Recently, the Supreme Court ruled that the names of jurors could be published or made public in a move to open up the judicial process further. Not long ago this author spent an entire day waiting to be selected as a jury member, but despite the fact that 150 were called and 45 were interviewed, only 6 were actually selected that day to serve on a trial. This collection of randomly selected citizens, who had been chosen by driver's license data and zip codes, included a cross section of men and women, from heavily tattooed hard hats to college professors, journalists, self-employed entrepreneurs, and retired citizens.

Whether one is a victim of a crime or the perpetrator who committed the crime, both are guaranteed representation in a court of law where the process will be enacted before a judge, a jury, or a panel of judges. The judicial branch of government is actualized through communication between these various factions according to a body of laws that have the force of the state but are open to interpretation, appeals, and sometimes revisions. While the process of conducting a trial or filing an appeal is very complex, some experts say that the whole outcome is dependent on whether or not the principal players present a good story. Let us turn our attention to the jury and how rhetorical tactics may work in that arena.

PERSUASION AND THE JURY

Anyone who depended on a jury to decide their fate may have reason to be fearful if they knew how bad jurors' memories really are. Reid Hastie, Steven Penrod, and Nancy Pennington (1983) conducted a postdeliberation study which showed that individual jurors' memory on trial facts was approximately 50 percent accurate and their memory of the judge's instructions was less than 30 percent accurate; other studies show findings similar to these. Such errors continued into the deliberation process. First, they also found that 90 percent of jurors had already decided on "a story model" of what had happened between the litigants before beginning deliberation (Call, 1996, p. 20). Their study showed that people are information seekers and story builders who attempt to make sense of what they see or hear based on what they already know about the world. Second, the "factual" information that a juror assimilates includes their beliefs about certain knowledge, for example, the effects of a certain drug and how it would impact an eyewitness's memory. These "facts" may be either accurate or inaccurate. Third, jurors' use of "strategic" knowledge—what is inside the juror's head and includes their style of thinking and how they organize and analyze data to reach a conclusion—forms the trial story for them. Jurors spend only about 20 percent of the time discussing the law in deliberations (Call, 1996, p. 20). In summary, jurors only remember half of the facts in a trial accurately, and they remember the judge's instructions less than 30 percent of the time. They have already formulated a storyline in their heads before they go into deliberations. This composite consists of what they remember from the trial and what they already thought they knew when they came into the trial.

STORYTELLING IN TRIALS

Murray Ogborn (1995) wrote an article entitled "Storytelling throughout Trial: Increasing Your Persuasive Powers," in which he analyzed the importance of telling stories that resonate with the jurors' own stories or life experiences. He identified three primary channels of delivery: verbal (words), vocal (how the message is delivered), and nonverbal (facial expressions, eye movements, or body positions) (p. 63). In communication theory we combine **vocalics,** that is, vocal properties such as pitch, dialect, resonance, and rate, as a nonverbal property; but Ogborn noted that jurors are generally biased in favor of one of these three channels: either what they see, hear, or feel, which can be observed as early as the jury selection process, or *voir dire*. Experts see three tasks to be performed at that stage: (1) information gathering, (2) indoctrination, and (3) creation of rapport (Ogborn, 1995, p. 64). The attorney must listen to the jurors and the stories they tell so that they can determine how to relate the narrative of their client during the trial. For instance, if a juror is a nurse who worked in an emergency room, she would be prone to understand a medical negligence case.

Gerry Spence wrote in the *ABA Journal* in 1986:

> Of course it is all storytelling—nothing more. It is the experience of the tribe around the fire, the primordial genes excited, listening, the shivers racing up your back to the place where the scalp is made, and then the breathless climax, and the sadness and the tears with the dying of the embers, and the silence. . . . The problem is that we, as lawyers, have forgotten how to speak to ordinary folks . . . lawyers long ago abandoned ordinary English. Worse, their minds have been smashed and serialized, and their brain cells restacked so that they no longer can explode in every direction—with joy, love, and rage. They cannot see in the many colors of feeling. The passion is gone, replaced with the deadly droning of the intellect. And the sounds we make are all alike, like machines mumbling and grinding away, because what was once free—the stuff of storytelling—has become rigid. (Spence, 1986, p. 62)

In a society that suffers from information overload, there is also information anxiety that deals with how overwhelmed we feel by the mass of it and our inability to access it, process it, or be comfortable with it. Attorneys should use scripts that are consistent with those that already exist in the heads of the jurors. Ogborn wrote: "Scripts are also a memory structure in that they let us act more or less by rote, without our being fully aware that we are using them. They are storehouses of knowledge we have about certain situations. They are collections of old experiences against which we measure new experiences of the same type" (Ogborn, 1995, p. 63). Storytelling achieves five goals in a trial:

1. To illustrate a point
2. To make the listener feel one way or another
3. To make other people experience certain sensations, feelings, or attitudes vicariously
4. To transfer some piece of information in our head into the head of the listener
5. To summarize significant events (Ogborn, 1995, p. 64)

The various stages of the trial enable the attorneys to present their story or drama with vivid imagery and language and to make it memorable for jurors, whose memories are faulty.

OPENING STATEMENTS

The **primacy-recency theory** of communication states that we remember best those facts that are made first and last in a presentation. In a courtroom, that means that the opening and closing arguments should be powerful. This primacy theory should be applied at trial because most people have developed a first impression in the first four minutes of the opening, Ogborn (1995) stated. The main story must be presented in the opening statement to jurors as early as possible for it to be effective, persuasive, and remain with them throughout the trial. The lawyer should use present tense and active verbs to engage jurors. Further, the rule of threes should be used, meaning that jurors understand information packaged in threes such as "faith, hope, and charity" or "life, liberty, and the pursuit of happiness" (Ogborn, 1995, p. 66). The opening statement is the first opportunity to give the jury the client's whole story and to set the stage for what is to come.

The direct examination phase of the trial is the epitome of storytelling, where the lawyer anticipates the questions from the jury and must ask the witness those questions during the process so that the story is compact, simple, and direct. If expert witnesses are used, their credentials should be presented as a storyline also. Frequently attorneys offer experts' credentials as something to be gotten out of the way, but the jurors would rather know why the engineer spent three years in Saudi Arabia than saying he spent three years in the Middle East (Ogborn, 1995, p. 65). The cross-examination phase of the trial exists to discredit the witness for the opposition, but that is not enough if the jury has no clue what story has been told or how the facts fit overall.

Roger Schank said memory is composed of memory organization packages (**MOPs**), which consist of context-dependent parts of memory of common experiences such as going on a date, having to go to the emergency room and fill out papers, or going to the dentist's office. These experiences conjure up immediate visual and auditory MOPs when only mentioned. Attorneys should attempt to elicit those MOPs that will lead to the desired persuasive efforts for their clients. Ogborn (1995) concluded that the final argument should retell the case story with appropriate morals and motives exposed. All three channels—visual, auditory, and kinesthetic—should be employed to complete the story so that the jury does not need to contemplate or reflect on the details; they must have already concluded that the plaintiff's story is most compelling.

Ogborn's practical advice is congruent with Walter Fisher's **narrative theory**, which simply states that humans have heard stories since birth and are conditioned to understand them even when they cannot follow Aristotelian logic. Ogborn's perspective is that a trial is an exercise in storytelling that requires skill in the timing, clarity, information flow, and persuasive strategies that are employed from the moment that the attorney sees the juror, gives the opening statement, examines the witnesses, cross-examines the opposition witnesses, and moves to the closing argument. Like a great work of literature, the characters are clear, the action, ills, and motives are identified, and the remedies should be self-evident.

CLOSING STATEMENTS

The closing arguments become definitive when the attorney is trying to get compensation for a client who has suffered a tragedy. Clients who have been injured by negligent drivers, hurt or killed in medical malpractice situations, or accidentally killed because of product failure need lawyers who can make technical jargon concrete and meaningful for jurors. Some effective tactics are to use analogies to clarify issues, to use repetition to reinforce juror's memories, and to use down-to-earth language that jurors can understand regardless of the issues in conflict. Here is an excerpt from a closing, showing an attorney's use of analogy to make a point about a client who was injured when a Southern Freightways truck struck her car and hurled her Volkswagen the length of a football field; then the defense attorneys for State Farm Insurance argued that she had a preexisting condition, so they were not responsible for her back injuries. Russ M. Herman, American Trial Lawyer Association (ATLA) president from New Orleans, included this analogy in his closing statement (the client's name has been changed for confidentiality reasons):

> With our common sense, let's suppose there is a pickup truck parked at a construction site where they are going to demolish something, and some dynamite caps are in that truck.

An out-of-control cement mixer trashes the pickup, and it explodes, and two or three houses in the neighborhood are damaged. The cement company says, "Wait a minute, I didn't know there were dynamite caps in that pickup, so I don't owe you anything. If the truck had been empty, your house wouldn't be damaged."

Is that a fair argument? Does that make sense?

That's what the 18-wheeler and State Farm are saying about Linda. "Linda had this condition, and she shouldn't have had it, so we're not responsible. We're only responsible," they say, "when we crash, bash, and trash a completely healthy person." Is that fair? (Turbak, Herman, Habush, Shar, & Gibbins, 1996, p. 54)

While this is a short excerpt, the rest of his closing was equally vivid with other stories that demonstrated the responsibility of the company to pay restitution to his client because they had injured her and done permanent damage to her which should be compensated because she had been victimized in the accident and then again by her own insurance company. He used an orange to demonstrate that, when one removed a slice from it, what looked whole on one side was in fact compromised by 10 percent, just like his client who was diminished in body function by a 10 percent disability. He used everyday activities and examples to reach the jury like eating breakfast, buying a painting, or taking care of one's family to establish his case that his client's life was compromised after the accident.

Often the attorney will use emotional appeals (**argumentum ad miseracordium**) or appeal to pity while denying the use of this tactic. Their pleas are always characterized as a call for justice. Numerous studies reported that jurors and certainly judges are not particularly impressed when attorneys rely heavily on pathetic appeals to win sympathy. The facts must speak for the need to redress a plaintiff's situation. Notice in the following excerpt from an actual trial the use of repetition of the word "money." The case involved the birth of twins in which the first infant was born healthy but the second one was deprived of oxygen and suffered brain damage during a 35-minute delay before the surgical team appeared to complete a cesarean section. Marcus Z. Shar of Baltimore, in his closing statement, told the jury:

Ladies and gentlemen, it is true that money will not give Bobby back the life that was so unfairly and unnecessarily taken from him just 35 minutes before he was born. It is true that money will not allow him to get out of his wheelchair and walk like other children. It is true that money will never take away the pain and the anguish that will now be his lifelong companions. But it is also true that money is the only form of justice that our system allows. At least give him that. (Turbak et al., 1996, p. 16)

A skilled attorney must be a practitioner of the fine art of persuasion, which employs logical arguments, appropriate emotional appeals, and the image of a competent, sincere professional. The impact that the arguments have on the jury is a holistic impression that will lead to their responding with more sympathy and credibility to one side than the other based on complex interrelated dynamics of communication from all parties, past experiences, and interpersonal relationships.

TRIAL AS THEATER

Mark I. Bernstein and Laurence R. Milstein go further than seeing a trial as a good story; they wrote an article, "Trial as Theater," in which they drew a lengthy parallel between a drama and a trial. "Both trials and live theater educate as they persuade by linking a series of events that appeal to human emotion" (Bernstein & Milstein, 1997, p. 64). It would be more accurate to say that a trial represented Aristotelian theater, or the well-made play, which has a beginning, a climax, and an end or resolution, because much of theater today is episodic and not orderly at all. A trial must have an orderly progression that leads inexorably to a conclusion for the client. A trial differs in two significant ways from a play—the characters are real, with genuine grievances, and, most significantly, the end of the drama is written not by the playwright or lawyer, to keep the analogy, but by the jury. This country has embraced trials as theater from its inception with the Salem Witch trials during colonial times, the Chicago Seven trial during the 1970s on antiwar riots, and in past decades the trials of Dr. Jack

Gloria Allred is known for her legal success in defending family rights and feminist causes against celebrities like O.J. Simpson, Michael Jackson, and even the Catholic church.

Kevorkian concerning physician-assisted suicide (Bernstein & Milstein, 1997, p. 64). The analogy is well developed and appropriate. They wrote:

> Both trials and theater afford us the opportunity to scrutinize private details of others' lives and to learn from them. The world's fascination with the O. J. Simpson trial attests to our cathartic and voyeuristic needs. Domestic violence, money, fame, murder, interracial relations, government conspiracy, perjury—could Euripides have devised a more intriguing plot? Once pulled in, our imaginations captured, we are ready to be educated and perhaps even enlightened.
>
> Not every trial provides the opportunity to reexamine social norms on a grand scale. Nonetheless, each trial contains a challenge to educate and influence an audience of jurors. Like the dramatic actor, the trial attorney has a story to tell. To do so, the courtroom's enormous opportunity for persuasion is available. Similar to a live theater, the physical courtroom provides a conducive setting for audience receptivity and, ultimately, identification with the properly presented story, theme, and characters. (Bernstein & Milstein, 1997, p. 64)

The courtroom sets the stage for the majestic play with the ornate oak walls, and the elevated position of the judge in the black robe situated as the seat of authority and wisdom. A transformation occurs when the judge ascends the bench and each juror is elevated to the role of public official. The ceremonial procedure adds to the solemnity of the event as the jurors become the conscience of the community. While the lawyer becomes the "producer, director, and actor" . . . "[S]he builds the story to its climax" (Bernstein & Milstein, 1997, p. 65). All the communication channels are engaged to make the performance credible, with the audience receiving 55 percent visually, 38 percent audibly, and 7 percent verbally (Mehrabian & Wiener, 1967, p. 108). Since a majority of the communication messages that a jury receives are carried on the nonverbal band, we should look at this form of communication more carefully.

NONVERBAL COMMUNICATION AS EFFECT

Mehrabian's formula, which stated that meaning is derived primarily through nonverbal means, motivates us to understand either those skills that communicate power, confidence, and authority, if that is what we want, or those skills that communicate rapport, trust, and likability when that is what we desire. Mary E. Ryan (1995), in an article "Good Nonverbal Communication Skills Can Reduce Stress," demonstrated her battle plan by outlining a strategy to effectively analyze what we hope to achieve in any given contingency. The first step was to set a goal, which would ultimately involve winning the case for the client in court, but there are incremental goals that must be achieved along the way that push the parties in that direction. The second step is analysis of the other person and of the environment in which the communication takes place. We know that the communication context is significant in that professional protocol is dictated by the setting. For example, the courtroom environment is adversarial between the prosecution and defense attorneys, formal, rule-driven, and recorded, where other settings may involve informal, confidential messages between cooperating parties, such as lawyer–client meeting or judge–attorney conferences.

The third step that Ryan outlined was the action phase where the lawyer either selects actions that will enhance his or her power, confidence, and authority or selects actions that will enhance rapport, trust, and likability.

We know from the animal kingdom that the territorial imperative is a powerful one that necessitates the defense and possession of personal space. Humans have learned to mask their defense and aggressive signals, but sometimes these actions, like dirty looks, marking space with personal possessions, or using civil inattention by treating another as a wall, are insufficient signals. Humans have moved beyond marking their territory like dogs with urine, but sometimes their possessive moves are about as overt as those of other primates. The body behaviors that Ryan (1995) outlined that increase the perception of power involve the use of territory and the interaction that occurs within a designated territory. She recommended the following:

1. Relaxation—especially lower body relaxation (for example, relaxed knee joints)
2. Purposeful movements—few extraneous gestures, little self-grooming (for example, playing with hair, fixing clothes)
3. Large silhouette—gestures that protrude to the sides of the body
4. Open-face posture—slightly raised chin, raised brow and widened eyes, relaxed mouth (Ryan, 1995, p. 73)

Territoriality is a basic set of behaviors that shows possession or defense in humans just as it does in animals, and we know that some animals dominate a scene while others are subordinate to them. In clashes such as the adversarial relationship between the prosecution and defense attorneys, the client wants to believe that their representation is equal to or superior to the opponent's. Powerful people control their space by appearing to be comfortable in it and not giving ground to another, whether in an intellectual or physical manner.

If the goal is to increase rapport, trust, and likability rather than demonstrating power, then the behaviors are different nonverbally. One way to establish rapport is to mirror the behaviors of the person with whom you are interacting. This does not mean mimicry, which would be an insult, but complementary behaviors. For example, a very calm and low-keyed person would be made uneasy by a hyperkinetic type who spoke loudly and was in constant motion. Nonverbal feedback is one way to build rapport (Ryan, 1995). Show the other person that you are listening to them with direct eye contact, backchanneling, like "Yes," or "Go on," and behaviors that build trust. Subtle cues, like checking your watch, tell another that they are out of time or you are rushed so the interaction is terminated.

There is no easy prescription for appropriate nonverbal communication since the rules are dependent on the context, the party with whom you are interacting, the culture in which you are interacting, and the relationship between the interactants. We do know that nonverbal messages are believed over verbal ones because our bodies are more honest than our mouths. However, in a courtroom or a legal proceeding, where credibility is everything, one can only be effective if they know that both verbal and nonverbal messages travel together to achieve the goal of winning adherence for your case and winning the respect of the judge and jurors.

THE ETHOS OF THE LAWYER

Of the three classic appeals in rhetoric, Aristotle believed that *ethos*, or the character of the speaker, was most important. It is the attorney's job to present a morality play in which the plaintiff is the good guy who has been wronged, and the defense is the bad guy who should be punished for his wrongdoing. The lawyer uses the opening statement to make a good impression. The jurors size the attorneys up immediately, because this impression management is composed of infinite details—how attractive the attorney is, how similar they are to the juror, how they dress, speak, move, and appear to treat them. Attorneys can "steal the thunder" of the opposition in the opening by inoculating the jurors against any bad news that is coming from the defense's side. John Call explained the inoculation process in this way:

> The inoculation concept derives from research that shows that listeners' resistance to persuasion increases if they are given a weakened version of an opposing argument and then shown how it may be refuted. In this instance the attorney provides the counter arguments to jurors and immunizes them against opposing counsel's persuasive attempts. (These techniques can also be used in persuasive writing such as trial briefs.) (Call, 1996, p. 21)

The use of forewarning and **inoculation** against a damaging piece of evidence enhances the credibility of both the attorney and the defendant. Similarly, when a witness raises a damaging piece of evidence about himself during testimony, it enhances his credibility. This would be **reluctant testimony**, which most people believe enhances credibility because we reason that a person would not voluntarily offer harmful information about himself unless it were true. This strategy allows the person offering the damaging material the opportunity to frame the argument, to refute it, and to minimize the power that would result from the opposition controlling the information and the context in which it is exposed.

Jurors remember emotional material better than they do factual material, so attorneys should present emotional arguments first and save the more boring details for later. The effects of two strong witnesses back to back can minimize their impact on the jury, so spacing such testimony and timing such testimony can work to advantage. The primacy-recency principle dictates that both the opening and closing presentations should be dramatic. "Scientific data also indicate that people better remember what they learn at the beginning (primacy) and at the end (recency) of a presentation. Key testimony should be placed in these locations" (Call, 1996, p. 23).

A lawyer's persuasiveness is associated with two qualities—credibility and attractiveness. Of the two, credibility is more important. Credibility is composed of intelligence, competence, trustworthiness, and good will. One's speaking style is part of establishing competence. Disfluencies and mispronunciations can signal lack of preparation, while a dynamic speaker comes across as powerful, knowledgeable, and enthusiastic. Hedges like "I think," or qualifiers such as "well," "you know,"or "I guess" are perceived as powerless speech, and studies show that awards to plaintiffs are negatively affected by this form of communication. Hesitation forms such as "uh," "um," and "well," or an intonation that signals a question by a rising inflection at the end of sentences, show uncertainty. Polite forms of address such as "Sir," "Madam," or "Please" show deference or a power hierarchy, and qualifiers such as "very," "definitely," and "surely" can be overused and show the speaker lacks weight and is not to be taken seriously (Conley, O'Barr, & Lind, 1979, p. 1375).

The "**Pygmalion effect**" involves a behavioral style that attorneys should use to signal that they expect to win based on auto-suggestion and **self-fulfilling prophesy,** which influences jurors to reach this belief also (Call, 1996, p. 26). In Greek legend we know the story of a king of Cyprus who fell in love with the statue of a maiden, who was brought to life after hearing his prayers; later, the George Bernard Shaw play *Pygmalion* (1912) showed how Eliza Doolittle was transformed from a vulgar flower girl to a refined, beautiful lady. So the Pygmalion effect involves a transformation of an object, person, or thing into the desired outcome. The attorney who creates and presents a case with the expectation that they will win the support of the judge and the jury is more likely to do so, making their fervent hope a self-fulfilling prophesy or reality.

Attractiveness is a component of credibility, because physically attractive people are thought to be more intelligent, friendly, and persuasive than less attractive others. This phenomenon is obvious even in kindergarten, where this "halo effect" leads teachers to believe that pretty children are smarter, nicer, and less likely to misbehave. The stigma of ugliness or obesity is often denied, but still both conditions are evident in America where attractiveness is associated with youth and beauty. The opposite can be true as well, where people with extraordinary good looks are thought to be superficial and vacuous, or "airheads."

Daniel Linz, Steven Penrod, and Elaine McDonald (1986) found that the greater an attorney's trial experience, the greater their misperception regarding how they affected jurors in their opening statements in relation to communication skills, organization, and arrogance (Call, 1996, p. 27). Surprisingly, as lawyers become more comfortable and confident in their work, they may lose sight of themselves and their effect on others. Such self-monitoring could be expanded through video-taping presentations and peer review in continuing education opportunities. Linz et al. (1986) reported that, generally, prosecuting attorneys ranked higher on communication skills than defense attorneys did. They wrote:

> The finding that greater trial experience actually leads to greater inaccuracies in self-perception among defense attorneys might mean that in the absence of accurate feedback, defense attorneys are adopting feedback strategies that result in an inflated perception of their performance. Defense attorneys may be attending to and remembering feedback that confirms rather than disconfirms positive conceptions they have of themselves (Swann & Read, 1981a, 1981b). Even when they receive feedback that disconfirms their self-conceptions they may interpret it in ways that minimize its impact (Crary, 1966; Markus, 1977; Shrauger & Lund, 1975). It is also possible that defense attorneys actively create self-confirmatory environments around themselves (Swann & Read, 1981a, 1981b). Once these self-impressions are created they may be highly resistant to subsequent change (Rosenhan, 1973; Ross, Lepper, & Hubbarad, 1975; Walser, Berscheid, Abrahams, & Aaronson, 1967). (Linz, Penrod, & McDonald, 1986, p. 299)

In summary, attorneys should adopt strategies that will establish their credibility and competence immediately in the trial. This impression is composed of a broad mixture of verbal, nonverbal, and interactive dimensions of communication, which includes the juror's perceptions of how attractive, trustworthy, and dynamic the attorney is based on cognitive, attitudinal, and behavioral messages sent and received.

PERSUASION AND THE JUDGE

Courtroom shows like *Judge Judy* and *Judge Joe Brown* have led to negative behaviors in the actual courtrooms. Professor David Papke said that such courtroom shows have led to ruder parties and less respect for both the court and the judge (Hoskins, 2007, p. 1). One judge was so upset that he wanted to censor and suppress such shows because he thought they were harmful to courtroom decorum. In a conference in Illinois, judges told Papke that they instruct jurors not to expect what they see on television in such dramas as *Perry Mason*, *Law and Order*, and *CSI*.

No one can deny the effect that pop culture has on the courtroom, since opinions and arguments often integrate characters from television like *Animal House*, *American Pie 2*, *Hogan's Heroes*, and *Borat*; however, not everyone is enamored of pop culture references in legal proceedings. They are more persuaded by productions from law libraries than from The Juilliard School. In a July 2005 opinion, Court of Appeals Judge Michael Barnes wrote a dissenting opinion in the case *Breeding* v. *Kyle's Inc.*, in which he reminded the court that the controversy was over a contract for the rental of a hall and not a contract for disc jockey services. Barnes, in a footnote, cited the songs "Heard It through the Grapevine," "(I Can't Get No) Satisfaction," and "Let It Be"—among others (Hoskins, 2007, p. 1). The most frequent

The television show *Law and Order* fascinated the American public by depicting the prosecution and defense of criminals and presented current stories found in headlines.

artists quoted for song lyrics are Bob Dylan, Bruce Springsteen, the Beatles, as well as others like Paul Simon, Woody Guthrie, the Rolling Stones, the Grateful Dead, Simon and Garfunkel, and R.E.M. (Hoskins, 2007, p. 1). The problem with such references is that the lyrics are not meaningful for all generations. In one such gangsta rap reference, the court reporter wrote "hoe" as a garden tool, when the reference was to a "ho," a term with which she was not culturally or semantically familiar.

It seems obvious that lawyers should respect the judge who will preside and referee the proceedings that can become heated and complex at times, but some attorneys take liberties that can backfire on their clients and impugn their own professional standing. Some lawyers are so concerned with the witnesses or the jury that they forget to pay attention to the judge. Jenny Davis (2002) spelled out what RESPECT means in the courtroom in an article, "Winning Ways with Judges." Her advice is outlined in the June issue of *ABA Journal*. Showing respect for the judge throughout the proceedings is a fundamental concept like "gravity and relativity." If the attorney can customize and streamline the presentations, it can save time and be effective. Judges are persuaded by the same things that jurors are, such as visual aids, analysis of the credibility of evidence, and appeals to rationality. The attorney should avoid flip comments or extemporaneous answers such as, "that's absurd," "that's preposterous," or beginning sentences with "clearly." Practicing law is not just about having quick answers or applying labels, but about knowing the law and having the facts of the case. If the attorney makes a mistake, an apology coupled with a remedy may work well with the judge, who will be spared having to take more drastic measures. When challenged on evidence, if the source of the information is cited, this action highlights the data and makes the clash more professional and less personal. For example, "Judge, this isn't coming from me, it's what the 8th

 circuit said" (Davis, 2002, p. 54). Honesty is the best policy if the attorney is unable to answer a question or makes a mistake. "Honesty means you don't quote part of a holding and end the quote before the word 'however'" (Davis, 2002, p. 55). That would constitute citing out of context, or if the finding has been overruled or distinguished you simply accept the fact that you cannot know all the answers and admit this to the judge. Davis's last piece of advice was "don't take abuse." Some judges enjoy their power, but if you treat the judge with respect, they should treat you with respect as well. Irving Greines, a Los Angeles appellate lawyer, advised attorneys to take a courteous, sincere stance and suggested the following approach when there is impatience from the judge: "Your honor, it seems to me that you're losing your patience with me. I am here to represent my client the best that I can, but I believe you may be angry with me" (Davis, 2002, p. 57). Greines's admonition was not to let the hostility of one judge throw you off track. He said that a 2–1 decision is still a win.

SUMMARY

Forensic communication goes back to the ancient Sophists, who taught their pupils to argue both sides of an issue and to be persuasive in their examination of cases. Aristotle discussed crimes according to motives, victims, and the kinds of proof that should be used to both prosecute and defend citizens. Legal communication includes the day-to-day proceedings in courts across the land, the record that is established to be studied and reviewed as artifacts, what media communicates about the justice system, and regulations on communication such as defamation, First Amendment challenges, and federal statutes. Sometimes there are conflicts between the First Amendment, which guarantees free speech and press, and the Sixth Amendment that guarantees a fair and speedy trial. We see these conflicts in high-profile cases wherein the judge has the discretion to impose a gag rule, move the trial, or close some stages of the trial and open others or impose restrictions on how access will be gained by the media. Legal studies have drawn analogies between trials and theater or story-telling where the characters have conflicting roles that must be resolved by the end of the drama; the difference between theater and trials is that the characters are real people and the jury gets to write the end of the play. The principle vehicle for enacting this drama is to offer prosecution and defense teams who are in charge of producing and directing the action, scenery, and storyline. The strategic method of communicating the lines is through rhetorical address, which means that one side must be more persuasive than the other side to win the case. The judge is supposed to be a wise and impartial referee for the process, which enlists jurors or ordinary citizens as the conscience of the community who enforce the rules of justice, forgiveness, or fair compensation. The opening and closing statements of the trial are most memorable and deserve special attention to design and plot. While courtroom presentations are dramatic, they are not like television renditions where everything has to be solved in 60-minute episodes. The wheels of justice turn slowly, and some find themselves out of resources before the process addresses their grievances. The statue of the blind lady of justice with a scale in one hand speaks to the need for the balance of evidence to tip according to weight and preponderance of fact regardless of race, class, or power, since none of us is either above or below the law that she is supposed to symbolize.

APPLICATIONS

1. Research the O. J. Simpson trial and the public reports of it at the time it was held. What caused such divergent views between white Americans and African Americans about the verdict?
2. Attend a criminal trial at your local courthouse, and pay particular attention to the opening arguments, the behavior of the jurors, and the communication skills of both the prosecutor and the defense attorney. What communication strategies could you identify that the parties used to adapt to the jurors in the trial?
3. Discuss the effect of cameras in the courthouse. Do you think the presence of the media affects the performance of the judge or the attorneys?

REFERENCES

Aristotle. (1932). *The rhetoric of Aristotle* (L. Cooper, Trans.). New York: Appleton-Century-Crofts, Inc. (Original work 330 BCE)

Bernstein, M. I., & Milstein, L. R. (1997). Trial as theater. *Trial, 33*(10), 64–69.

Call, J. A. (1996). Making the research work for you (Jury Persuasion). *Trial, 32*(4), 20–27.

Chandler v. Florida 449 U.S. 560 (1980).

Conley, J. M., O'Barr, W. M., & Lind, E. A. (1979). The power of language: Presentational style in the courtroom. *Duke Law Journal, 1978*(6), 1375–1399.

Crary, W. G. (1966). Reactions to incongruent self-exiences. *Journal of Consulting Psychology, 20*, 246–252.

Davis, J. B. (June 2002). Winning ways with judges. *ABA Journal, 88(6)*, 50.

Drucker, S. J. (2005). Legal communication: A review in search of a field. *Legal Communication, 5(1)*, 12–24.

Hastie, R., Penrod, S. D., & Pennington, N. (1983). *Inside the jury*. Cambridge, MA: Harvard University Press.

Hoskins, M. W. (2007). Pop culture's place in law: Attorneys, judges use movies, music to supplement legal arguments. *The Indiana Lawyer*, February 21. IBJ Corporation. Retrieved May 17, 2007, from http://wf2la7.webfeat.org/KSeoH1237/url=http://web.lexis-nexis.com/universe/printdoc.

Johnstone, C. L. (2006). Sophistical wisdom: *Politike Arete* and *"Logosophia." Philosophy and Rhetoric, 39(4)*, 265–289.

Linz, D., Penrod, S., & McDonald, E. (1986). Attorney communication and impression making in the courtroom: Views from off the bench. *Law and Human Behavior, 10(4)*, 281–302.

Markus, H. (1977). Self-schemata and processing information about the self. *Journal of Personality and Social Psychology, 35*, 63–78.

Mehrabian, A., & Weiner, M. (1967). Decoding of inconsistent communication. *Journal of Personality and Social Psychology, 6(1)*, 109–114.

Ogborn, M. (1995). Storytelling throughout trial: Increasing your persuasive powers. *Trial* 31.n, 8, 64. Retrieved May 17, 2007, from http://find.galegroup.com/itx/infomark.do?&contentSet=IAC-Documents&type=retrieve&tabID=T0020&prodId=EAIM&docId=A17218543&source=gale&srcprod=EAIM&userGroupName=upitt_main&version=1.0.

Rosenhan, D. L. (1973). On being sane in insane places. *Science, 179*, 250–258.

Ross, L., Lepper, M., & Hubbard, M. (1975). Perseverance in self-perception and social perception: biased attributional processes in the debriefing paradigm. *Journal of Personality and Social Psychology, 32*, 880–892.

Ryan, M. E. (1995). Good nonverbal communication skills can reduce stress. *Trial, 31(1)*, 70–75.

Shrauger, J. S., & Lund, A. K. (1975). Self-evaluation and reactions to evaluation from others. *Journal of Personality, 43*, 94–108.

Spence, G. L. (1986). How to make a complex case come alive for a jury. *ABA Journal, 72(4)*, 62–67.

Swann, W. B., & Read, S. J. (1981a). Acquiring self knowledge: The search for feedback that fits. *Journal of Personality and Social Psychology, 41*, 1119–1128.

Swann, W. B., & Read, S. J. (1981b). Self verification processes: How we sustain our self-conceptions. *Journal of Personality and Social Psychology, 17*, 351–372.

Turbak, N. J., Herman, R. M., Habush, R. L., Shar, M. Z., & Gibbins, B. (April 1996). Closing arguments: Persuasive endings (Jury Persuasion). *Trial, 32(4)*, 48–60.

Walser, E., Berscheid, E., Abrahams, D., & Aaronson, V. (1967). Effectiveness of debriefing following deception experiments. *Journal of Personality and Social Psychology, 6*, 371–380.

CHAPTER 8

RELIGION AND PERSUASION

KEY WORDS

anomie	logology	conversion
apocalyptic rhetoric	millennium	discernment
creation narrative	modernity	exile
eschatology	mortification	praise
establishment clause	naturalism	secularization
evangelists	nonviolent resistance	Tanakh
free will	postmodernism	theism
ideology	rhetoric of:	utopian
Koran	communion	

PREVIEW

In 1957 **evangelist** Billy Graham announced his "crusade" in New York City, which he nicknamed "Sodom on the Subway," referring to the cities of Sodom and Gomorrah in biblical times that were destroyed by fire because of the sinfulness of the people living there (Butler, 2006, p. 51). Graham hoped for a "revival" that would reawaken the religious devotion from an earlier America. Where in this nation might we find more diversity in religious practices than in New York? Christians, Jews, Muslims, Haitian practitioners of voodoo, Hindus, and Sikhs are creating or redefining sacred spaces. Part of the explanation for religion's survival is **syncretism**, or the combination and reconciliation of differing beliefs and philosophies that generations have merged. For example, enslaved Africans would merge Christian beliefs and African traditions such as the response-and-call practices into their services in the African American communities. African Cuban immigrants made cramped apartments into sacred spaces in New York and New Jersey, shaping their environment to serve their needs (Butler, 2006, p. 57). Other denominations refused assimilation and isolated themselves, building like-minded communities in America.

Reverend Billy Graham called New York City "Sodom on the subway" and preached to thousands there in 1957.

This chapter explores the confrontations and compromises that religious positions impose upon public discourse in this country through the examination of Judeo-Christian **ideology** and the challenges to traditional religious practices or beliefs by atheists, agnostics, and competing religious groups. As diversity in religions emerge, debate regarding fundamental rights and tolerance for this diversity engulfs the public sphere. The most intense battles have always been over competing values, so it is not surprising that the public schools and town halls have become the territory for heated debates and legal interventions. Religious rhetoric can be divided into two major categories—**utopian** and **apocalyptic**—which may be seen as two sides of the same vision. When the promise of a heaven on earth does not materialize, then visions of the end times are resurrected and prophesied. When Thomas More created the word "utopia" he drew from two possible Greek prefixes, with one meaning "no-place" and the other meaning "good place" (Schultze, 2003, p. 50). We know that humans through the ages have searched for the perfect place, but none exists on this earth, although utopian rhetoric assumes that humans can strive to make progress toward that world. In American religious thought we find recurring references to "A City upon a Hill," which is taken from Jesus's Sermon on the Mount, and Puritans in New England saw the frontier as a society transformed according to Christian ethics (Mixon, 1989, p. 1). The opposite vision involves the coming of the apocalypse, which the Puritans inherited from the millennial beliefs in western Europe. In theology, the **millennium** is the thousand years when Satan is prophesied to be bound and Christ will rule the earth. The sermons of John Cotton, delivered in Boston between 1634 and 1641, examined the book of Revelation as a blueprint for God to take control of the earth (Mixon, 1989, p. 2). Let us examine the characteristics of apocalyptic rhetoric as manifested in earlier America and heard as recently as the year 2000 when the Y2K scare shook our technological base.

THE RHETORIC OF THE FIFTH MONARCHY: APOCALYPTIC RHETORIC

Eschatology is that branch of theology that deals with end things like death, resurrection, immortality, and judgment day. In other words, eschatology focuses on those mysteries that can only be known through belief in the sacred texts or that "leap of faith" that is required to accept that which is beyond human experience during this life. A movement emerged in England following the death of Charles I in 1649 called The Fifth Monarchy that was based on the book of Daniel, the seventh chapter, which divided world history into four kingdoms, or monarchies, with the fifth one ushering in the kingdom when Christ would come to rule directly over human affairs. This belief in the Fifth Monarchy, the rule of Christ, gained currency with some prominent colonists. Reverend John Cotton, a prominent minister of that time, preached a series of sermons from 1639 to 1641 in Boston that reflected ideas from the New Testament book of Revelation. Puritans believed that at long last God would achieve a complete reformation in the wilderness that would conform to his divine plan (Mixon, 1989, p. 2).

Frederick Kreuziger offered a functional analysis of apocalyptic rhetoric. Kreuziger stated that apocalyptic rhetoric is best explained in the "language of disjunctive expectation." Disjunctive logic offers an either/or condition of alternative realities. Apocalyptic rhetoric begins with a promise. When that promise is broken or does not materialize, there is disillusionment. This disillusionment can be expressed in three kinds of expectations: first are simple expectations, which see the future as an extension of the present; the second expectation is a future where the present efforts have a cause–effect relationship on the outcome; and finally, a third expectation that is neither an extension of the present nor a cause-and-effect relationship, but something entirely different that includes the apocalyptic expectation, such as the end of life as we know it. The disjunctive expectation is to offer hope toward the fulfillment of the promise that is "imminent," breaking at any moment without further warning (Mixon, 1989, pp. 2–3).

Now how does apocalyptic rhetoric relate to Puritan beliefs? They had expected the Reformation in Europe to return the church to a new covenant with God, but that did not happen. Thus they grew disillusioned when England, which had offered the greatest hope for them, failed. They believed that the stage was set for their "city set upon a hill" to offer a reformation that was both sudden and dramatic, not a continuation of the present nor a slightly engineered change from the status quo. Reverend John Cotton believed the millennium was at hand as the current calamities ushered in the apocalypse, which he dated to come in 1655. "He predicted the quick emptying of the last two vials, followed by Armageddon, when God's enemies would be subdued, ushering in the full glory of the gospel and inaugurating a church policy for which New England Congregationalism was a prototype" (Mixon, 1989, p. 4). Other Puritans turned to affairs that they could actually manage, while others seemed to believe that even if the prophesies were accurate, the time frame was God's and not properly theirs to control. Cotton continued to express the apocalyptic visions up to the time of his death in 1652, but the belief in the Fifth Monarchy waned throughout his lifetime, and 1655 passed undramatically. The apocalyptic vision continued with prophesies that the government would continue to grow more and more corrupt until Christ would come to reign, with God taking control of human affairs—even if God's timetable was different from that of the believers (Mixon, 1989, p. 4).

Apocalyptic rhetoric has continued into contemporary affairs, such as global warming, the Y2K rollover in 2000, when all computers were predicted to fail, and the current terrorist threat to the United States, with radical Islamists leading the attack in 2001 in New York. Barry Brummett (1991) explained the origin of the word "apocalyptic," which means "lifting the veil, or revelation" (p. 31). Brummett wrote:

> It is derived from the Greek *apo*, from or away, and *kalupsis*, covering, or *kalumma*, veil" (Robinson, 1985, p. xii). What is revealed is the secret order or structure actually underlying what has lately seemed to be a chaotic world. Apocalypse therefore "means the unveiling of secrets; and apocalypse means the unveiling of secrets about this 'other' age, this 'other' world" (Barrett, 1953, p. 138). (Brummett, 1991, p. 31)

Apocalyptic discourse thrives when there is great change or perceived disorder or "from a resulting sense of **anomie**, disorientation, lawlessness, and impending chaos" (Brummett, 1991, p. 23). Brummett described the context that nurtures apocalyptic rhetoric. First, the threat or change is *unexpected*. Second, the change must be *inexplicable*. That is, standard systems of belief or explanations of history fail to bring meaning, and there is a "perceived collapse of social order and authority" (p. 25). All of these taken together result in a "sense of *anomie*, of lawlessness and chaos." Brummett discussed the cosmic vision that is characteristic in apocalyptic rhetoric. First, "history is linear and telic," meaning that history proceeds toward a final goal (pp. 32–33). The Christian and Jewish ideology embraces the assumption that "there is a whole purpose of God for the universe from the creation to the end-time" (Russell, 1960, p. 97; Brummett, 1991, p. 33). This notion means that "everything is predetermined and all human decisions are only sham struggles" (Buber, 1957, p. 201). For example, writers like LaHaye (1972) assert that the future of the Middle East was clearly predicted by the prophet Ezekiel; Kirban believed the book of Revelation prophesied the ecological woes of today (Brummett, 1991, p. 36). One prevailing characteristic of apocalyptic rhetoric is that when the world seems to be in such a chaotic state that no traditional comprehension of what path to follow is clear, then audiences embrace a master plan that was there all along but now gains fervent belief. According to

Brummett (1991), there exist both premillennial and postmillennial strategies in apocalyptic discourse. He wrote:

> The apocalypse is both a change and a revelation. It is the moment in which history culminates, and is culminating, the grand plan underlying history is revealed. I would stress that in any view, the apocalypse is a *moment*; it is sudden, decisive, and quickly finished (although nothing remains the same hereafter). For Christians, the apocalypse occurs at the Second Coming of Christ (the parousia). For Jews, it is the arrival of the Messiah. For New Age mystics, it is the moment in which full enlightenment and thus complete spiritual unity are achieved. For economic apocalyptists, it is when the current economic system collapses totally. For ecological apocalyptists, it is a climactic moment in which the damaged environment changes suddenly. (Brummett, 1991, p. 48)

Premillennialists are concerned with the events before the apocalypse, which they expect to come soon. Premillennial adherents believe history is about to climax, and a joyful age is coming. Postmillennialists are vague about history and tend to disguise their discourse by defining a gradually evolving new age with discourses such as Marxism or Nazism (Brummett, 1991, p. 52). Billy Graham was a typical apocalyptic preacher who spoke of the chaos in the world and suffering of people, but the good news was that they ultimately will be delivered from it. Graham told audiences to expect pain and suffering, but that by facing up to the pain in the long term, they will be saved because God is still in control of their destiny: "He has a plan" (Brummett, 1991, pp. 54–55).

Utopian visions and apocalyptic prophesies continue as major themes in religious rhetoric, with other variations on these two major paradoxes. We examine five of these genres that were identified by Quentin J. Schultze.

THE RHETORIC OF CONVERSION, DISCERNMENT, COMMUNION, EXILE, AND PRAISE

Quentin J. Schultze (2003), in *Christianity and the Mass Media in America*, identified five forms of rhetoric used by Christian groups to attract, engage, and convert people through the use of mass media organizations. These themes included the rhetoric of **conversion, discernment, communion, exile,** and **praise.** Here, we examine each of these forms further.

THE RHETORIC OF CONVERSION

The rhetoric of conversion is most prominent in sermons that call for a turn away from the sinful ways of the world and toward the path of righteousness. This form of persuasion is most dominant in all sermons. The rhetoric of conversion, according to Alvin W. Gouldner, replaced the ritual of mass with the exhortation of the sermon which was a paradigm of energetic and righteous persuasion intended to mobilize men to deeds (Schultze, 2003, p. 10). This rhetoric included both faith and commerce, which used persuasion, propaganda, and evangelism to further the Protestant impulse through sermons like Jonathan Edwards's graphic appeals to be saved from eternal damnation in colonial America.

The Four Horsemen of the Apocalypse that are described in the book of Revelation represent war, famine, disease, and death.

The rhetoric of conversion continued into the twenty-first century through televangelists who co-opted the methods of ad men to spread their messages to anonymous millions through television ministry. The most enduring metaphor used in the utopian vision of the Protestant earthly paradise was the City upon a Hill, which Governor John Winthrop of Massachusetts defined for Puritans, and this vision was revived by Ronald Reagan three centuries later to describe a beacon of liberty to the rest of the world where communists and other villains threatened the New Jerusalem (Schultze, 2003, p. 13). In this form of rhetoric, America is the new promised land where there is an opportunity to build a utopian society that is God- fearing, just, and free from the old world miseries of class consciousness and royal corruption.

THE RHETORIC OF DISCERNMENT

The rhetoric of discernment is used by religious groups to differentiate their brand from others as the tensions and disagreements grow in our multicultural society. Both Protestants and Roman Catholics participate in efforts to gain financial support as well as solidarity in a society that is increasingly driven by special interests according to "gender, sexual orientation, leisure activities, political issues such as gun control and abortion, and probably thousands of others" (Schultze, 2003, p. 17). These differences can be transcended as long as they do not challenge the "sacred" nonnegotiables that are fundamental to Americans, such as hope and freedom or the fundamental tenets of the faith. Other religions, like Islam, are challenging the dominance of Christians in America through international networks. Black Muslims in the United States experienced growth through the last four decades, often converting prisoners to the faith, like Malcolm X, who became a leader and spokesperson for the group in the United States before he was assassinated. Other, more sinister sects are fundraising for such endeavors as terrorism to eradicate the "infidels" or the entire United States under the guise of benign organizations. There are threats to the Judeo-Christian paradigm both within the United States and abroad.

THE RHETORIC OF COMMUNION

The rhetoric of communion supports the need for unity amid growing cultural and ethnic diversity. St. Augustine wrote that we reside in two worlds, the "City of Man" and the "City of God" (Schultze, 2003, p. 24). This dual allegiance can be threatening, so mass media was enlisted to build cohesion.

> The mainstream media's rhetoric of communion entered the cultural contest for social status as well, creating a phenomenal national system of fame, celebrity, and popularity. Although the secular media pay attention occasionally to national religious figures such as Billy Graham, they focus primarily on entertainers, newsmakers, and experts. Americans were inclined to identify themselves with particular consumption communities as much as with religious, ethnic, or other traditionally defined groups. (Schultze, 2003, p. 26)

When religious leaders began to use mass media in the early days of radio, their intentions were to reach small congregations within signal reach, with statistician Roger W. Babson urging them to pattern their outreach efforts after chain stores (Schultze, 2003, p. 164). The Federal Communication Commission opened up the less desirable FM stations to nonprofit groups such as religious broadcasters. By 1973 there were 111 radio stations in the United States that offered religious programming, but by 1976 there were 341 such stations; by 1970, 449 religious stations; and by 1983, 1,052 religious stations in America (Schultze, 2003, p. 165). In the early days of Christian broadcasting, it was believed that the programs had to be as universal as possible, nonsectarian, with the goals "to promote the spiritual harmony and understanding of mankind and to administer broadly to the varied religious needs of the community" (Schultze, 2003, p. 158). With the growth in religious media outlets, narrowcasting occurred, with programs explicitly designed for various interest groups.

THE RHETORIC OF EXILE

Many twentieth-century Christians felt a growing alienation from the national consumer culture. The rhetoric of exile reflects the core values of Christians, who believe that the cultural environment is hostile to their faith community; like the exile of the Old Testament Jews, they are attempting to communicate their traditions to future generations but need to find a new "rhetorical vernacular" (Schultze, 2003, p. 30). The conflict between the materialistic culture and the life of faith almost forces them to forsake their distinctive beliefs to participate fully. Richard Neuhaus referred to this "religiously compromised society" as the "naked public square" where there is an absence of God or even people who believe in God so that any religious interests must be kept private. Those who profess any sacred beliefs are seen as fanatics or as interlopers (Schultze, 2003, p. 30).

> Over the last few decades, some of the most distraught and agitated religious outsiders have fought for their own piece of the public square. From Rev. Jerry Falwell's Moral Majority to Rev. M. G. "Pat" Robertson's Christian Coalition, evangelicals have led tribal attacks on mainstream politics, Hollywood, the Supreme Court, and beyond. Sometimes these

right-wing religious attacks elicit left-wing religious counterattacks, such as those led by Norman Lear's People for the American Way. . . . A rhetoric of exile identifies the enemies, coalesces the tribe, and directs tribal action toward a "reclamation" of American life. (Schultze, 2003, p. 32)

Those who have had to defend their positions in society most vigorously have organized, like evangelist, author, and radio personality James Dobson did, through his Focus on the Family organization and Family Research Council to become political forces. They have been attacked both overtly and covertly. For example, Jerry Falwell was featured in a Campari liquor ad that claimed that his first sexual experience was with his mother in an outhouse while he was drunk. Reverend Falwell sued *Hustler* magazine, which carried the parody, for "libel, invasion of privacy, and intentional infliction of emotional distress" (*Hustler Magazine* v. *Falwell*, 485 U.S. 46, 1988). While the two lower courts upheld Falwell's claim and awarded damages amounting to $200,000, the Supreme Court reversed their decisions, saying that in order for a public-person plaintiff to prevail, they had to prove actual malice, deliberate falsehood, and that the source portrayed them in a false light. According to the Supreme Court, the advertisement was a "ridiculous parody" which no reasonable person would believe, so it did not meet the actual malice test. This case points to the scorn that high-profile Christians endure from secular society under the banner of First Amendment protection of free speech. Frequently religious leaders are the object of satire in comedic skits, like "the Church Lady" on *Saturday Night Live*, some of which they have brought upon themselves because of their overindulgences, as did Jim and Tammy Fay Baker with their air-conditioned dog houses and his licentious lifestyle.

THE RHETORIC OF PRAISE

In media culture, success, legitimacy, and market share determine the value of an enterprise, including religion. Schultze (2003) wrote:

Evangelistic rhetoric, too, sometimes equates mere popularity with success in the marketplace. As one manager of recording artists in the Christian music industry told an industry gathering, the goals of ministry and marketing are "exactly the same—market share." Popularity becomes a public vehicle for establishing the praiseworthiness of people, artifacts, and organizations. American rhetoric about the media turns pundits and celebrities into icons of praise. Popular culture in a market system offers a widely shared arena for expressions of public praise. (p. 36)

Tocqueville wrote of religion in America as "democratic and republican," with the American Roman Catholics forming the most democratic class in the new nation (Schultze, 2003, p. 39). Thomas Jefferson used these same words—democratic and republican—to predict that most Americans would become Unitarian, but they did not.

Protestants became very individualistic; with the wall between church and state growing to protect them from any state religion, they were free to decide who and what was praiseworthy. This wide range of Christianity found voice in both televangelists, like Oral Roberts, and pop cultural icons like Janis Joplin, each of whom prayed for grand rewards. Oral

Roberts, the evangelist, warned on January 4, 1987, on his television program *Expect a Miracle,* that if he could not raise $8 milliion to "provide full scholarships for medical missionaries who would be sent to Third World countries," then God would call him home. Other insiders wrote to Roberts, noting the discrepancies in his reports to the media on how his capital campaign was doing and funds that they knew he had already raised for the missionaries (Cloud, 1990, p. 1). With such dramatic tactics, it is difficult to separate the television personalities of the holy men from the pop cultural personalities like Joplin, who simply prayed for a good car and a night on the town. The lyrics come from her song "Mercedes Benz" found on the *Pearl* album (1971), but she would die at age 27 before it was released:

> Oh Lord, won't you buy me a Mercedes Benz?
> My friends all drive Porsches, I must make amends.
> Worked hard all my lifetime, no help from my friends,
> So Lord, won't you buy me a Mercedes Benz?
> (Joplin, 1971)

Roberts used supplication to find the rewards in this life for some greater good, even though some saw his appeals to be just as crass as Joplin's and perhaps less honest. Roberts's faulty prophecy was exposed by credible ministers who had tracked the success of his fundraising to do God's work by auditing the donations that rolled in. Not all religions are equally legitimate; not all practitioners are equivalent in their intentions or their service. But the decision on which religion to follow belongs to the people; our Constitution promised through the First Amendment to neither facilitate nor hinder the practices of religion in America.

ORTHODOXY VERSUS MODERNITY

Religion is generally equated with beliefs, dogma, or worldview, but religion includes three aspects: (1) beliefs, (2) "doing," and (3) "being" (Anderson, 2004, p. 33). These three dimensions of religion explain our relationship with a supernatural world, which for Christians includes the presence of God; define how we should act or what we ought to do, which includes personal, political, and social actions; and, finally, addresses the individual's moral and ethical character (Anderson, 2004, p. 33).

As our society has become more pluralistic, cultural conflicts have arisen about how, where, and when groups may practice their religions. The public square, the workplace, the military and prisons, but especially public schools, have become the territories where disputes have erupted. These controversies have been labeled culture wars between believers and nonbelievers, or others who simply do not claim to know either way. Further, people exist in all three categories who believe that religious matters should be relegated to the home or the places of worship and not interjected into the public debate at all, so their approach is to espouse compartmentalization of the issue. Yet public debates continue as advocates argue that the First Amendment addresses two issues concerning religion. While it prohibits the establishment of a state religion, it also guarantees the "free exercise" of religion, thus assuring that individuals will not be denied the right to practice their faith as they see fit.

As the United States has become more pluralistic, with more Muslims now than Jews in America (Anderson, 2004, p. 2), the former notion that Protestants, Catholics, and Jews made up the dominant religions of the United States is changing. Various Eastern and Native American religions are notable, with the total percentage of Christians remaining fairly constant. According to Anderson, three worldviews exist: theism, naturalism, and postmodernism (Anderson, 2004, pp. 27–29).

Theism is common among various cultures that have the following perspectives:

God exists—is personal, infinite and sovereign.
God created the cosmos.
People are created in the image of God.
God communicates with people.
There is life after death.

Whitney Houston's life represents the tension between the life of the sacred and the profane with a singing career that began in church and ended after meteoric success in secular music with her found dead from drowning with cocaine in her system in February 2012.

Ethics have their origin in the character of God.

History is linear with fulfillment of God's purpose for people. (Anderson, 2004, pp. 27–28)

Naturalism is another perspective that exists in the modern age, and it supports the following beliefs:

Matter exists, and that is all there is.

Personality is an outgrowth of chemical and physical properties.

Death is extinction of personality and individuality.

History is linear but has no overarching purpose.

Ethics are derived only from people. (Anderson, 2004, p. 28)

Postmodernism, which has many different interpretations, offers yet another worldview, which has the following characteristics:

It generally rejects the idea that major attention should be given to metaphysical considerations. Some postmodernists recognize that we all hold some views on first things, but argue that we cannot justify them objectively—especially to other people—so we just have to live with our differences and accept that we will have a clash of faiths.

There is no predetermined purpose for life, and we are liberated—free to create our own purpose. We should not make anyone or anything divine, but depend upon ourselves to establish meaning and purpose for ourselves. (Anderson, 2004, p. 29)

The first view supports religious orthodoxy, where a body of beliefs regarding a deity, creation, and human's place in the universe exists, although each religion defines these ideas differently. The second view has come to be regarded as secular humanism, where rationality is the key, with humans exercising judgment about how to use their faculties and ultimately accepting responsibility for their ethical and moral life. The third view focuses on tolerance and freedom from the orthodoxy of perhaps a God of wrath or an evil spirit personified by the devil. Even if these forces existed, we could not know them with any certainty or explain them to others. The first category of beliefs, which have orthodox dogma to explain the concept of God, or a supreme being by any other name, offers the greatest conflicts for outsiders and between faith groups.

FREEDOM OF RELIGION FROM THE ESTABLISHED ORDER

At the time of the American Revolutionary War, there were at least 8 established churches in the 13 colonies, and there were established religions in 4 of the remaining 5 colonies (Bosmajian, 1987, p. 12). Thomas Jefferson and James Madison opposed all religious establishments by law or principle, placing all religious groups on equal footing in the United States. In their words:

[T]he people [in Virginia], as elsewhere, reached the conviction that individual religious liberty could be achieved best under a government which was stripped of all power to tax, to support, or otherwise to assist any or all religions, or to interfere with the beliefs of any religious individual or group. (Bosmajian, 1987, p. 99)

The First Amendment provides that "Congress shall make no law respecting an establishment of religion, or prohibiting the free exercise thereof . . ." (Bosmajian, 1987, p. 104). So, from the beginning, the government could neither advance nor inhibit religion and should avoid any entanglements with religion. Jefferson's concept of the **establishment clause** was intended to erect "a wall of separation between Church and State" (Bosmajian, 1987, p. 99). There was to be no distinction between believers and nonbelievers in government action.

Thomas Jefferson wrote to John Adams, predicting that Unitarianism would become the religion of a majority of Americans because it was rational and democratic, but he was mistaken (Victor, 1996, p. 3). Jefferson's image of a wall between the church and the state can be found regarding prayer in schools, resistance to pledges, and other such cases. The founding fathers constructed guarantees against an oppressive state religion in our constitutional framework, reinforcing it in the First Amendment. Yet our cultural heritage exhibits prominently the institutional evidence of the faith of the founding fathers with religious artifacts, like the Ten Commandments on courthouses, such as the Allegheny County Courthouse in Pennsylvania, or Old Testament prophets like Moses or Solomon in federal buildings, and affirmations of faith on our coinage—"In God we trust." Congress opens each session with a prayer, and with few exceptions our presidents and members of Congress are sworn into office with oaths on the Bible.

With increasing frequency these artifacts, oaths, and prayers are being challenged by agnostics, non-Christians, and strict constructionists who believe that religious ideology has invaded government, businesses, and public schools. The pledge of allegiance that includes the phrase "under God," the national mint where coins are stamped, and public buildings that display biblical images have all been the subject of lawsuits brought to remove any testimony to religious content. At the same time that a movement exists to secularize society, there has been a resurgence of fundamentalist religions. During the 1950s, when the Protestant denominations were experiencing tidal growth, Fundamentalists were seen as the poor or poorly educated, but 40 years later the Protestant denominations are experiencing a drastic decline in membership while charismatics and Fundamentalists have been attracting hundreds of thousands of people. Jeffrey S. Victor (1996) wrote in *The Humanist*:

The question that I want to discuss here is one I have thought about for many years now without finding a satisfying answer. It involves the contradiction between two types of social change in religion: increasing secularization in society on the one hand, and increasing supernaturalism in personal belief on the other. One direction of social change is a constant decrease in manifestations of supernatural belief in the public institutions which influence everyday life. Yet there is also a constant resurgence of belief in all sorts of supernatural phenomena—from evil demons to angels to miracles, as evidenced in public-opinion polls and in the growth of fundamentalist forms of religion around the globe.

This contradiction is nothing new. The contradiction goes back centuries, long before the time of Jefferson. It has its origins in the Enlightenment, when European intellectuals— politicians, scientists, artists, and medical doctors—strove to separate their activities in the public institutions of society from the creedal constraints of religious supernaturalism. Before their time, religious ideology had dominated every aspect of daily life like a totalitarian social system. Indeed, it is still useful to think of that struggle as quite similar to the struggle to free society from a totalitarian ideology. (Victor, 1996, p. 20)

There has been a reduction in the supernatural in institutions like the economy, government, science, medicine, and education, since rarely is religion used to explain making or spending money, going to war, or giving AIDS relief (Victor, 1996, p. 20). Theologian Paul Tillich suggested that art, more than religion, reflected the spiritual needs of the times by exploring the moral dilemmas and pain of people in society. Victor (1996) noted:

Modern art and literature rarely make any reference to supernatural themes anymore. It is indicative of the religious condition of our times that we can find expressions of supernaturalism only in folk art and in popular culture, in Christian and New Age books. However, these products of folk culture have no influence whatsoever upon the gate keepers of the elite intellectual culture. It is that culture which creates the ideas of the dominant institutions of society. (p. 20)

Yet only 3 percent of people claim to be atheists and agnostics in the United States, compared to 40 percent in France; and 60 percent of Americans affirm a belief in the devil as an evil supernatural force (Victor, 1996, p. 21). Fundamentalist religion is spreading through the United States, with Christian colleges booming, mass media networks with television and radio stations growing, and Christian Fundamentalist political organizations exerting influence within the Republican Party (Victor, 1996, p. 22). There has been a drive to return to supernatural religion and away from institutional religion to revitalize Christianity in the face of what is perceived as an alien way of life. Victor (1996), the sociologist, wrote:

These are revitalization movements aimed at restoring a long-lost way of life in which beliefs and values based upon supernatural preconceptions guided much of everyday life. In this sense, fundamentalist religious movements are much like the Ghost Dance religion of Native Americans in the 1880s, which hoped to restore the vitality and power of the native American religion in the West after it had been vanquished by a very defensive posture against an alien world. (p. 22)

Victor (1996) compared institutional religion to folk religion, saying that institutional religion was maintained by "the word"—texts, doctrines, and interpretations—while folk religion is maintained through personal experience—magical and mystical experiences of childhood which are repeated throughout life. Institutional religion is passed on by elite members who are educated by the wisdom of ancients, whereas folk religion is passed through family, communities, and charismatic leaders. Because the elite leaders are educated and constantly informed by new sources of knowledge, institutional religion can change quickly, but folk religions are impervious to new ideas and to change because the followers are not educated, nor do they claim different ways of knowing (Victor, 1996, p. 23). Religious cults and New Age religions have arisen from the folk religions. The revival of American Fundamentalism can be seen as an attempt to return to the "Anglo-American rural cultural values and folkways. Now that it is armed with modem communication technology, it is doing quite well" (Victor, 1996, p. 23). Such "religious awakenings" have arisen during times of great change and social disruptions. The influx of immigrants from every center of the globe, who are bringing their own religions with them, along with the growing **secularization** in American culture, threaten both institutional and folk religions as practiced in America. Religious institutions fulfill the following functions:

1. Advocate ideology through teaching, preaching, and interpreting sacred scripts.
2. Support the religious community through funds, social functions, and interaction, including political action.
3. Perform rituals in births, marriages, deaths, and sacred rites such as baptisms, inductions, and ex-communication or shunning.
4. Communicate both internally and externally to members of the in-group and to the greater society to recruit, retain, and defend the group and its goals.
5. Manage resources of personnel, assets, and liabilities including special projects like missions, seminary, schools, hospitals, hospice, churches, synagogues, or temples.

 Functions 1, 3, and 4 are primarily communication functions of a rhetorical nature. First, regardless of whether the denomination is Christian, Jewish, Muslim, or Hindu, there is a body of beliefs that followers must embrace and support. These beliefs in the words of holy prophets or creators give laws or codes for living, which are explained in the texts of each religion. Each religion contains oaths, ceremonies, or instructions on how to conduct the rituals or sacraments, whether this means sacrifices on an altar or keeping one day as the holy day, which have meaning for the believers. Communication devices vary from face-to-face services in an outdoor arena, a tent, or temple to electronic sermons sent at the speed of sound or light. Most religions have a messianic urge to proselytize and expect service in that direction. They also explain our origin or the creation. Kenneth Burke explained the dramatistic version of the creation narrative by examining the way language created the negative that explained all the "thou shalt nots" to keep the Covenant or contract with God.

THE JUDEO-CHRISTIAN *CREATION NARRATIVE*

Kenneth Burke (1961), in *The Rhetoric of Religion: Studies of Logology*, examined the foundations of the Judeo-Christian belief system through an analysis of the language used to explain the Genesis narrative. Burke stated that creation implies a creator who is the author of creation and the authority over it. The creator, God, is the highest authority with the most radical sovereignty over creation, which includes a Covenant with man, who, unlike stones, trees, or things, can violate the contract with the creator. Things do not understand agreements or commands, but man does. Man was created in the image of God and put into

Eden, the garden of paradise, where he fell from grace when he ignored the Covenant, which included the injunction to avoid the tree of knowledge of good and evil. Eve, the first woman—who was created from Adam's rib and was subordinate to him—tempted him to eat of the forbidden fruit. This "fall" from the state of unity with God required punishment for Adam's and Eve's disobedience (Burke, 1961, p. 175). The idea of punishment implied the possibility of redemption and a redeemer or agent who could bring about a restored condition of grace (Burke, 1961, pp. 175–176).

Burke (1961) wrote that the hereditary sins of Adam implied the principle of the Covenant, which contained both the seeds of temptation and redemption, with the word "justice" equating to payment that was proper for the sin and "mercy" being disproportionate to the severity of the offense in favor of the offender (p. 178). The **Covenant** could be seen as a kind of contract between God and man that included a code of conduct, rules regarding how disobedience should be judged and punished, and some mechanism for redemption or restoration to unity and grace. The first Covenant created by God was a permissive one, with only one forbidden command, which Adam broke when he ate of the tree of knowledge. The second Covenant created by God was to impose a penalty on all of mankind.

Burke (1961) stated that the word "Covenant" is insufficient to analyze the Genesis of man and the fall from grace because there is no negative for the word, but "Order" implies "Disorder" and offers the kind of word necessary to understand the theological relationship as well as the socio-political order of society. There is the natural order of the cosmos, such as the wind and tides, and there are orders that can be obeyed or disobeyed. The idea of God's authority is combined in both of these ideas. Burke wrote:

> The biblical myth pictures natural things as coming into being through the agency of God's Word; but they can merely do as they were designed to do, whereas with God's permission though not without his resentment, the seed of Adam can do even what it has been explicitly told not to do. The word-using animal not only understands a thou-shalt-not; it can carry the principle of the negative a step further, and answer the thou-shalt-not with a disobedient NO. Logologically, the distinction between natural innocence and fallen man hinges about this problem of language and the negative. Eliminate language from nature, and there can be no moral disobedience. In this sense, moral disobedience is "doctrinal." Like faith, it is grounded in language. (Burke, 1961, pp. 186–187)

Clearly, then, religion and rhetoric are inextricably bound to one another, since Burke wrote of "The Word" that was delivered from God in the beginning, and the words that we use to explain the supernatural like Satan, angels, and eternity—those dimensions that are beyond the experience of man, except as we name them and give them a reality.

Free will exists as the dividing line between obedience and disobedience; free will allows humankind to follow the Covenant or to disobey God with action that is freely chosen (Burke, 1961, p. 187). Unlike the motion of a rock, man is motivated or shows intentions to act according to his will. Burke noted that **mortification** is the word that needs to be reclaimed, meaning "subjection of the passions and appetites, by penance, abstinence or painful severities inflicted on the body" (Burke, 1961, p. 190).

Mortification is a severe form of self-control or exercise of virtue in the face of temptation that reaffirms the divine order, whereby disobedience, or saying yes to disorder, is giving license (luxuria) to fornication and other excesses (Burke, 1961, p. 190). The ultimate mortification is death, to return to the dust from which Adam was made. Purification can be found by projecting one's sins upon a sacrificial vessel or a scapegoat that will cleanse the guilt within the mortified agent. In Christian ideology, Christ was the perfect "victim" to be crucified for the first sin committed by Adam against the first authority, God (Burke, 1961, p. 191). Burke said Christ represents both sovereignty and subjugation—two poles of government found in the same figure—Christ as king and Christ as servant.

This narrative is so well known that it functions as a cultural premise that can be identified as a communal myth that weaves the fabric of social consciousness in America. A speaker can mention any portion of the story, for instance the Garden of Eden or the forbidden fruit, and audience members are able to fill in the rest of it, so it functions as an enthymeme. The narrative is basic to Judeo-Christian beliefs that are integrated into literature, from John Milton's *Paradise Lost* to glitzy cinema that depicts bargains with the devil for one night with

 a beautiful woman or the next fix of heroin. Evil becomes the manifestation of disorder or disobedience against the authority of the Covenant with God in theology—and in the social-political realm, crime is committed when the contract with the tribe, community, or state is violated.

The notion of natural law, as defined in the Judeo-Christian tradition, unites the roots of religious institutions and civil society or the state through this foundation. An uneasy truce exists between these underpinnings that rest on religious foundations supported by faith in the belief system and tolerance for other worldviews. In the public sphere laws reflect the values that arise from the Judeo-Christian ideology that were established through rational deliberations and integration of values grounded in natural law. Obedience to legitimate authority, justice and mercy, recognition of human dignity, and frailty are all part of the social contract. This sense of freedom to choose through the exercise of free will and the responsibility to uphold the covenant with God, or at least to support the social contract in a civil society, is at the heart of a just and ordered nation. There were many religious laws that imposed grave remedies for disobedience, including death and eternal damnation, wherein God was presented as a vengeful master who exacted a tortuous price.

RELIGION IN A POSTMODERN WORLD

Max Weber predicted the inability of religion to survive the onslaught of **modernity**, and Sigmund Freud wrote of the undesirability of religion as a force in modern society. According to Jon Butler, Weber and Freud saw the incompatibilities between religion and modern life in the roots of "urban, multi-ethnic, multi-religious, multi-national, economically globalized, bureaucratic, technologically-driven, popular yet not necessarily democratic politics and a demand for power and control made more alluring by the apparent possession of real means to desired ends" (Butler, 2006, p. 53). Yet religion has shown an amazing ability to adapt to modern conditions despite the secular and materialist culture in America.

The Supreme Court decision of June 28, 2013 struck down the portion of the Defense of Marriage Act that restricted gay couples from receiving equal benefits from tax laws, retirement funds, and inheritance benefits awarded to other married couples.

The polarization of Americans can be seen with secularists blaming religion for the worst atrocities in history while religious leaders call for a return to the discipline and righteousness that their religious foundations demand. Despite prophesies of the demise of religion as a force in America and the secularization of society, scholars are puzzled by the resurgence and revival of religious fervor in the United States. Both Presidents Jimmy Carter and George W. Bush called themselves born-again Christians and laced their rhetoric with references to the belief in an omnipotent God, good works born of compassion, and faith in divine interventions.

The presence of religion is evident by the churches, synagogues, and temples throughout this nation, although some of the old houses of worship have been converted to chic restaurants with such endearing names as Angel's Corner where wine flows not as part of a sacrament but of everyday secular life. Jon Butler (1990), in his book *Awash in a Sea of Faith: Christianizing the American People*, wrote:

> Throughout this book, religion is taken to mean belief in and resort to superhuman powers, sometimes beings, that determine the course of natural and human events. This is what philosophers of religion call a "substantive" rather than a "functional" conceptualization. It describes what religion is rather than what religion does, and it is based on the work of the anthropologist Melford Spiro. With minor modifications in Spiro's formulation, religion here is associated with supernaturalism, with supernatural beliefs, and with the conviction that supernatural beings and powers can and do affect life as humans know it. Those who hold such views are taken to be religious. Those who reject or ignore them are not taken to be religious. (p. 3)

This definition of religion as the belief in the supernatural is a good working definition for this chapter on the rhetorical powers of religion and the controversies that arise from the believers and nonbelievers in everyday affairs. A Middle East news agency claimed that

President Bush said God spoke to him about invading Iraq, which the president denied as inaccurate, but the White House did not deny reports that he consulted with conservative religious groups about the nominations of Harriet Miers, who stepped down from the nomination, and Samuel Alito, who was confirmed, for Supreme Court vacancies. Both Weber and Freud would have found the position of religion at the center of political debate unbelievable; nineteenth-century religious leaders would have been pleased even if perplexed (Butler, 2006, p. 54).

When we speak of religion in America, it is not entirely clear what we are examining from an historical point of view because most scholarly history was denominational history, meaning each group wrote of their group identity, doctrine, and ecclesiology (Butler, 2006). Then Perry Miller wrote of the Puritans, which changed both the methods and status of studying religion as history.

> . . . Miller lifted Puritans from their status as anti-modern sectarians to intellectuals of not inconsiderable conceptual achievement and elevated the discussion of Puritanism and religion generally, or at least American Protestantism, to unprecedented heights.
>
> In the wake of Miller's achievement, Henry May tied religion to the shaping of the American industrial order and progressivism, even if he found its efforts more than wanting. Timothy L. Smith linked urban revivals to the power of antebellum reform in education, women's rights, and abolition, and challenged the portrait of American religion as rural and retrograde. Later histories celebrated the religious origins of the civil rights crusades of the 1950s and 1960s (but expressed puzzlement about the religious foundations of the New Christian Right). These books superseded the old denominational histories because they concentrated not on religious institutions but placed religion at the very center of American culture. (Butler, 2006, pp. 47–48)

In matters of social movements, religious groups have figured prominently from the beginning of our nation's history. Most notable among these are the abolitionist movement, the anti-saloon movement, the civil rights movement, antiwar movements, pro-life and pro-choice movements, and others too numerous to name here. Some issues like abortion and gay rights have split denominations because there have been religious advocates on both sides of the debate. But the 1988 Republican presidential nomination of Pat Robertson demonstrated that the nation is not ready to have a televangelist in the White House yet, even though Robertson made a second-place showing in the Iowa primary before his campaign folded (Foege, 1996, p. 15).

EVOLUTION OF A GOD OF WRATH TO A PLASTIC JESUS

Religion in America has been treated with great devotion as the center of the universe by true believers, but for others, religion and sacred icons are simply another part of pop culture, as the song by Ed Rush and George Comarty demonstrated:

> I don't care if it rains or freezes
> long as I got my plastic Jesus
> ridin on the dashboard of my car.

Through all trials and tribulations,
We will travel every nation,
With my plastic Jesus I'll go far. (Cromarty & Rush, 1957)

This secularized and profane view of the trinity exists alongside sacred Christian rituals assimilating the Catholic saints who champion lost causes as well as islanders' tribal voodoo, sorcery, and charms. Thus, religion has been manipulated and morphed to suit the needs of those who claim to be religious by adapting the language or rhetoric of religion to address their lives and philosophies of living and dying. That is not to say that all versions of religious doctrine are equally acceptable. There exists institutional religion and idiosyncratic derivatives of each sect, which varies from the ridiculous to the sublime, capturing the majesty of the old cathedrals with their spires reaching to the heavens as a testament to God and the plastic Jesus on the dashboard, right along with the St. Christopher medal and the fuzzy

Pop star Madonna co-mingles religious themes with worldly images intentionally by exploiting sacred artifacts like wearing rosaries as jewelry, dressing as a nun and singing lyrics "Like a Virgin" and "Poppa Don't Preach."

dice. The pop star Madonna made millions singing "Poppa Don't Preach" and "Like a Virgin." She used religious references in her music in an oppositional manner that stirred controversy as she gloried in her materialism by exploiting sacred artifacts. Madonna wore rosaries as jewelry and dressed as a nun while her husband dressed as a pope, thriving on the provocation of Catholics. This form of exhibitionism is only meaningful because audiences comprehend the power of the symbols being desecrated. She has depicted the three types of women defined in drama as the holy mother (*the* Madonna), the prostitute, and the wife, comingling the three roles indiscriminately. As the folk singer Woody Guthrie once said, "I ain't prejudiced. . . . I offend everyone equally." So Madonna's rosaries became "bling," or jewelry for her and those who emulated her styles of dress. What today is protected by the First Amendment as art would have in earlier times been grounds for heresy against the Divine and a death sentence. Early theologians like Jonathan Edwards warned of the inferno that awaited wayward sinners. His sermons were dramatic examples of the rhetoric of conversion that was mentioned earlier.

JONATHAN EDWARDS'S GOD OF WRATH

Jonathan Edwards, on July 8, 1741, delivered a sermon to the Calvin congregation in Enfield, Connecticut, with such earnestness that he had to admonish the parishioners to refrain from groans of agony so that he could continue. Edwards's sermon was called "Sinners in the hands of an angry God." He said:

> The God that holds you over the pit of hell much as one holds a spider or some loathsome insect over the fire, abhors you, and is dreadfully provoked; his wrath towards you burns like fire; he looks upon you as worthy of nothing else but to be cast into the fire; he is of purer eyes than to bear to have you in his sight; you are ten thousand times so abominable in his eyes as the most hateful and venomous serpent is in ours. You have offended him infinitely more than ever a stubborn rebel did his prince: and yet it is nothing but his hand that holds you from falling into the fire every moment. 'Tis ascribed to nothing else, that you did not go to hell the last night; that you was suffered to awake again in this world after you closed your eyes to sleep; and there is no other reason to be given why you have not dropped into hell since you arose in the morning, but that God's hand has held you up. (Edwards, 1741)

Edwards called all souls to be converted to avoid the wrath of Almighty God and give up their hardened hearts and blindness of mind to be gathered up with the saved and blissful. Edwards's God was an angry God who condemned "children of the devil" as readily as he did adults to the everlasting pits of hell. His parishioners grew weary of his demands of them emotionally and spiritually, so he left for the frontier town of Stockbridge, where he was in charge of the Indian [sic] mission. Edwards was later called by the Commissioners in Boston to serve as president of the College of New Jersey, which became Princeton University.

In Edwards's sermon the ideology of fallen man, a vengeful God, with strict adherence to a code of virtue and conversion to be saved from hell was evident, but his imagery was vivid and grew increasingly unacceptable to the flock. Evangelists continue to hold to these beliefs in conversion and salvation from hell.

Edwards saw pride as the basest of sins, and he detailed his faults to the commissioners, despite the fact that he had an able intellect and some ranked him with Benjamin Franklin as the other great prose writer of the eighteenth century in America.

Edwards's wrathful God continued in the preaching of self-styled men of the cloth who pointed to the "gob-piles" of the Appalachian coalfields that belched sulfurous fumes as flames licked the night skies dwarfing the company houses and small churches; they admonished sinners to fall down before the altar and repent or burn eternally in the pits of hell. The dramatic effect of the burning sulfur and flames erupting from the slag heaps that smoldered from internal combustion was a powerful visual threat.

JOHN WOOLMAN'S GOD OF EQUALITY

At the same time that Edwards was delivering fire-and-brimstone sermons to his uneasy flock, others were turning their attention to the ills of society as well as introspectively examining their souls. John Woolman, a Quaker in faith, who lived the life of the Friends, refused a request to draw up a bill of sale for a slave because he believed that owning slaves was morally wrong. He traveled and preached primarily in Pennsylvania, but he was appointed to serve as representative for the Friends in England.

In 1774 Woolman had to give up his business and worldly affairs when he began to preach against slavery and capitalistic exploitation and to preach to the Native Americans. In his diary he wrote of people becoming indebted and then being sued, of their wearing costly apparel, consuming "spiritous liquors" that clouded their minds, and he refused to write wills that passed slaves from parents to their children. He wrote:

> It is clear to me, that I would not be the scribe where wills are drawn, in which some children are made absolute masters over others during life. . . . I could not write any instruments by which my fellow-creatures were made slaves, without bringing trouble on my own mind."
> (Woolman, 1774, p. 41)

In one instance, when he refused to write such a will, the owner set the slave free. Woolman, who had been away from home 24 days and had ridden 316 miles, according to his diary, understood his duty to stand against convention that subjugated one human to another. The abolitionist movement was taking roots in the voluntary singular deeds of one man acting in conscience as he understood the prophet Jeremiah's message. "His Word was in my heart as a burning fire shut up in my bones; and I was weary with forbearing, and could not stay" (Woolman, 1774, p. 45). Woolman was willing to forgo his profitable business and to accept the calling to preach to the Society of Friends and Native Americans alike the message of equality, compassion, and tolerance. He used moral persuasion to deter fellow colonists from owning or passing on slaves as inheritance to their children.

The impact of religious leaders on social movements has a long tradition. Perhaps one reason that religion has survived and continues to thrive is that religious leaders have become political forces by addressing social ills such as the discrimination against blacks, women, and gay members of society. Dr. Martin Luther King Jr. was one who combined the words from Old and New Testament prophets as readily as he did the words of philosophers to petition for a righteous resolution to the oppression of his people. Dr. King combined the **nonviolent resistance** of Gandhi with the civil disobedience of Henry David Thoreau and the sit-down strike tactics of John L. Lewis's labor movements from the early 1930s. But his most powerful weapon was the words of the scriptures that rolled from his tongue in a cadence of urgency that tied the sins of bondage and oppression not to kings of old, but to city mayors, sitting presidents, and lunch counter managers in the South.

DR. MARTIN LUTHER KING JR.—THE PHILOSOPHY OF NONVIOLENT RESISTANCE

Dr. Martin Luther King Jr., leader of the civil rights movement, mobilized the Montgomery bus boycott in the basement of his Dexter Avenue Church in Alabama, which would gain him national recognition as a spokesperson for the movement. Other ministers, like Dr. Ralph Abernathy and A. W. Wilson, participated in the organizational meetings. Dr. King pondered how to confront the racist establishment in Montgomery, Alabama, and yet not fuel hatred and resentment (King, 1969, p. 115). Dr. King was familiar with the teachings of Mahatma Gandhi, the leader who freed 400 million from British rule in India, and Henry David Thoreau, who protested against the Fugitive Slave Laws and was imprisoned for his peaceful resistance (Metcalf, 1970, p. 7). Dr. King was fascinated by Gandhi's life and campaigns of nonviolent resistance.

> "The whole Gandhian concept of *satyagraha* (*satya* is truth which equals love, and *graha* is force; Satyagraha thus means truth-force or love-force) was profoundly significant to me," he wrote. "As I delved deeper into the philosophy of Gandhi, my skepticism concerning the power of love gradually diminished, and I came to see for the first time that the Christian doctrine of love operating through the Gandhian method of non-violence was one of the most potent weapons available to oppressed people in their struggle for freedom." (Metcalf, 1970, p. 708)

Dr. King had been moved to action following the arrest of Mrs. Rosa Parks on December 1, 1955, when she refused to give up her seat to a white man who boarded the bus, since black passengers had to sit in the back of the bus and to yield seats to whites. Dr. King found his first opportunity to employ the philosophy of nonviolent resistance in the organized bus boycott that followed Mrs. Park's arrest. According to his wife, Coretta Scott King, he believed:

> Religion deals with both heaven and earth. . . . Any religion that professes to be concerned with the souls of men and is not concerned with the slums that doom them, the economic conditions that strangle them, and the social conditions that cripple them, is a dry-as-dust religion. (King, 1969, p. 113)

Dr. King's religion was an activist one that combined fomenting for change with passive resistance to confrontations with the establishment. The Christian ministry provided the leadership that the civil rights movement required, and "Christian ideals were its source"

(King, 1969, p. 113). When Abernathy and King went to the Holt Street Baptist Church on Monday following their plan to boycott the Montgomery city buses, they found a terrific traffic jam and 5,000 people filling the streets singing "Onward, Christian Soldiers." Dr. King said, "That night I understood what the older preachers meant when they said, 'Open your mouth and God will speak for you'" (King, 1969, p. 117). He began to speak by telling his audience that he understood how tired they were of being oppressed, how patient they had been, and how they must be guided by the "highest principles of law and order" (p. 118). He continued:

> Our method must be persuasion, not coercion. We will only say to the people, "Let your conscience be your guide." . . . Our actions must be guided by the deepest principles of the Christian faith. . . . Once again we must hear the words of Jesus, "Love your enemies. Bless them that curse you. Pray for them that despitefully use you." If we fail to do this, our protest will end up as a meaningless drama on the stage of history and its memory will be shrouded in the ugly garments of shame. . . . We must not become bitter and end up by hating our white brothers. As Booker T. Washington said, "Let no man pull you so low as to make you hate him." (King, 1969, p. 118)

With his thoughts turned to history, he said that if they protested courageously and with dignity and Christian love, historians would say of them, "There lived a great people—a black people—who injected new meaning and dignity into the veins of civilization" (King, 1969, p. 118). There were death threats against Dr. King, but he admonished his followers

Rosa Parks refused to give up her seat to a white rider on the bus in 1955, and her arrest sparked the Montgomery bus boycott that elevated M. L. King to leadership of the civil rights movement.

that even if he were murdered they must continue without retaliation to protest with dignity and restraint (King, 1969, p. 123).

As the movement broadened to include other major American cities, various groups coalesced to add their support to the demonstrations against discrimination. People who were willing to go to jail for participating in civil disobedience had to sign a commitment card that read:

I hereby pledge myself—my person and my body—to the nonviolent movement. Therefore, I will keep the following ten commandments:

1. Meditate daily on the teachings and life of Jesus.
2. Remember always that the nonviolent movement in Birmingham seeks justice and reconciliation—not victory.
3. Walk and talk in the manner of love; for God is love.
4. Pray daily to be used by God in order that all men might be free.
5. Sacrifice personal wishes that all men might be free.
6. Observe with both friend and foe the ordinary rules of courtesy.
7. Seek to perform regular service for others and for the world.
8. Refrain from the violence of fist, tongue, and heart.
9. Strive to be in good spiritual and bodily health.
10. Follow the directions of the movement and of the captains on a demonstration. (King, 1969, pp. 218–219)

This code of conduct was a tall order given the threats of violence that prevailed in major cities. In January 1963, Dr. King, Dr. Ralph Abernathy, and Fred Shuttlesworth met with President John F. Kennedy, whom they perceived to be sympathetic to their cause. The president said that he could not propose legislation in the civil-rights area because it would divide Congress on other important legislation he had to have passed (King, 1969, p. 219). The leaders decided to continue the confrontations with authority to get justice, and both Dr. King and Dr. Abernathy were arrested in Birmingham and taken to jail. Robert Kennedy, the attorney general, and President Kennedy both eventually talked with Mrs. King to reassure her that they had been in contact with her husband in Birmingham and that while Bull Connor was hard to deal with, maybe a new city government would take over Birmingham and change would come (King, 1969, pp. 225–226).

The demonstrations continued when Dr. King was released, but the media had released stories that confirmed the fact that he had the ear of the president of the United States. This did not stop the violence. Medgar Evers was shot in the door of his home in Jackson, Mississippi, on June 12, 1963. Dr. King continued speaking and demonstrating for civil rights legislation. In Los Angeles 25,000 came, in Detroit 200,000 demonstrated, and on August 28, 1963, the leaders of the movement planned to march down the Mall from the Washington Monument to the Lincoln Memorial, where Dr. King would speak (King, 1969, p. 235). Coretta King said 250,00 people lined the Mall all the way back to the Washington Monument. Dr. King delivered his most famous speech, "I Have a Dream," which he concluded by saying:

This will be the day when all of God's children will be able to sing with new meaning, "let freedom ring." So let freedom ring from the prodigious hilltops of New Hampshire; let freedom ring from the mighty mountains of New York. But not only that. Let freedom ring from Stone Mountain of Georgia. Let freedom ring from every hill and molehill of Mississippi, from every mountainside.

When we allow freedom to ring from every town and every hamlet, from every state and every city, we will be able to speed up that day when all of God's children, black men and white men, Jews and Gentiles, Protestants and Catholics, will be able to join hands and sing in the words of the old Negro spiritual, "Free at last! Free at last! Great God Almighty, we are free at last! (King, 1969, p. 240)

Dr. King moved forward with his agenda to reform the country and to bring forth equal rights for his people. His rhetoric and strategy of nonviolent resistance following the demonstration in Washington, D.C., made him the uncontested leader of the civil rights movement at that time; however, his position was being challenged by more radical voices who called him an "Uncle Tom" or spurned his peaceful methods. Some were ready for a revolution in the late 1960s as violence sparked, especially in Detroit and Watts, but most major cities experienced racial unrest. His speech has become the most quoted address from the twentieth century, but it was not enough to heal the breach that existed in race relations. On September 15, 1963, four little black girls died in a Sunday School room when the Sixteenth Street Baptist Church in Birmingham was bombed, and on November 23, 1963, President John F. Kennedy was assassinated in Dallas, Texas. Both events were tragic in their own right, but leaders saw them as particularly tragic for the civil rights movement. As the King family watched Jacqueline Kennedy mourn her husband, they steeled themselves for what was to come. Dr. Martin Luther King Jr. was assassinated on April 4, 1968, but his message lived on. President Lyndon Johnson pushed civil rights legislation through Congress that JFK had not been able to propose or to have passed. Benjamin Mays, president emeritus of Morehouse College, Dr. King's alma mater, eulogized him, saying:

Surely this man was called of God to do this work. If Amos and Micah were prophets in the eighth century, BC, Martin Luther King, Jr., was a prophet in the twentieth century. If Isaiah was called of God to prophesy in his day, Martin Luther was called of God to prophesy in his time. If Hosea was sent to preach love and forgiveness centuries ago, Martin Luther was sent to expound the doctrine of nonviolence and forgiveness in the third quarter of the twentieth century. If Jesus was called to preach the Gospel to the poor, Martin Luther was called to give dignity to the common man. If a prophet is one who interprets in clear and intelligible language the will of God, Martin Luther King, Jr. fits that designation. (Mays, 1968, in King, 1969, p. 356)

Many said that the bullet that killed him did not still Martin Luther King Jr.'s voice because more people heard his message in 4 days of mourning than had heard it in his 12 years of preaching (King, 1969, p. 334). His speeches outlined a course of action that needed to rewrite the contract with black Americans, and his I Have a Dream speech created the vision that ideally all could embrace with inspiration and dedication. Dr. King's rhetoric used the call to conversion, but unlike Edwards, who called for individuals to repent, King intended to reform a whole culture, not one sinner at a time. His rhetoric included the notion of exile as well, with blacks separated by Jim Crow laws from the mainstream of America; King called for the NSF check that was written to his people to be cashed and paid in full. The sacred texts from the Old and New Testaments were foundational to his rhetoric. His letter from Birmingham Jail (see Chapter 4) gives further insight into his leadership and communication skills.

RELIGIOUS DIVERSITY

In December 2006, the first Muslim Congressman, Keith Ellison, a Minnesota Democrat, was installed in Washington, D.C., using not the Christian Bible but the Muslim Koran to administer his oath of office, creating a firestorm of criticism. The **Koran** used in the ceremony reportedly came from the library collection of Thomas Jefferson along with arguments that Jefferson was not a Christian at all but a Deist. Dennis Prager, a Jewish holocaust survivor, said Ellison should not be allowed to use the Koran: "America is interested in only one book, the Bible. If you are incapable of taking an oath on that book, don't serve in Congress" (Sacirbey, 2006, p. 1). We now know that Ellison was not the only member of Congress to use a book different from the Bible, but he was the first to use the Koran. Debbie Wasserman Schultz, Florida Democrat, used the Hebrew Bible, a **Tanakh**, in 2005 for her oath, and Linda Lingle, Republican Governor of Hawaii, used the Tanakh in 2002 as well. In 1825 John Quincy Adams used a law book instead of a Bible, and Herbert Hoover, citing his Quaker beliefs, did not use a Bible either. Members of the ACLU and others noted that there was no religious test required as a qualification for public office in the United States, so Muslims should not have to perform a religious ritual that they do not support (Sacirbey, 2006, p. 2). Congressman Ellison said that his family roots go back to 1742 and that he is not an immigrant but an African American who planned to focus on minimum wage legislation and health insurance. He said, "The fact that there are many different faiths, many different colors and many different cultures in America is a great strength" (Sacirbey, 2006, p. 2). Religious differences continued to be hotly debated in the 2008 election as Governor Mitt Romney confronted the issue of religious pluralism when it became evident that many Americans consider Mormonism to be a cult, not a mainstream religion at all. His father, George Romney, represented moderate Republicans in 1968 when he campaigned for the presidency, but his presidential ambitions did not progress far enough for this religious debate to become national. In 1968 race riots, burning cities, and antiwar protests were primary concerns. Mitt Romney's answer to criticism about Mormonism in the 2012 campaign for the presidency was to point to his family, to his achievements in political life, and to promise to attend to the affairs of state, leaving religion for others to worry about. Confrontations of ideology sometimes erupt, but in Ellison and Romney's cases, they both focused on common ground or similarities, not differences.

When John F. Kennedy ran in 1960, he had to reassure Americans that the presidency would not be influenced by the Pope or the Vatican if he were elected as the first Catholic to that office. It is a myth that religious tolerance came to the colonies with the new immigrants, since the long stretch of the Church of England's traditions came with the appointed governors. The prosecution of colonists for heresy, including the Salem Witch trials, bear evidence to the intolerance for any deviation from the norm. When the Bill of Rights was adopted, religious doctrine that was at variance with the majority was to be protected, but irreverence was still punished, as the 1811 case of Mr. Ruggles showed. He was convicted in the New York Courts when he called Jesus a "bastard" and his mother Mary a "whore" (*People v. Ruggles*, 290 N.Y. 1811). The judge in the *Ruggles* case made it clear that he did not have to protect religions other than Christianity. Since those of "Mahomet or of the Grand Lama . . . [are] impostors" (Pfeffer, 1967, p. 665).

The controversies regarding religion are often contingent on such legal rulings as time, place, and manner. Charles R. Kniker (1997) wrote about religious displays in schools, which demonstrated the compromises regarding artwork and symbols:

> A child does a finger painting in Sunday School class and wants to bring it to school for "show and tell" on Monday. Permissible? Yes. A Michigan public high school wants to have a permanent display of religious art, including a picture of Jesus Christ, in one of its hallways. No, said a U.S. district judge. Can the Ten Commandments be posted in a public school? No, said the Court. Religious artwork and use of symbols, such as a cross, menorah, or crescent, legal voices are saying, may be used in the schools if they have an instructional purpose and if they are on display temporarily. (p. 50)

Religious symbols in schools must be for instructional purposes, and any displays must exist only during that length of time that the activity requires. Recent controversies deal more with the free exercise clause of religion than they do with the establishment clause. Often the cases articulate more clearly what is not permitted. Churches do not have the right to amplify sound that will disrupt neighbors or functions like education during school hours, and preachers do not have the right to obstruct traffic, whether vehicular or pedestrians, in the public square. Citizens have a right to be left alone in their homes, in the airport, and in their businesses. Religious institutions exist on a continuum that contains elite spokespersons for the learned scholars from the best seminaries to folk religions that have charismatic leaders who often have confrontations with the law, like Jim Jones and David Koresh.

CULTS AND UTOPIAN VISIONS—JONESTOWN AND THE BRANCH DAVIDIANS

The idea of a Christian utopia is planted in the biblical narrative of Genesis, according to Quentin Schultze (2003):

> In the biblical book of Genesis, human beings are created to be coworkers with the Creator. God tells Adam and Eve to plant and care for the garden that God made for them. God then blesses humankind and gives people the power to act upon their God-created role in the world as caretakers of Creation. As one observer puts it, the "power of the Creator's blessing enables [human beings] to grow up and grow into technical and

technological activities. It is both the gift of God and the fruit of human work and thought. Humankind is empowered by God to work with the world and to create" (Marshall, 1984, p. 5). In addition, the technical work that humankind begins in the Garden of Eden will end in the city, the New Jerusalem. "The life of humankind through fall and redemption . . . involves shaping and forming the earth, moving from the garden to the city." (Marshall, 1984, p. 5) (p. 51)

Jonestown, a settlement that was cut out of the jungle of Guyana, South America, started as an ideal society, but it ended in a tragedy that would record 911 members of the People's Temple dead in a mass suicide, which Jones called a revolutionary act. Jim Jones was a charismatic preacher who became a successful reformer, gathering followers who believed in his preaching, his social work to feed the hungry, and his desire to build a color-blind society. Jones's attempts to establish such a community was part of the utopian vision that many Christians have espoused in the past. Congressman Leo Ryan went to Guyana to investigate abuses that families reported to him. When Americans saw the newsreels that his cameraman continued to record while bullets rang out during the confrontation between the unarmed California congressman and the men from Jonestown who shot and killed him, they were mortified with reports that 911 people died there following that incident, including women and children of all ages. Sixteen People's Temple members defected to fly out with Congressman Ryan, consisting of the Parks and Bogue families from Indiana. The Parks family ran the Jonestown medical clinic, while Jim Bogue was the agricultural manager and a founding member. Jones beseeched them to remain, but when they left, he called them traitors and lamented that when people leave, they tell lies about the place (Wessinger, 2000, p. 46).

JIM JONES

Jim Jones began his ministry in California in the 1970s as a reformer who promised racial harmony, Christian love, and a sense of belonging. In other words, his flavor of rhetoric was utopian. While today his blood son, now 50-some years old, would tell you that his father was a "monster" in his last psychotic days, he would also tell you that Jonestown was a grand experiment that his father, mother, and loyal followers cut out of the jungle of Guyana, South America. Both Stephen and his adopted brother, who carried Jim Jones's name and claimed that his adopted father brought him back from the dead, were away the day that the mass suicides occurred. Faith healings and miracles were part of Jim Jones's repertoire, and as his adopted son stated, it was difficult not to feel indebted to and awestricken by someone who had that kind of power. But some saw through the fraud and wished to leave the settlement, and that is why the congressman had gone there to investigate conditions.

Some People's Temple members survived because they were away on a field trip the day that Ryan came to Guyana to investigate charges that Jones was holding family members against their will and that other abuses were occurring. A documentary was released in

Jim Jones began his career as a reformer gathering blacks and whites together to form a utopian community in Guyana, South America, where he preached Marxist ideology and presented himself as a God figure.

February 2007 named *Jonestown: The Life and Death of People's Temple*. It was reviewed by Barry Paris in the *Pittsburgh Post-Gazette*, who wrote:

> Jones, after all, was a bona-fide civil rights pioneer, who practiced as well as preached integration as early as the '50s. A large majority (80 percent) of his followers were African-American. His was really a black church led by a white minister. He built a congregation that promised food, clothing, shelter and retirement homes to its people—and delivered. Sure, folks had to give a 20-percent tithe (which evolved into giving all their money and possession) to the church, but that wasn't so unusual and they did it voluntarily. In the utopian-community business, a deal's a deal. . . . Unknown to the rank-and-file utopians was that, as a child in Indiana, their color-blind leader had evidenced a morbid fascination with death and charismatic religion from age 5, stabbing and solemnly burying cats for his rituals. (Paris, 2007, p. W-24)

Jim Jones had supported San Francisco Mayor Moscone's campaign and was rewarded by being named to the city's housing commission. He moved his operation to Guyana, South America, where he bought a large tract of land on which he built a settlement that housed 1,000 people, where he isolated them. When Congressman Ryan went to investigate charges of coercion, financial corruption, and sexual abuse, members of the compound shot Ryan and other members of his party. Then Jones "announced they were under attack and ordered everyone to escape the misery that would befall them by 'going over' to the other side, where they would find peace" (Paris, 2007, p. W-24). The members were lined up, children first, and given cyanide-laced strawberry Flav-R-Aid, while others were shot in the head. As one former People's Temple member said, "No one ever goes and joins a cult. They join a church" (Paris, 2007, p. W-24). So Jim Jones began gaining power by using utopian rhetoric that promised absolute equality, security, love, and belonging—basic needs for people who were disenfranchised. Then, as his paranoia and drug use increased, his sermons turned to apocalyptic rhetoric that their paradise could not survive in Guyana because "they" would never leave them alone to succeed. He practiced drills called "White Nights" in case they were attacked, and he demanded absolute devotion. He had loyalty drills where the members practiced the suicide ritual that would finally be enacted. He would rather see the whole community die than be brainwashed by the capitalists and other corrupt invaders, as he described them. With the murder of Congressman Ryan, he knew that his reign was over, so he chose to end it all, blaming the defectors for the act that was to follow. His son Stephen said in an interview with Ron Csillag:

> Q: You state in the film that your father knew he was sick and believed he was a fraud. Did he ever move to the point where he really believed he was a kind of messiah?
>
> A: Tough to say. I doubt it. The delusion at that point, the level of drugs he was taking toward the end, especially, I can't say. I think there was always part of him that knew he was a fraud, part of him that was deeply insecure. His whole agenda was about trying to drown out that voice with as much adulation as he could conjure and cajole out of people. . . . (When) it became clear that people were tuning him out, and many of them were likely to go back and let others know what they had experienced, his world unraveled. He had no reason to continue living. He was destroyed. And so he took a lot of people with him. (Csillag, 2007, p. 2)

Jonestown had begun as a utopian community where all would contribute to the socialist commune cut from the jungle. Jones tightened his control over the members, performing sex with women and men alike, refusing to allow children to go to their parents or others to leave the compound, and finally annihilating the whole group of them. His message had long passed persuasion and entered into perpetual propaganda, coercion, and fear-inducing rituals. His commune at Jonestown was no longer about creating a heaven on earth, but sustaining his hellish control over his followers, many of whom would have gone away if given that choice. The last gathering at Jonestown was audiotaped with Christine Miller, a 60-year-old black woman arguing with Jones that "where there is life, there is hope" and that she was not ready to die nor should the children be killed. Jones's reply showed that he still believed himself to be a savior of all of them, but his incoherent rant reflected his agitated state:

> "I've saved them. I saved them, but I made my example. I made my expression. I made my manifestation and the world was not ready, not ready for me. Paul said, 'I was a man born out of due season.' I've been born out of due season, just like all we are—and the best testimony we can make is to leave this goddamn world [applause]" Christine Miller complained that people were becoming hostile toward her, but Jones encouraged her to speak and said that she was not a traitor: "I know you're not a runner." But miller decided to stop arguing: "That's all I have to say." Christine Miller chose to die with her community. (Wessinger, 2000, p. 51)

Other members spoke of how crossing over to the other side "feels good." Jones's last words on the audiotape were, "We got tired. . . . We didn't commit suicide, we committed an act of revolutionary suicide protesting the conditions of an inhumane world" (Wessinger, 2000, p. 51).

Annie Moore, a nurse who was the last to die, left a note that stated that the children there were free from the streets where they could be run down by cars; the elderly were treated with respect and given little garden patches to tend, and those who were sick were given the best medical care. She concluded by writing in a different colored ink, "We died because you would not let us live in peace. Annie Moore" (Wessinger, 2000, p. 52).

Jones had preached that the United States would be destroyed by a nuclear holocaust, but surviving elites would establish a new socialist order, a second Eden. His revolutionary style of apocalyptic rhetoric included him as the embodiment of Christ. He told followers that he was no longer a man but a principle.

> Jones warned that a cataclysmic period of race war, genocide, and ultimately nuclear war was nearing. He taught that Nazi fascists and Ku Klux Klan white supremacists would put people of color in concentration camps. As the messiah, Jones offered a place of refuge in his church and ultimately the "promised land" in Jonestown. Utilizing the powerful metaphor from the book of Revelation in the New Testament, Jones taught that American capitalist culture was irredeemable "Babylon." There was no point in trying to reform its corrupt institutions. Instead, the elect had to withdraw to a place of safety to survive the destruction, after which they would emerge to establish the perfect communist society." (Wessinger, 2000, p. 33)

Despite Jones's success in creating the commune of Jonestown and establishing a devoted following, death did not come from the fulfillment of any prophesies from Revelation or the holocaust that he had predicted for July 15, 1967, then changed to a secret date (Wessinger, 2000, p. 38). Death came to Jonestown through the execution of Jim Jones's own design to either control all the residents there or have them die in his jungle Eden, a very corrupted paradise.

THE BRANCH DAVIDIANS

David Koresh of the Branch Davidians reached his position of power and control through a different set of circumstances. Vernon Howell, who renamed himself David Koresh in 1990, offers perhaps the best and most dramatic example of apocalyptic rhetoric, because he presented himself as a messiah anointed by God to interpret the Seven Seals of the book of Revelation. Koresh claimed that the prophesies of Revelation were revealed to him in 1985:

> In Revelation 10, an angelic figure is told to "seal up" and not write the mysteries of seven "thunders," which are equivalent to the events of the Seven Seals. Yet this figure has in his hand a "little book," and he is given all the "mystery of God as declared to the prophets."

This messenger, whom Koresh claimed to be, is subsequently told, "You must prophesy *again* before many people, nations, and tongues, and kings" (emphasis added). (Tabor & Gallagher, 1995, p. 16)

The *Waco Tribune-Herald* had begun in February, 1993, publishing articles that claimed David Koresh, whom they called "The Sinful Messiah," was guilty of bizarre sexual practices, child abuse, and paramilitary activities that included having an armed arsenal (Tabor & Gallagher, 1995, p. 2). A former convert, Marc Breault, who was a candidate for the ministry in the Seventh-Day Adventist church from which the Branch Davidians had splintered in 1930, came to Mount Carmel and became a trusted and loyal lieutenant to Koresh. When Koresh announced that a "new light" had been revealed to him in which he was to propagate a family from his seed which gave him the right to have sexual relations with any woman in the community, including married ones and girls who had barely reached puberty, Breault left Mount Carmel and became Koresh's arch opponent. Breault went to Australia and began to expose Koresh's behaviors to media sources; he reported sexual abuse, which culminated in one of the minor girls, Keri Jewell, being taken by her father out of the compound to Michigan where he had moved. Her mother, Sherri Jewell, would remain behind and die in the massive fire that consumed the whole compound April 19, 1993, where 74 Branch Davidians were found dead, 21 of whom were children under age 14 (Tabor & Gallagher, 1995, p. 3). Only 9 Branch Davidians escaped the fire, but in the initial raid, 4 Bureau of Alcohol, Tobacco, and Firearms (BATF) agents were killed and 20 were wounded, with 6 Branch Davidians shot and others wounded. David Koresh was wounded in the shoot-out, but on Monday following the Sunday raid he began a series of interviews, taking hundreds of hours to explain his view of the world. The substance of these messages, which most saw as either delaying tactics or boring monologs, contained "his understanding of the biblical apocalyptic significance of the situation in which he found himself" (Tabor & Gallagher, 1995, p. 3). Koresh believed that he was anointed by God, as the second messiah, to interpret the meaning of the Seven Seals, or the end times. The negotiators from the government who pleaded with the Branch Davidians to surrender and come out of the compound saw their mission as one of "hostage rescue." But the Branch Davidians saw the moment as a fulfillment of the apocalypse when the righteous ruler of the earth would come to reign. According to James Tabor and Eugene Gallagher, who conducted interviews with members of the Branch Davidians and gave Koresh some credibility as a theologian, or at least a sincere seeker of divine answers, the Davidians saw this moment as a confrontation with the Babylonians:

> In their view, the federal agents represented an evil government system, referred to in the book of Revelation as "Babylon." The idea of "surrendering to proper authority," as the government demanded throughout the next seven weeks, was absolutely out of the question for these believers unless or until they became convinced it was what God willed. As they saw it, their group had been wantonly attacked and slaughtered by government agents whom they understood to be in opposition to both God and his anointed prophet David Koresh. Their fate was now in God's hands. (Tabor & Gallagher, 1995, p. 4)

McLENNAN CO.
SHERIFF'S OFFICE
WACO, TEXAS
58022   1103 77

David Koresh, called the "evil messiah" by reporters said he was a prophet, and he was obsessed with the apocalypse and the book of Revelation.

The BATF agents reported that conversations with Koresh were often three or four hours long and not really negotiations but sermons wherein he used religious rhetoric preaching to them. He told them that that God had told him to wait and that he would not surrender until he received "word from God" because the group perceived that they were in the period of the Fifth Seal, which must be placed into context from the book of Revelation.

In its opening chapters the book of Revelation describes a scene in which a mysterious book or scroll sealed with seven wax seals is introduced. The question is then raised: "Who is worthy to open this sealed book?" Koresh understood the sealed book to be the entire Bible, particularly the prophetic writings. Accordingly, to open the book is not only to explain it but also to orchestrate the events it sets forth, leading to the climax of human history, the end of the world. According to the book of Revelation, only one person can open this book, a figure called "the Lamb," whom Christians have always understood to be Jesus of Nazareth. Koresh, however, had an elaborate set of arguments to demonstrate that a figure other than Jesus was intended here, a second Christ, or Messiah, whom Koresh claimed to be. This second Messiah he found prophesied in many passages in the Bible, but particularly in the Psalms and in Isaiah, where he is called "Koresh," the Hebrew name for Cyrus, the ancient king of Persia who conquered Babylon. David Koresh, born Vernon Howell, claimed to be this special figure, sent before God's final judgment upon the world to open the Seven seals of the book of Revelation and thus reveal to the world the full mysteries of the entire Bible. (Tabor & Gallagher, 1995, p. 8)

The Branch Davidians believed that they were living in the moment of the Fifth Seal, because the book of Revelation spoke about those who were slain because of their faithful testimony to God and how their blood would be avenged. The Sixth Seal revealed a time of disastrous earthquakes and heavenly signs that would mark the arrival of the Seventh Seal. As paranoid as the rest of the world may have viewed Koresh to be, the action of the Branch Davidians confronting the BATF and the earlier deaths fulfilled the Fifth Seal prophesy, wherein they believed if they waited a little while, the rest would be slain and their martyrdom would lead to the Sixth Seal, which would bring the judgment of God to earth (Tabor & Gallagher, 1995, p. 10). So their delaying tactics were consistent with their worldview, according to scriptural prophesy as preached by Koresh, their self-proclaimed messiah. He had predicted the confrontation with Babylon to occur in 1995, not in 1993, but not all the details were clear to him. Tabor and Gallagher (1995) wrote:

> Koresh was convinced that the attack on February 28 was related to the final sequence of events foretold in the Bible, but, given these ambiguities, he was uncertain of what he was to do. Although the apocalyptic Text was fixed, like a script written in advance, the Interpretation and the precise Context were variable. Koresh was waiting because he believed that God had told him to do so and because he understood a waiting period to be required by the "fifth seal." In the meantime he was seeking his "word from God," which would clarify the ambiguities and uncertainties inherent in the changing outside situation. (p. 12)

Koresh had sent Livingstone Fagan, who had a graduate degree in theology and was an avid supporter of Koresh, out of Mt. Carmel to act as religious interpreter for the Davidians. Fagen told the agents that the outcome of the confrontation was not predetermined but depended on the government's response to Koresh's messages. "Fagan saw the Mount Carmel siege as a kind of spiritual trial, or test, for our culture, to determine whether or not we would listen to God's final messenger" (Tabor & Gallagher, 1995, p. 13). Meanwhile the BATF agents were presenting arguments to Janet Reno, attorney general under President Clinton, to take immediate action, and the evidence presented to her cast Koresh in the light of a master manipulator and con man. Meanwhile, Koresh did begin work on his interpretation of the Seven Seals, and he wrote a letter to his lawyer, Dick DeGuerin, stating that once he finished his writing and interpretation, he would be free of his "waiting period" and then he would stand to be judged regarding his action. He said the first manuscripts would be given to his lawyer, but many scholars and religious leaders would want to publish them. Koresh said that would not be the case because he wanted everyone to have them. Koresh had promised to come out on March 2, but he changed his mind. Meanwhile, experts who ruled on Koresh's mental state thought him to be extremely paranoid, or just delaying the ultimate confrontation, so Janet Reno gave the approval for the CS gas operation that involved punching holes into the walls of the compound with tanks to deliver the gas that was intended to evacuate the compound. Ruth Riddle, who survived the fire, had acted as Koresh's typist and stenographer that Sunday night before the fire. She carried a computer disc with approximately 28 pages of manuscript on it, which indicated that Koresh was working on the interpretation that he had promised. He was totally committed to sharing the apocalyptic scenario of the book of Revelation with the world in order to save souls. He envisioned himself as the messiah who would confront Babylon, but his end would arrive sooner than he envisioned. Some believed that if the federal agents had stepped into the ideology of David Koresh to negotiate, a different outcome may have been possible, but others saw the death of federal agents and Koresh's refusal to yield at least everyone else in the compound up to the federal agents as sufficient evidence of his last-ditch effort to manipulate and control his followers. Kenneth Newport, in *The Branch Davidians of Waco* (2006), reported that Koresh held counsel with selected males in the compound that may have led to the Branch Davidians themselves setting the fire, which would bring the fulfillment of their prophesies that a great wall of fire would burn their flesh and "take them up" and where their last act would be one of faith and obedience to God rather than an act of cowardice or "surrender to the beast" (Newport, 2006, p. 322). In other words, Koresh chose to be "taken up" on the flames that he predicted rather than be "taken out" by the agents of Babylon. Perhaps the fatal fire could have been prevented had the government seen Koresh as something other than a cult personality but Mt. Carmel as "a fully functioning interpretative community" (Newport, 2006, p. 322).

Such cases bring troublesome questions regarding the government's role in protecting our citizens from opportunistic exploitative personalities and at the same time respecting the sanctity of beliefs in the afterlife and the sacred texts of people who view the world in a very different light than mainstream America. The similarities between Jones and Koresh are multiple: each presented himself as a prophet or messiah with special powers to prophesy the future; both gathered disenfranchised followers with promises of a utopian society; both claimed privileges regarding sexual partners and rights of the followers to leave; and both leaders used propaganda to indoctrinate their flock.

There were other religious cults during the 1970s who espoused apocalyptic rhetoric, with each embracing different versions of the end times, and some have ended in group suicides, like Heaven's Gate, while others have thrived. Some of the more visible ones were the Hare Krishnas and the Moonies. Reverend Sun Myung Moon, the South Korean evangelist who enlisted an army of teenagers and young adults, was indicted for tax evasion and conspiracy after depositing approximately $1.6 million in cash in Chase Manhattan Bank of New York. These accounts earned $112,000 in interest, which he failed to report, and the organization said he was just holding them for the Unification Church ("Of Moon and Mammon," 1981, p. 1). The question that many raised was, what appeal did the 3 million members of the Unification Church find in following Moon when many parents charged him with kidnapping or brainwashing their children? The Moonies could be found at ballgames, airports, and Fourth of July celebrations selling candy or flowers late into the night. The tragedies of Waco, Texas, and Jonestown, Guyana, are case studies in cults controlled by irrational leaders who isolated their members, controlled their lives totally, and came to a dismal end with only a handful surviving the mass murders or suicides. Scholars predict that mass suicides will continue unless we understand the ideology of the true believers based on their prophesies and interpretations of sacred texts. These visionaries, like Jones and Koresh, become absolute masters over their sects or cults by claiming divine gifts or powers from God. They interpreted the Scriptures to suit their own desires, but the followers would deny that they were brainwashed or coerced into submission. Many of the Branch Davidians were educated men and women with advanced degrees, with some coming from successful businesses. So how can we explain this contradiction between being men and women of the world in a rational sense and belonging to a society that lives for the second coming of Christ and envisions all events as fulfillment of that inexorable move toward the Millennium? For them, the believers, the promises were clearly written, and the signs of Babylon were all around them. The agents may come as Congressman Ryan, as the Bureau of Alcohol, Tobacco, and Firearms agents, or as the Internal Revenue Service came to challenge their devotion to their leader, beliefs, and practices, but their commitment to beliefs are so devout that hundreds are willing to die for them rather than join the larger society.

SUMMARY

We can see that religion and rhetoric are inseparable, since "The Word," as Burke analyzed the Judeo-Christian story, has been assimilated into the foundations of our society through laws, literature, moral codes, and various religious denominations. The wall that Jefferson created as a metaphor, that separates church and state, has grown taller and wider in the recent past with challenges to prayer in school, intelligent design, and abortion debates occurring in the courts. The rhetoric of religion takes two dominant themes— utopian and apocalyptic. Utopian rhetoric promises the ideal society through the resurrection of the "shining city on a hill." When the promise of that ideal society does not materialize, then apocalyptic rhetoric is adopted, which relies on the prophesies from the Old and New Testaments that warn of the end of the world as we know it. The arrival of the Millennium is to usher in the age of Satan chained and Christ to reign on the earth for Christians or in Jewish ideology for the messiah to arrive. Other genres that can be analyzed are the rhetoric of conversion, discernment, communion, exile, and praise. Religious diversity will continue to grow with challenges to the dominant sects in America. Muslims are a growing population with an increasing presence in society, now including Congress.

 Religious leaders have been instrumental in challenging injustices such as slavery, segregation, and sexism. Such social movements are worthy of books on their own merit, but in this chapter we have only introduced some of the rhetoric that leaders used to expose the core issues.

The power of persuasion is at the very heart of any religious enterprise. Some teach through interpretations of sacred texts, and theological seminaries continue to sustain this scholarship. Others use the lessons from the profane world and establish belief systems that splinter from the dominant institutions of religion. Freedom of religion is one of our most sacred rights, but no one is above the law. As the examples of Jonestown, Guyana, and Waco, Texas, show, the government has a right to intervene to protect individuals from abuse of fanatics or psychotic leaders. The line between the right to be left alone to exercise religious freedoms and the role of government to intervene to prosecute crimes against citizens, to expose theft, and expose pedophiles or other predators has not been established in black-and-white terms. Each case that makes its way to the Supreme Court has to be decided on the merit of the evidence, but as Waco shows, controversy surrounds findings regarding the time, place, and manner in which the parties conducted their religious activities. Ongoing challenges are increasingly taken to our courts, where Richard Neuhaus's "naked square" may become the only one that everyone can agree to inhabit. We have not reached that state yet, but the counting of Christmas trees, menorahs, and other religious symbols to see which religion will prevail as the most visible one in public space, and legal battles over these issues, may ultimately remove all evidence of the sacred canopy that covers us through life except in our homes, temples, or churches. These divisive debates are referred to as the "culture wars," and the outcome will depend on who has the legitimacy and power to have the last word.

APPLICATIONS

1. Interview a religious leader—minister, rabbi, or priest—concerning what they consider to be the primary obstacle to making their religion a viable one today.
2. Review a recent court case that concerns a religious issue—clothing, symbols such as crosses in the workplace, teaching intelligent design instead of evolution in schools, religious group meetings on school property, etc. Analyze the arguments that are presented by the parties on both sides of the issue. Which do you find to be most persuasive? Why?
3. Study the Waco, Texas, case of the Branch Davidians. Do you believe that the government acted properly in using CS gas on the compound where the Branch Davidians were barricaded? What criteria should be used before religious compounds are forced to open their doors or permit outside inspection or investigations?
4. What distinguishes folk religions from institutional religions?
5. As a theoretical question, how strong should the "wall" between church and state be? Hold a debate that presents arguments for the "establishment clause," which forbids the government to establish a state religion, and for the "free exercise" of religion, which permits the presence of religion in the public square, churches, work, government functions, etc. What are the issues? Why does this separation of church and state exist? Whom does it protect?
6. Complete research on a social movement and describe the role that religious leaders and religious issues played in the controversy: Abolitionist movement, the Anti-Saloon movement, the Civil Rights movement, The Abortion movement 1965–1973 and beyond, or the Gay Rights movement.
7. Identify the primary characteristics of Apocalyptic rhetoric and apply it to a contemporaneous situation, such as global warming, terrorism, Wars in the Middle East, natural disasters like Hurricane Katrina, etc.
8. Identify the primary characteristics of Utopian rhetoric and apply them to some community or group who has attempted to establish the perfect society. What was their belief system or ideology? Who led the group? What did they achieve? What happened to them?

REFERENCES

Anderson, R. D. (2004). *Religion and spirituality in the public school curriculum*. New York: Peter Lang Publishing.

Bosmajian, H. A. (Ed.). (1987). *Freedom of religion*. New York: Neal-Schuman Publishers.

Brummett, B. (1991). *Contemporary apocalyptic rhetoric*. Praeger Series in Political Communication. New York: Praeger.

Buber, M. (1957). *Pointing the way*. London: Routledge & Kegan Paul.

Burke, K. (1961). *The rhetoric of religion: Studies in logology*. Berkeley: University of California Press.

Butler, J. (1990). *Awash in a sea of faith: Christianizing the American people*. Cambridge, MA: Harvard University Press.

Butler, J. (2006). December theory and God in Gotham (Theme Issue). *History and Theory, 45*, 47–61.

Cloud, D. W. (Ed.). (1990). Oral Roberts' false prophecies. *O Timothy Magazine, 7*(3), 1.

Cromarty, G., & Rush, E. (1957). *Plastic Jesus* [song lyrics]. Retrieved March 1, 2007, from http://www.reverendcolin.com/PlasticJesus.html.

Csillag, R. (2007). *10 minutes with . . . Stephan Jones*. Personal interview, Toronto, Canada, March 14.

Edwards, J. (1797). Sinners in the hands of an angry God. A sermon preached at Enfield, July 8, 1741, at a time of great awakening; and attended with remarkable impressions on many of the hearers. By the late Reverend Mr. Jonathan Edwards, President of the College of New Jersey. New York: Printed by G. Forman 1797 for C. Davis, No. 94, Water-Street. Retrieved March 10, 2011, from Eighteenth Century Collections on line via Gale: http://find.galegroup.com/ecco/start.do?prodID=ECCO.Foege, A. *Hustler Magazine v. Falwell*. 485 U.S. 46, 1988.

Joplin, J. (1971). *Mercedes Benz* [song lyrics]. *Pearl* album, Paul A. Rothschild, (Producer). New York: Columbia Records.

King, C. S. (1969). *My life with Martin Luther King, Jr*. New York: Holt, Rinehart & Winston.

Kniker, C. R. (1997). Religious practices in public schools. In T. C. Hunt & J. C. Carper (Eds.), *Religion and schooling in contemporary America: Confronting our cultural pluralism*. New York: Garland Publishing.

LaHaye, T. (1972). *The beginning of the end*. Wheaton, IL: Tyndale House.

Marshall, P. (1984). Is technology out of control? *Crux, 20*(3), 5. Cited in *Christianity and the mass media in America*, Q. J. Schultze (2003). East Lansing: Michigan State University Press.

Mays, B. E. (1969). Eulogy of Dr. Martin Luther King, Jr. In C. S. King (Ed.), *My Life with Martin Luther King, Jr*. (pp. 352–359). New York: Holt, Rinehart & Winston.

Metcalf, G. R. (1970). *Black profiles*. New York: McGraw-Hill.

Mixon, H. (1989). "A city upon a hill": John Cotton's apocalyptic rhetoric and the Fifth Monarchy Movement in Puritan New England. *The Journal of Communication and Religion, 12*(1), 1–6.

Newport, K. G. C. (2006). *The Branch Davidians of Waco: The history and beliefs of an apocalyptic sect*. New York: Oxford University Press.

Of Moon and Mammon. (October 26, 1981). *Time* in Partnership with *CNN*. Retrieved February 26, 2007, from http://www.time.com/timeprintout/0,8816,924992,000.html.

Paris, B. (2007). Countdown to Doomsday: Jonestown Documentary Leads Unflinchingly To Horrific Ending. *Pittsburgh Post-Gazette*, February 22.

People v. *Ruggles*, 290 N.Y. 1811.

Pfeffer, L. (1967). *Church, state and freedom* (rev. ed.). Boston: Beacon.

Robinson, D. (1985). *American apocalypses: The image of the end of the world in American literature*. Baltimore, MD: Johns Hopkins University Press.

Russell, D. S. (1960). *Between the testaments*. Philadelphia: Muhlenberg Press.

Sacirbey, I. (December 9, 2006). Conservatives attack use of Koran for oath. *Religion News Service.* Retrieved February 26, 2007, from http://www.washingtonpost.com/wp-dyn/content/article/2006/12/08/AR2006120801482.html.

Schultze, Q. J. (2003). *Christianity and the mass media in America: Toward a democratic accommodation.* East Lansing: Michigan State University Press.

Tabor, J. D., & Gallagher, E. V. (1995). *Why Waco? Cults and the battle for religious freedom in America.* Berkeley: University of California Press.

Victor, J. S. (1996). Forecasting the future of religion: The next 50 years. *The Humanist, 56*(3), 20–23.

Wallace-Wells, B. (May 20, 2012). George Romney for President, 1968. Retrieved from: http://nymag.com/news/features/george-romney-2012-5

Wessinger, C. (2000). *Now the millennium comes violently: From Jonestown to Heaven's Gate.* New York: Seven Bridges Press.

Woolman, J. (1774). Journal. *In the works of John Woolman: In two parts.* Philadelphia. (pp. 1–250). Retrieved from Eighteenth Century Collections Online. (M.DCC.LXXIV. Retrieved March 10, 2011, from Eighteenth Century Collection Online via Gale: http://find.galegroup.com/ecco/start.do?prodId=ECCO.)

CHAPTER 9

ART AS PERSUASION: VISUAL RHETORIC

KEY WORDS

apotheosize	homoerotica	stigmatized
cinematic messages	misogynistic	symbol
conventions	pornography	visual rhetoric
elaboration likelihood model	sign	
	SLAP test	

PREVIEW

This chapter addresses Sonja Foss's theory of visual rhetoric and discusses some examples of how works of art—sculpture, photographs, film, and music videos—communicate with diverse audiences. Charles Kostelnick and Michael Hassett's rhetoric of visual conventions is discussed also, in relation to how conventions are supported by the community that uses them, but conventions can be used as a point of departure as well as a model to which artists conform. In Chapter 6 on political rhetoric, we offered J. Anthony Blair's (2004) analysis of a pre–World War II political cartoon, which he believed clearly made a proposition, or a claim, about the precarious nature of all of Europe if Czechoslovakia were to fall. The focus was particularly on the consequences for England and France if that event were to occur, and it did, so that the slippery slope argument that the cartoonist made came to pass. Blair stated that visual rhetoric could offer propositions that could be either proved or disproved, so that despite ambiguity, visual rhetoric can make arguments just as verbal statements do. Sonja K. Foss wrote of visual rhetoric as a communicative artifact. Let us begin by examining Foss's theory of **visual rhetoric**.

SONJA FOSS'S THEORY OF VISUAL RHETORIC

Sonja Foss (2005) stated that not every visual object qualifies as visual rhetoric. There are three characteristics that must be present for a visual image to be considered as visual

As visual rhetoric, Lady Gaga wore a meat dress to the 2010 Video Music Awards to protest the "Don't ask, don't tell" policy of the military at that time.

rhetoric: "The image must be symbolic, involve human intervention, and be presented to an audience for the purpose of communicating with that audience" (p. 144).

In order for the image to qualify as visual rhetoric, the image must not serve as a **sign**, like thunder means that a storm is coming or falling leaves mean that fall has arrived; it must be symbolic, like the red stop sign, which is only " indirectly connected to its referent" (Foss, 2005, p. 144). The shape of the sign and the color of it have meaning only because we have been taught that it means "Stop." There must be human intervention for an object to qualify as visual rhetoric—that is, someone has to determine the color, form, media, and size of an artifact. Someone must intentionally transform, say, a pine tree into a Christmas tree by adding angels, ornaments, or lights, or make an oak tree into a welcome-home banner by adding a yellow ribbon. Without such decoration, the tree remains a pine tree or an oak tree, which one may appreciate as a natural thing of beauty but not an intentional instrument of communication. Human intervention is essential in either the production of the creation or in the interpretation of what it means (Foss, 2005, p. 144). Visual rhetoric requires an audience that is either real or imagined, although the creator of the image or work may paint, write, or design the artifact with himself or herself as the audience. Foss said in this case it is the "I" talking to the "Me," as Mead noted. Foss (2005) summarized her definition as follows:

> Visual rhetoric as artifact, then, is the purposive production or arrangement of colors, forms, and other elements to communicate with an audience. It is symbolic action in that the relationship it designates between image and referent is arbitrary, it involves human action in some part of the visual communication process, and it is communicative in its address to an audience. As a tangible artistic product, such a visual artifact can be received by viewers and studied by scholars as a communicative message. (p. 145)

Foss not only included the visual artifact that the creator offered to the audience as a first part of her theory, but she also noted that visual rhetoric can refer to the perspective that scholars may take to analyze a visual image. In this sense Foss noted that when we include the second part of her theory on perspective, the possibilities are limitless. What distinguishes the notion of perspective from the visual image is that the focus is on a rhetorical response rather than an aesthetic one. Aesthetics deals with the beholder's perceptual encounter with the colors, design, or form; visual rhetoric's perspective is on understanding the rhetorical responses to the work (Foss, 2005, p. 145).

For example, on perspectives that scholars may take, we can analyze the response to political cartoons that a Denmark paper carried. When the newspaper printed a series of 12 cartoons including one of Mohammed with a bomb in his turban, the Islamic world was extremely offended. First they were offended because the political cartoons implied that the religion was a violent one composed of terrorist intentions, and second the prophet is not supposed to be visually depicted at all. The political fallout was powerful following this cartoon's publication in 2006 and the other 11 that accompanied it in the paper. There were death threats made against the cartoonists, several of whom went into hiding. Five thousand Muslim immigrants living in Denmark took to the streets with Muslim organizations demanding an apology, which the editor, Carsten Juste, rejected saying, "We live in a democracy" (Belien, 2005). The Danish imam Raed Hleyhel stated, "This type of democracy is worthless for Muslims. Muslims will never accept this kind of humiliation. The article has insulted every Muslim in the world" (Belien, 2005). The cartoons did make a political statement, as Blair (2004) illustrated (in chapter 6) using a pre–World War II cartoon, and it did make a statement about radical Islamists in today's world, which illustrates Foss's second type of visual rhetoric, regarding the perspective that the scholar takes. The international audience did interpret the cartoon as a statement about the violence perpetrated by radical Islamists, which was deserving of being elevated to the plane of discussion. Devout Muslims saw the cartoon as desecration of a sacred **symbol**. In retaliation, a Muslim immigrant depicted the Virgin Mary with naked breasts, which drew protests from Catholics, although he needed not fear for his life since he received a subsidy from the Denmark Ministry for Culture to create this image (Belien, 2005). Al-Qaeda websites listed *Jyllands-Posten*, the Danish newspaper that printed the cartoons, as a possible terrorist target. Pictures of bombs with blood covering the paper circulated from a group calling itself "The Glorious Brigades in Northern Europe" (Belien, 2005). As the foregoing example shows, political cartoons do take a perspective on worldly affairs, and the meaning can be read by the audience—in this case, the international audience.

Another feature of the rhetorical perspective on visual imagery is that the audience is not assumed to have any technical knowledge, according to Foss. They are viewed as a lay audience who interpret the work based on their own experiences from living in the world. The rhetorical perspective that scholars may explore includes attention to three elements: the nature of the image, the function of the image, and the evaluation of the image. The nature of the image includes both presented elements—the size of the image, media used or materials applied—and suggested elements—the ideas or themes that the work might evoke. The function of the image deals with the way it works for the audience, not the purpose that was intended by the creator, since none of this material may be available to the scholar. Scholars who take a rhetorical perspective on visual artifacts believe that the image exists independently of the creator. Finally, the evaluation of the image is part of the perspective scholars may take in assessing an image (Foss, 2005, pp. 146–147).

Foss noted that scholars may apply either deductive or inductive methods to visual imagery. Using the *deductive* method scholars assume that visual imagery possesses the same characteristics that discourse does, although Foss noted that propositions exist only because viewers attribute them to the visual image. Blair made this argument earlier as well, that is, that visual images are interpreted much as symbols in communication, and this allows for an expansive selection from rhetorical theories that already exist to be used. Some examples that Foss cited were works that applied rhetorical analysis to Benjamin Franklin's commemorative medal, *Libertas Americana*, as epideictic, deliberative, and apologetic rhetoric; and to New York's Central Park as epideictic rhetoric focusing on "repose, rhetorical sensibility, emblem and allegory, and ornamentation" (Foss, 2005, p. 148). Scholars who use the *inductive* approach on visual imagery do not assume that visual images generate propositions or arguments, as discursive symbols do. First, one cannot isolate a single element that would function as a word might, and language is general and abstract whereas images are concrete, Foss noted. Scholars who use the inductive approach focus on the properties of the image to decipher meaning from it and then attempt to construct a rhetorical theory to explain its symbolicity (Foss, 2005, p. 150). Scholars who use the inductive approach to visual imagery may create new kinds of knowledge about all forms of art.

In summary, Foss's theory proposes that, in order for an artifact to qualify as visual rhetoric, it requires symbolic action and human intervention regarding the image's creation and assumes an audience that could appreciate or interpret its meaning. Through deductive reasoning, the audience or the scholar who analyzes the artifact could interpret the work as making a claim or proposition with truth value and apply existing rhetorical theories to the perspective they employ. Through inductive reasoning, the audience or scholar would focus only on the characteristics of the image itself to derive meaning or its rhetorical significance. Scholars analyzing the artifact could take multiple perspectives, including known rhetorical theories, or invent new theories arising from the visual image itself.

KOSTELNICK AND HASSETT'S CONVENTIONS

In order for an audience to interpret or derive meaning from visual rhetoric, there must be some conventional understanding within the field that can be relied on to make judgments. Messaris and Moriarty (2005) called this ability visual literacy. Paul Messaris and Sandra Moriarity wrote of "visual literacy theory," which not only recognizes theories of visual rhetoric but defines the skills inherent in decoding meaning. They quoted Deborah Curtiss (1987):

> Visual literacy is the ability to understand the communication of a visual statement in any medium and the ability to express oneself with at least one visual discipline. It entails the ability to: understand the subject matter and meaning within the context of the culture that produced the work, analyze the syntax—compositional and stylistic principles of the work, evaluate the disciplinary and aesthetic merits of the work, and grasp intuitively the Gestalt, the interactive and synergistic quality of the work. (Messaris & Moriarty, 2005, p. 482)

Despite the field-specific tools that we use to analyze visual rhetoric, some scholars have looked for common ground that is applicable across fields. In Charles Kostelnick and Michael Hassett's (2003) book, *Shaping Information: The Rhetoric of Visual Conventions*, the authors identify some conventional practices that would help explain the "pervasiveness, malleability and context-dependent nature" of visual images (p. 5). The **conventions** that they identify are as follows:

1. *Conventions prompt rather than stifle invention* (p. 5).

They noted that conventions are not etched in stone, but rather they invite adaptation and improvisation. Conventions are dynamic, with their fate resting in the community that supports them, the technology that facilitates them, and the cultural values that find meaning in them.

2. *Conventions pervade all forms of design* (p. 6).

The capital letters at the beginning of every sentence and the period at the end are a convention. Even when designers flaunt or ignore conventions, readers acknowledge their existence when expectations are not met. Conventions permeate all forms of information design, sometimes combining a number of conventions, such as diagrams with instructions, technical grids such as electrical designs, and other forms coexisting together, cutting across fields.

3. *Conventions operate in social contexts where users control them* (p. 6).

Kostelnick and Hassett wrote that conventions are not sent from a platonic domain of preexisting forms; rather, conventions are learned, imitated, and codified—socially constructed. Because they rest within the hands of their users, who can either reject or alter them, they are kept alive in shared communities who interpret them, deploy them, and "behave less like monarchs than like elected officials" (p. 6).

4. *Conventional practice is intrinsically rhetorical* (p. 6).

Conventions are not inherently prescriptive, since the designer must select them based on the ability of receivers to interpret them. "This process of selection, adaptation, and integration requires rhetorical judgment. Even when a convention demands strict conformity, and the designer acquiesces to that authority, the convention carries the rhetorical weight of the discourse community that sanctions it" (p. 6). In other words, the receivers must be able to "read" the visual language.

The conventions that Kostelnick and Hassett (2003) identified can be applied across fields of communication just as readily as they can information design, and they can account for the contextual interpretation of visual rhetoric that gives rise to so many different perspectives on how works of art, advertising, film, graphic design, photographs, and images communicate or make propositions that have truth value. Throughout their analysis of the rhetoric of visual conventions, they note that culture, organization, and discipline all overlap in discourse communities (Kostelnick & Hassett, 2003, p. 27). Given this breadth of interpretation, we can write of either macro- or micro-levels of rhetorical influence. That is, we can look at the idiosyncratic variation or the system of design that serves as a foundation that is either reinforced or used as a point of departure.

One example of departure from expectations would be Maya Lin's Vietnam Veterans Memorial design, which sparked so much controversy that it elicited two follow-up sculptures to be placed in close proximity to the black granite wall. Two elements were very conventional about the memorial—the black granite material that constituted the wall and the listing of the names on the wall. In little towns throughout America, one can view memorial parks where walls of some substance, often granite, hold the names of local heroes from past wars, and these memorials may have statues of doughboys, World War II soldiers or marines, flags, benches, picnic areas, wreaths, or other commemorative symbols. The Vietnam memorial, so plain and devoid of these traditional symbols, invites visitors to decorate the memorial space as they see fit in accordance with their idiosyncratic interpretation of that place and those who are memorialized in the black granite.

THE VIETNAM VETERANS MEMORIAL

The Vietnam Veterans Memorial wall was created through the funds that veterans of that war raised and was designed more than 30 years ago by Maya Lin, a Chinese-American Yale undergraduate student. The memorial consisted of two long walls of black polished granite with the names of 58,249 service men and women engraved on it. Lin entered the competition to complete a requirement for an architecture course. She visited the future site of the memorial on the National Mall in Washington, D.C., to visualize her design. She said, "I thought

Maya Lin said the Vietnam Veterans Memorial represents a rift in the earth that never heals.

about what death is, what a loss is. . . . A sharp pain that lessens with time, but can never quite heal over. The idea occurred to me there on the site. I had an impulse to cut open the earth. The grass would grow back, but the cut would remain" ("Vietnam Veterans Memorial"). She completed the design in three weeks. It caused great controversy when Lin's design was selected for the war memorial. It was unlike any other in its simplicity and power to evoke personal remembrances or responses to the list of names. Many veterans hated it, and 27 Republican congresspersons tried to block the plan to complete Lin's memorial. To placate critics, a conventional bronze statue was installed with three soldiers and an American flag nearby; a women's memorial was added later. The memorial space continues to evolve as additional names are being added to a memorial plaque of dead and MIA soldiers not included originally.

In 2006, what Lin called a "rift in the earth" and one brigadier general called "a scar of shame" was selected by the American Institute of Architects for a work that has stood the test of time (McGuigan, 2007, p. 59). The criteria that designers had been given was: "The design must be reflective and contemplative, it must be harmonious with the site, it must be inscribed with the names of the dead and missing, and it must make no political statement about the war" ("Vietnam Veterans Memorial").

Today the Vietnam memorial wall is the most visited memorial in Washington, D.C. What is most notable about the work is the response that it evokes in all who behold it. Some trace the names with their fingers, and others leave letters, flowers, rosaries, or pictures at the base of the wall. School students who visit the wall write poems or essays telling of their walks there with their fathers or grandfathers and the stories that the tribute evoked from them. Anyone who stands beside the wall and observes the visitors who linger there will see friends and family members touch the names, shed tears, or call out the name in pain or pride, but no one passes there untouched.

Following a rain, red-brown sand washes over the lip of the wall which encourages observers to wipe it clean, to keep it pure, for the hallowed men and women whom it honors. Like the war that it commemorates, the wall has brought controversy and passionate resistance from its inception to the present day. Critics said the V-shape of the wall was a peace sign and made a political statement. No one can give the wall their thoughtful attention without feeling the loss and the confusion that the war brought to America. With her minimalist design, Maya Lin captured something that visitors respond to in their own unique way based on their impressions of the war or their experiences during that time if they were alive. Those who knew the GIs that returned will recall their stories of Agent Orange and the health problems it caused, the napalm bombs, the loss of life and hope in the jungles or on the rivers there. One critic said the memorial was "neither a building nor sculpture," like those from the past, but McGuigan wrote: "Yet few public projects have had such a profound hold on our national consciousness, and it's cast a long shadow over the design of major memorials ever since. Lin created not just an object to revere but an evocative sense of place" (McGuigan, 2007, p. 59).

It is difficult to find a place to put grief, whether it is born in this instant or over a quarter of a century ago; the power of the wall is that it gives each of us permission to deal with grief and loss in our own way. The black granite can be seen as a collective of all the gravestones that mark the resting place of these brave souls or simply a marker to remind us that our lives should be full because of the empty spaces left by these fallen mothers and fathers, lovers and friends. The black granite speaks to us of the passions of life and the solitude of death. What message does the wall whisper to us as we see our own faces reflected in it? It causes us to question the meaning of our own lives where each fills in the blanks about what we will do with this gift. Lin's unconventional design motivates the most conventional of human responses in a very powerful way. The ambiguity of the wall was indeed fitting, with nothing more than the names of those recorded on it. The wall offers no traditional sculpture to give the victims form or substance; that narrative was to be supplied by each mourner who traveled there. For those who demanded more material evidence of the struggle and loss, two additional sculptures were added featuring men and women in realistic poses, but nothing can capture the whole story or purge all the demons that fill the nightmares of some who remember too much. Lin's goal was to relieve the pain and allow the healing to begin through this tribute. It remains a haunting place that marks unfinished lives with indelible etching of their names in stone. In that black shining wall, they, the fallen, have become immortal.

Maya Lin used conventional materials in a very novel way. Each culture has elaborate rituals to deal with death and remind us of the lessons to "memento mori" (remember death) and "fugit hora" (time flies), as Robert Morris noted (2006) in an essay called "Death on Display," but other artists are less concerned with contemplation of eternity and very much absorbed with pleasures of the flesh. Like Mya Lin, Robert Mapplethorpe's photographic exhibits brought a furor of controversy to the art community and prompted political action—all of which increased the value of his work as well as instigating record museum attendance.

MAPPLETHORPE'S EXHIBIT: *THE PERFECT MOMENT*

Robert Mapplethorpe achieved notoriety for his photographs of male nudes that celebrated and documented New York's gay community in the late 1970s. His images explicitly depicted sexual organs and bondage equipment, and often they included both black and white men. Mapplethorpe's exhibit, called *The Perfect Moment* collection, raised the ire of Rev. Donald Wildmon's conservative American Family Association as well as Senator Jesse Helms, Republican from North Carolina, which would ultimately result in congressional action to limit public funds to the National Endowment for the Arts (NEA). Deborah A. Levinson wrote:

> Helms has objected most forcefully to those photographs that he and others regard as pornographic. The senator has a standard packet of four Mapplethorpe photos he shows to reporters questioning him about his stance on "obscene" art. These include "Man in Polyester Suit," depicting a polyester-clad torso of a black man, his uncircumcised penis dangling from his fly, and "Rosie," a two-or three-year-old child caught on film—her crotch exposed. Helms claims the latter is a clear example of child pornography. Both photographs are part of the Perfect Moment collection. (Levinson, 1989, p. 1)

Perhaps the debate on pornography vs. art would not have been so vigorous had Mapplethorpe's exhibit not followed on the heels of the work of Andres Serrano, another photographer, whose exhibit included a work he called "Piss Christ"—"a murky, muddy photograph of the crucified Christ submerged in the artist's urine" (Levinson, 1989, p. 1). The NEA had funded Serrano's work with a $15,000 grant, and similarly part of Mapplethorpe's exhibit had been funded by the NEA. Congress appointed a commission to study the issue of artistic freedom and to examine the procedures by which the NEA awarded funds (Berman, 1991, p. 258). Arguments of "cultural equity" arose when some found that the NEA favored large cities while others found that NEA funds supported Eurocentric art while our population is becoming more diverse, with blacks and Latinos underrepresented.

The political fallout from the congressional inquiry would result in the Corcoran Gallery of Art in Washington, D.C., canceling the exhibit of Mapplethorpe's work in June 1989. The D.C. artists retaliated by showing a slide presentation of the explicit photographs on the marble façade of the building. When the *Washington Post* reviewed the show from its catalog, the demand to see the show then exploded. The Washington Project for the Arts (WPA), which funded the exhibit following this controversy, generally had only 40 visitors on weekends, but two weeks after the Corcoran Gallery cancelation WPA found 4,000 visitors crammed into the small gallery (Levinson, 1989, p. 2). What made Mapplethorpe's nudes so controversial? Beside the nudes who were shown in **homoerotic** poses, he included crosses, altars, and other religious symbols. Levinson's review states:

> But Mapplethorpe had a style all his own. Raised in a strict Catholic family, Mapplethorpe was influenced by the rigidity of his religion in his later work in every way. Often in the exhibit, one sees carefully geometric layouts, as in the two gigantic mirrors "Star" and "Black X." Both are sectioned as precisely as a Good Friday mass, the "X" most symbolically so with a tan cross reaching from apex to apex across the carbon-black mirror.
>
> The cross imagery and its accompanying symmetry also appear dramatically in his 1987 construction, "Andy Warhol," where a photograph of the enigmatic artist is framed inside a square-shaped cross. Warhol, his silver wig surrounded by a glowing halo, has a look on his face like a Christ stunned at the revelation of his own godhood. Religious sentiments figure strongly in "Tie Rack" as well, with stickpins piercing stigmata on a figure of the Virgin Mary and a crucifix suspended from floss wound around the pins. (Levinson, 1989, p. 2)

Mapplethorpe said that he was a Catholic boy who was influenced by the magic and mystery of church, and this shows in how he arranges things: "It's always altars" (Levinson, 1989, p. 2). He placed male genitals upon his altars, and often he featured models without a head, with attention to particular body parts—chest, legs, or if the head is visible, the eyes are downcast. His nudes, unlike those of the ancient Greeks who deified them, included body hair, scars, and imperfections. Robert Asen (1998) wrote:

> Whether as formal objects of appreciation or erotic objects of desire, Mapplethorpe's models are passive figures who pose for the enjoyment and pleasure of the viewer. In a number of his photographs, Mapplethorpe crops the heads of his models, focusing instead on body parts. *Charles* (1985) is representative of this type of Mapplethorpe nude. The photograph shows the torso of a muscular white model. The model poses as a body builder. His arms are raised and cropped, revealing his full chest for the viewer. We cannot see Charles' face nor can he see us. Instead, Charles is an object that we respond to in various ways. In other photographs, whole bodies are shown. Yet in these instances, the models almost always avoid the eye of the camera and viewer. Averted glances and closed eyes substitute for direct engagement with the camera. (Asen, 1998, p. 52)

The men are presented as beautiful objects, with dramatic lighting, which is a Mapplethorpe characteristic, and symmetry. Asen stated that viewers may respond to the nudes as objects of beauty that represent the human form as the classical Greeks appropriated the images of nudes in sculpture. Aristotle said that art presents a thing as it might be in idealized form, whereas history presents what has actually been. The Italians **apotheosized** the nude in Michelangelo's *David*, which no one perceived as pornographic, but Mapplethorpe's nudes made a statement:

> Mapplethorpe's nudes appropriate the sadomasochistic imagery of his earlier work and interpersonal relations that contest heterosexual norms and subject them to an

Robert Mapplethorpe's exhibit caused a political debate about what constitutes art and what constitutes pornography.

> analogous refashioning. The nude mitigates some of the "danger" of this invoked eroticism, making desire "safe" by orienting it to an aesthetic tradition of detached appreciation. (Asen, 1998, p. 54)

Mapplethorpe's nudes are presented as erotic objects, not pornographic images. Roland Barthes argued that pornography is always without intention "and manages to half conceal, delay or distract," while erotic imagery is mediated (Asen, 1989, p. 56).

Mapplethorpe, who died from AIDS in his forties in 1989, challenged the art world with his images, and he challenged the politics of Jesse Helms, Hilton Kramer, and Pat Buchanan, his antagonists, "where the mere presence of homoerotic themes in art is taken as prima facie evidence of **pornography** and obscenity. . . . Mapplethorpe's photography stands as a powerful statement of the beauty and dignity of those whose lives have been denounced as morally bankrupt and baneful" (Asen, 1989, p. 61).

Mapplethorpe's photographs, including sadomasochistic images and homosexual sex acts, were the subject of a pornography suit in Cincinnati in 1990 where the jury cleared the Contemporary Arts Center and its director of the obscenity charges brought against them. The debate over what constituted art and what constituted pornography raged while Mapplethorpe's works were popularized, making his posters, postcards, and catalogues best sellers. Attendance in art museums and galleries increased geometrically, with overflow crowds going to see what all the fuss was about.

It is evident that what Mapplethrope's images represented to the beholder depended on what attitudinal, spiritual, and physical ground the viewer held. Some felt like voyeurs peering into a world where a secret relationship existed between the photographer, Mapplethorpe, and his subject of that moment—like a window blind half raised onto the studio. For others the images represented pornographic pictures that would fail the **SLAP test** developed in the *Miller* v. *California* case of 1973 on pornography. They saw the photographs lacking any Social, Literary, Artistic, or Political value. In other words, for those like Jesse

Helms, the exhibit failed the Supreme Court's standard for decency. The Robert Mapplethorpe Foundation donated $5 million to the Solomon R. Guggenheim Museum in New York City with the stipulation that they show his work in an exhibit every two years (Guggenheim, 1993, p. 1).

Whether he intended to or not, Mapplethorpe instigated a heated debate on all art—what constituted art, how it should be funded, what the content should be, and where it should be shown. It was the content portion of the debate that involved First Amendment proponents who saw the tempest as a barometer of how far our society has sunk into the abyss of political correctness or sensitivity to diversity. James Fitzpatrick, from the law firm of Arnold and Porter in Washington, D.C., specializes in constitutional and public policy issues; in a commencement address entitled "The Sensitive Society," given at the Corcoran School of Art, he stated:

> In our Sensitive Society, comment, observation, satire, reportage, editorials, cartooning, caricature, playwriting and painting—all are now supposed to take into account the sensibilities of the reader or observer. This is not the world of Mark Twain, Ambrose Bierce or H. L. Mencken. . . . Historically a speaker's rights under the First Amendment have not been limited simply because they might cause outrage in the audience. It was only when a speaker's comments could create a severe public disturbance that one might consider a limitation on the speaker's voice. And even in those circumstances, the government would be required to have sufficient force on hand to protect the controversial speaker. (Fitzpatrick, 1995, p. 1)

Fitzpatrick concluded that there are better ways to arrive at truth than to silence the speaker or to ban the artist and their work. Mapplethorpe's exhibit was canceled in June 1989 from the Corcoran Gallery in Washington, D.C., but when the Washington Project for the Arts picked it up, over 50,000 people came to see the show. Record numbers of crowds would attend the seven different exhibits held across the country, with over a half-million people seeing Mapplethorpe's *The Perfect Moment*. It would be hard to claim in the face of this phenomenon that his work lacked either artistic or political value. Mapplethorpe used the conventions of photography—form, light and shadow, texture, composition, space, and color—to communicate his message to the world; it was his rhetorical perspective that aroused such resistance from critics in Congress and other institutions. Using Foss's theory we can see that Mapplethorpe did engage in visual rhetoric by presenting artifacts, photographs, in a "purposive production or arrangement of colors, forms, and other elements to communicate with an audience" (Foss, 2005, p. 145). Further, the perspective that the audience took varied from legal action to close the exhibit and congressional intervention to change the way that the NEA awarded grants or made decisions on what was worthy art, to vigorous defense of Mapplethorpe's freedom of expression and the aesthetics of his work. It was the content of his photographs that sent the combative message, "Here we are; take it or leave it." Mapplethorpe recorded his perspective on the world and his place in it by presenting *The Perfect Moment* when the clock of time had already stopped for him.

VISUAL RHETORIC IN CINEMATIC MESSAGES OF CHANGE:
BROKEBACK MOUNTAIN

While Mapplethorpe's work generated much controversy throughout his short life, his trail-blazing in photography made it more acceptable for others to complete works that explored homosexual themes. We know that attitudes are generally not bent or changed in a revolutionary moment but are influenced through time so that what was once considered shocking becomes less so with additional exposure. For example, the television series *Will and Grace*, which presented likable characters in everyday comedic situations, has been instrumental in normalizing homosexuality to mass audiences, and newer characters continued to do the same thing, like the gay lawyer in the television series *Brothers and Sisters*. The character Kevin Walker was portrayed first as a family member with brothers, sisters, nieces, and nephews who love and accept him with whom he interacts; second as a man trying to connect romantically in a meaningful way with another; and finally as one who has political views and makes decisions that are not always mature or wise. In 1993 Tom Hanks starred in the film *Philadelphia* and was awarded an Oscar for Best Actor; so homosexual protagonists are not new.

Years later, what made *Brokeback Mountain* unconventional was that it was presented as a conventional love story. The movie was nominated for three Oscars (for Best Actor, Best Supporting Actor, and Best Actress in a Supporting Role), and it actually won three Oscars for (Best Director to Ang Lee, Best Original Score to Gustavo Santaolalla, and Best Adapted Screenplay to Larry McMurtry and Diana Ossana). By industry standards, the movie was a great success, but the impact that the film had on attitudes toward homosexual romance would be harder to measure. It is safe to say that mainstream attitudes have shifted substantially since 1993, because as the entertainment industry treats such issues as sexism, racism, and mental illness with increasing sensitivity, audiences have become more tolerant of the issues and more sympathetic with characters portrayed in the works of art, whether photographs, film, or literature.

Brokeback Mountain took eight years to make it to the silver screen from the Pulitzer Prize winner E. Annie Proulx's original short fiction, which was described as a story that "had been sitting there for years, waiting to be told" (Turan, December 9, 2005). The protagonists were a pair of 19-year-old cowboys, played by Jake Gyllenhaal and Heath Ledger. The story is a "deeply-felt, emotional" love story that deals with the uncharted, mysterious ways of the human heart just as so many mainstream films have before it. "The two lovers here just happen to be men" (Turan, 2005). Screenwriters McMurtry and Ossana found the script "scary and sensitive," so it required time for them to strike the right balance. Some audience members found the story slow-moving, while others believed that the rhythm was just right to allow the full story to sink in. The two youthful cowboys, Ennis del Mar (Ledger) and Jack Twist (Gyllenhaal), meet at a trailer where they were seeking summer work in the mountains of Wyoming as sheep herders. Ennis wanted to be a rancher, and Jack wanted to be a rodeo bull-rider; both were trying to make some money to accomplish their plans. Movie reviewer Kenneth Turan (2005) wrote:

> Alone in nature's grandness, they are drawn to each other almost without their knowing it's happening. When the intimacy between them takes hold, it is graphic, candid, unapologetic.

As Proulx writes of a later kiss, passion seizes them "easily as the right key turns the lock tumblers." Yet, as the film is at pains to insist, it is a lonely passion that has no place in their world. Theirs is a bond unlike anything either man has known before; not because it's a same-sex relationship but because of the strength of the feelings involved. Their closeness perplexes, confounds and confuses Ennis and Jack; it's something they can neither explain nor control. (Turan, December 9, 2005)

After they've had sex for the first time, Ennis declares, "I'm not no queer." Jack adds, "Me neither. A one-shot thing. Nobody's business but ours." They know the penalties for being "different" in Wyoming in the early 1960s; Ennis tells a story about one man having been beaten to death for having a gay relationship. That admonition is to be a foreshadowing of what is to happen to Jack later in life:

> When he was nine years old, his father forced him to view the battered corpse of Earl, a gay man, beaten to death and castrated. This harsh lesson from his father teaches Ennis that sexual intimacy and love between two men are forbidden and may get one killed. Although we are told nothing about his mother, we do know that this memory of his father is indeed brutal. For all Ennis knows, his father is one of the perpetrators. Certainly one can assume that Ennis never received from his father nurturance, affection, and love. (Rose & Urschel, 2006, p. 247)

In *Brokeback Mountain* we see that in this case of visual rhetoric "[c]onventions prompt rather than stifle invention" (Kostelnick & Hassett, 2003, p. 5). The conventional love story is given a different twist with the old themes of forbidden fruit, two cowboys, and unrequited love, which is confounded by time and place, but portrayed with great power and depth of character. If we were to look for a tragic flaw in the protagonist, perhaps it would be that he lacks the courage to admit who he really is, and through his denial of self he extends his net of illusions to his entire family, who exist then in his web of lies. Ennis visits Jack's parents after Jack is beaten to death, and all he can do is touch Jack's shirt reverently as though it were a sacred garment from a crucified man. He mourns in stoic silence and regret.

Attention was paid to the marketing of the film's release. The film first opened in select theaters with demographics that would guarantee sophisticated viewers and a large gay community, but audiences and critics described it as "the modern day Romeo and Juliet—the tragic love story of contemporary America" (Stone, 2006, p. 51). But how did heterosexual males respond to it? Alan Stone, a Touroff-Glueck Professor of Law and Psychiatry at Harvard University, wrote in *Psychiatric Times*:

> What is the male audience supposed to think and how are they supposed to feel? Director Ang Lee's answer seems to be that they should be able to suspend their own sexual taboos and accept with tolerance what they see on the screen. As for what they should feel, there are only 2 minutes of homoerotic activity and no frontal nudity in this slow moving film that lingers over the beauty of the tree-capped mountains and the pristine wilderness. Hopefully, heterosexual men will feel neither the excitement of arousal and attraction nor the repulsion of dismay and disgust. That, at least, seems to be Lee's directorial formula and perhaps that

is why *Brokeback Mountain* was able to make it out of select theaters in urban America and continue to draw large attentive audiences in the red states and around the world. (Stone, 2006, p. 51)

Stone's questions regarding how straight men were supposed to respond to the movie gets at the heart of the question of why art, in this case film, is so persuasive. The theater is dark, it is nonthreatening because after all it is just a fictional story, and one can always do a parody of the two gay cowboys to alleviate discomfort if necessary, as most late-night talk show hosts did following the release of the film. Many in the gay community complained about the fact that neither of the lead actors nor the director were gay and that Lee had shown too much restraint. But "for mainstream audiences, *Brokeback Mountain* was gay enough, and its star-crossed lovers evoked compassion and tolerance" (Stone, 2006, p. 52). Homosexuality has existed as a great stigma in straight society, but attitudes are being altered through normalization of homosexual relationships, media portrayals that are sympathetic with likable characters, and everyday interactions with gay men and women who are visible in government, corporations, and schools. Other issues, such as mental illness, have been explored through literature and film and similarly have been defused as **stigmatized** conditions with further exposure to the subject.

PORTRAYALS OF MENTAL ILLNESS IN FILM

In earlier parts of the twentieth century and before that, the mentally ill were hidden away in homes or placed in institutions because of the fear and stigma attached to mental illness. Movies like *The Three Faces of Eve* (1957), *Rain Man* (1988), *Forrest Gump* (1994), *Nell* (1994), and *A Beautiful Mind* (2001) have explored such conditions as dissociative identity disorder, autism, schizophrenia, and developmental delays. Many others have portrayed sociopathic or psychopathic personalities. Often the portrayal induced fear and confusion in the minds of theatergoers rather than enlightening them.

Joanne Woodward's depiction of Eve is that of a young, mousey housewife who emerges with three separate personalities but is treated with hypnosis and comes to understand former

Brokeback Mountain portrayed a homosexual romance between two virile cowboys that ultimately proved to be deadly.

abuse and to heal. Such simplistic solutions to complex illness are laughable by any measure of realism, but the movie opened dialog concerning dissociative identity disorder. In *Rain Man*, Dustin Hoffman portrays a man who has been institutionalized by his father for autism and apparently for endangering his younger brother, played by Tom Cruise, who did not know that Raymond, his real name, existed until after their father's death. The movie offers comedic situations as "Rain Man" is deinstitutionalized and taken across country by his younger brother, who learns that Rain Man can do mathematical equations and easily win at poker. We learn that he is obsessive about his corn curls, television programs, and about being touched, but his younger brother invents ways to desensitize Rain Man, such as a kiss from a sexy girl in an elevator. When she asks how it was, Rain Man replies, "wet." Audience members left the theater perhaps more curious about autism, but they would have to read and pursue the topic further to learn that there are levels of autism that are only mildly obvious while others are totally disabling. Hoffman won an Oscar for his portrayal in *Rain Man* in 1989, having visited mental institutions for a year to study residents who suffered from mental illnesses. The character Forrest Gump became a champion in indescribable ways, but he was endearing as he frequently quoted his mother, who told him, "Life is like a box of chocolates; you never know what you're going to get." Forest, who has a low IQ, has "gumption," which is a southern term meaning tenacity, ingenuity, and integrity, that leads to emotional and spiritual revelations throughout the movie, which earned 13 Oscar nominations (Fables, 1995).

A Beautiful Mind is a movie based on Sylvia Nasar's book exploring Nobel Prize-winner John Nash's true story as he struggled with schizophrenia, a mental illness that affects one in 100 people across cultures (Kadlecek, 2002). Nash suffered the same symptoms that others do: "delusions, frequent auditory hallucinations, illusions that messages are being sent to him through television or newspapers, a skewed view of reality leading to paranoia. And, like many who have struggled to live functional lives with the illness, he has watched his personal relationships dissolve, his career interrupted and his life disintegrate" (Kadlecek, 2002, para. 2). What makes Nash different is that he shared the Nobel Prize in 1994 for the doctoral thesis he completed at Princeton University on game theory in 1950. Nash did recover after his breakdown that lasted 25 years. The movie, which starred Russell Crowe, reached more people than Nasar's book would have and had a greater impact on public perception.

> "Cases like Nash's help us know that people may have a mental illness but still have a lot to contribute to society," Says Roberto Gil, assistant clinical professor of psychiatry and head of the Schizophrenic Research Unit at the New York State Psychiatric Institute at Columbia Presbyterian Medical Center. "I'm encouraged by the general public awareness [created by Nash's story]. Most times mental illness in general and schizophrenia in particular comes [to] the public's attention only when behaviors are bizarre or violent. But we still have a long way to go in helping educate families and remove the stigma." (Kadlecek, 2002, para. 9)

The power of cinema as an art form to educate and influence the public is irrefutable, as all of the foregoing examples demonstrate. Blair (2004) noted that films empower arguments primarily by constructing credible narratives (p. 56). Walter Fisher noted in his narrative theory that in order for a story to be credible, it must have coherence and fidelity—that is, it must hang together and ring true. But that raises the question: If these positive results occur because of the persuasive power of cinema or entertainment forms, are we equally influenced by the sex and violence that dominates movies and television? In general, the courts have found that there is no direct link between video games like *Grand Theft Auto* and violent movies and violence in society. It is contradictory that we claim positive effects on the one hand and deny the negative impact on the other. A definitive answer to these cultural questions can only be answered by extensive studies that include more than college students in the samples. Professionals in the field of mental health certainly do believe that literature and movies are influential in shaping attitudes and behaviors. Michael Grinfeld wrote:

> Battling the societal stigma that enshrouds brain diseases is difficult, and the ability to overcome centuries-old biases is often thwarted by the stereotypical representations of mentally ill individuals, as well as psychiatrists, psychologists and other therapists. The issue is nothing new, but the latest spate of movies, books and TV shows that involve mental health issues renews concerns that rather than progression there is a backslide into prejudice that militates against understanding. (1998, p. 1)

Professional organizations such as the National Stigma Clearinghouse (NSC) have begun to advocate for change in the damaging stereotypical depictions of mental illness in the media. Jean Arnold, president of the NSC, said that the producers do not mean to be hurtful, but they see the stereotypes as a short route to understanding. She said that the entire mental health community needs to be more active in taking on the entertainment industry when it portrays hurtful and inaccurate images or situations (Grinfeld, 1998, p. 1).

Grinfeld wrote that Glen Gabbard, medical doctor and author of the book *Psychiatry and the Cinema* (1987), testifies to the power that cinematic images and story lines have to influence the public regarding our understanding of mentally ill people:

> Movies, to the American public are like what Greek drama was to ancient Athenians. They shape our culture and they shape our attitudes," said Gabbard, the Callaway Distinguished Professor at the Menninger Clinic in Topeka, Kansas. "Ever since McLuhan, we know how influential the electronic media is in shaping the culture." (Grinfeld, 1998, p. 2)

According to Gabbard, neither therapists nor mentally ill clients have fared well in the cinema. He mentions three movies that portray therapists sympathetically—*I Never Promised You a Rose Garden* (1977), *Ordinary People* (1980), and *Good Will Hunting* (1997). Most movies are more like *Wag the Dog*, where actor Robert DeNiro portrays a mentally ill soldier who is always popping antipsychotic medication into his mouth and is killed while committing a rape (Grinfeld, 1998, p. 3). People with mental illness are consumers of books, movies, and all forms of media. These negative stereotypes make it less likely that they will seek treatment. It damages their self-esteem and their confidence in themselves and the therapies that are available to them. Dr. Gabbard said that the media can be used to educate the public about mental health, but as long as movies use stereotypes of patients and therapists to entertain audiences, the situation will not get better. As long as the box office determines the storylines, there will be no improvement in the inaccurate portrayals of psychiatrists.

The fact that organizations are lobbying for a change in the inaccurate and hurtful content of movies and other literary depictions of the mentally ill verifies the power of the medium to influence audience members, particularly those who have mental health issues. The 2007 murder rampage at Virginia Tech University created stress for the entire population, but for the mentally ill such events can trigger hospitalizations or real crises.

> Otto F. Wahl, Ph.D., a clinical psychologist and professor of psychology at George Mason University in Fairfax, Va, said the cumulative effect of constant negative depictions of the mentally ill profoundly impacts not only the general public but also those who suffer from mental illnesses. The most significant misrepresentation, he told *Psychiatric Times*, is the link created by entertainment media between mental illness and violence. The appearance of "psycho killers" in movies, books and children's television programs is at epidemic proportions. (Grinfeld, 1998, p. 2)

Let us imagine that art forms were more accurate in their portrayal of stigmatized subjects; would that alleviate the distortion and suffering that occurs because of stereotypes? It would help, but distortion exists in news stories and in everyday living. For example, look at the news story that involved the tragic shootings at Virginia Tech. Cho Seung-Hui, the South Korean student who shot 32 people—2 professors and 30 other students—in April 2007 before killing himself, was no movie character but a leading news story. He blamed the victims for his outrage and the assassinations; he said:

> You had everything you wanted. Your Mercedes wasn't enough, you brats. Your golden necklaces weren't enough, you snobs. Your trust fund wasn't enough. Your vodka and cognac weren't enough. All your debaucheries weren't enough. Those weren't enough to fulfill your hedonistic needs. You had everything. ("Killer's Manifesto," April 18, 2007)

Investigators pored over his computer to see what kinds of sites he visited, interviewed suitemates to discover what kinds of video games he played and what kind of music he played. There was one game that he seemed to play over and over, yet other students play video games repeatedly without committing murderous crimes. Clearly, the impact that any media, including movies, have on audiences depend on what else the viewer has been exposed to and how they relate to the multiple stressors of life in general. Evidently, the man was a loner who had stalked female students, avoided all contact or interaction with other students, had been referred for mental health counseling but had refused to continue contact; then he bought guns and ammunition before completing his planned assault on innocent victims on campus and in classrooms. He mailed a video with pictures of himself holding guns and spewing hate-filled threats to NBC after he murdered two students in West Ambler Johnston Hall dormitory but before he began the final assault in Norris Hall that would end with his own suicide. NBC played the video, and others followed, while Fox and a few other stations refused to expose the mass audience to the violent images and messages. Debates on the ethics of giving a mass murderer what he wanted or allowing him to have the last word incensed some of the victims' parents as well as general audience members. What about copycat killers who would emulate his example to get their own stories in the news? The channels were saturated with the story for a week. Does this kind of notoriety motivate other unbalanced individuals to try to establish a new record? Many fear that it does and call for tempering the public discourse to tame the savage beast of psychotic imagination to do harm. A former neuroscience graduate student, James Holmes, armed himself and shot 12 people in Aurora, Colorado, in the summer of 2012 at the midnight showing of *The Dark Knight Rises*. In his initial court appearance, he wore bright red hair like the Joker and seemed totally detatched from the proceedings. The crimes were the result of a man who was known to the mental health professionals at his school. His action evoked this response from Ty Burr, a movie critic: "Don't blame director Christopher Nolan or star Christian Bale. But maybe it's worth having a discussion about an entertainment culture that excels at selling violent power fantasies to people who feel powerless" (Btburr@globe.com).

What effect do such tragedies have on the general population—and, more specifically, what effect do such events have on those who are mentally ill? We probably cannot answer the first question with any force of certainty, much less the latter one. George Gerbner in his cultivation theory, which was explained in earlier chapters, researched and wrote about the cultivation of values through images of sex and violence. He stated that the Electronic Storyteller, television, has replaced the institutions of religion, family, and education with disastrous results since profit-driven producers and directors have taken over our "Cultural Environment."

From the beginning of motion pictures we have known the powerful effects that they have. President Wilson, after viewing his first film, *Birth of a Nation*, described the film as being "like history written in lightning" (Black, Bryant, & Thompson, 1998, p. 153). By 1915 it was evident that motion pictures had great emotional and propagandistic powers not only to entertain audiences but to alter attitudes on the cognitive, affective, and behavioral level. On every front, cinema as an art form has the capacity to educate, to exhort, to distort, and to inspire audiences on every subject imaginable. The medium has not used its tremendous power as affirmatively as it should, but as the foregoing examples demonstrate, the narratives, characters, and perspective that producers take do influence public opinion.

MUSIC AS PERSUASION

While music may seem miscast as part of visual rhetoric, we understand that music videos are a major part of the industry today. Further, advertising relies heavily on music as an attention-getting tool as well a memory device to have audiences remember the ad and the product. Political campaigns and conventions rely on concerts to raise money, to create enthusiasm at the conventions, and to represent campaign issues. Music is inseparable from religious ceremonies and the classical works that we celebrate every holiday, but music also is used as a marker in Christian identity ranging from the Jesus freaks, celebrated in the contemporary Christian music of dc Talk's (1995) record-breaking album entitled *Jesus Freak*, to the protest song of the civil rights movement, "We Shall Overcome." Neo-Nazi groups like the skinheads rely on heavy metal bands at their recruiting meetings, where beer flows freely while anti-Semitic, anti-black lyrics fill the air. Social movements have relied heavily on music to represent identity, cohesion, and a call to action. Frequently, musical lyrics articulate the hopes and anguish of a nation before policymakers become attuned to social conditions such as poverty, AIDS, and homelessness.

GANGSTA RAP

In the last two decades the musical genre drawing the most criticism has been gangsta rap, which is characterized by **misogynistic** lyrics that portray women as hoochies and hos while glorifying sexual promiscuity, drugs, and violence. As Don Imus found on April 4, 2007, the language created in the hood should stay in the hood. In other words, rappers like Snoop Dog and others have become wealthy using such denigrating terms, as have the record executives who market them, but mainstream America is forbidden to speak in those terms. Imus commented on air, "Man, they've got tattoos and. . . . That's some nappy-headed hos there, I'm going to tell you that now . . ." (Kosova, 2007, p. 26). He crossed a line by attacking the young women of the Rutgers basketball team. For years, Imus had been insulting everyone from Vice President Cheney, whom he called "Pork Chop Butt," to *Washington Post* reporter Howard Kurtz, whom he called a "boner-nosed, beanie-wearing Jew Boy" (Kosova, 2007, p. 26). Obviously, Imus crossed the line of decency often in his broadcasts. He underestimated the cumulative effect of anti-Semitic racist, sexist, toilet humor. He certainly did not anticipate the eloquence of the Rutgers women's basketball coach, C. Vivian Stringer, who spoke on television to say that Imus could not possibly know the girls whom he had insulted because they had struggled so hard to achieve their place in the NCAA championship game and that they were classy women, professional, and intelligent. Coach Stringer was the epitome of composure, articulate speech, and dignity. When Imus met with the team to apologize, after being fired from his talk show, one of the players told him, "I don't want

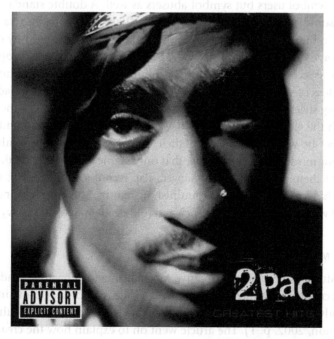

Tupac Shakur's rap music commented upon poverty, racism, and social injustices.

you to think that I question myself because of what you said. I'm a classy woman at a great university. I will pray for you" (Kelly, Starr, & Conant, 2007, p. 33). Imus started the process to sue his employer, because his contract called for him to be confrontational and controversial, but nothing in the contract empowered him to denigrate and embarrass private citizens—college girls who had done nothing to deserve his racist remarks. But where did the language of "nappy-headed hos" originate? Gangsta rap lyrics are filled with such references; Imus did not invent the words. He was just emboldened enough to use them, not anticipating the backlash that his words would stir. Are lyrics persuasive? Are lyrics strong cultural interpretations of social reality? What makes it more acceptable for artists to use racist, violent, incendiary rhetoric while mainstream speakers cannot? The desensitization that occurs through exposure to language, behavior, and lifestyles cannot be ignored. Just as the movie *Animal House* decades ago made crude, lewd, and rude behavior seem acceptable on college campuses, gangsta rap lyrics have made women easy targets for repulsive labels and stereotypes. The Imus controversy motivated Al Sharpton, Jesse Jackson, and others to claim that they had spoken against the rhetoric of rap artists, but unlike others, like the Women's Black Caucus in the 1990s, which did take political action to bring change, no one remembers hearing Sharpton or Jackson condemn them directly. Gangsta rap occupies a prominent place in record sales, and the artists defend their right to say anything they wish to say under the protection of the First Amendment. Now a new twist has occurred; some rappers claim that they "own" the words, that they are racist and misogynistic only if white people use them because of the oppressive history of slavery. Here is a news flash. No one owns the language; you only own the consequences of using abusive language. As Kenneth Burke said, we are not only symbol users but symbol abusers as well. A double standard of speech has emerged, with some claiming that it is alright for them to be obscene, racist, sexist, and violent in speech, but it is not alright for the same language to be used by other people. It sounds like George Orwell's Newspeak with meanings being twisted, co-opted, and copyrighted as long as economic profits keep accumulating. Language pollution has consequences, regardless of who brandishes the words. Gangsta rappers have had an impact on language, clothing styles, and general culture. Part of their appeal was the "otherness" that they represented with the glorification of the outlaw ideology, sexual prowess, and denigration of women or others who were not members of their "gang." Many artists were either murdered or went to prison for misdeeds, but for a time that only seemed to strengthen the mystique that loyal fans felt for them and their work. Gangsta Rap record sales are down, so perhaps that means the form has reached the point of diminishing returns. Music genres long before gangsta rap have created whole movements, like rock and roll, Beatlemania, and heavy metal bands.

CREATIVITY, MUSIC, AND PERSUASION

In an article, "Music as Persuasion: Creative Mechanisms for Enacting Academe," Bostrom et al. noted that creativity is a way to "generate plans, ideas, knowledge, and information that differ significantly from those in common use and are part of our general culture" (Bostrom, Lane, & Harrington, 2002, p. 1). The article went on to explain how the creative process fed into the process of persuasion with the focus on music:

In order to contribute to creative thinking in communication we will first define creativity—allowing ourselves a bit of creative license as we peruse the literature and provide a context from which creativity can be interpreted and processed. In doing so, we discuss metaphors as creativity, creativity as persuasion, and song lyrics as persuasive communication. Ultimately, our claim is that music is a form of persuasion and thus is a creative mechanism for academics to use that has an impact on how listeners subsequently enact their procession. (Bostrom et al., 2002, p. 2)

Often, emotional responses are invoked through supplementing the cognitive content of a message with presentational elements such as music and art. Motion picture scripts and song lyrics are used to communicate in business and professional settings. "James Gleick (1993) has pointed out that *Sesame Street*, the Doors, and *Monty Python* are all replacing Greek and Roman classics in our popular culture" (Bostrom, Lane, & Harrington, 2002, p. 5). They also wrote:

> Persuasion certainly is not confined to messages delivered in straightforward ways. John Lennon may have been a more effective persuader (in the long run) than John Kennedy. Clearly Bruce Springsteen has stimulated many to consider the plight of the poor and Willie Nelson has done the same for American farmers. In the newspapers, comic strips were once designed for amusement only—but Burke Breathed of *Bloom County* and Gary Trudeau of *Doonesbury* consistently have made political material highly salient.
>
> In Nazi Germany in the 1930s, the propaganda minister, Dr. Joseph Goebbels, had complete control of the artistic life of the state. He commissioned the talented filmmaker Leni Riefenstahl to use her artistic powers to produce a number of films supporting the government, many of which are classics today. Goebbels encouraged Wagner and discouraged American jazz, especially the work of George Gershwin (who was considered not only decadent, but an "animal" because he was Jewish). At the same time the Soviet Union was producing films like *Alexander Nevsky,* in which the considerable talents of Eisenstein and Prokofiev were combined to a Pro-Russian, anti-German message. And we should remind ourselves that the use of the arts in persuasive activity is not necessarily a bad thing. Some of George Bernard Shaw's best plays (e.g., *Major Barbara*) were frankly propagandistic. And who can forget Robin Williams in *Good Morning, Vietnam*? (Bostrom et al., 2002, p. 6)

Frank Capra was enlisted by the State Department during World War II to create propaganda films for the United States to persuade citizens to accept war rations, to buy war bonds, and to support the sacrifices of death and scars from that war. Disney characters were transformed into dictators, which audiences enjoyed seeing whacked as the buck-toothed ToJo, mad Mussolini, or a mustached, goose-stepping Hitler.

SHANNON AND WEAVER VERSUS TONY SCHWARTZ

An examination of music as persuasion warrants breaking out of the Shannon and Weaver (1949) model of communication that is linear based on electronic systems which transmitted electrons, thus giving rise to the label, "information flow." Similarly, our nervous system is composed of pathways of neurons and synapses that give validity to this linear flow of messages transmitted and received. The linear paradigm does not always seem to apply to human interaction (Bostrom et al., 2002, p. 3). Frentz and Farrell (1976) believed that it was more fruitful to focus on all the elements of a communication transaction that are likely to be episodic, meaning that nonverbal components such as facial expressions, posture, and other cues are more likely to reveal the true feelings of the participants. The episodic view of communication is more dramatic with more holistic images, much like a stage presentation with motion, music, and voice as components.

Tony Schwartz (1983) believed that most of what we know about communication theory is mistaken based on the linear model, and he proposed a resonance model of communication. He said the resonance theory is based on hearing that evokes something already in a listener's experience. The transportation theory of communication means "getting something across" like mail or Western Union, in keeping with the electronic theories of Shannon and Weaver. The resonance theory holds that meaning is an interaction between the material one receives and what is stored in the minds of the receivers. This is the age of reception of instant messages. Schwartz wrote:

> The resonance theory of communication is based on the phenomenon of hearing. It concentrates on evoking responses from people by attuning the message to their prior experience. Marshall McLuhan said that "instant information creates involvement in depth." The depth to which he referred is the depth of the mind, and the instant he referred to can be as little as the time difference between reacting to reading and reacting to hearing and seeing. (Schwartz, 1983, p. 14)

Tony Schwartz used to record the sounds of New York, including children's games, street vendors, and sidewalk musicians, and he used such cues as a baby crying or someone laughing to evoke the desired response to his commercials.

Anyone who has experienced a recurring refrain from a song they heard running through their head all day can attest to the power of music. In the film *Amadeus* (1984), based on the life of Wolfgang Amadeus Mozart, we learn in a speech by Salieri that music is the "mouthpiece of God." Salieri laments that he has studied everything there is to learn about music, yet the sniveling, childish Mozart has all the talent. Salieri believes that it is through music that the common man communes with God and is elevated above the worldly cares that shatter the human spirit. Mozart began composing music at age four, minuets by five, and symphonies by age nine. He was gifted as his name implied; Amadeus means "beloved by God." The significance of music in the life of everyone is the theme in many artistic works, especially film.

In the movie *The Shawshank Redemption* (1994), Andy Dufresne, the lead character who is unjustly accused of murder, defies the prison warden by locking the door to the library and broadcasting "Duettina Sull'Aria," from the Italian opera *The Marriage of Figaro*, into the prison yard. The music transports the prisoners momentarily into a world of culture that has never existed for them as they stand transfixed by the beautiful aria that floats over the sea of blue denim prison suits. In the movie, the narrator, Red, says:

> I have no idea to this day what those two Italian ladies were singin' about. Truth is, I don't want to know. Some things are best left unsaid. I like to think they were singin about something so

beautiful it can't be expressed in words and makes your heart ache because of it. I tell you, those voices soared, higher and farther than anybody in a gray place dares to dream. It was like some beautiful bird flapped into our drab little cage and made those walls dissolve away. And for the briefest of moments, every last man at Shawshank felt free. (Darabont, 1994)

After the warden threw Andy into the hole (solitary confinement) for a month to punish his disobedience, Andy tells his friend Red that he was not alone; Mr. Mozart kept him company and continued to give him hope because there are places in the head and in the heart that even the brutal world of prison could not negate. Andy speaks of hope that transcends the prison walls, which Red argues is a dangerous thing that could drive a man insane. The episode of the opera visually demonstrates the emotional power of music to elevate the spirit of even the most oppressed of men, even for a brief moment, to another plane.

Music genres include everything from classical compositions to country ballads with complex scores or simple chords, but for every occasion and every taste there is an appropriate musical selection. LeCoat quoted various scholars through time to demonstrate that musical works reflect the conventions of their time. He wrote:

When Henry Peacham, in the 1620s, presented music as an art of persuasion, he was obviously thinking of the art of music as it was practiced in his own time. For Peacham's contemporaries, the function of music was essentially to furnish the listener with archetypal images for human moods and passions in view of creating in him specific psychological effects. With regard to the interrelation of rhetoric and poetic during the Renaissance, Sister Miriam Joseph points out that rhetoric was concerned "with the communication of ideas directly from mind to mind," and poetic "with the communication of experience indirectly by the creation of illusion," but that in both cases the emphasis was on the intelligibility of the communication. This statement is perfectly applicable to the interrelation of rhetoric and music. (LeCoat, 1976, p. 158)

LeCoat wrote that musicians adopt their art using the three appeals of classical rhetoric—logos, ethos, and pathos—especially when tonal and verbal patterns are combined, but instrumental works require a more complex approach of analysis.

A recurring theme in *Shawshank Redemption* was the power of music to elevate the soul and to transcend the torture of prison life.

MUSIC TELEVISION

The contemporary music scene has been researched as well, with music videos viewed as possible arguments that are exceptionally malleable and open to audience interpretation. On August 1, 1981, the Music Television (MTV) cable network was launched. Gregg Walker and Melinda Bender conducted a study to see if subjects perceived music videos to be making arguments using the definition given by Rieke and Sillars (1984, p. 5) that argumentation was the "process of advancing, supporting, modifying, and criticizing claims so that appropriate decision makers may grant or deny adherence." As Foss noted in her theory of visual rhetoric, the audience here was the "ordinary person," college students, viewing the videos to decide if they were influenced by them. The Walker and Bender study asked these research questions:

1. To what extent do viewers perceive music video as argument?
   a. Do they see dominant messages or claims in music videos?
   b. Do they believe that music videos seek viewer agreement (adherence with their central message)?
2. To what extent do viewers see music videos as influential?
   a. Are viewers influenced by music videos?
   b. Is liking a video associated with its influence?
   c. Do viewers judge videos as attempting to influence attitudes or behavior?
   d. What are viewers' content perceptions?
   e. Do they regard music videos as social or political messages?
   f. Do they perceive visual and lyrical message content in music videos?
3. How do judgments about adherence and influence relate to liking a video and finding its content understandable? (Walker & Bender, 1994, p. 70).

The researchers used a seven-point scale, with 1 being not at all and 7 being yes, very much; the findings were:

> The viewer responses display that seven videos, with strong dominant message consensus and mean values greater than 5.7 on a 7-point scale, are highly argumentative. Michael Jackson's "Man in the Mirror" (about social responsibility and peace) and 2 Live Crew's "banned in the USA" (about freedom of speech) generate 6.45 message agreement ratings (with standard deviations about 1) and strong consensus regarding the presence of a dominant message (99% and 97% respectively). "Self Destruction" by the Stop the Violence Movement (about gang violence, drugs), Neneh Cherry's "I've Got You Under My Skin" (about AIDS and safe sex), MC Hammer's "Pray" (about prayer, spirituality), Psychefunkapus' "We Are the Young" (about political and social responsibility), and "Tick Tock" by the Vaughan Brothers (about cultural diversity) combine 93 percent or greater dominant message consensus with a mean of 5.7 on the question of the video seeking viewer agreement with its dominant message. (Walker & Bender, 1994, p. 72)

Other videos did not rank as high, such as Midnight Oil, Queen Latifah, Queensryche, and Poison measuring in the 5.02 ratings, with heavy metal and nonargument/entertainment videos ranking lowest as forms of argument with 2.62 ratings (p. 72). The conclusions of the study generalize that it is appropriate to consider some music videos as persuasive discourse. Others, like Leland (1992), have studied rap music and consider that genre as being socio-political persuasive communication.

Viewers are not hapless, passive receivers of these messages, but they interpret them according to their own perceptual frames. The **elaboration likelihood model** (ELM) explained earlier established that receivers may examine stimuli critically through the central processing unit (CPU) of the brain if they have the knowledge to examine the stimulus with detail or elaborate on what they are perceiving, but when they lack that ability, they may process the stimulus through the peripheral processing unit (PPU), which attends to more extrinsic details such as images, color, number of arguments, or the appearance of the presenter rather than the intrinsic worth of the artifact. This theory is helpful in understanding how we accept and appreciate some forms of art or visual artifacts, or we may rely totally on someone else to explain or critique the same artifact to us.

Increasingly, young viewers get their news from such stations as MTV and from comedians such as Jon Stewart. To ignore the influence of the entertainment industry or of art in its multiple forms would be a major mistake in the attempt to understand attitude formation, views on the political and social world, and adoption of appropriate behavior.

SUMMARY

Visual rhetoric according to Foss involves an artifact that was created with the intention of communicating something through the choice of media, color, shape, or size that has an audience in mind that must be able to decipher meaning from the symbols presented. Scholars who study visual rhetoric focus either on the rhetorical perspective presented by the work itself, such as Mapplethorpe's *The Perfect Moment* exhibit, or on the response that the work evokes from the audience, whether a congressperson, the mass audience, or experts in the medium. According to Kostelnick and Hassett, each field has conventions that can serve as either a model to be followed or as a point of departure that frees the artist or creator to do unconventional things, like Maya Lin did with the Vietnam Veterans Memorial in Washington, D.C. Each art form brings communicative powers to evoke significant responses in receivers. In films we have discussed how homosexual romance was presented in *Brokeback Mountain*, which took a conventional love story but treated it in an unconventional way. A number of films have portrayed such stigmatized subjects as mental illness, with the effect of initiating dialog about various conditions and the people who suffer from them. These works of art have been instrumental in attitude change in the general public. The capacity of music to touch our soul is unquestioned. LeCoat stated that music is persuasion that uses the classical appeals of rhetoric—logos, pathos, and ethos, that is, logic, emotion, and character—which employ the conventions of the time period to communicate effectively with audiences. Every genre offers a different avenue to explore, from gangsta rap to Mozart's symphonies.

When we look at the entertainment and art worlds, we are mindful that they have a great influence on our attitudes toward myriad subjects because they present truths to us, with which we sometimes vehemently disagree, that have a significant impact on our thoughts, our feelings, and our behavior. Aristotle's definition of rhetoric, as the art of discovering in any given situation the available means of persuasion, includes what today we call visual rhetoric as sculptures, photographs, films, music videos, and many other forms not reviewed in this chapter. Each form brings not only its intrinsic value as art, but another opportunity to present truths or propositions about which we can discuss the validity of the perspective presented and the value that it has for us.

APPLICATIONS

1. Review the Academy Award nominations for this year and analyze the topics portrayed in the films. Were any of them advocacy pieces?
2. Select a controversial artist and report what critics say about his or her work; include any insights the artist offers about what he or she intended to do.
3. Identify and analyze antiwar lyrics by identifying the time, place, and intended audience for the music.

REFERENCES

Asen, R. (1998). Appreciation and desire: The male nude in the photography of robert mapplethorpe. *Text & Performance Quarterly, 18*(1), 50–62.

Belien, P. (2005). Jihad against Danish newspaper. *Brussels Journal,* October 22. Retrieved April 20, 2007, from http://www.brusselsjournal.com/node/382.

Berman, R. (1991). Lobbying for entitlements: Advocacy and political action in the arts. *Journal of Arts Management & Law, 21*(3), 258–266.

Black, J., Bryant, J., & Thompson, S. (1998). *Introduction to media communication* (5th ed.). Boston: McGraw-Hill.

Blair, J. A. (2004). The rhetoric of visual arguments. In C. A. Hill & M. Helmers (Eds.), *Defining visual rhetorics* (pp. 41–61). Mahwah, NJ: Lawrence Erlbaum Associates.

Bostrom, R. N., Lane, D. R., & Harrington, N. G. (2002). Music as persuasion: Creative mechanisms for enacting academe. *American Communication Journal, 6*(1), 1–11.

Burr, T. (2012). Fantasy, masks, and James Holmes, the *Dark Knight Rises* killer. Retrieved October 30, 2012, from: http://www.boston.com/ae/movies.

Curtiss, D. (1987). Introduction to visual *literacy.* Englewood Cliffs, NJ: Prentice-Hall.

Darabont, F. (1994). (Screenwriter). *The Shawshank redemption.* Film. F. Darabont (Director). Burbank, CA: Warner Brothers/Castlerock Entertainment.

Fables—Forrest Gump and the "new disability." (1995). *Rehabilitation International Interaction, 9*(2). National Council on International Disability, Australia. Retrieved April 24, 2007, from http://www.rehab-international.org/publications/filmcat/fables.html.

Fitzpatrick, J. F. (1995). The sensitive society. *American Theatre, 12*(1), 88.

Foss, S. K. (2005). Theory of visual rhetoric. In K. Smith, S. Moriarty, G. Barbatsis, & K. Kenney (Eds.), *Handbook of visual communication: Theory, methods, and media* (pp. 141–52). Mahwah, NJ: Lawrence Erlbaum Associates.

Frentz, T. R., & Ferrell, T. B. (1976). Language-action: A paradigm for communication. *Quarterly Journal of Speech, 62,* 333–349.

Gabbard, G. (1987). *Psychiatry and cinema.* Washington, DC: American Psychiatry Press.

Grinfeld, M. J. (1998). Psychiatry and mental illness: Are They Mass Media Targets? *Psychiatric Times, 15*(3), 1–6. Retrieved April 23, 2007, from http://www.psychiatrictimes.Com/p980301a.html.

Kadlecek, J. (2002). Sylvia Nasar discusses her book, *"A Beautiful Mind"*; Psychiatrist Roberto Gil: Schizophrenia and recovery. Retrieved November 7, 2010, from http://www.columbia.edu/cu/news/02/01/beautiful_mind.html.

Kelly, R., Starr, M., & Conant, E. (April 23, 2007). A team stands tall. *Newsweek, 149*(17), 32–33.

Killer's manifesto: You forced me into a corner. Retrieved May 3, 2007, from http://www.cnn.com/2007/US/04/18/vtech.shooting/index.html.

Kosova, W. (April 23, 2007). The power that was. *Newsweek, 149*(17), 24–31.

Kostelnick, C., & Hassett, M. (2003). *Shaping information: The rhetoric of visual conventions.* Carbondale, IL: Southern Illinois University Press.

LeCoat, G. G. (1976). Music and the three appeals of classical rhetoric. *Quarterly Journal of Speech, 62*(2), 157–166.

Leland, J. (June 29, 1992). Rap and race. *Newsweek, 119*(26), 47–52.

Levinson, D. A. (1990). Robert Mapplethorpe's extraordinary vision. *The Tech, 110*(31), 12–14. Retrieved November 7, 2010, from http://tech.mit.edu/V110/N31/mapple.31a.html.

McGuigan, C. (February 12, 2007). Where memory endures: After 25 years the Vietnam veterans memorial casts a long shadow. *Newsweek, 149*(7), 59.

Messaris, P., & Moriarty, S. (2005). Visual literacy theory. In K. Smith, S. Moriarty, G. Barbatsis, & K. Kenney (Eds.), *Handbook of visual communication: theory, methods, and media* (pp. 481–502). Mahwah, NJ: Lawrence Erlbaum Associates.

Morris, R. (2006). Death on display. In L. J. Prelli (Ed.), *Rhetorics of display* (pp. 204–226). Columbia, SC: University of South Carolina Press.

Rieke, R. D., & Sillars, M. O. (1984). *Argumentation and the decision making process.* Glenview, IL: Scott, Foresman.

Rose, J., & Urschel, J. (2006). Understanding The Complexity Of Love In Brokeback mountain: An analysis of the film and short story. *The Journal of Men's Studies, 14*(2), 247–252.

Schwartz, T. (1983). *Media the second God.* Garden City, NY: Anchor Books/Doubleday.

Shannon, C., & Weaver, W. (1949). *The mathematical theory of communication.* Urbana, IL: The University of Illinois Press.

Stone, A. A. (2006). Best picture: How far will Hollywood go? *Psychiatric Times, 23*(10), 50–55.

Turan, K. (2005). The new frontier of "Brokeback" Is Vast And Heartfelt. Movie review. *Los Angeles Times,* December 9. Retrieved April 20, 2007, from http://articles.latimes.com/2005/dec/09/entertainment/et-brokeback9/3.

Vietnam veterans memorial: Evolution of the memorial. Retrieved February 12, 2007, from http://www.nps.gov/archive/vive/memorial/evolutionprint.htm.

Walker, G. B., & Bender, M. A. (1994). Is it more than rock and roll? Considering music video as argument. *Argumentation & Advocacy, 31*(2), 64–80.

CHAPTER 10

ADVERTISING: INTEGRATED MARKETING COMMUNICATION (IMC)

KEY WORDS

advertising	FDA	SEC
AIDA approach	FTC	Stone Age brain theory
branding	IMC	subliminal advertising
cease and desist	niche	technological Darwinism
demographics	product placement	third-person effect
digital advertising	product positioning	unique selling position
endorsements	product promotion	(USP)
FCC	psychographics	U.S. Postal Service

PREVIEW

This chapter focuses on the rhetorical aspect of advertising, which is the influence that advertising has on receivers who interpret multiple messages daily from sponsors who hope to sell their goods and services or to manage customer relations in a positive manner. William F. Arens (2002) defined advertising in the book *Contemporary Advertising*:

> **Advertising** is the structured and composed nonpersonal communication of information, usually paid for and usually persuasive in nature, about products (goods, services, and ideas) by identified sponsors through various media. (p. 7)

Advertising is first of all a form of communication that has the goal of persuading consumers to buy a designated good or service, and it is very structured, using both verbal and nonverbal elements to fill time and space that is paid for by a sponsor, such as GM, Kmart, or a local business. Media is essential to advertisers to link them to producers through multiple channels such as newspapers, magazines, billboards, radio, television, and the Internet. Direct selling occurs through mailings and interactive media as well as nontraditional media such as "shopping carts, blimps, and video-cassettes" (Arens, 2002, p. 9). The messages can be autobiographical, where the speaker tells the imaginary audience why he chose a particular golf club, or a narrative message that relates a story about others, or a drama that engages characters who play roles in the ad. There are *ideological campaigns*, which focus on ideas and changing the public's perception on issues such as civil rights, gay rights, or the environment. Similarly, there are *political campaigns*, which sponsor a candidate for a specific office and end when the candidate is either elected or rejected by the electorate. This chapter focuses on commercial campaigns that sponsor products, although one political ad is discussed that used subliminal components.

Advertising is tied to marketing, which develops an overall strategy to aid through market research, sales, and distribution of the goods. Before an ad campaign can be mobilized, there must be a target audience. Generally, there is a multilayered strategy developed that requires specific steps or tactics along the way. All of this planning is motivated by the sponsor's desire to sell their product, idea, or services to the consumer. The Pepsi Generation did not just happen, it was invented, just as the Clydesdale horses who pull the Budweiser beer wagon were conceived, presented, and given certain attributes such as power, tied to an all-American product, beer, with associational references to Middle America where the men enjoy competition, a robust lifestyle, and a brew that came to America with their ancestors.

Advertisements do much more than give product information; ads sell illusions, fantasies, and dreams. All ads contain information, but their primary function is to persuade consumers to buy a featured product. As the Latin translation (*advetere*: to turn) tells us, ads are supposed to turn our heads toward the sponsored product or arrest our attention. The number of ads that Americans see per day has doubled since the 1970s, so we are inundated by advertisements that attempt to connect with the consumer. Part of this proliferation exists because new media has opened new channels for advertising on the Internet; these channels are stealing market shares from more traditional venues like newspapers, radio, and television.

Every morning, advertisements fall out of our newspapers, which subsidize the price of our paper and inform us of sales in department stores, incentives at car dealerships, and professional services ranging from pharmacies, to lawyers, to local restaurants. As we wind our ways to work, we are inundated with billboards along the highways and jingles on our car radios that play through our heads that day. That evening as we watch our favorite television shows, there are products embedded in the scenes with our favorite stars, like designer clothing, expensive cars, and beverages. This is called **product placement**, or entertainment advertising.

This chapter addresses one theory of advertising, which states that advertisements need to appeal to our most basic instincts, such as reproduction, survival, and security from threatening situations, because we still have a Stone Age brain. Advertising has many functions, which are discussed as well, including the need to link consumers to producers, to inform consumers of new products, and to generate liking, preferences, and choices for products. One major job that advertising performs is cutting through all the competing stimuli to make a product stand out from the rest in some way by establishing a **unique selling proposition** For example, a recent ad featured the successful reattachment of "lucky" rabbit's feet with casts of various colors on the rabbits to underline their transformative surgeries

Pictured here is the Aston Martin featured predominantly throughout the James Bond series, starting with *Die Another Day*. Critics claimed the movie should have been called "Buy Another Day" because of product placements.

with the ultimate message that we cannot rely on luck but rather should purchase a designated insurance that will provide security for us in an uncertain world. Various strategies are discussed, such as **branding**, **niche** marketing, and market research such as **demographics** and **psychographics**. Some dysfunctions that are attributed to advertising are discussed also, including deception, exploitation, and corruption of values and culture.

Because of questionable practices in business, the government established a number of regulatory agencies to assure the welfare of consumers. That means that advertisers cannot just say anything they choose about their products. Commercial speech is regulated and does not have the same standard of protection that political speech does in the arena of First Amendment rights. Consumer safety requires that products such as drugs, cosmetics, and foods be safe for U.S. citizens. Further, advertising agencies are held to standards of accuracy to protect consumers from deception in advertising. Various fraudulent schemes emerge that guarantee instant wealth, and other scams abound, such as oceanfront property for sale at bargain-basement prices. Federal agencies have evolved to enforce regulations in commerce and advertising; these include the **Federal Food and Drug Administration (FDA)**, the **Federal Trade Commission (FTC)**, the **Federal Communications Commission (FCC)**, the **U.S. Postal Service**, and the **Securities and Exchange Commission (SEC)**. These agencies are explained briefly, along with the safeguards that they provide.

Advertisements are so much a part of television that viewers now tune into Super Bowl Sunday to see which ads were the funniest, most memorable, or likely to be rated the best overall. Ad agencies walk a fine line between recognizing the complexities of our society and still supporting their client's products. How do you think The Boeing Company adapted to the political climate after September 11, 2001? After the silver birds that the technology giants were so proud of portraying in their ads were misappropriated by the terrorists who flew into the Twin Towers in New York City, the last thing Americans wanted to see featured was the lift-off or sheer power of supersonic jets. Corporations must be sensitive to threat appeals or the psychology of the masses to successfully present their products in an acceptable manner. This chapter discusses the perils of social-political forces in the national psyche and the effect that social chaos has on marketing strategies. Persuasive discourse, including advertising, requires an awareness of the attitudes, values, and beliefs of the audience as well as their hopes and fears.

ADVERTISING STRATEGIES AND TACTICS

The history of advertising shows that the same strategies were used in ancient civilizations that are still used today to promote goods. The method of delivering the message was quite different, though. Examples of product **branding**, *positioning, placement, promotion,* and *endorsements* can be found long before mass consumers were addressed through the use of printing. Products are given names that are identified as the brand that should result in "brand equity," which is "the number of people who will buy the brand with the least thinking" (Du Plessis, 2008, p. 197). Further, the brand is associated with brand liking, or what kind of positive emotions are associated with it. The advertisement creates a name and image, and the hope is that consumers remember these when they stroll down the supermarket aisles, and if a positive image has been created they will purchase the product. The next time they shop, buyers remembers whether or not they liked the product, and, if so, they purchase it again. Erik Du Plessis (2008) explained the process this way:

> All these activities lay down memory traces to some degree; everything we experience does that, to at least some degree. Over time the natural processes of neuronal recruitment (in other words, the formation of memories and concepts) takes place. This passes through the limbic system, and results in the development in the brain of what we called a soma (positive or negative). In other words, the exposure to the product causes the person to have an emotional attitude to the brand: he or she feels well disposed towards it (brand liking) or if the experiences have been bad, the product poor, feels negatively disposed towards it (brand dislike, we might call it). (Du Plessis, 2008, pp. 197–198)

There are many ways to establish a brand in commercials—images, logos, advertising themes, slogans, and jingles, for example (Du Plessis, 2008, p. 175). When we see a Clydesdale horse, we think Budweiser beer, but an actor who says "Wasuup" can evoke the same beer. Cute kids from diverse nationalities singing "Oh, I wish I were an Oscar Mayer wiener," sometimes off key with snaggley baby teeth, make the brand memorable and establish a positive attitude toward the product. These were successful campaigns.

Product positioning is the stage in the life cycle of the campaign when the product is classified and differentiated from all other products. "The basic goal of positioning strategy is to own a word in the prospect's mind. Levi's owns 'jeans.' FedEx owns 'overnight.' And Volvo owns 'safety'" (Arens, 2002, p. 182). Positioning allows the product to occupy a segment in the market.

Product placement is a controversial practice of paying a fee to have a product written into a movie where the actor or actors wear or use the brand and audiences associate the product with top actors or movies. Placement can appear in any work of art, for that matter, but most recent examples appear on television or in movies. For example, Nokia paid close to $1 million for placement of mobile phones in the movie *Mission Impossible* in 1996 where Tom Cruise discussed the features of the telephone. Similarly, Mercedes-Benz featured their new all-activity vehicle in *The Lost World: Jurassic Park* (Arens, 2002, p. 602).

Product promotion includes all the communication means used to reach consumers with information about the goods or services being offered. Since the 1970s the integrated marketing communication model (IMC) has been used, which means that advertising campaigns have been coordinated to focus on the customer based on database forces that include demographics, psychographics, purchase data, and attitudes about the brand (Arens, 2002, p. 243). Wang and Schultz developed a seven-stage planning model, which is summarized by Arens:

1. Segment customers according to brand loyalty or purchase behavior.
2. Analyze the database to plan the time, place and situation to communicate with customers.
3. Set marketing objectives based on analyzed data.
4. Identify what changes in attitude are necessary to reinforce or change purchase behavior.
5. Establish communication objectives and strategies for influencing consumer behaviors, attitudes, and beliefs to encourage desired behaviors.
6. Change product, price, and distribution based on stage five if necessary.
7. Determine communication campaign to reach customers—media advertising, direct selling, publicity, sales promotion and special events (Arens, 2002, p. 244).

In a survey of Fortune 500 companies with 122 participating, most understood the concept of IMC and agreed with the benefits of integrated marketing (Arens, 2002, p. 244). The idea that successful advertising is based on understanding the past behavior of customers and analyses of current attitudes, beliefs, and behaviors, and then constructing a communication model to appeal to that audience seems to be the perfect use of feedback to adjust messages to gain the desired effect.

Promotions can include anything from direct mailings with coupons, new television commercials, or distribution of samples through mail, to sponsoring NASCAR drivers or special events.

Endorsements are testimonials from celebrities or other attractive spokespersons who are intended to have appeal for mass audiences. For example, athletes who sport the milk mustaches with the simple message "Drink milk" imply that in order to be successful at tennis or other sports, all you have to do is drink milk. These endorsements from celebrities only work as long as the audience finds the celebrity to be attractive or appealing in some way. For example, Michael Jordan, a spectacular basketball player, had credibility and appeal as a role model for youngsters who loved basketball so that the Nike tennis shoes he advertised sold despite the price tag, which was around $170. Douglas Kellner wrote:

Jennifer Aniston's Smartwater ad is a spoof on advertising tactics that exploit sex, animals, babies, and physical violence.

In fact, Jordan is so handsome that he has often been employed as a model and his good looks and superstar status have won him countless advertising endorsements for products such as Nike, McDonald's, Gatorade, Coca-Cola, Wheaties, Hanes shorts, and numerous others. A Gatorade ad tells the audience to "be like Mike," establishing Jordan as a role model, as the very icon of excellence and aspiration. In anti-drug ads, Jordan tells the nation to just say no, to avoid drugs, to do the right thing, and to be all you can be, mobilizing the very stereotypes of conservative postindustrial America in one figure. As Andrews points out (1995) [sic, Andrews, 1996], Michael Jordan is a paradigmatic figure of the "hard body" (Susan Jeffords) that was the ideal male image of the Reaganite '80s, a model of the powerful bodies needed to resurrect American power after the flabbiness of the 1960s and 1970s. (Kellner, 2002, p. 10)

Jordan was challenged to comment on Nike's exploitation of Third World workers, but he remained aloof when social or political controversy erupted. When he was asked to comment on the Rodney King beating in Los Angeles in 1992, he replied that he was more concerned with his jump shot. One commentator, Todd Boyd, stated that no one was asking Jordan to become a Malcolm X, but when an opportunity came to assert leadership on black issues in the political arena he should not run from it (Kellner, 2002, p. 16). Jordan made his millions doing what he did best, which was playing basketball and exploiting his celebrity status to become the highest paid athlete at that time.

Some celebrities have lost contracts for advertising when their name became blemished for criminal acts or their reputations were otherwise tarnished. Michael Jackson, O. J. Simpson, and Kobe Bryant are celebrities who lost contracts because of charges of criminal behavior. Jackson was accused of molesting children; Simpson was prosecuted for murdering his wife and her friend, Ronald Goldman, and Bryant was accused of rape. Although none of the three were found guilty of these crimes, their reputations were no longer appealing for advertisers. Reversals in celebrities' standing have become so frequent, like supermodel Kate

Moss being linked to cocaine use, that Lloyd's of London offers a "Death and Disgrace" policy to protect companies who have invested in a publicity campaign that must be withdrawn from substantial losses ("Lloyd's Comments," 2006). Celebrity status comes and goes, just as the bumpy life of Paris Hilton shows.

Paris Hilton, who made an ad for Hardees, made executives very nervous, but apparently the ad worked when she appeared in a scanty bathing suit washing a car. Since Hilton's stint in jail for driving under the influence and ignoring summonses to appear in court, it is doubtful that a family establishment will invite her to advertise for them in the near future, despite the fact that she claims to have found God while in jail. Hilton has stated that she will use her experience to become an advocate for the welfare of women who have been imprisoned, and the media that created her seem to be anxious to see what she does next. Perhaps Hilton's commercial campaigns will convert to ideological campaigns that replace product sponsorship with advocacy for a worthy cause such as prison reform.

Lance Armstrong lost millions in endorsements when he admitted that he had used performance-enhancing drugs during the Tour de France races.

Tiger Woods's wholesome image has been tarnished by his multiple extramarital affairs, exposed late in 2009, and sponsors have rescinded contracts because they simply do not want a spokesperson who does not appeal to family values. The famous golfer was in hiding to be treated for sex addiction, and in a long-delayed public statement he apologized for his moral lapses and asked the media to respect his and his family's privacy. Many viewers wanted the sordid details of the affairs, but some of his sponsors had seen and heard enough to disassociate themselves from him.

The advertising strategies of branding, positioning, placement, and endorsements have a long history in product campaigns and continue to evolve according to the media channels that carry the messages to consumers. There are parallels between commercial campaigns, ideological campaigns, and political campaigns, but there are primary differences as well. We focus primarily on product campaigns.

HISTORY OF COMMERCIAL SPEECH: ADVERTISING

The basic methods of advertising have not changed all that much, but the channels that deliver the messages have certainly broadened. John Hood (2005), in *Selling the Dream: Why Advertising Is Good Business*, gave examples of ancient practices that continue in today's marketing. While the Romans were not selling Big Macs, they still used brand names to make their products memorable. For example, a fish sauce called *garum*, made of the meat and entrails of sardines, mackerel, and other fish from the Mediterranean, was offered under various name brands during the Roman Empire but was sold with phrases such as "best available" and the "essence of the best mackerel" (p. 12). Product positioning was seen as Romans attempted to differentiate their various kinds of wine, most of which were identified by the grapes used in the processing, the region from which they came, or the name of a famous winemaker, similar to the California wineries today. One Roman tavern promoted its wine by appealing to elite taste or those who like only the best: "If you will give the sum of two donkeys, you will drink better wines; if you will pay four, you will drink Falernian wines" (p. 12). The idea that if you really care you will give the very best has continued into present-day advertisements like the Hallmark card ads. Product placement, where writers and artists implant the names of consumer goods in books, art, and television programs, has been seen as a "sellout" or a questionable practice, but ancient Roman poets such as Martial and Virgil appear to have done the same thing. The poet Horace wrote: "What would I rather do on the festival of Neptune? Come on, Lydia, hurry and bring forth the stored Caecubian [wine]" (Hood, 2005, p. 13).

Shopkeepers and politicians engaged in advertising by using town criers who were paid to promote products or campaigns before printing made mass ads available. The "sandwich board" form of advertising was said to have originated from sea captains who would send sailors or slaves into the city who wore advertisements for their ship's cargo. Product endorsements go back to the city of Pompeii, where archeologists have found toy chariots with the names of famous charioteers on them. Lamps and bowls have been found with the names of famous gladiators on them (Hood, 2005, p. 13). In Europe *Acta Diurna*, or "Daily Events," was attributed to Julius Caesar in 59 BCE as a means to promote his various military campaigns. For advertising to come of age, though, there would need to be large masses of people to attend to the signs, town criers, or ads placed on statues or works of art. Various developments were essential for advertising to grow, such as large cities with aggregates of people and a means to transport the wares across distance. The printing press ushered in a new age in communication of all kinds, including commercial speech.

The printing press allowed merchants to print handbills promoting products. Then newspapers evolved and were made affordable when Dennis Day decided to sell advertisements in the United States, which dropped the price to a penny per paper. Slick magazines like *Ladies' Home Journal*, *Saturday Evening Post*, and *Life* began to carry targeted stories, pictures, recipes, and advertisements. The Industrial Revolution brought together economic forces that would enable commerce to flourish. The growth of the publishing industry was a primary vehicle for communication, but without the development of the steam presses and the steam locomotives that carried the commodities and the printed ads across the country, there could not have been the level of success that occurred. The railroads were an essential part of this robust growth of our national economy. The combination of mass printing, mass transportation, and public education, which produced a literate nation that would deliver mass consumers for advertisers, meant that commercial culture would be tied to the mass media culture. This early alliance that formed during the print era would continue into the electronic age of radio and television and accelerate with interactive new media made possible by the Internet. Advertising evolved according to the channels that were available to carry the messages, beginning with the town crier, to handbills, newspapers, magazines, radio, television, and the World Wide Web.

The Golden Age of magazines accelerated the union of advertising and segmented markets, with specialty magazines emerging for various groups. In 1883, Cyrus and Louisa Curtis renamed their *Tribune and Farmer* magazine the *Ladies' Home Journal* and priced it at 25 cents while their competitors were charging $3 to $4 for *Harper's* and other magazines. Cyrus Curtis explained his view of media to a convention of advertisers:

> Do you know why we publish the *Ladies' Home Journal*? The editor thinks it is for the benefit of American women. This is an illusion, but a very proper one for him to have. But I will tell you the real reason, the publisher's reason, is to give you people who manufacture things that American women want and buy a chance to tell them about your product. (Hood, 2005, p. 30)

According to Curtis, mass media existed to find consumers for the manufacturers' products, and this view was more recently expressed by Kathleen Hall Jamieson for the twenty-first century as well. Curtis bought the *Saturday Evening Post* in 1897 for $1,000, and by 1909 it had a readership of over one million that doubled by 1913 (Hood, 2005, pp. 30–31). The Curtis Publishing Company set up a research division in 1910 to study consumer habits, and the advertising industry began to evolve into the **integrated marketing communication (IMC)** model that we see today with specialized research for testing ad copy on customers, creating graphics and color ads, and coordinating the total campaign.

The Procter & Gamble company hired a young economist, Paul Smelser, who began to focus on customer behavior rather than commodity markets. His door-to-door interviewers did not write down answers, but they had standardized questions that they had memorized.

They did not want the consumers to be self-conscious when answering the questions. Companies like P&G and General Motors were developing the commercial culture in America by doubling the per capita spending on advertising between 1880 and 1900, and again between 1900 and 1929, when advertising expenditures as a share of gross domestic product (3.3 percent) and personal income (4 percent) reached the highest point in American history before or since (Hood, 2005, p. 36).

Integrated marketing communication evolved to coordinate multiple efforts for companies to strengthen the relationship with their customers. Arens (2002) defined IMC:

> Integrated marketing communications is the process of building and reinforcing mutually profitable relationships with employees, customers, other stakeholders, and the general public by developing and coordinating a strategic communications program that enables them to have a constructive encounter with the company brand through a variety of media or other contacts. (p. 240)

According to Arens (2002), the IMC model focuses on such qualities as having a unified image (e.g., 3M); having a consistent voice that coordinates messages to different audiences such as customers, suppliers, or others (e.g., Coca-Cola); being a good listener that seeks feedback through toll-free numbers, surveys, and other communication opportunities like trade shows (Saturn, Gateway); or being a world-class citizen that is focused on the wider community through environmental policies, social awareness, and a strong company culture (Ben and Jerry's, Apple, Honda) (p. 240). The IMC model emphasizes the role of education, feedback, and reciprocity—a wider view that includes corporate responsibility to the citizen and the world. One cannot separate the functions neatly in such an approach, and clearly this communication model includes not only communicating or advertising products, goods, and services to consumers, but also public relations functions, which are discussed more fully in the next chapter.

EXPANDED CHANNELS FOR ADVERTISING

In the past decades a few global giants dominated television or print advertising and managed the placement of ads for their clients, but a more complicated advertising terrain has evolved with **digital advertising**. Ajaz Ahmed, chairman and co-founder of the independent digital marketing agency AKQA, said, "The agency of the future will be half a software company and half an entertainment company because that's the new landscape" (Steel, 2007). Even though the old media companies have a presence on the Web, companies like Google Inc. and Yahoo! Inc control much of Internet media. Now Web marketing has claimed a major portion of advertising budgets with $16.9 billion, or 5.9 percent of the $285 billion total U.S. advertising market in 2006, which is a 1.2 percent increase over 2005, according to the Interactive Advertising Bureau (Steel, 2007).

Newspapers are losing their readership and similarly they are losing advertising revenues. The Newspaper Association of America reported that advertising fell 1.7 percent to $46.6 billion in 2006, outweighing their 31.5 percent increase in online advertising, which was $2.7 billion (Sutel, 2007).

Television advertising has lacked precision in targeting their audiences. For example, young women may be predicted to watch *Grey's Anatomy* on ABC, where we have male characters called "McDreamy," so advertisers would promote their products there. But audience data are based on a limited number of households and therefore not very accurate. By contrast, online advertisers can trace the viewing habits of customers. For example, if a consumer visited two car sites and then visited the website for a magazine, a car ad might be placed on the magazine site. Independent marketers like Tacode Inc. or Revenue Science Inc. can track consumer Web habits and can recommend that the ads appear before a consumer who may respond even though the site has nothing to do with cars. Further, the advertiser only pays the online site when a consumer has clicked on their spot. This makes online advertising more affordable for smaller companies who have to optimize their budgets (Steel, 2007). Also, the feedback is more precise with online advertising. Digital advertisers can gauge how many people viewed the ad, how long they spent with it, and what the surfer did after viewing the ad. If they find that the ad is not working, they can alter it quickly and easily with the click of a button. On television, the marketers surveyed the audiences before and after the ads ran to check the effectiveness of their campaigns.

Online advertising has expanded the channels for communication. Smaller companies can use these services and have contributed to the growth of them. The online advertisement sites can be monitored for the number of hits and how long the consumer spends with the ad, and if the ad is ineffective, it can easily be changed. Further, research firms trace the viewing habits of the surfers and can suggest additional sites on which to display certain ads. Overall, the targeting, feedback, and alteration of ads is much easier with online advertising than with print or television advertisements.

RECURRING COMPLAINTS AGAINST ADVERTISEMENTS

There are four standard complaints about advertising that contribute to the view that it is often intrusive, deceptive, unethical, and demeaning or corrupting of culture. Let us examine these complaints:

1. Advertising is intrusive. We cannot avoid advertisements from the wall murals in cities, to laser lights in the night skies, and even banners flying on the beach crafts as we soak up the summer sun.
2. Advertising is deceptive. Ads either explicitly or implicitly promise to improve our lives through the mere purchase of some commodity. Using the "if . . . then" strategy suggests that if a woman uses a certain cosmetic, men will follow her everywhere.
3. Advertising exploits children. The average American child sees 40,000 ads per year, twice the number viewed in 1970, while other countries have banned ads aimed toward children altogether, like Norway and Sweden and the Canadian province Quebec.
4. Advertising demeans and corrupts culture. Advertisers use the persuasion model of arresting attention, creating interest, stimulating desire, and then motivating action to obtain the product or service—the AIDA model. This stimulus-response form of advertising has been seen as corrupting children by convincing them that their happiness is tied to some product. The problem evolves when being a good mother is tied to buying a particular detergent or purchasing a "happy meal" for her child.

Values can be corrupted when they are tied to the mere consumption or possession of some product. When did loving one's husband become associated with a clean shirt that did not have "ring-around-the collar"? Or how do parents feel who cannot afford a computer for their child when ads tell them that a failing child can become a straight-A student simply by having a computer purchased for them to use for their schoolwork? When did teenagers need to wear a label on their backside that advertised an expensive blue jean like Tommy Hilfiger, Ralph Lauren, or Calvin Klein? Should not the company pay the teen for advertising space, especially if the teen happens to be an attractive model who creates the image of status and popularity for that particular piece of clothing? Belonging to the "in" crowd and being a "cool" person is tied to possessions, such as designer jeans and purses. Remember following Hurricane Katrina, when $2,000 debit cards were issued for victims of the disaster to purchase basic clothing or food and one recipient spent the money on a $2,000 Louis Vuitton purse? Some others gambled the funds away or spent it on prostitutes or even for breast implants. Where did that insanity originate which motivated someone to value a single purse over essential goods like clean clothes? Perhaps their logic was that, regardless of how they spent the government aid, there would be more where that check originated. What kind of ethics were displayed when some school children were attacked or even killed for their Air Jordan tennis shoes? Some say that the world of advertising has taught us that unless we can own certain status-encrusted items like designer clothing or electronic gear or games and have a certain address, then we are nobody. Arens wrote:

> Critics claim advertising manipulates us into buying things by playing on our emotions and promising greater status, social acceptance, and sex appeal. It causes people to take up harmful habits, makes poor kids buy $170 sneakers, and tempts ordinary people to buy useless products in the vain attempt to emulate celebrity endorsers. Again, they claim advertising is so powerful consumers are helpless to defend themselves against it. (Arens, 2002, p. 37)

Many people believe that it is not the government's role to protect people from their own vices or stupidity, but that the primary role of government is to protect the people from predatory others who, through either force or criminal intent, would do us harm. It became evident in the early twentieth century that the government needed to assume a role in the regulation of business, including advertising. Abuses occurred with deception in claims and even dangerous drugs being sold, so federal agencies were created to protect consumers from unscrupulous practices. The old warning *caveat emptor*—buyer beware—was altered to include sellers beware, too, since the regulatory agencies were empowered by the courts to prosecute criminal behavior, to monitor mailings to customers and advertisements for products, food, and drugs, and to impose fines or take legal action against violators.

REGULATORS OF ADVERTISEMENTS

THE FEDERAL TRADE COMMISSION (FTC)

The Federal Trade Commission was established in 1914 to prevent unfair methods of competition in commerce as part of the effort to "bust the trusts" (Federal Trade Commission, 2010).

The FTC is engaged in both consumer protection and competition jurisdiction in the U.S. economy. The agency's role was strengthened in 1922 when they won a suit against a company for deceptive claims that their stockings were woolen, when they contained less than 10 percent wool. In 1938, Congress passed legislation prohibiting "unfair and deceptive acts or practices," and this extended the FTC's powers to include supervision of advertising. The commission has since been directed to administer a wide variety of consumer protection laws. In 1975, the FTC received from Congress the authority to adopt industry-wide trade regulation laws. The FTC published their top 10 consumer complaints for 2010, and identity theft topped the list for the 11th year in a row. Last year the commission heard 250,854 complaints, or 19 percent of all action, on identity theft. The list of complaints also included the following in descending order: debt collection (11%); Internet services (5%); prizes, sweepstakes, and lotteries (5%); shop-at-home and catalog sales (4%); imposter scams (4%); Internet auctions (4%); foreign money/counterfeit check scams (3%); telephone and mobile services (3%), and finally credit cards (2%). For the first time, imposters who posed as relatives, friends, and government agencies to get consumers to send them money made the list—there were 60,158 of those complaints to the FTC. These crooks have learned the fine art of deception, and they prey upon innocent consumers. The FTC is there to protect our interests.

 What does all of this have to do with persuasion? Con artists are by necessity slick persuaders who prey upon the trust or naivety of others. Advertising sells a lot more than consumer goods. Ads sell sex appeal, promises of success, status, and immortality, and we accept "puffery" or "get-rich-quick" schemes as part of the national communication clutter. Federal agencies set standards, and they punish violators with everything from warnings to cease and desist orders intended to shut them down. C. Lee Peller, who is now president and CEO of the National Advertising Review Council, served on the FTC for 33 years. He said he saw the FTC evolve from being called the "Little Old Lady of Pennsylvania Avenue" because of its ineffectiveness in the 1960s to the "Tyrranosaurus Rex of federal regulatory agencies" in the 1970s, and now it is one of the most respected consumer protection agencies in the government (Metropolitan Corporate Council, 2007, p. 19). Much of this improvement came from working with the National Advertising Division (NAD) of the Council of Better Business Bureaus (CBBB) and the National Advertising Review Council (NARC).

THE FOOD AND DRUG ADMINISTRATION (FDA)

The Food and Drug Administration is the oldest consumer protection agency in the United States. Its origins go back to 1848 when Lewis Caleb Beck was appointed to carry out chemical analyses of agricultural productions, a duty that would later fall under the authority of the newly created Department of Agriculture in 1862. The Pure Food and Drugs Act passed in 1906 began the regulatory functions of what became the FDA in 1930 (FDA, 2011).

Recently new pressure has been placed on the FDA because of the pet food that killed many pets and sickened others, creating great emotional and financial losses for families who have dogs and cats, some of whose pets died painful deaths from kidney failure and paralysis that shut down vital functions.

Taco Bell pulled an ad that made fun of party poopers who brought veggie trays to game day because a Twitter campaign was launched against Taco Bell's anti-vegetable perspective.

PepsiCo removed a Mountain Dew commercial that critics called the most racist one in history that stereotyped and degraded African Americans by depicting a line up to identify the perpetrators of gang related violence against a white woman.

Perhaps the best known case of public endangerment came when Tylenol was tainted September 28, 1982, but the Johnson & Johnson Company took immediate action to remove all the supplies of Tylenol from store shelves and changed forever how over-the-counter medicines would be packaged and sealed to protect us from tampering. Their CEO addressed the emergency immediately and assumed responsibility for the safety of their customers, even at a great loss of revenue to the company. His courage and ethical behavior gave that case a prominent place in case histories that students of business ethics would read for decades to come. Johnson & Johnson's bold action created much credibility and good will between the company and consumers, and the company's lost market shares were recovered.

With the importation of all manner of products—especially tainted foods, medicines, and pet foods from China—the FDA needs to revise and adapt to the overwhelming task of guaranteeing Americans that these products are safe or, if not, taking the appropriate measures to have them removed from our markets. The FDA has undergone a metamorphosis since its inception, both in terms of the science it utilizes and the products it regulates, yet its stated mission remains that same as it was in 1906: to protect the public health of our citizens.

THE FEDERAL COMMUNICATIONS COMMISSION (FCC)

Maybe the only time you think of the FCC is when a "wardrobe malfunction" occurs, as when Janet Jackson exposed a breast during the Super Bowl game several years ago, or when some shock jock goes too far with his insults, and then a public outcry renews discussion of media censorship. The Federal Communications Commission was established by the Communications Act of 1934, but many other acts to regulate radio waves preceded this move. The sinking of the Titanic drew attention to the need to regulate ship-to-shore and ship-to-ship communication to save lives, and that regulation has extended to interstate and international communication. Today the FCC has jurisdiction over 50 states, the District of Columbia, and U.S. possessions. The five commissioners are appointed by the president and serve for five years—only three can be from the same political party.

The FCC regulates radio, television, wire, satellite, and cable communication, and the agency is responsible for licensing and renewals, processing complaints regarding deception or decency in communication media, and conducting investigations. The FCC exists to monitor the airwaves and wireless transmission to ensure that a citizen's public interest, convenience, and/or necessity are served. Since radio frequencies and satellite transmission are essential for day-to-day broadcasts, the commission also addresses public safety and homeland security issues such as emergency and disaster management.

The FCC exercises considerable power over the content of messages, including advertisements. Herbert Hoover feared that radio would lose its program appeal in the 1920s, when news and classical music "became the meat in a sandwich of two patent-medicine advertisements" (Hood, 2005, p. 67).

It would be advertising agencies, and not the networks, that created and produced radio and television shows. Popular radio dramas were named "soap operas" because they were generally sponsored by detergent-selling companies like Procter & Gamble; these shows became a primary vehicle for selling household goods to the listening audience and then on television to the viewing audience. Procter & Gamble sponsored *Ma Perkins*, while General Mills's Betty Crocker character sponsored *Today's Children*, and through these kinds of alliances, programming and advertising began a symbiotic business model emerging from radio and continuing for two more decades on television (Hood, 2005, p. 72). So the early notion that radio would only serve to carry news and public service announcements or highbrow classical music was soon confronted by the necessity to find sponsors to fund such programming. Along with these sponsors came passionate stories of love affairs made and broken or power struggles for inheritances with commercial breaks that feature little ditties about "Super Suds" or Betty Crocker cakes and bread. While this was not the "public interest, convenience, or necessity" that the FCC was formed to protect, everyone settled in for a long ride with commercial interests driving the media train, audiences brought aboard by tales of lust, intergenerational conflict, and every dysfunction known to humans. While complaints mounted against Madison Avenue and advertising—Thorstein Veblen's theory of "conspicuous consumption" became an evident societal malady, and Vance Packard's eight hidden needs were exploited—the agencies adopted a *laissez-faire* posture concerning programming unless it contained obscene material, but from time to time they flexed their muscles in the direction of truth in advertising or consumer safety.

Veblen, a Yale-educated philosopher, coined the phrase "conspicuous consumption," which addressed the reason why consumers bought items that had little utility, little relationship to rationality, and supported whim or status rather than functionality. Veblen's work reflected the new Darwinian theory of evolution—survival of the fittest. In his book, *Theory of the Leisure Class* (1899), Veblen explored how the wealthy exhibited their status through artifacts such as homes, expensive clothing or ornamentation, and sumptuous meals. Their wealth insulated them from the need to labor for these goods, so he wrote of "pecuniary emulation," which meant that the leisure class did not buy goods to benefit their health or comfort but rather gave them status or impressed their peer group (Veblen, 1899). The common concept of "keeping up with the Joneses," or competitive bidding for possessions, captures the phenomenon of consumers buying material goods beyond their means simply to create the appearance of being wealthy or well heeled and to achieve status among their neighbors. This urge to possess finery or unique artifacts continues to drive some consumers to bankruptcy, to credit debt that is unending, and to indulge family members who believe that designer labels will somehow fill any needs that they have resulting from personal insecurities and inadequacies.

Vance Packard's "Eight Hidden Needs," taken from his book, *The Hidden Persuaders* (1957), were discussed fully in Chapter 4, but a review of Packard's categories will show where advertisers find fertile ground for implanting appeals to satisfy these needs. Packard indentified them as: emotional security, reassurance of worth, ego gratification, creative outlets, love objects, sense of power, sense of roots, and immortality (Packard, 1957, pp. 61–70). Packard's work shed further light on the power of advertisers to sell products that promised extraordinary effects—longevity, power, sex appeal, or instant success. Similarly, A.H. Maslow's Pyramid of Needs (1987), which consisted of five levels—beginning with physiological needs, safety needs, belonging needs, esteem needs, and finally, self-actualization needs—reflect his insight into human motivation and personality attributes that predispose people to exhibit attitudes, beliefs, and behaviors that market research exploits in advertising campaigns. For example, if an ad implies that if you do not use deodorant you will have no friends, it is obvious that the message has focused on our need to belong and to be accepted. It would be difficult for the FCC to attack such an ad unless it promised some secret ingredient that guaranteed a particular set of outcomes. Most ads use vague language such as "virtually," "like," and "seem," which only imply a successful result.

Advertisers do not "make" us do anything; we buy products because we believe they will satisfy our needs or gratify us in some way. As Packard's work shows, we are not fully aware of what drives or motivates us to choose one product over another one, even if it costs more or seems more frivolous.

THE SECURITIES AND EXCHANGE COMMISSION (SEC)

Following the stock market crash of 1929, a series of measures were created to protect the public from fraudulent advertising for stocks and bonds. The agency required a truthful and complete disclosure before a security could be offered for sale. Anyone who had been deceived by buying a security that was inaccurately advertised could bring legal action against the firm that sold it. More recently, insider trading received wide attention and scrutiny with the prosecution of Enron's CEO and of Martha Stewart for unethical business practices, but what happens under cover often remains there for the unsuspecting investor or shareholder. With the economy unstable going into 2010, there was a cry to buy gold, a return to a more stable commodity. Insecurity in stocks and bonds motivate investors to return to gold as a historically secure commodity.

THE U.S. POSTAL SERVICE

One way that citizens are protected from receiving obscene material in the mail or receiving deceptive advertisements is through the regulations that surround the U.S. Postal Service. The post office can impound inappropriate materials and bring criminal charges against those who attempt to fraudulently use the mail services, which can result in fines or prison terms.

Although these descriptions are brief, we can see that a number of federal agency networks exist to assure that advertisements adhere to some ethical standards of truth in advertising, safety in products, and responsible business practices. Despite these measures, we regularly find that elderly citizens have been victimized by an unethical contractor who gave them an estimate for a remodeling job and then charged thousands of dollars that the client lacked the ability to pay. Similarly, we hear of terminally ill patients going abroad for treatments that have not been approved in the United States or for cosmetic surgeries that are considered unsafe to perform or have questionable outcomes. In other words, the government cannot protect people from themselves if they choose to buy from black market sources or to go abroad for alternative treatments. Yet the search for hope and immortality are well-documented human desires.

Given all these government safeguards, we may ask ourselves, what makes consumers so gullible? Why do beautiful bodies seem to be so persuasive in advertisements? Why are young women willing to starve themselves or develop health problems just to emulate the emaciated figures that are portrayed regularly in teen magazines? First, we must note that not everyone is affected in the same way by advertisements and, second, remember what Tony Schwartz stated—that it is not what the message implants into the receiver's brain, but rather it is the messages that are evoked through an emotional link to something already resident there. Advertising involves a transactional process between the source, message, and receiver just as any communication does. Questionable practices in advertising have framed a vigorous debate about the value of commercial speech and the need to protect the vulnerable from unethical appeals. Some theorists see consumer behavior linked to survival strategies that we thought had been left to our earlier ancestors. Evolutionary psychology posits that humans are still driven by survival mechanisms from the Stone Age.

THE STONE AGE BRAIN THEORY

Evolutionary psychology suggests that we have a Stone Age brain that is composed of certain functions to enable us to adapt to the specific tasks of our ancestors. According to this theory, the best advertising strategies speak to the solutions to universal concerns such as reproduction, power, speed, and survival by outmaneuvering or exploiting animals, plants, and other people. Marks and Neese (1994) noted that most human fears come from ancient forces such as "snakes, spiders, heights, storms, thunder, lightning, darkness, blood, strangers, social scrutiny, separation, and leaving the home range" (Cary, 2002, p. 103). People do not fear dangers inherent in sports utility vehicles or electrical outlets, even though their chances of being harmed from these are greater than from being killed by a snake or spider. Cary suggested that when strategists plan a political campaign, they should choose fear appeals that touch our evolutionary past and evoke a strong gut reaction. Perhaps that is why the "War on Terror" was such an effective political appeal during the 2004 election, because it touched a nerve with citizens who feared that their basic security had been breached and continued to be endangered. Automobile ads show crash dummies lurching forward in tests, but testimonials reassure us that the airbags and anti-locking brakes are the safest features on the market.

According to Cary, the Stone Age brain dictates to a degree what men and women want and how advertisers should adapt to deliver the promise to fulfill their needs. We certainly assume that "sex sells," or we would not see so much of it in advertisements. Cary wrote:

> Men want women of high reproductive value and use resources—power, status, food, possessions—to attract these women. From a biological point of view, sex with a woman taking birth control pills should be quite unsatisfying, since there is no possibility of offspring. However, men's minds are not wired to understand such recent developments; instead, their minds respond to the traditional markers of fertility—youth, good health, and physical attractiveness.
>
> Women seek men who have resources and will invest them in their offspring. They seek healthy mates with the energy and cleverness to succeed in contests with other men. Women are less concerned than men with physical attractiveness and more concerned with resources and emotional support. (Cary, 2000, p. 103)

During the Stone Age, a woman's value to a man depended on her reproductive value, which was evident by the features of youth—"full lips, clear, smooth skin, clear eyes, lustrous healthy hair, good muscle tone, and high energy levels" (Cary, 2000, p. 103). Today's fashion magazines display all manner of cosmetics or aids that guarantee these qualities, in other words, to increase their reproductive value, in Stone Age parlance. Advertisements for men are most effective when they promise to enhance resource acquisitions. Just as this was true with the warrior-hunter it is also true in business and sports. Men's success is signaled through artifacts such as expensive cars, spacious homes, and other expensive items (Cary, 2000, p. 104). The metaphors for the names of the products harken back to the Stone Age, when speed and dexterity were primary—Mustang, Jaguar, and Impala. Women are more persuaded by ads that promise extended reproductive capacity, extended kinship, and support in raising the offspring. Cosmetic counters display brands like Beautiful, Diamonds, and Youth Dew along with other anti-aging formulas.

Whether consciously or not, Cary says, people attribute personalities to products and brands, and similarly they have a relationship with that personality or brand. Advertisers attempt to segment customers according to their emotional relationship with brands. Further, Cary stated that advertisers should adapt scripts to Stone Age language, which means using words and metaphors that the Stone Age brain understands. For example, a telephone becomes a device to "reach out and touch someone" rather than a transmitter of signals in digital packets. Like the Jedi Knight's weapon, the lighted sword was simply a fancy stick, much like primates used to retrieve food when they needed an extension or tool. "High technology has been assimilated to Stone Age warfare" (Cary, 2000, p. 104). It is easy to analyze the military campaigns of "shock and awe" with "smart bombs," but everyday products use the same illusory power to persuade consumers of the sheer superiority and earth-shaking effects of the secret ingredients or engineering excellence of an XKE, for example, or other products so special that they use code to symbolize their essence since they are beyond words.

Whether we agree with the evolutionary psychology of the Stone Age brain or not, much of the language and imagery of modern advertising seems to aim at reproductive success, or at least the promise that is implied in sexual references. The types of sexual content that have been studied in advertising research include nudity or the amount of clothing worn in ads, sexual behavior such as flirting or body language, hugging or kissing, physical attractiveness including facial beauty or physique, sexual referents through objects or events, and sexual embeds like subconscious words, objects, and small images of body parts (Reichert & Lambiase, 2003, p. 14). Appeals that involve affect and arousal appear to be central to ads that use sexual content. The elaboration likelihood model of persuasion allows for persuasion to occur through both the central processing unit, where there is high involvement with critical components, and the peripheral unit, where there is low involvement. Sexual information may influence consumers if they analyze the brand in terms of sexual promises and benefits and find those promises compelling (Reichert & Lambiase, 2003, p. 33). Sexual information in ads is commonplace because it does attract attention, position the product as a sexual one, and suggest benefits that would be hard to refute or to prosecute. In other words, sexual ads sell promises and fantasies. But some recent research reported in the March 2007 issue of *Applied Cognitive Psychology* suggests that sex does not sell, but rather creates excitation that causes viewers of such shows as *Sex and the City* to ignore commercials altogether (The Big Turnoff, 2007). Viewers failed to remember what they had seen regarding the product compared to those who viewed more mundane shows like *Malcolm in the Middle*.

Research from Stanford University, Carnegie Mellon, and the Massachusetts Institute of Technology published in *Neuron* demonstrated that various parts of the brain mediated whether or not to buy an object. The research showed that consumers engage both the lizard-like brain that is driven by instinct and the cerebral cortex, which is the CEO that makes decisions. Brain mapping using magnetic resonance imaging (MRI) has enabled these researchers to see brain activity when subjects view an object for four seconds and then the price of the object for four seconds.

The experiment . . . showed that the more subjects liked a product, the greater the activity in the pleasure-seeking nucleus accumbens. But once the price flashed before their eyes, activity shifted to the pain-sensing insula, says Carnegie Mellon's Scott Rich, who co-authored the report. If the price was less than they had expected to pay, blood also flowed to the medial prefrontal cortex, where the CEO calculated the cost benefits of buying. If the greatest amount of blood flow was in the insula, the study participants balked at the purchase; if it was in their pleasure centre and the prefrontal cortex, they bought. The pattern was consistent enough that researchers were able to predict when subjects would close a deal and when they would take a pass. (Abraham, 2007, p. 50)

There was some fear expressed about advertisers and marketers using this research for even greater powers of persuasion when North America's credit card debt is already staggering. Rich said perhaps it is easier for consumers to slap down a Visa card than to pay cold, hard cash. This new research indicates that there are primitive parts of the brain at work when we make decisions, but there is also the frontal lobe or cerebral cortex that deliberates between immediate gain and future pain or vice versa. These interacting parts could explain why consumers react differently to advertising or product purchases. Clearly, "tightwad" controls were visible in these exercises in decision making as well as Nike's urge to "Just do it!"

Despite the neuroscience of brain mapping, Antonio Rangel, a neuroeconomics expert at Caltech University said, "If you define neuromarketing as the use of neuron-technologies to improve the effectiveness of advertisements or sales, I have not yet seen a single instance of success" (Mitchell, 2007, p. 10). Marketers have said they see nothing that suggests that they have to change everything that they have been doing. Just because we can observe the brain activity or neural firing, we still do not know what thoughts were being processed, although the researchers could predict selections with accuracy based on what they observed. Market research has been around now for a century, and advertisers still do not control consumers' behavior although they wield great influence on our purchases. The fear of **subliminal advertising** has been around for some time.

SUBLIMINAL ADVERTISING

Wilson Bryan Key wrote a book, *Subliminal Seduction* (1973), in which he claimed that advertisers used hidden sexual messages by embedding images or words on models, in ice cubes, or other artifacts in ads that unconsciously motivated viewers to buy the product. Most academic studies have discredited Key's claims because the experiments that he described have never been duplicated in laboratory settings. Further, no one has established a link between the word "sex" embedded in a Ritz cracker and a voracious appetite for Ritz crackers.

Subliminal advertising came to the public's attention in 1957, when Jim Vicary claimed to have conducted an experiment in which he flashed the words "drink Coca-Cola" and "eat popcorn" on a movie screen at a speed that could not be seen consciously, yet he claimed that sales increased substantially because of these unconscious messages. Later, Vicary admitted that the results of his experiment were fabricated when no one could duplicate them.

This did not quiet the fears that advertisers could trick consumers into buying things by manipulating them unconsciously (Rogers & Seiler, 1994, p. 1). In 1994, 75 to 80 percent of the U.S. population believed that subliminal advertising existed, despite denial by the industry. The FCC in 1974 set policy that if a TV station knowingly ran subliminal messages, they could lose their license for violation of the public trust (Teinowitz, 2000, p. 4). Wilson Bryan Key's writing and presentations kept the concept alive and appealed to consumers who believed that advertisers did use hidden persuaders to have them buy their products.

In 1994, Martha Rogers and Christine Seiler conducted a national survey of advertising industry practitioners and their clients to determine if companies did use subliminal advertising. They sent mail surveys to 750 companies that consisted of a four-page booklet-style questionnaire to investigate their beliefs and experience with subliminal advertising. They defined subliminal advertising as "the use of words, pictures, and shapes that are purposely inserted in advertising materials so that the viewers of the material cannot process the imagery at a conscious level, but rather at a subconscious level" (Rogers & Seiler, 1994, p. 4). There was a 36.1 percent return rate, netting 256 completed surveys. Not all questions were answered as directed, but almost 43.4 percent of the respondents had been employed in the advertising industry at least sixteen years, which correlated with the time period when

SkechersGOrun2 running shoes used social media to launch the 2013 Super Bowl campaign and an animals vs. humans theme that showed a man outrunning a cheetah.

subliminal advertising was receiving the most attention. Nearly all of them were aware of the concept of subliminal advertising before they received the survey, and 66 percent of them believed that advertisers do use subliminal messages in ads even though respondents themselves had not used it. They were split evenly on the question of whether or not it was effective to use subliminal ads, with 119 saying yes and 120 saying no. It was clear from the answers of 30.4 percent of the responses that some respondents did not know what subliminal advertising was since they described it as "probably built into creative message[s]" or "to emphasize extreme youthful appearance, high level energy, etc. showing elderly in unflattering manner" (Rogers & Seiler, 1994, p. 7). They confused subtle with subliminal, which indicated some confusion in the industry about the concept of subliminal ads. When asked the question, "To your knowledge, did the firm you formerly worked for ever use subliminal messages or imagery in your advertisements or in those of a client?" only 13 of the 189 who had worked for a different company said "yes." The remaining 93.1 percent said "no." They listed the reasons that it was not used as being ineffective, or irrelevant (i.e., an issue that never came up for discussion), or that it was unethical to use it (Rogers & Seiler, 1994, p. 7). Some respondents attached letters or margin notes stating that they thought subliminal ads were a myth and that it was not used in the industry. The researchers found that younger individuals with less than 19 years in the industry were more likely to believe that subliminal advertising was used, which indicated that these views were not based on industry practices but were coming from "other sources, allegations, and possible misinformation" (Rogers & Seiler, 1994, p. 7). This study concluded that subliminal advertising was not widespread and rampant in the advertising industry, as 90.63 percent of those surveyed denied any use or knowledge of the use of "words, pictures, or shapes that are purposely inserted in advertising materials so that the viewers of the material cannot process the imagery at a conscious level, but rather at a subconscious level" (p. 9). Of the remaining 9.3 percent, only one had a correct definition of subliminal advertising and had actually used it as a spoof or "an inside joke" (p. 10).

This study and others like it have not quelled the rumors or the widely held belief that subliminal appeals are used in both commercial and political ads. The latest tempest was created in a political ad that flashed the word "RATS" on the screen for one-thirtieth of a second in a spot that criticized Al Gore's prescription drug plan in the 2000 election. The ad was produced by National Media political ad executive Alex Castellanos, and it renewed the debate on the efficacy and ethics of subliminal advertising. Ira Teinowitz wrote in *Advertising Age*: "In the strangest political ad controversy yet this year, prominent Democrats charged they didn't just smell a rat when they saw the latest Republican National Committee commercial—they saw one" (Teinowitz, 2000, p. 4). Castellanos told CNN that he was not aware that the word "RATS" appeared and there was no intent to use subliminal advertising. The executive vice president of American Association of Advertising Agencies, Hal Shoup, said: "Subliminal advertising is a myth. . . . There is nobody I know that has experience in its use. There is absolutely no interest in it from the commercial side of advertising" (Teinowitz, 2000, p. 4). George Bush said that he believed the spot was not intended as a subliminal advertisement, only that Castellanos tried to make the word "bureaucrats" more interesting visually and "it was just a coincidence that the letters appearing first spelled out 'rats'" (Crowley, 2000). When candidate Bush was asked if the ad would be pulled, he said it was already coming out of rotation, but it ran 4,400 times in 33 markets, at the cost of $2,576,600 for the National Republican Committee (Crowley, 2000). That is a lot of cash to spend on a political ad that was treated as a mere visual mistake. The ad promoted Bush's Medicare prescription plan and said that Al Gore's plan would be run by bureaucrats. Gore protested that he had never seen anything like the RATS ad, which he said spoke for itself and its sponsor, whom he never named as either Bush or the NRC. Candidate Joe Lieberman said the ad was disappointing and strange, while Republicans like Representative J. C. Watts of Oklahoma said he took Bush at his word that it was inadvertent. This incident rekindled the debate on subliminal appeals in advertising and assured that during the 2008 presidential campaign critics would be inspecting all ads for such embeds.

Political advertisements that go beyond acceptable practices include the memorable ads like Lyndon Baines Johnson's "Daisy" commercial, George H. W. Bush's "Willie Horton" ad, and the "RATS" ad by George W. Bush. The Daisy ad tied Barry Goldwater to nuclear war, the Willie Horton ad implied that the Democrats were soft on murderers, and the RATS ad labeled Gore's healthcare bill nonsense. The RATS ad caused an uproar that motivated the FCC to investigate the following issues:

> As a result the FCC sent letters to 217 television stations asking (1) whether they aired the advertisement; (2) the dates it aired; (3) how many times it aired; and (4) whether officers, directors, or employees were aware that the advertisement contained the word "RATS." Of the 179 responding stations, 162 were not aware the advertisement contained the word "RATS" (Tristani, 2001), an unsurprising finding considering the nature of subliminals. (Stewart & Schubert, 2006, p. 107)

LeDoux and Phelps (2004) explained the effects of subliminal or precognitive primes as being processed by the "low road," which is tied to the autonomic nervous system, hormonal, and behavioral responses. The "high road" allows for systematic analysis of stimuli "as information moves from the sensory thalamus to the sensory cortex, where conscious thought occurs, and from there to the amygdala" (Stewart & Schubert, 2006, p. 104). The high road controls decision making and behavior, but the individual does not need to be aware of stimuli to be affected by them (Damasio, 1994; LeDoux, 1996, pp. 53–63; Marcus, Neuman, & Mackuen, 2000, pp. 35–41; Stewart & Schubert, 2006, p. 104).

While practitioners in advertising deny the use of subliminals or their effectiveness, the researchers named previously give credence to the emotional impact of subliminals or precognitive primes. "Specifically, the RATS precognitive prime was related to diminished trust in the Democrats to protect the Medicare system and to reduced support for Al Gore" (Stewart & Schubert, 2006, p. 109). The number of subjects in the Stewart study involved only fifty-five students selected from an Introduction to American Government class, but the attitudinal impact of such ads was supported by other researchers in more extensive tests as well. Social science research has become an integral part of campaigns of every type—product, political, and ideological.

MARKET RESEARCH

Social science research entered business seriously in the late 1920s with innovative minds like that of Edward Bernays, called the father of public relations, who approached selling or public relations campaigns with statistical findings regarding attitudes, impediments to positioning the product, and attributes that needed to be advanced.

Demographic research focuses on the characteristics of a population which includes such facts as age, income, education, gender, party affiliation, geographic location, race, religion, family size, and other profiles. Such research reveals that "women make 85 percent of retail purchases, with working women between the ages of 40 and 60 forming the largest market. Although a few companies, including Nautica and Banana Republic, feature mature models in ads or catalogs, older women remain largely invisible in print ads" (Gardner, 1999, p. 18).

Psychographics is the study of lifestyles or group identity generally referred to as VALS—values, attitudes, and lifestyles. Psychographic research began to appear in the 1960s and 1970s when target or segmented marketing emerged as a predominant business strategy. Computer data analysis allowed large numbers of subjects to be studied, which gave general results that could be processed and interpreted (Clark, 2004, p. 1118). This research is more about how the consumers identify themselves than the facts included in demographic profiles. For example, what do you think the profile of a Harley Davidson motorcycle purchaser would be? What kind of person would purchase a Coach purse? Dewars scotch? A pet rock? A thong bathing suit? You have read about baby boomers, generation Xersm and nexters, but this trend of trying to stereotype or categorize consumers is meeting resistance as one 23-year-old male stated:

> As my fellow "Xers" will surely agree, enough already! We have endured an endless parade of labels artfully created and enthusiastically promoted by their originators: Baby Busters, Slackers, Flyers, 13th Gen, Twenty somethings, Grungers, Cocoes, ad infinitum. Each week continues to bring forth new "designer labels," and yet these endless epithets do surprisingly little to characterize the roughly 46 million consumers born between 1965 and 1976. Ironically, my generation continues to be frequently misunderstood despite such extensive "group psychoanalysis." (Morrison, 1994, p. 27)

Morrison (1994) protested the psychographic labels intended to provide clarity because that approach depends on a priori assumptions that are inaccurate or dated. Two tendencies were noted. First, the "snapshot factor," and second, "market diversity." The snapshot factor leads to inaccuracies because generational lifestyles, language, and attitudes are constantly changing and labels quickly become obsolete. Market diversity means that to assume that 46 million peers are similar is as inaccurate as "to erroneously generalize that every Baby Boomer was at Woodstock" (Morrison, 1994, p. 27).

The challenge in the twenty-first century is to establish individual psychographics in a market that is growing in multiculturalism and segmentation.

> According to U.S. Census Bureau estimates, African-American, Hispanic and Asian population growth will continue to outpace that of whites. By 2050, the white population will

represent 53% versus the current 72%. As the white segment loses its majority status and as our population becomes increasingly multiracial and multicultural, lines of demarcation are going to blur. The term ethnic minority will lose its relevance and use.

Due to growing sophistication and complexity of consumers and how they define themselves, the model of segmentation has to evolve to a much more psychographic and personal approach that plumbs beneath attitudes and lifestyles to get to the core of each individual's desired self-image. (Burrell, 2000, p. 18)

The diversification of the population and the use of new media will challenge advertisers to make their ads more personal with agents that specialize in ethnic marketing. Statistics from the Myers Group in 2000 showed marked increases in projected advertising targeted at ethnic groups, with Hispanic, African American, and Asian consumers receiving substantially more media focus, but the Hispanic market represents the fastest growing group for advertising attention and funds (Burrell, 2000, p. 18).

Arens (2002) outlined 10 categories of lifestyle that were analyzed to determine what kinds of financial services consumers would need. These represent classic types of psychographic profiles (Table 10.1).

Whether you find yourself or your family in one of these categories should not concern you since there were 40 other profiles in the original research, but it is informative to note the attention to details and the labels applied in an effort to know customers, their needs, and the abundance or scarcity of their resources. Research is essential for advertising campaigns, since any effective communication with an audience requires that the source must know whom they are addressing. Increasingly advertisers are looking for a special place in the market to place their product and ads for it. That means looking for a **niche**.

NICHE MARKETING

The word "niche" derives from the Latin word for "nest" (Lindsay, 2007). A nest is cozy and built exclusively for the inhabitants of it. Mature economies eventually head toward specialized products for a narrowly defined market. The "one size fits all" philosophy is no longer satisfying to most consumers. As one Wal-Mart official noted, "no customer today will stand to be treated as part of a mass market anymore" (Lindsay, 2007). No superstore is more massively marketed than Wal-Mart, yet planners understand that a major shift in marketing has occurred.

Modern technology allows marketers to know more about consumers than ever before, and this technology allows interactivity with a level of contact and customization for consumers unlike any former times. Today marketing can optimize segmentation by filling the niche that consumers demand. "It's pure survival of the fittest—but with technology such as DVRs and the World "Live" Web it will feel like economic Darwinism at the speed of light. The only marketers that survive and thrive will be those that quickly embrace the principles of this new economy's nichecraft" (Lindsay, 2007, para. 2). In the nineteenth century, Social Darwinism led to excesses in wealth and a growing divide between the "haves" and the "have-nots" as the Knob Hill elites exploited immigrant workers and gained obscene wealth through their labors. **Technological Darwinism** will have global implications in the marketplaces all over the world as continents dissolve with neural networks joining consumers

TABLE 10.1 CONTEMPORARY SOCIAL CLASSES

Upper Crust	Social Security
Metropolitan families, very high income and education, manager/professionals; very high installment activity.	Mature/seniors. Metro fringes, singles and couples, medium income and education; mixed jobs, very low credit activity
Midlife Success	**Middle of the Road**
Families, very high education managers/professionals, technical/sales High income; super-high installment activity	School-age families, mixed education, medium income, mixed jobs; very high revolving activity, very high bankcard accounts
Movers and Shakers	**Trying Metro Times**
Singles, couples, students, and recent graduates, high education and income, managers/professionals, technical/sales average credit activity, medium–high installment activity	Young, seniors, ethnic mix, low income, older housing, low education, renters, mixed jobs, low credit activity, medium–high retail activity
Successful Singles	**Low-Income Blues**
Young, single renters, older housing, ethnic mix, high education, medium income, managers/professionals; very high bankcard accounts, very high installment activity, very low retail activity	Minorities, singles and families, older housing, low income and education, services, laborers; low credit activity, medium–high retail activity
Stars and Stripes	**University USA**
Young, large school-age families, medium income and education, military, precision/craft; average credit activity	Students, singles, dorms/group quarters, very low income, medium–high education, technical/sales; low credit activity, high percent new accounts

The groups outlined in this exhibit are just 10 of 50 Microvision lifestyle segments defined by National Decision Systems. This division of Equifax wants to know what financial services various consumers are likely to need.

Source: Arens, 2002, p. 153.

and providers of goods and services. Regulation and controls are yet to emerge from this free-for-all, but perhaps the movement toward particularity and customization of products to suit a narrow demand is a symptom of a movement away from the massification of commerce toward a more satisfying relationship with an exclusive group of loyal customers. However robust and global the marketplace, regulations are still essential, as the 2007 pet food tragedy reminded us when gluten from China contained chemicals used in manufacturing plastics that was fatal to many dogs and cats and made others seriously ill. Product safety is a major concern in the United States, which means that agencies must adapt to the globalization of products.

Target, Starbucks, and Apple began as narrow niches to satisfy a band of limited potential customers. Now these corporations have become household words and national neighbors. Lindsay (2007, para. 20) wrote:

> Offerings that resonate with the target for which there are few alternatives create a loyal customer base with all the benefits; more predictable revenue streams, lifetime value and word-of-mouth advocacy on your behalf. This, along with consumer-generated content and online communities, create marketing efficiencies that further drive growth and profitability.

You have to wonder what demographic or niche Kmart's "Ship My Pants" ad was created to address, which promises free shipping to customers.

The product that the marketer offers must satisfy some need, which sometimes requires a large imagination to conceive and to actualize. So the concept of niche marketing does not mean thinking "small" but "narrow." Lindsay concluded, "It's like the old saying: If you are on the wrong train to begin with, every stop along the way is the wrong stop. . . . So how do you get on the right train? Ask the niche for directions" (2007, para. 24). Everyone remembers the anomaly of the Volkswagen Beetle in the 1960s, when American cars were huge and laden with all manner of metal ornamentation. Today we see hybrid cars that are half the size of the SUVs that dominate the highway. The hybrids satisfy a group of consumers where the large SUVs satisfy a larger market, but the circumstances of foreign oil and rising gas prices may make the hybrid car niche an attractive one. The niche may be to be the smallest, to be the best, to be the most affordable, or simply to be first.

AGE/GENDER-SENSITIVE ADVERTISING

CHILDREN AS CONSUMERS

The debate on the efficacy and ethics of advertising to children is a heated one, but children between the ages of 4 and 12 spend about $23 billion annually, according to Janet Bodnar (1999). Those who defend advertising to children say that they learn important product information, that advertising does not have a direct stimulus–response effect, and that with training, children can become savvy consumers with critical skills (Acuff & Reiher, 1997; Guber & Berry, 1993; Neeley & Schumann, 2004). On the other side of the debate, many see advertising as dangerous and unethical because "it is deceptive and manipulative, stimulates wants, promotes consumerism and poor nutritional habits, and encourages children to nag their parents for products, creating dissention and stress in the home" (Bandyopadhyay, Kindrea, & Sharp, 2001; Bergler, 1999; Neeley & Schumann, 2004, p. 7).

Advocacy groups such as Stop Commercial Exploitation of Children (SCEC), Commercial Alert, Alliance for Childhood, and the Center for a New American Dream want more federal regulation to protect them from advertising. Sabrina Neeley and David Schumann (2004, p. 7) wrote:

Governmental agencies such as the Federal Trade Commission (FTC) and the Federal Communications Commission (FCC) typically advocate self-regulation (Furchtgott-Roth, 1998), whereas organizations such as the Children's Advertising Review Unit (CARU) of the Council of Better Business Bureaus (CBBB) works with businesses to ensure that advertising directed at children is accurate and sensitive to the audience. One recent historical analysis of advertising and children suggests that the relationship between advertiser and child is more complex than society recognizes, and calls for research examining this relationship. Cross suggests that one area of needed research is an examination of the form and content of advertising directed at children. (Cross, 2002, p. 445)

There is a concern that cartoon-like characters have a great capacity to influence children, especially preschool children. American children are avid consumers of media, with the average 2- to 11-year-old watching 21 hours of television per week with 81 percent of these shows carried on cable television (Neeley & Schumann, 2004, p. 7).

While very young children lack the ability to store and retrieve information, television offers color, sound, animation, and sound effects that increase attention in preschool-aged children (Alwitt et al., 1980; Fowles, 1976; Hays & Birnbaum, 1980; Huston-Stein & Wright, 1979; Wright & Huston, 1983). The visual and auditory complexities of the message cut through the child's "attention inertia and increase both attention to, and retention of, information" (Neeley & Schumann, 2004, p. 8). So, clearly, spokescharacters increase attention to ads. Young children often confuse products, name brands, and other information on the product. Since they cannot read, young children generally can recognize the cartoon spokescharacter that promotes the product and identify the product that the character advertises. The ability to recognize products increases with age (Neeley & Schumann, 2004, p. 9). Bahn (1986) found that children four to five years old associate the character-spokesperson with the characteristics of the product itself. For example, those products that are endorsed by a cartoon character are just for kids, they believed, while those that lack the cartoon character were for adults only.

Before Old Joe Camel who promoted Camel cigarettes was banned, a study revealed that 30.4 percent of three-year-olds to 91.3 percent of six-year-olds were able to match Old Joe with the Camel cigarettes. The researchers concluded that Old Joe was as recognizable to this age group as Mickey Mouse, and they asserted, "intentions are irrelevant if advertising affects what children know" (Fischer et al., 1991, p. 3148). Yet Mizerski (1995), who tested three- to six-year-olds, found a strong negative relation between liking Joe Camel and liking cigarettes, so he concluded that the characters did not appear to have a strong impact on whether they liked or disliked the product.

According to developmental psychologist Piaget (1929/1951), children two to seven cannot process information logically or abstractly (Neeley & Schumann, 2004, p. 10). This includes the inability to compare attributes of persons or objects, but numerous studies found that familiarity with a product was associated with children's preference and choice for those products (Shamir, 1979; Swanson, 1987). Children's preferences for products, toys, or activities can be very fickle and inconsistent. In the detailed study that Neeley and Schumann conducted they found that spokescharacters did generate attention, character recognition and liking, and product recognition and liking; however, this recognition and liking did not necessarily transfer to product preference and choice (Neeley & Schumann, 2004, p. 18). Advocates against targeting children in advertisements say that parents have lost control over their children's viewing because of media proliferation. They worry about online ads using spokescharacters or those that may become part of media games. A whole new arena has been opened for online advertisement where controls are still emerging or being tested. If advertisement to children were banned, programming revenues would suffer that support educational television too. Better regulations to control deceptive and inappropriate advertisements would help.

The American Psychological Association has debated the value of using psychological research to pitch toys, video games, snack food, and other products to children. In 1999 over 60 psychologists signed a letter calling for the association to probe the use of research and to draft a code of ethics that would address the issue. Some saw the manipulation of the young as unethical. Dr. Krasser, an associate professor of Psychology, said:

"When advertisers are using psychological principles to sell products to children, they are not only selling that product, but they are also selling a larger value system that says making money and using your money for the purchase of material things will make you happy." He said, "That's what is really behind almost every commercial message, that this product will make you feel happy, or loved, or safe and secure. My feeling is that it is manipulation to use children's needs to get them to buy these products." (quoted in Hays, 1999, p. C6)

Other psychologists, such as Dr. Acuff, who co-wrote *What Kids Buy and Why* (Acoff & Reiher, 1997), believed any action to block advertising to children was "anti-free enterprise." Acoff discussed the stage of neocortical development when children begin to develop logic and reasoning, which permits them to separate fact from fantasy (Hays, 1999, p. C6). These same techniques that enable advertisers to sell to children permit them to wage campaigns that are socially redeeming like anti-alcohol or anti-smoking campaigns.

The FTC set a public hearing for July 18, 2007, to discuss advertising that targets children including the use of character spokespersons. The snack food industry has been challenged to change the $10.39 billion-a-year enterprise by reducing calories and eliminating transfats and sugars to combat obesity and heart disease. "They're trying to take enough steps so Congress won't pass laws and they won't get sued," said Margo Wootan, Nutrition Policy Director at the Center for Science in the Public Interest (Tong, 2007, p. A-9). The FTC planned to survey 44 food and drink companies regarding their advertising to children. Some have begun to use a white check mark over a green dot that indicates that these products have less fat, sugar, or sodium and offer other health benefits. The new area of combat for advertisers is to show improved nutritional values and to show that they do not exploit children. Federal agencies attempt to protect children and teens from predatory practices in advertising and to sometimes protect them from indiscretions such as TMI—too much information—which they receive and are willing to divulge about themselves.

The privacy issue is one of the big challenges for advertisers on the Internet, according to Peeler, who worked for the FTC for more than 30 years. Young people do not use discretion in their postings often, and they may be more gullible than adults concerning ads. New media like YouTube allow for demonstrations and information that challenge traditional regulatory practices, but the Electronic Retailing Association supports self-regulation to evaluate honesty in core claims in national direct response advertising. Some agencies, like the Council for Responsible Nutrition, which is a trade association for dietary supplements manufacturers, have hired a full-time attorney to monitor dietary ads found on the Internet (Metropolitan Corporate Counsel, 2007). The area of diet supplements is a very large market that requires regulation for safety since in the past products have been found to contain life-threatening ingredients, like Ephedra. With America's obsession with thinness, the diet supplements deserve special monitoring. The average model in the beauty magazines is about 5 feet 11 inches tall and weighs about 111 lb., an impossible combination for a healthy female to attain. The influence or persuasive value of such magazines can be seen in the increase in eating disorders such as anorexia nervosa and bulimia that continue to rise, including in children as young as nine or even younger. Heightened awareness is coming with such educational videos as *Killing Us Softly 3: Advertising's Image of Women* (Jhally, 2002) that expose the indoctrination of young children that being razor thin is the path to beauty and stardom, when often teens develop life-threatening medical conditions that require hospitalizations to survive. Jean Kilbourne has studied the effects of advertising for over 20 years, and she created a series of videos that analyzes the impact of advertising on body image and unrealistic expectations that lead to all manner of self-esteem issues. The airbrushed Photoshop-finished models are actually making those who emulate their beauty sick from starvation or splurge-and-purge bulimic episodes.

GENDER STEREOTYPES

Advertising and mass media in general distort both male and female images to focus on power, competition, and resources for men and focus on beauty, sex appeal, and youth for women. Marilyn Gardner wrote in *The Christian Science Monitor*:

> Three decades after the women's movement offered women greater equality and expanded roles, a small chorus of media critics laments what it sees as a one-dimensional portrayal of women by Madison Avenue, characterized by nudity, extreme thinness, sensuality, even bondage. With their dual emphasis on physical perfection and sexuality, such ads, these critics say, can create body dissatisfaction, fuel addictions, and subtly legitimize violence and bondage. "The emphasis is so completely on women's bodies," says Jean Kilbourne, who for 20 years has been lecturing on images of women in advertising. "The ideal has always been unattainable, but now it's even more so." She attributes some changes to the ability to alter photographs with computers—to elongate bodies or put one woman's head with another woman's body. "The ideal is no longer a real woman," she says. "It's a composite." (Gardner, 1999, p. 18)

Gardner discussed one such ad for French designer clothing that shows an "ultra thin model [who] wears nothing but sunglasses, black gloves, and a velvet skirt low on her hips." Another shows a "long-limbed woman clad only in a sequined black bikini under her mink coat. She strikes a come-hither pose." The final ad she addressed was for a website that shows a naked model with only computer cord wrapped around her chest and hips (Gardner, 1999, p. 18).

While the statistics on eating disorders have reached epidemic proportions, girls who were interviewed by Elizabeth Massie for a documentary video denied that they were influenced by media that features skinny models, but they admitted that their friends were influenced by them. This **third-person effect** was named for the common attitude that media affects other people's attitudes, behaviors, and values, but we lack the self-awareness or honesty to see that it influences us also.

SENIOR CITIZEN ADS

Not all advertisements hit the mark, and such ads alienate receivers because the messages and images do not reflect the attitudes of the target consumers. Research conducted by Robert Wilkes in 1992 found that older women (age 60 to 79) believed that age was associated negatively with fashion interest, entertainment activity, and cultural activity. It is difficult to discern the best approach to developing products that serve certain segments of the population without stigmatizing them. Generally, older models are not used in ads unless they feature denture creams, adult diapers, retirement villages, or estate planning information. Advertisements aimed at men frequently feature erectile dysfunction drugs or blood pressure medicines. Many older citizens find these ads stereotypical and distorted because many older citizens engage in "defensive aging" consumption, that is they purchase goods based on their self-image developed in early life, even if this image is not considered valid by others (Moschis & Bernhardt, 2006, p. 340). Some older Americans will not use senior discounts even when it will save them money because they do not want to buy into the "old age" label. The older consumers are, though, the more likely they will engage in old-age-targeted communication. This communication includes "old-age-appropriate products, interest in senior discounts, and sensitivity to older spokespersons in advertisements" (Moschis & Bernhardt, 2006, p. 340). Many advertisers refuse to use older models in ads, fearing that this will alienate the younger segment of the market, which further alienates older consumers. Tepper (1994) found that people between 50 and 54 avoided senior discounts so as not to be labeled old. Those between 55 and 65 showed moderate resistance to such labeling, while those 65+ were not that concerned with being labeled old by using discounts or age-relevant products.

Certainly, market research should reflect the fact that age is more than a number. First, there is the chronological age of the consumer, which is their actual age. Next, there is their subjective or psychological age, which includes how old they feel or how they want to be identified. Finally, the functional age of the consumer defines what they are able to do. For example, running shoes are associated with young people who are in good shape, but some are unable to walk because of an infirmity or an accident which demonstrates that a young person may have the same functional age as someone who is 65 or 75. Older adults are loyal to stores and brands, Moschis (1992) found, so ads should appeal to brand loyalty rather than to age, which is stigmatized in a country where youth and power are revered.

It is obvious that the age of the consumer is a primary consideration in the type of messages and graphics that are appropriate or ethical. To say that something is effective as a sales pitch is not the same as saying that it is ethical. Children can be manipulated, but some adults can be misled as well. Most of us are willing to concede that mass media is a powerful force in shaping perceptions and cultural expectations, but few of us are willing to admit that we are personally affected by such a ubiquitous presence. The young women who are starving themselves to death are generally intelligent people, so where did the cult of thinness originate? Take a look at the magazines and tabloids at the supermarket and newsstands and count the number of them that feature a new diet drug, diet plan, or celebrity food/ workout routine on the cover. The obsession with thinness coincides with the portrayal of emaciated models on television, in the movies, and in magazines. Advertisers have turned our heads toward unattainable standards of beauty with airbrushed images, elongated bodies, and other distorted composites while simultaneously offering more calorie- and fat-laden foods than ever before. The rate of obesity has climbed to threatening proportions as the masses sit before their televisions or computer screens to absorb more tempting commercials for snacks or fast foods. One pundit recently stated that Super Bowl Sunday is a paradoxical situation where 22 overworked, exhausted men on a field are locked in combat and are in dire need of rest while millions of fans sit at home watching them who are in dire need of exercise.

Perhaps it is time for advertisers to internalize the purposes for mass media communication according to the FCC—to serve the "public interest, convenience, and necessity." Advertising agencies are not immune to public pressure or action such as protests and boycotts of products. Neither are they immune to social or political events that affect the national psyche. When a national tragedy or disaster occurs, the business establishment is affected in some unpredictable ways, but those who create ad copy or commercial messages must be sensitive to the social-political milieu in which they operate. To be insensitive to the event would be an affront to those who suffered losses, but to exploit the situation by tapping into the fear or unrest left in the wake of a disaster would be seen as unethical too.

ADAPTIVE ADVERTISING STRATEGIES FOLLOWING DISASTERS

There are many kinds of disasters that can shake the foundations of a nation, and the United States is not immune to such chaos. During the 1930s and 1940s the advertising industry had to adjust to the Great Depression, the New Deal, and World War II. Each social and economic challenge required unique attempts at adjustments from the advertisers. During World War II, movies were preceded by newsreels from Europe and pleas for citizens to continue their conservation of gasoline, rubber, aluminum, sugar, and other commodities and to purchase war bonds to support the war effort. How does a company sell commodities to a nation where most of the men between 18 and 45 are absent and there are shortages of all manner of supplies? Patience and sacrifices were values that brought Americans through that time to the postwar boom where everything was in demand from houses to cars, but patriotism was a winning appeal to the nation's consumers. Postwar advertisers could address those experiences of denial by selling home freezers to store food, which were communicated as a savings and convenience for households, but research showed that consumers bought freezers because they feared shortages and deprivations that they had known during the war years.

Natural disasters such as floods, hurricanes, or earthquakes require the government and civilians alike to pitch in and help with distribution and acquisition of supplies as well as emergency services. As brutal as these disasters can be, Americans generally respond with courage and goodwill. How should advertising agencies address those who have just lost their homes, personal effects, and sometimes family members? Disaster victims need everything, yet they lack resources to purchase what they need.

What happened on September 11, 2001, was unlike anything in our history in that the terrorist attack was complex, involving multiple targets, a successful surprise attack, and an ambitious operation beyond description. Our own technology was turned against us as commercial airliners were used as bombs to attack the Pentagon, the World Trade Center, and another, undisclosed, destination. A stunned nation watched news coverage, aghast at what we were witnessing without any comprehension of who planned it and why, or how this series of attacks came to pass. In the days that followed, the scope of the tragedy became more apparent, and the emotions of anger, depression, and loss settled in for months to come with the holiday season approaching when the most vigorous selling opportunities should have been realized. How could advertisers acknowledge the tragedy that we all felt and at the same time promote their goods and services without appearing to put profit above compassion or sensitivity to the national mood?

Gwendolyn Bounds wrote in the *Wall Street Journal* on February 5, 2002:

> Marketing after a tragedy is tricky business. Allude to it, and risk alienating those who think the promotion capitalizes on misfortune. Ignore it, and there's a danger of seeming out of touch. "In one sense I don't want anyone to forget what happened on that day," says Jennie Farrell who lost her brother in the World Trade Center attack and has co-founded Give Your Voice for families of victims. "But it's also an open wound for us. You can't watch the Super Bowl without it being right there. And I would hope and pray that everyone's intentions are honorable and for the greater good and not to commercialize it for one reason or another." (p. B-1)

How do advertisers adapt to such tragedies? During Super Bowl Sunday different companies handled the thorny issue in different ways. Bounds reported:

> . . . Anheuser-Busch Cos. aired an ad showing its Clydesdale horses trekking to ground zero and bowing their heads in respect. Siebel Systems Inc. is selling software it dubs "Siebel Solutions for Homeland Security." One recent ad pairs a fuzzy security camera image of two dark-haired men in an airport with the stark question: "Who are the Mohamed Attas of tomorrow?" And this past weekend, designer Kenneth Cole published a newspaper insert with text including "On September 12, people who don't speak to their parents forgot why. . . ." The ad, which promotes items including $98 sateen pants, concluded: "Today is not a dress rehearsal." (2002, p. B-1)

The Clydesdale horses presented an image of patriotism and respect for a place that has become hallowed ground and represents an icon for the twenty-first century. The viewer

Anheuser-Bush created a Budweiser Clydesdale Salute to 9/11 that was aired only once on Super Bowl Sunday as a tribute to the victims of 9/11 and their families.

could complete the narrative that was not offered because we all knew the story; the horses simply offered a silent moment of reflection upon an event that, despite all that had been said and written about it, could not be captured in words. This graphic picture was an example of visual rhetoric that evoked a powerful emotional response from viewers.

Siebel Systems used a mild threat appeal by reminding us that there is a need for homeland security and implying that their technology can offer a solution to terrorists who may pass unnoticed. Generally, threat appeals work only if there is a sense of empowerment that the audience can do something to address the threat, and in this case, surveillance was the solution Siebel offered. Such threat appeals can backfire if the audience wishes to avoid the painful memory or fears associated with it and if they feel powerless to cope with the dangers.

The Kenneth Cole ad focused on the importance of relationships because life is to be lived fully in the present since it is not a "dress rehearsal" or contrived theatrical performance defined only by costumes, staging, or illusions. Cole managed to advertise their $98 sateen pants and other items, but the ad reminded us that some things are more important. They implanted the idea that connections to other human beings, like parents, transcend more material possessions when we reflect on the impermanence of life in a post-9/11 world. The ad presented the product, but it implied in the script that "things" were secondary to our September 12 priorities, which should optimize the gift of life and family.

Alan Brew, an owner of Addison Branding & Communications in San Francisco, warned that for advertisers to tie their product into a tragedy only works as long as consumers feel tied to the event. Further, when Siebel used the Atta reference, they dragged consumers back into that horrific moment which they really wanted to forget. Erich Joachimsthaler, chief executive officer of Brand Leadership Company, cautioned that companies should not use ads that they are unwilling to have follow their brand identity for the long term (Bounds, 2002, p. B-1).

Boeing adjusted to the tragedy in their advertising by focusing on freedom from the fears of terrorism. The ad reminded us that we needed to exercise the liberties that we possess in this country: "The freedom to go where you want to go, when you want to go, is a precious liberty. And . . . the nation's skyways are once again ready to help you make the most of that freedom" (Bounds, 2002, p. B-1). Rob Britton, who was supervisor of the advertising and marketing planning of AMR Corp.'s American Airlines, explained why the ads would not feature their planes.

> One thing the commercial doesn't show: planes. "You can guess why not," Mr. Britton says. "The imagery is something we've always used, the silver birds were a point of distinction and pride. But the image that flowed from the misappropriation of those vehicles was pretty powerful." (Bounds, 2002, p. B-1)

During the 2001 holiday season, the ads would focus on family ties with small children walking through airports with their little suitcases wheeling behind them with icons of New York like the Statue of Liberty displayed behind them. Families still had to travel to reunite with loved ones and to complete holiday plans that had been made months in advance. Images of innocent children replaced the surging jets and smoldering ashes from the World Trade Center. The Pentagon was rarely pictured, even in news stories about the attack, because no one wanted to be reminded that the bastion of military might had been struck without any effective defense mounted. Advertisements for air travel returned to themes of patriotism, appeals to freedom to come and go as we please, to family unity, and the holiday season.

As the foregoing examples show, advertisers must be cognizant of the pulse of the people, their fears, and their hopes. Some images are powerful for the history or narrative that each evokes. Iconic images like the Twin Towers in New York have come to represent shorthand messages that unravel complicated tales to viewers. Advertisers have to guide the narrative and to manage the response by thoughtfully constructing the images and messages that they create for us.

SUMMARY

Advertising is a form of communication that aims to both inform citizens and persuade consumers to buy a product, elect a candidate, or to join an ideological movement. The integrated marketing communication (IMC) model demonstrates the complexity of the many strategies and tactics necessary to effectively initiate a product campaign. The customer is central to this effort so that every attempt is made to understand their needs, beliefs, and behaviors and to link them to the product by appealing to their sense of value, propriety, and satisfaction. We know that not all purchases are practical, but customer gratification may be based on some hidden desire such as status, reward for past deprivation, or to compensate for some felt inadequacy.

Social science has been applied to marketing so that information processing theory on how messages are received, stored, and retrieved is related to consumer behavior. Recent studies on brain mapping may take this research further, but experts in advertising have not seen any reason to change their methods yet. The **Stone Age brain theory** posits that advertisers should speak the language of survival, reproduction, and power because those are prime motivators for humans. The age-old techniques of brands, product placement, positioning, and endorsements continue to be used while the channels that carry advertisements have broadened. Subliminal advertising has been denied by over 90 percent of practitioners in the business, yet in 2000 a political ad created a furor and enlivened the debate on the effectiveness of hidden images, words, or objects in political ads. The government regulatory agencies exist to protect consumers from deception, unsafe products, and unethical business practices. Global commerce is challenging our agencies' ability to control products that are no longer clearly produced in the United States, since additives or ingredients may be manufactured elsewhere without the standards of safety and inspection that we exercise in this country.

The effectiveness of advertising depends on the selective perception and behavior of each receiver. Whether or not they purchase the product depends on how they define "value," which is an idiosyncratic decision crafted from their perspective. But the AIDA model of advertising posits that first you must get the consumer's attention and maintain their interest, then create desire to possess the product, then move them to action, which would be to purchase the good or service. The process could break down anywhere along the way.

All communication exists in a social-political context that is reflected in the national psyche, and advertising agencies must grapple with the fine line between pandering to people's fears and prejudices and presenting tasteful messages. The post-9/11 holiday advertisements presented challenges for various companies who did not wish to appear crass or overly driven by profit, but at the same time, they did not want to dwell on tragedy or arouse further mourning and fear. We are exposed to a constant battery of advertisements, and we are unaware of these sensory stimuli unless one stands out for its excellence or affronts our sensibilities. When we reflect on the complex dynamic between a sponsor's desired goal and the diverse nature of the consumer base, we can appreciate an ad that really resonates with the masses.

APPLICATIONS

1. Look for subliminal messages or images in advertisements and bring them to class for discussion. What images were you able to find and to identify? How did these images enhance the advertisement?
2. Bring in a variety of magazines and analyze the cover of each, paying attention to the people featured there and the articles that they announce in that issue. How many covers announced articles on diets, sex, cosmetics, and celebrities?
3. Analyze an ad according to the market segment that you believe the ad is addressing. Whom do you perceive to be their targeted consumer? Was the ad effective?
4. Compare online advertising with traditional channels such as radio, television, newspapers, magazines, and billboards. What advantage does the Internet offer?
5. Research a regulatory agency and a case that was recently prosecuted by that agency. What was the charge against the advertiser or company? How was it resolved?

REFERENCES

About the FCC. (2011). Retrieved March 13, 2011, from: http://www.fcc.gov/aboutus.html.

Abraham, C. (2007). Your brain on Gucci: Economists used to think consumers made rational purchasing decisions. But a new field of research is revealing neural forces that leave classical theorists scratching their heads. *The Globe and Mail*, a division of CTVglobemedia Publishing Inc., p. 50.

Acuff, D. S., & Reiher, R. H. (1997). *What kids buy and why: The psychology of marketing to kids*. New York: Free Press.

Alwitt, L. F., Anderson, D. R., Pugzles Lorch, E., & Levin, S. R. (1980). Preschool children's visual attention to attributes of television. *Human Communication Research, 7*(Fall), 52–67.

Andrews, D. L. (1996). The facts of Michael Jordan's blackness: Excavating a floating racial signifier. *Sociology of Sport Journal, 13*(2), 125–158.

Arens, W. F. (2002). *Contemporary advertising* (8th ed.). Boston: McGraw-Hill.

Bahn, K. D. (1986). How and when do brand perceptions and preferences first form? A cognitive developmental investigation. *Journal of Consumer Research, 13*, 382–393.

Bandyopadhyay, S., Kindrea, G., & Sharp, L. (2001). Is television advertising good for Children? Areas of concern and policy implications. *International Journal of Advertising, 20*(1), 90–116.

Bergler, R. (1999). The effects of commercial advertising on children. *International Journal of Advertising, 18*(4), 411–425.

Bodnar, J. (1999). *Dollars and sense for kids*. Washington, DC: Kiplinger Books.

Bounds, G. (2002). Psychology Of Marketing: Marketers Tread Precarious Terrain—Ads Alluding To Sept. 11 Risk Taint Of Commercializing Tragedy To Push Products. *Wall Street Journal*, February 5 (Eastern Edition).

Burrell, T. J. (2004). Make It Personal. *Advertising Age, 71*(7), 18.

Cary, M. S. (2002). Ad strategy and the Stone Age brain. *Journal of Advertising Research, 40*(1/2), 103–104.

Clark, C. (2004). Psychographics. *Museum of broadcast communications encyclopedia of radio, (AN20997565) 3*, pp. 1118–1119.

Cross, G. (2002). Values of desire: A historian's perspective on parents, children, and marketing. *Journal of Consumer Research, 29*, 441–447.

Crowley, C. (2000). Bush says "rats" ad not meant as subliminal message. *CNN.com*, September 12. Retrieved June 29, 2007, from: http://archives.cnn.com/2000/ALLPOLITICS/stories/09/12/bush.ad/.

Damasio, A. R. (1994). *Descartes' error: Emotion, reason, and the human brain*. New York: Putnam.

Du Plessis, E. (2008). *The Advertised mind: Ground-breaking insights into how our brain responds to advertising*. Philadelphia: Kogan Page.

FDA (U.S. Food and Drug Administration). (2011). Retrieved March 13, 2011, from: http://www.fda.gov/AboutFDA/WhatWeDo/History/default.htm.

Federal Trade Commission protecting America's consumers. (2011). Retrieved March 13, 2011, from: http://www.ftc.govftc/about.shtm.

Fischer, P. M., Schwartz, M. P., Richards, J. W., Goldstein, A. O., & Pojas, T. H. (1991). Brand logo recognition by children age three to six years: Mickey mouse and old Joe the camel. *Journal of the American Medical Association, 266*, 3145–3148.

Fowles, B. R. (1976). Moppets in the market place: Evaluating children's response to television advertising. In B. B. Anderson (Ed.), *Advances to consumer research* (pp. 520–522). Provo, UT: Association for Consumer Research.

Furchtgott-Roth, H., Commissioner of the Federal Communication Commission. (1998). Speech before the American Advertising Federation, March 25. Cited in Neeley & Schumann, *Journal of Advertising, 33*(3), 7–23.

Gardner, M. (1999). Body by Madison Avenue: Women make 85 percent of all retail purchases. *Christian Science Monitor*, November 24, p. 18.

Guber, S., & Berry, J. (1993). *Marketing to and through kids*. New York: McGraw-Hill.

Hays, C. L. (1999). A call for restrictions on psychological research by advertisers into products for children. *The New York Times,* October 22, Late Edition, East Coast.

Hays, D. S., & Birnbaum, D. W. (1980). Preschoolers' retention of televised events: Is a picture worth a thousand words? *Developmental Psychology, 16*(5), 410–416.

Hood, J. M. (2005). *Selling the dream: Why advertising is good business.* Westport, CT: Praeger Publishers.

Houston-Stein, A., & Wright, J. C. (1979). Children and television: Effects of the medium, its content, and its form. *Journal of Research and Development in Education, 13,* 20–31.

Jhally, S. (Producer, Director, & Editor). (2002). *Killing us softly 3: Advertising's image of women* [DVD]. Created by J. Kilbourne. Northampton, MA: Media Educational Foundation.

Kellner, D. (2002). The sports spectacle, Michael Jordan, and Nike: Unholy alliance. Unpublished manuscript. Retrieved July 7, 2007, from: http://www.gseis.ucla.edu/faculty/kellner/papers/MJNIKE.htm.

Key, W. B. (1973). *Subliminal seduction.* New York: Signet.

LeDoux, J. (1996). *The emotional brain: The mysterious underpinnings of emotional life.* New York: Simon & Schuster.

LeDoux, J. E., & Phelps, E. A. (2004). Emotional networks in the brain. In M. Lewis & J. M. Haviland-Jones (Eds.), *Handbook of emotions* (2nd ed.). New York: Guilford.

Lindsay, M. (2007). Today's niche marketing is all about narrow, not small. *Advertising Age,* June 4. Retrieved November 9, 2010, from: http://adage.com/cmostrategy/article?article id11705.

Lloyd's Comments On Celebrity Advertising Campaign Coverage. (2006). Retrieved July 3, 2007, from: http://www.insurancejournal.com/news/international/2006/06/29/69966.htm.

Marcus, G. E., Neuman, W. R., & Mackuen, M. (2000). *Affective intelligence and political judgment.* Chicago: University of Chicago Press.

Marks, I., & Nesse, R. M. (1994). Fear and fitness: An evolutionary analysis of anxiety disorders. *Etology and Sociobiology, 5*(6), 247–261.

Maslow, A. H. (1987). *Motivation and personality* (3rd ed). New York: Harper & Row, Inc.

The Metropolitan Corporate Counsel. (2007). Self-regulation: The advertising industry's commitment to truth and substantiation in advertising. *The metropolitan corporate counsel,* May 3, Northeast Edition, *15*(5), p. 19. Retrieved June 5, 2007, from: http://www.dglaw.com/images_user/newsalerts/150519DavisUrbach-Peeler.pdf.

Mitchell, A. (2007). Advertisers turn to science to get inside consumers' heads BRANDING; Neuroscience is shedding new light on how people respond to marketing, but can it be used to change behavior, asks Alan Mitchell. *The Financial Times Limited,* January 5 (London, England). Retrieved June 13, 2007, from http://wf2la7.webfeat.org/G5NyH1352/url=http://web.lexis-nexisi.com/universe/document?.

Mizerski, R. (1995). The relationship between cartoon trade character recognition and attitude toward product category in young children. *Journal of Marketing, 59,* 58–70.

Morrison, D. A. (1994). More than new label, gen X needs research. *Advertising Age,* October 24. Retrieved June 11, 2007, from https://sslvpn.pitt.eduuniverse/, DanaInfo=web.lexis-nexis.com+printdoc.

Moschis, G. P. (1992). *Marketing to older consumers: A handbook of information for strategy development.* Westport, CT: Quorum Books.

Moschis, G. P., & Bernhardt, A. (2006). Older consumer responses to marketing stimuli. *Journal of Marketing Research,* September, 339–346.

Neeley, S. M., & Schumann, D. W. (2004). Using animated spokes-characters in advertising to young children. *Journal of Advertising, 33*(3), 7–23.

Packard, V. (1957). *The hidden persuaders.* New York: David McKay Company, Inc.

Piaget, J. (1951). *The child's conception of the world.* London: Routledge and Kegan Paul. (Original work published 1929.)

Reichert, T., & Lambiase, J. (2003). *Sex in advertising: Perspectives on the erotic appeal.* Mahwah, NJ: Lawrence Erlbaum Associates.

Rogers, M., & Seiler, C. A. (1994). The answer is no: A national survey of advertising industry practitioners and their clients about whether they use subliminal advertising. *Journal of Advertising Research, 34*(2), 36–45.

Shamir, J. (1979). Children's consumer information processing: The development and training of product choice strategies and information use. Doctoral dissertation, University of Minnesota.

Steel, E. (2007). Advertising's brave new world. *The Wall Street Journal,* May 25, Business News Section. Retrieved November 7, 2010, from: http://www.commercialalert.org/news/archive/2007/05/advertisings-brave-new-world.

Stewart, P. A., & Schubert, J. N. (2006). Taking the "Low Road" with subliminal advertisements: A study testing the effect of precognitive prime "RATS" in the 2000 presidential advertisement. *The Harvard International Journal of Press/Politics, 11*(4), 103–114.

Sutel, S. (2007). Print advertising revenues at U.S. newspapers falls 1.7 percent in 2006. *Associated Press Financial Wire,* March 15. Retrieved November 9, 2010, from: http://www.seattlepi.com/busi.

Swanson, K. J. (1987). The effects of familiarity on children's product choices: An information processing perspective. Doctoral dissertation, Texas A&M University.

Teinowitz, I. (2000). Ad creates a "rat" problem for GOP. *Advertising Age, 71*(39), 4.

Tepper, K. (1994). The role of labeling processes in elderly consumers' response to age segmentation cues. *Journal of Consumer Research, 20*(4), 503–519.

The big turnoff. (2007). *The Economist* (U.S. Edition), March 3. Retrieved June 13, 2007, from: http://www.economist.com.

Tong, V. (2007). Food makers put snacks on a diet: Manufacturers slim-size junk, reacting to demand, regulation fears. *Tribune Review,* June 21.

Veblen, T. (1899). *The theory of the leisure class.* New York: Macmillan Company.

Wilkes, R. E. (1992). A structural modeling approach to the measurement and meaning of cognitive age. *Journal of Consumer Research, 19*(2), 292–301.

Wright, J. C., & Houston, A. C. (1983). A matter of form: Potentials of television for young viewers. *American Psychologist, 38,* 835–843.

CHAPTER 11

PUBLIC RELATIONS: ENGINEERING PUBLIC CONSENT

KEY WORDS

asymmetrical
Chappaquiddick principle
Excellence Study
image restoration
integrated communication
  model (ICM)

press agentry
public relations
Public Relations Society of
  America
spin

symmetrical
transparency
weak propaganda

PREVIEW

Edward Bernays, who was Sigmund Freud's blood nephew, combined the theories of sociology and psychology to win adherence to his ideas and to create campaigns for his clients. He is known as the "father of public relations," which is an appropriate honor, but according to Bernays's autobiography, the Nazis used his book, *Crystallizing Public Opinion* (1929), without his approval as a guide for gaining support for their program against the Jews. Public relations involve communication strategies that can be used for good or ill purposes, as the Nazi example shows, but Bernays defined public relations as "engineering public consent." Bernays devoted his life to helping our government and corporations by influencing public opinion. His ideas were used to mount the first government propaganda campaign during World War I. He said:

> The conscious and intelligent manipulation of the organized habits and opinions of the masses is an important element in democratic society. Those who manipulate this unseen mechanism of society constitute an invisible government which is the true ruling power of our country. . . . We are governed, our minds are molded, our tastes formed, our ideas suggested, largely by men we have never heard of. (quoted in Harman, 2007, p. 1)

Edward Bernays developed the disciplines of marketing and public relations, which have become university majors and influence everything from presidential campaigns to funny commercials we see on Super Bowl Sunday.

Edward Bernays believed that manipulation of public opinion created an invisible government in a democratic society by engineering consent.

Public relations (PR) is a management function that aims to create and maintain a positive impression of a government or organization and to restore a positive image when damage has resulted from an action or event that has diminished public perception of the reputation of the product, organization, or people who represent them. Kevin Moloney defined PR this way:

> Modern PR is competitive communication seeking advantage for its principals and using many promotional techniques, visible and invisible, outside of paid advertising. Defined thus, it is consistent with advocacy and adversarial types of communication (Barney & Black, 1994). Since the last quarter of the nineteenth century, it has been political, commercial and social messaging for dominant interests and elected governments in maturing liberal democracies. (Moloney, 2006, p. 165)

Moloney went on to say that public relations is "weak propaganda," but this label generates controversy because no one wants to say that they are paying for or sending out propaganda. Since Bernays wrote his early book on which he called PR propaganda, the word "propaganda" has taken on a pejorative connotation. The ideological struggles against fascism and communism that used covert sources, misinformation, and psychological manipulation co-opted the word propaganda. Today, no public relations practitioner wants to be identified with propaganda—even **"weak propaganda."** Moloney wrote:

> PR propaganda is the one-sided presentation of data, belief, an idea, behaviour, policy, a good or service in order to gain attention and advantage for the message sender. It seeks attention and advantage through attitudinal change and then through behavioural compliance. It intends to persuade through the use of selective facts and emotions in its message construction. Merton indicates how the factual and emotional elements can be combined in the least manipulative, if not non-manipulative, way. He writes (1995, p. 271) that "mass persuasion is not manipulative when it provides access to the pertinent facts. It is manipulative when the appeal to sentiment is used to the exclusion of pertinent information." (Moloney, 2006, p. 167)

Today the term most often associated with public relations or manipulation of public sentiments that manages communication at the expense of full disclosure is "**spin**." Moloney addressed the idealism of the Grunigs, whom he said ignored some facts in their Excellence Study that is covered in the next paragraph. Moloney stated that the Grunigs "have become associated with PR as communicative idealism" (2006, p. 168). He said PR is not a discipline "in search of an altruism or moral ideal. It is rooted in the pluralist, self-advantaging promotional culture associated with liberal democracy and free markets. Above all, it is communication designed to further the interests of its principals" (p. 168). These principals could be anyone from Britain's royal family to celebrities in sports, the arts, or politics.

In a 1984 textbook, *Managing Public Relations*, Grunig and Hunt established four models to describe historical developments in the United States and to describe ideal types based on how public relations is practiced.

> These four models were called press agentry/publicity, public information, two-way symmetrical, and two way **asymmetrical**. Press agentry/publicity and public information both are one-way models. Practitioners of **press agentry** [emphasis added] seek attention for their organizations in almost any way possible, whereas public information practitioners are journalists-in-residence who disseminate accurate, but usually only favorable, information about their organization. With the two-way symmetrical model, practitioners use research and dialogue to bring about symbiotic changes in the ideas, attitudes, and behaviors of both their organizations and publics. (Grunig, 2001, pp. 11–12)

While the four models have received criticism from other scholars, they have offered teaching tools in the United States and guidance for developing countries in the world. Critics claim that the **symmetrical** (two-way) approach means that organizations could not pursue their self-interest, which is unrealistic. Grunig defended the symmetrical model by stating that organizations do better when they serve the public "because organizations get more of what they want when they give up some of what they want" (Grunig & White, 1992, p. 39). Persuasion runs from the organization to the public and from the public to the organization regarding changes in attitudes and behaviors. The symmetrical model has been critiqued as utopian because it is based on assumptions of "liberal pluralism." James Grunig and Larissa Grunig have extended their work on public relations to strategies to empower activist groups, who pay little attention to mediated messages but respond to personal communication. They suggested **asymmetrical** communication like media advocacy, government lobbying, and litigation as a means to convince organizations that the public's problem is also their problem. Once such action has been taken, public relations strategies can return to **symmetrical** communication to build long-term relationships between the organization and activist groups.

While there is no neat definition for public relations, Professors James and Larissa Grunig, both now retired from the University of Maryland, issued a series of books that grew out of the **Excellence Study** they conducted on public relations, which was intended to find out what theories and practices best exemplified excellence in the field. Many academicians believed that it was the best scientific research in the field. In 1991, the Grunigs drew distinctions between marketing and public relations by stating, "[T]he marketing function is concerned with products, services and customer markets. Public relations, in contrast, is concerned with all relevant publics of that organization. . . . Whereas marketing's purpose is to make money, public relations strives to save money for the organization by managing threats to its mission or mobilizing support for it" (Dozier, Grunig, & Grunig, 1995, p. 263). The Grunigs separate marketing from the public relations department. This separation flies in the face of the **integrated communication model** that was described in earlier chapters, which coordinates all research, education, and communication functions. The Grunigs argued that such separation of those departments was necessary so that public relations practitioners could focus on strategic problem solving, and any attempt to combine departments of marketing and public relations would diminish the importance of communication in organizations where less than excellent practices were already in place (Hallahan, 2007, pp. 299–336).

Critics of the Grunig's work found that public relations is too complex with too many variables to be fit into four neat models, and they recommended a contingency approach that addresses specific publics at a particular time based on a continuum from pure accommodation to pure advocacy. In an article entitled "It Depends: A Contingency Theory of Accommodation in Public Relations," scholars identified 87 variables that affect the degree of accommodation undertaken by public relations practitioners. Their study found that the whole enterprise is too complicated to fit into the normative theory of the excellence reports and must take into account antecedent, mediating, and moderating variables as an alternative approach to the two-way symmetrical model. The best approach depends upon too many variables to be pushed into four boxes but rather depend upon antecedent conditions, current pressures and opportunities (Cancel, Cameron, Sallot, & Mitrook, 1997).

The controversy over where marketing or public relations fit on the organizational chart and whether public relations should be taught in business or communication curricula continues. Matt Shaw, vice president of the Council of Public Relations, said, "It turns out that when advertising grows up it wants to be public relations" (Shaw, 2007). Shaw stated that the public relations toolbox was being pilfered by other disciplines claiming turf that was not called public relations by the perpetrators. He said:

> What I'm seeing these days is a lot of coveting (and more) of our turf. There have been many pieces written in the past year or so on why this is the right place, right time for public relations firms to excel. In large part, it's because public relations is the one business discipline that has always been about social influence. The global world of commerce is coming around to public relations, recognizing that social rules—transparency, relationships, meaningful conversation—favor public relations practitioners. (Shaw, 2007, para. 7)

Shaw stated that the industry showed a 13.9 percent growth in 2006 and a projected compound growth of 11 percent through 2012, according to the Veronis Suhler Stephenson report. He added that since 1990 there had been a 44 percent growth in head counts in public relations, which is three times the growth rate of advertising professionals. Shaw stated that public relations was changing so rapidly and dramatically that some marketing consultant predicted that they would no longer be referred to as "PR firms" in 15 to 20 years but "they" will have morphed into something new, so he cautioned his members to "Be Bold. Be Smart" (Shaw, 2007, para. 18). Because of new media and rapid growth in the industry, there are turf battles emerging, with efforts to define the paradigm shift in favor of public relations rather than advertising. Lou Capozzi, Public Relations Corporate Communications Group Chairman Emeritus, told his peers to "add a zero to the (public relations) budget and call advertising a public relations tactic" (Shaw, 2007). All of this dialogue tells us that the integrated communication model is not all that integrated after all but still resisted by conventional organizational charts.

Kirk Hallahan came down on the side of integrated communication when he wrote:

> Future research must look beyond public relations as a specialty function to consider how public relations activities—including relationship building and strategic communication— are undertaken by the entire organization. Stated another way, the level of the analysis used in studying public relations management needs to expand from the department level to the organization level, and must recognize that public relations activities are not carried out only by people who call themselves public relations practitioners. (Hallahan, 2007, p. 319)

A Commission on Public Relations Education was formed in 1992, comprised of 47 members who represented eight organizations: the Public Relations Society of America and its Educator Academy, The Institute for Public Relations, the National Communication Association, the Association for Women in Communication, the International Association of Business Communicators, the International Communication Association, and the International Public Relations Association. That commission recommended that public relations programs should teach students the following:

- Communication and persuasion concepts and strategies
- Communication and public relations theories
- Relationships and relationship building
- Societal trends
- Ethical issues
- Legal requirements and issues
- Marketing and finance
- Public relations history
- Use of research and forecasting
- Multicultural and global issues
- Organizational change and development
- Management concepts and theories (Wright & VanSlyke Turk, 2007, p. 580)

According to Wright and VanSlyke Turk (2007), the Commission identified the skills that would be necessary to enter the profession of public relations:

- Research methods and analysis
- Management of information
- Mastery of language in written and oral communication

- Problem solving and negotiation
- Management of communication
- Strategic planning
- Issues management
- Audience segmentation
- Informative and persuasive writing
- Community relations, consumer relations, employee relations and other practice areas
- Technological and visual literacy
- Managing people, programs and resources
- Sensitive interpersonal communication
- Fluency in foreign language
- Ethical decision making
- Participation in the professional public relations community
- Message production
- Working with a current issue
- Public speaking and presentation
- Applying cross-cultural and cross-gender sensitivity (p. 580)

The Commission's primary focus was on undergraduate education, but some consideration was given to graduate education as well. Clearly, the skills just listed are essential for any student graduating with a degree in communication, but most certainly they are essential for anyone who wishes to have a successful career in public relations.

FUNCTIONS OF PUBLIC RELATIONS

While there is broad disagreement about how to define public relations, there is more consensus of what public relations should accomplish. Robert Heath (2001), editor of *The Public Relations Handbook*, identified the rhetorical context in which public relations operates and what needs are addressed by the practitioners:

- Need to increase or decrease awareness of an organization, a problem, an issue, a product, a service, an issue advocate, an action, a fact (information), a value, a policy, and so forth
- Need for understanding or agreement on the part of an organization, stakeholders, or stakeseekers regarding a fact (information), a value premise, or a policy position
- Need to build, repair, or maintain mutually beneficial and satisfying relationships
- Need to create, sustain, repair, or apply identification
- Need to create, repair, and maintain a clear and coherent persona (voice) for the organization
- Need to understand and implement appropriate standards of social responsibility
- Need to accept stewardship by taking issue stands (p. 34)

Heath noted that in a utopian society there would be no need for either rhetoric or public relations, but there are dissensions in society that require "discourse that lead to the co-creation, co-management, or co-definition of meaning (zones of meaning) that reconcile strains and alienation and foster mutually beneficial relationships (2001, p. 35). The following statement from the Public Relations Society of America may clarify their goals:

> Public relations helps our complex, pluralistic society to reach decisions and function more effectively by contributing to mutual understanding among groups and institutions. It serves to bring private and public policies into harmony. . . . To achieve their goals, these institutions must develop effective relationships with many different audiences or publics such as employees, members, customers, local communities, shareholders, and other institutions, and with society at large. (quoted in Heath, 2001, p. 36)

Not only corporations enlist public relations firms—foreign governments do also. Some of the most talented spokespersons have been enlisted by foreign governments.

PUBLIC RELATIONS GIVES GOVERNMENT SUPPORT ABROAD

In 2007 Ogilvy Public Relations Worldwide joined with JL McGregor & Company, an existing premier research and advisory company, to offer the Chinese government support and services in public relations, communications, and commerce. James McGregor, CEO of JL McGregor & Company, said, "This strategic alliance allows us to leverage our joint talent pool, operational experience and network of business and government relationships to help clients successfully execute the right business strategy for the China growth opportunity" (Ogilvy Public Relations Worldwide). McGregor is a Mandarin-speaking former journalist who turned his expertise to business after living in China for decades. He authored the book *One Billion Customers: Lessons from the Front Lines of Doing Business in China*, which became a best seller. He had headed the *Wall Street Journal* bureau in China and was chairman of the American Chamber of Commerce in China. Ogilvy Public Relations Worldwide has offices in more than 60 cities around the world and provides expertise to clients across "consumer marketing, corporate, healthcare, technology, public affairs, social marketing and entertainment practices" (Ogilvy Public Relations Worldwide). William McCahill, who is a former American Foreign Service officer and was instrumental in developing the U.S.–China bilateral World Trade Organization agreement, works with Ogilvy in China. The cultural, linguistic, and business acumen of the personnel whom China has hired to develop and promote trade across the world is impressive. Hiring a public relations firm certainly is one step toward solving some of the China's troubles following the pet food and toothpaste contaminations with ingredients that killed pets and endangered U.S. consumers. China's action was rather draconian; the head of the one factory where the products were manufactured was summarily executed following the investigation, and one factory was dismantled. This action did little to reassure Americans that China's products were safe and met quality control standards. *Newsweek*, on July 23, 2007, reported that China is the third largest food supplier to the United States, after Canada and Mexico. "It is a primary supplier of seafood, garlic seasonings, apple juice, citric and ascorbic acid (Vitamin C) and various spices" (Stern, 2007, p. 58). Linda Stern reported in *Newsweek:*

> In May, pet food carrying the industrial chemical melamine killed dozens of pets across the United States. Then there were lead-painted toy trains, toothpaste contaminated with

The 2008 Olympic Games held in China were spectacular and choreographed from start to finish to show that the Chinese government could successfully manage as host.

dry-cleaning chemicals and drug residues in seafood. Most recently, Robert's American Gourmet Food recalled Veggie Booty, a snack food popular with kids, after salmonella bacteria found in the Chinese-made seasoning ingredients was said to have sickened 57 people in 18 states. (p. 58)

Clearly, such mistakes cannot be repeated and much damage control will follow these scandals so that confidence can be restored in China's exports to America and across the world. It is hoped that governmental action will be taken with the proper regulatory practices put into place, because no amount of "spin" can or should divert life-threatening situations, and the top-tier public relations and research teams of Ogilvy and McGregor & Company, which the Chinese government has hired, would lose credibility if they were to do anything but advocate change in the policies that allowed this scandal to happen. China demonstrated their seriousness in enforcing State Food and Drug Administration policies by executing the former head of the agency for accepting bribes from drug makers and falsifying documents. Zheng Xiaoyu's conviction for taking cash and gifts worth $832,000 was explained by Yan Jiangying, agency spokeswoman, "The few corrupt officials of the SFDA are the shame of the whole system and their scandals have revealed some very serious problems" (Chang, 2007). Other agents have been prosecuted and sentenced to death, as the agency works toward more transparency and tighter controls, and the government has closed factories where problems have been found. The Chinese government had to do damage control before the Beijing Olympics in 2008, and they must address the breaches of conduct that brought the U.S. FDA and similar agency representatives from other countries to contest their lack of safety in products.

AN INCONVENIENT TRUTH: PUBLIC RELATIONS AS EDUCATION

One of the primary functions of public relations is to educate the public on social issues. The **Public Relations Society of America**, which has 31,000 members, presented the Silver Anvil Award to the PR team who converted Al Gore's slide show on global warming into the Academy Award–winning documentary *An Inconvenient Truth.* Al Gore said:

> The public relations campaign created and implemented by this team helped to ignite a world wide conversation about climate change, and the cultural and social impact has been undeniable. . . . One can't turn on the news or pick up a paper without reading about the issue and the mobilization of people and corporations working to restore our planet's health. It's a dream come true for me to witness, and I know it would not have been possible without the movie. Publicity took that movie and helped make it into a movement. (Public Relations Campaign Team, 2007)

Megan Colligan (Paramount Vantage Executive Vice President of Publicity and Promotions); Buffy Shutt (Participant Productions Executive Vice President for Marketing); and Michael Feldman (Glover Park Group founding partner) produced the film as well as eco-friendly events for the premiere of it. They used invitations on recycled paper printed with soy ink, featured all-natural food, had living trees from around the world lit with energy-efficient lighting, and served food on reusable dinnerware to demonstrate their awareness of environmentally friendly events. They encouraged guests to take public transportation, with only 28 cars driven to the premiere that was attended by 400 guests. Here are the effects attributed to the film's release:

> The U.S. House of Representatives introduced the Safe Climate Act, 40 companies joined a Business Council to Address Global Climate Change; Wal-Mart revamped operations to comply with high environment standards; the band Pearl Jam donated $100,000 to renewable energy causes; California unveiled its Anti-Global Warming Plan requiring major industries to reduce greenhouse emissions 25 percent; and 22 of the world's largest cities vowed to cut greenhouse gas pollution. In addition, California Governor Schwarzenegger retired his beloved fleet of gas-guzzling Hummers; Arizona Governor Janet Napolitano signed an Executive Order to reduce greenhouse gas emissions; Prime Minister Helen Clark credited the film with sharpening public opinion and resolved to make New Zealand the first truly sustainable country; airline executive Richard Branson pledged $3 billion to fight global warming, 12 states sued the Environmental Protection Agency for failing to limit greenhouse emissions; General Electric, DuPont and 12 other corporations and environmental groups launched the U.S. Climate Action Partnership Coalition to rally for

Al Gore, who won the Silver Anvil Award for the documentary *An Inconvenient Truth* on climate change, raised awareness of a significant problem, which is one function of public relations.

compulsory federal emission standards; and two major bills were introduced in the U.S. Senate to reduce carbon dioxide emissions from power plants. (Public Relations Campaign Team, 2007)

The impact of the film, the premiere events, and the publicity surrounding Al Gore's donating 100 percent of the proceeds from the book and film to the Alliance for Climate Protection were a smashing success. There were free downloadable study guides for classroom use and other educational efforts along with philanthropic activities.

The Bush administration was criticized for ignoring environmental issues and even allowing agreements to lapse, but Al Gore's attention to the environment goes back to his 1990 campaign for the vice presidency with Bill Clinton running for president when

Gore wrote the book *Earth in the Balance*. Gore has been a constant voice for environmental issues, even though his lifestyle has been criticized by detractors as one of conspicuous consumption—jets, SUVs, and mansions. His amateurish slide show was converted by the public relations specialists to become a rhetorical event that will foster debate and political action for years to come. Global warming has been hotly contested in scientific circles for decades, since the first environmental movement in the 1970s, with some arguing that natural causes, such as the explosion of Mount St. Helens in Washington State, did more to pollute the United States than carbon emissions from cars or commerce in that area. Others note the catastrophic effect of only one or two degrees on our ecosystem. With the explosive growth in China and other nations across the globe, this issue will not go away. The movie was a great success that galvanized forces against climate change, which used to be called "global warming."

Public relations firms are at the forefront of many social and political controversies. In 2006, Bernadette Mansur, Senior Vice President for Communications for the National Hockey League, received an award for her handling communications and the fallout from the cancellation of the 2004–2005 hockey season. In 2005, Charles Conner, Senior Vice President, Communication & Marketing; Darren Irby, Vice President, Public Relations; and Deborah Daley, Vice President, Corporate Communications, for the American Red Cross received an award for their communication plan and program to prepare for the worst hurricane season ever predicted (Public Relations Campaign Team, 2007). You will note the different titles of these practitioners and the alliances that are formed to address issues dealing with corporate images, national disasters, and global issues. The Public Relations Society of America (PRSA) award in 2004 was given to the firm that rebuilt MCI's reputation after a corporate scandal that required them to reposition its brand. In 2003, Victoria Clarke, former Assistant Secretary of Defense for Public Affairs, U.S. Department of Defense, received the award for playing a major role in explaining the war on terrorism from the initial strike through the embedded journalists in Iraq who were attached to the military in the program called Operation Iraqi Freedom. In 2002 the award was given to Tim Doke, former Vice President of Corporate Communications for American Airlines, for creating a program to handle crisis communication when terrorists highjacked two of their jets and flew them in the terrorist attack of September 11, 2001.

The **Public Relations Society of America**, which is headquartered in New York City, has 109 chapters and 20 different professional interest groups "which represent business and industry, counseling firms, independent practitioners, military, government, associations, hospitals, schools, professional services firms and nonprofit organizations" (Public Relations Campaign Team, 2007). The award recipients demonstrate the types of crises that they are called upon to resolve or address for the various publics that they serve. Public relations cannot be neatly defined or packaged, since the professionals come from many disciplines and combine their talents to promote educational material, divert disasters, repair reputations and images, and plan for future challenges, whether economic, political, or social in nature. Public relations practitioners educate and manage public opinion through films, presentations, mass media releases, and special projects, as the former award winners show. They lobby, promote change, create, maintain, or restore images.

IMAGE RESTORATION

 Part of the human condition is to make mistakes or to use poor judgment, and some people practice questionable ethics or, at their worst, engage in criminal behavior. Torie Clarke (2006) wrote *Lipstick on a Pig: Winning in the No-Spin Era by Someone Who Knows the Game.* Torie Clarke is one of the nation's most recognized executives as former president of Bozell Eskew advertising and head of the Washington office of the public relations firm of Hill & Knowlton, as well as former president of the National Cable Telecommunications Association. She served as press secretary for George H. W. Bush's 1992 re-election campaign, and as Assistant Secretary of Defense for Public Affairs. She traveled with Defense Secretary Donald Rumsfeld and accompanied him on official visits on every continent to places like Baghdad, Kabul, and Moscow. Her credentials are unquestioned. In the first chapter of her book, she reminds us that you can put lipstick on a pig, but it is still a pig. She advises, "Deliver the bad news yourself, and when you screw up, say so—fast!" (Clarke, 2006, p. 1). We learned that simple truth in graduate school, at about the time a young Senator Ted Kennedy was dealing with the accidental drowning of Mary Jo Kopechne, and for my generation, the advice Clarke gave above came to be called the **"Chappaquiddick principle."** That is, there is never a good time to tell bad news, but the quicker that you do, the more likely that you will survive the fallout or be forgiven. Americans love confessions that are genuine, and they love to forgive the contrite sinner. Coming clean or confessing to former transgressions is the fastest way to exorcise demons that haunt public life and private relationships, but many choose to ignore, manage, or stonewall the public on troublesome events or actions. Clarke recounted the scandal that broke when Charles Keating, a powerful man who always had an entourage of lobbyists following him around, fell from his high place into a cesspool of "stupidity and corruption" (2006, p. 3). Keating had close associations with five senators, whose reputations were tarnished by their ties to Keating. They became known as the Keating Five, but John McCain, who was one of them, separated himself from the pack by holding a press conference in his home state of Arizona, answering every question, and returning journalist's phone calls. Senator McCain is known to have a short fuse or a hot temper when his honor is questioned, and this concerned Clarke, who was on McCain's communication staff. When McCain agreed to stay as long as he needed to answer questions, they agreed that Clarke would sit in the front row of the press conference, and if the senator seemed to be getting hot under the collar she would rub her nose and signal him to cool it. Clarke reported that she did not have to engage in that cautionary action because the senator was effective in addressing the crisis. Roger Mudd reported on the *MacNeil/Lehrer News Hour* in November 1989 that John McCain had said something that few senators ever say and that is that his meeting with Charles Keating was a "serious mistake" (Clarke, 2005, p. 6), while the other four— "Democrats Cranston of California, DeConcini of Arizona, Glenn of Ohio, and Riegle of Michigan had all been following a policy of stonewalling the press" (Clarke, 2005, p. 6). McCain's position was that while he had met with Keating, he had not abused his office because he always met with anyone who wanted to talk to him. Clarke summarized the approach that she and Senator McCain took to address the breaking scandal surrounding

Torie Clarke and Jon Stewart examined what "spin" is and how government's should be more transparent and forthright to shed light in dark places.

the Senator's association with Keating, who would be discredited for his role in the savings and loan scandal at that time:

- Own up. McCain should not have met with the regulators in the first place, giving the appearance of political favors and damaging his credibility.
- Stand up. McCain admitted to what he did by stating that he met with Keating, but he rebutted charges that he had asked regulators to back off from investigating Keating.
- Speak up. McCain spoke up early and often because *"charges unanswered are charges assumed to be true."* He did not hide behind staffers who might have made his case for him. (Clarke, 2005, p. 11)

Another maxim that Clarke expounded was **transparency** because "Transparency makes good things shine and bad ones go away" (p. 53). In the Information Age the fainthearted do not survive, so putting a constant spotlight on your good accomplishments is insufficient unless you are prepared to pursue your mistakes with the same aggressiveness. That enables the individual in crisis to solve the problem sooner, and telling the entire story is required, especially when it is complex and controversial (Clarke, 2005, p. 85). Other advice Clarke offered was: (1) be responsive—that means to answer all calls and to do so promptly; (2) be accurate with the news media—if you must choose between being fast or being accurate, choose accuracy; and (3) be truthful. This includes saying that you do not know or that you cannot say, because in some national security areas, one is not at liberty to discuss operational issues, just as in business there are proprietary issues that must be protected from the competition (Clarke, 2005, p. 91).

The public relations practitioner must have more than one weapon in their arsenal, because newspaper readership is down 11 percent since 1990, and traditional news channels have lost viewers by 28 percent since 2004, with ethnic media and online media showing growth during that time (Clarke, 2005, p. 96). Major news scandals like the *New York Times's* Jayson Blair affair and the Dan Rather report on George W. Bush's military service, based on forged documents, have soured the public's confidence in traditional sources of news. Clarke advised that the best tool in your arsenal should be a heavy dose of reality, which includes your ability to admit that your product or plan is a bad one. It is not just the packaging or the spin that counts, but a commitment to change the plan if necessary (p. 99). Clarke wrote:

> Think of the largest organization in which you've ever worked, and then reflect on the Pentagon for comparison. With about 2 million people as "employees" worldwide and a $400 billion plus annual budget, it dwarfs everything else, and the challenge of keeping your perspective is enormous. There is so much "incoming" on a daily basis—issues, meetings, e-mails, faxes, memos, calls—that it's hard for most people to look past the edge of their desks, much less have a grip on what's going on in the rest of the world. (Clarke, 2005, p. 107)

Practitioners must seek other perspectives by communicating with people outside the organization. Clarke used to call friends across the country to check the pulse by asking, "What's happening out there? What are people focused on? What are we missing" (Clark, 2005, p. 107)?

WILLIAM L. BENOIT'S THEORY OF IMAGE RESTORATION

Benoit's (1995) book, titled *Accounts, Excuses, and Apologies: A Theory of Image Restoration Strategies*, offered an analysis of how individuals, companies, or the government attempts to repair damages when they have done wrong or are perceived to have done something wrong. The field of public relations is focused on reputation and image creation and repair, but these strategies are used in personal situations as well as public ones. Benoit studied the Watergate incident and President Nixon's excuses, the Tylenol scare and how Johnson & Johnson dealt with the tampering with their pain relief capsules, Senator Kennedy's Chappaquiddick speech following the drowning death of Mary Jo Kopechne, and President Reagan's discourse on the Iran-Contra affair.

Benoit began to look at everyday excuses offered by students, friends, and even himself to explain away their failings. He explained how we attempt to avoid blame through denial, scapegoating (blaming someone else), or even attacking the source. Another defense mechanism can be to accept blame and to apologize. Further, the transgressor may take corrective action, as Johnson & Johnson did by repackaging all their products and removing all Tylenol from the shelf that may have been tainted. Benoit offered a workable model for analysis of serious public relations cases. He wrote, "Defensive utterances (justifications, excuses, apologies) are persuasive attempts to reshape another's beliefs, to change his or her belief that the act in question was wrongful, to shift his or her attribution of responsibility for that act" (Benoit, 1995, p. 6). He offered a typology of **image-restoration** strategies (Benoit, 1995, p. 95). Benoit said image-restoration strategies can be organized into five broad categories, three of which have variants: denial, evading responsibility, reducing offensiveness, corrective action, and mortification (Benoit, 1995, p. 74).

First, Benoit said *denial* may be attempted through two strategies: simple denial and shifting the blame. The rhetor may simply state that he did not commit the offensive act, or he may attempt to blame someone else or something else. A common ploy would be to claim that they never said or did whatever they are accused of doing or saying, but rather that they were set up or misquoted (Benoit, 1995, p. 75).

The second strategy is *evading responsibility* for the act, which includes four strategies. The first is to suggest that the act was committed because the actor was provoked to respond to a wrong committed against them, so they were justified in the action. Second, *defeasibility* pleads a lack of information or lack of control over the action or event. Because the accused lacked the ability to act, they should not be held responsible for it (Benoit, 1995, p. 75). Third is to make an excuse based on accidents. If we are late for a meeting, an unforeseeable traffic accident or some calamity at home can be blamed, thus reducing our responsibility for the offensive act. The fourth way to evade responsibility is to claim that the wrongful act was committed but that the actor had *good* rather than *evil intensions*. The outcome was not what was intended; and therefore, the blame should be mitigated on the basis of motives.

The third strategy for image restoration is *reducing the offensiveness of the act* in question. Benoit explained six variants on this theme, which were bolstering, minimization, differentiation, transcendence, attacking one's accuser, and compensation (1995, p. 77). *Bolstering* means that the accused tries to strengthen positive feelings toward the actor to offset the negative feelings about the act. For example, Exxon spent millions bolstering their image by demonstrating that their employees lived in those communities affected by the oil spill, and they wanted a clean environment also. Wal-Mart publicized their community involvement and scholarship funds when accused of hiring illegal immigrants as workers, exploiting their workers by denying them lunch breaks, or offering poor benefits. Another way to reduce the offensiveness of the action is to *minimize the negative effect* associated with the act. Walmart could claim that the complaints came from only a few disgruntled employees or that the employees did not really swipe their time cards correctly. Coal companies will claim that they restored hills or mountains to a state better than before their strip mines extracted the coal. A third way to reduce the offensiveness of the action is to *differentiate between the act in question and other, less desirable actions*—that is, to use contrast to show that a company or organization has a better record than comparable ones operating in the area. The next way to reduce the offensiveness of the act is through *transcendence*, which attempts to place the act in a broader context. For example, Benoit stated that the police officer who planted evidence on a defendant could appeal to the greater good of removing a dangerous criminal from the community (Benoit, 1995, p. 78). A common strategy in reducing the offensiveness of an act is to *turn on the accuser and attack them*. You will remember Hillary Clinton's defense of her husband, President Bill Clinton, during the Monica Lewinsky affair; she called the story a "right-wing conspiracy" to damage the President's reputation, but when he admitted having the illicit affair that created a new set of perceptions and restoration strategies. Finally, *compensation* through goods, services, and monetary sums are given as inducements to restore the damaged reputation of the agency under attack (Benoit, 1995, p. 78). Frequently, this action follows legal findings where the wrongs can no longer be denied or minimized.

Corrective action in image restoration is where the accused promises to correct the problem through a change of policy and gives future assurances that the problem will not occur again. Often this is done in conjunction with an apology. This strategy differs from compensation to counterbalance the wrong, because it addresses the cause of the problem and makes promises for future well-being.

The final means of restoring one's image is through *mortification*, wherein the guilty party confesses their guilt, asks for forgiveness, and offers a sincere apology (Benoit, 1995, p. 79). Kenneth Burke (1970) wrote of this redemption process and the means through which one can accomplish it not through denial or finding a scapegoat but by exercising self-control. Benoit's image-restoration theory can be applied in political, corporate, religious, and personal cases.

Many individuals have attempted to employ these strategies, as Pete Rose did when he denied betting on baseball, only to find that it did not work with his intended audience, the baseball commissioner. Years later, Rose went on to confess that he had gambled and to apologize for his behavior, finally employing mortification rather than denial as a strategy to win forgiveness. Most sports fans said it was too little too late, so the question remains whether or not Pete Rose will ever be inducted into the Baseball Hall of Fame, even though he was a very gifted athlete.

Benoit and his work with other researchers offered helpful tools for anyone who is trying to make sense of a very complicated social ill, such as an oil spill, corruption in government, or just everyday transgressions against family members.

His theory is well grounded and easily applied, as the cases of Exxon, Walmart, President Clinton, and Pete Rose demonstrated.

SUMMARY

Public relations is, as Edward Bernays said almost a century ago, "engineering public consent." The concept of what constitutes a public has grown to include employees, stockholders, Congress, the media, and the American public, but the need to educate, to persuade, and to create and to repair images is reliant upon practitioners who serve the organizations who employ them. Scholars are defining not only the territory and duties of the public relations specialist, they are also defining best practices to reach excellence in the public arena. Increasingly, governments use public relations specialists to win support for trade agreements, armed conflicts, and policies both domestic and foreign. Public relations is competitive communication that seeks an advantage for its principals and uses many promotional techniques, visible and invisible, outside of paid advertising, according to Kevin Moloney. He went on to call it "weak propaganda," but even though Bernays used the word "propaganda" in the early twentieth century, that term has negative connotations. The Grunig's four models describe the historical development of public relations in the United States through press agentry/publicity, public information, and two-way symmetrical and two-way asymmetrical communication. Most organizations use all of these models as they employ integrated communication to achieve their ends to build relationships and to strategically promote or defend their ties to their publics. New skills are demanded in the global arena, including fluency in foreign languages, cross-cultural and cross-gender sensitivity, ethical decision making, and technical literacy.

Public relations is far more than image building and includes education and goodwill. The best relationship is when both the organization and their publics benefit. As Torie Clarke (2006) said, "You can put lipstick on a pig, but it is still a pig" (p. 1). Clarke's condensed advice on handling scandal was: "Own up. Stand up. Speak up" (2006, p. 11). Ethical public relations practitioners employ many different communication strategies to accomplish the goals of their organizations and to avoid breaches of the public trust.

APPLICATIONS

1. Research and write a paper on a damage control campaign where the individual, corporation, or organization attempted to restore their image in the public's perception (e.g., John Edwards's 2008 extramarital affair, AGI executives partying on taxpayers' money, Governor Rod Blagojevich of Illinois, etc.).
2. Explore the public relations efforts of the Bush administration to "engineer public consent" for the Iraq War. Look at the embedded reporters in Iraq and Afghanistan, video news releases from the Pentagon, and news management from the White House.
3. Investigate a local issue that has caused controversy in the community and identify the attacks and defenses offered by various parties. Some recurring issues include landfills, drug rehabilitation facilities or halfway houses, abortion clinics, or school board decisions such as consolidation or closings.

REFERENCES

Benoit, W. L. (1995). *Accounts, excuses, and apologies: A theory of image restoration strategies.* Albany, NY: State University of New York Press.

Burke, K. (1970). *The rhetoric of religion.* Berkeley, CA: University of California Press.

Cancel, A. E., Cameron, G. T., Sallot, L. M., & Mitrook, M. A. (1997). It depends: A contingency theory of accommodation in public relations. *Journal of Public Relations Research, 9*(1), 31–63.

Chang, A. (2007). China puts to death official in fake drugs scandal: Beijing shows stern regard for product safety with execution. *The Oakland Tribune* (Inside Bay Area), July 11. Retrieved July 18, 2007, from: http://www.insidebayarea.com/

Clarke, T. (2006). *Lipstick on a pig: Winning in the no-spin era by someone who knows the game.* New York: Free Press.

Dozier, D. M., Grunig, L. R., & Grunig, J. E. (1995). *Manager's guide to excellence in public relations and communication management.* Mahwah, New Jersey: Lawrence Erlbaum Associates, Publishers.

Grunig, J. E. (2001). Two-way symmetrical public relations: Past, present, and future. In R. L. Heath (Ed.), *Handbook of public relations* (pp. 11–30). Thousand Oaks, CA: Sage Publications.

Grunig, J. E., & White, J. (1992). The effect of world views on public relations theory and practices. In J. E. Grunig (Ed.), *Excellence in public relations and communication management* (pp. 31–64). Hillsdale, NJ: Lawrence Erlbaum Associates.

Hallahan, K. (2007). Integrated communication: Implications for public relations beyond excellence. In E. L. Toth (Ed.), *The future of excellence in public relations and communication management: Challenges for the next generation* (pp. 299–336). Mahwah, NJ: Lawrence Erlbaum Associates.

Harman, W. (2007). The science of shaping opinion. *Daily Toreador*, February 23. Lubbock, TX: Texas Tech Press.

Heath, R. L. (Ed.). (2001). A rhetorical enactment rationale for public relations: The good organization communicating well. In *Handbook Of Public Relations* (pp. 31–50). Thousand Oaks, CA: Sage Publications.

Moloney, K. (2006). *Rethinking public relations* (2nd ed.). New York: Routledge.

Ogilvy Public Relations Worldwide/China JL McGregor Announce Strategic Alliance. (June 13, 2007). Ogilvy Public Relations World Wide, PR Wire Service U.S.

Public relations campaign team for Al Gore's Oscar-winning film "An Inconvenient Truth" Named public relations professionals of the year by 31,000-member public relations society of America. (2007). Business Wire, Inc., June 15. Retrieved July 9, 2007, from: http://wf2la4.webfeat.org/Jux711148/url-http://web.lexis-nexis.com/universe/printdoc.

Shaw, M. (2007). Advertising posing as PR: Why they want to be like us (and what to do about it). *Bulldog Reporter's Daily Dog,* March 22. Sirius Information, Inc. Retrieved July 9, 2007, from: http://wf21a4.webfeat.org/Jux711151/url=http://web.lexis-nexis.com/universe/printdoc.

Stern, L. (July 23, 2007). Where's the food from? *Newsweek,* Vol. CL 4, p. 58.

Wright, D. K., & VanSlyke Turk, J. (2007). Public relations knowledge and professionalism: Challenges to educators and practitioners. In E. L. Toth (Ed.), *The future of excellence in public relations and communication management: Challenges for the next generation* (pp. 571–88). Mahwah, NJ: Lawrence Erlbaum Associates.

GLOSSARY

AD ABSURDUM A fallacy that means reducing an argument to the absurd, illogical reasoning.

AD HOMINEM A fallacy that is characterized by personal attacks on the opposition, character assassination, or name calling.

AD POPULUM A fallacy that appeals to popular opinion or uses the opinion of the masses as proof.

ADVERSARIAL RELATIONSHIP A relationship characterized by opposition; the relationship between the media and government in the United States where the press is supposed to be the "watchdog" for the people.

ADVERTISING Structured and composed nonpersonal communication of information, persuasive in nature, about products, good, services, and ideas, paid for by identified sponsors through various media.

AFFECT DISPLAYS The nonverbal code that focuses on facial expressions responsible for communicating emotions and feelings like happiness, surprise, fear, anger, sadness, and disgust or contempt.

AGENDA SETTING To elevate an issue or idea to the plane of public discussion; a function of the media in the United States where journalists are supposed to tell us not what to think but what to think about. The selection and framing of public discourse that defines, interprets, and highlights some people, events, and issues while others are omitted or redefined.

AIDA APPROACH An advertising strategy that stands for attract Attention, create Interest, stimulate Desire, and promote Action; sometimes referred to as the motivated sequence of persuasion.

ALLEGORY OF THE CAVE An allegory from Plato's dialogue *The Republic* that represents the contrast between the world of sense perception and the world of light or the world of the Good.

ANALOGY A comparison to support or clarify a point or an idea.

ANOMIE A state of normlessness, disorientation, lawlessness, or impending chaos; a state that invites apocalyptic discourse.

APOCALYPTIC RHETORIC Discourse that is based on the belief that prophesy will be fulfilled when life as we know it will end and Christ will rule the earth; rhetoric concerning the end times. According to Barry Brummett, contemporary apocalyptic rhetoric arises from anomie or chaos with failed systems and collapsed authority, with humankind at the brink of annihilation when

Christ returns. Rhetoric that arises from ancient biblical prophecy, like the books of Revelation and Daniel, or contemporary conditions of threat and chaos.

APOTHEOSIZE To deify; to raise to godhood, or glorify.

A PRIORI From the beginning; an assumption made before examination or analysis; from cause to effect; based on theory.

ARGUMENTUM AD MISERACORDIAM A fallacy that is characterized by appeals to pity; an obvious play on emotions.

ARTISTIC PROOFS Arguments or evidence that the speaker creates to persuade the audience, according to Aristotle, based on the orator's knowledge, creativity, and judgment.

ASYMMETRICAL One-way communication used in public relations such as media advocacy, government lobbying, and litigation which contrasts with symmetrical or two-way communication between an organization and their publics—employees, stockholders, government, and the public.

ATLA American Trial Lawyers Association.

ATTITUDE A learned predisposition to respond in a consistently favorable or unfavorable manner with respect to a given object.

BALANCE THEORY A theory that posits that people seek psychological balance between ideas, people, and actions—Person A and Person B are in balance if both have a positive attitude toward C.

BELIEF DISCONFIRMATION PARADIGM When people are confronted with information that is inconsistent with their beliefs, they will engage in selective exposure by avoiding, rejecting, or distorting such information.

BIOGRAPHICAL CONVENTION FILM A media form that presents to the public the Republican and Democratic candidates at their respective conventions in the most positive manner to influence voters to support them and their platforms.

BLACK POWER MOVEMENT A social movement of the 1960s and 1970s to redefine stereotypes about African Americans by declaring that "black is beautiful."

BLOGS Web logs, a new form of media that goes directly to the public and bypasses conventional media outlets; an influential form of new media that extends access more directly to everyone with a computer.

BRANDING A strategy in advertising to create a unique selling position by naming or identifying a product or service.

CEASE-AND-DESIST ORDERS A legal action to guarantee truth in advertising that requires a company to stop deceptive or untrue advertisements, actions, or practices.

CHANNEL The medium used to send a message from a source to a receiver (e.g., face-to-face, telephone, television, or Internet).

CHAPPAQUIDDICK PRINCIPLE A concept derived from the accident involving Senator Ted Kennedy at the Chappaquiddick bridge where a young woman drowned, which threatened his position in Congress; based on the public relations maxim that there is never a good time to tell bad news, but the longer the delay, the worse the consequences in damage control.

CHARISMA The magic that some leaders have that causes others to follow them with great devotion; the ancient Greeks believed this quality was a gift from the gods.

CHRONEMICS The nonverbal code that focuses on time and timing related to punctuality, schedules; an abstract concept of time that is derived culturally, socially, or individually.

CINEMATIC MESSAGES Content that uses the art form of cinema to relay the message; meaning that is conveyed through the channel of movies; persuasion channeled through cinema.

CLAIM   A statement that needs to be supported by evidence to be accepted by a receiver. A debate topic or resolution.

CO-CULTURES   Cultures that coexist within the dominant culture in a country; for example, Little Italy, Chinatown, Polish Hill, and other ethnic groups.

COGNITIVE DISSONANCE THEORY   Based on the assumption that people desire to have agreement in beliefs, attitudes, and behaviors and where there is dissonance, there is psychological discomfort, which drives the person to restore a feeling of balance through adaptive steps like avoidance or change.

COHERENCE   The quality of being logically integrated, consistent, and intelligible.

COMMON GROUND   Those attitudes, beliefs, values, and experiences that people have in common that facilitate understanding and aid persuasion; synonymous with identification or alignment.

COMMUNICATION CONTEXT   Part of the Joseph DeVito communication model that consists of four parts in a communication transaction—time, place, social, and psychological aspects of the event.

CONNOTATION   Idea suggested or associated with a word; a more idiosyncratic meaning than the denoted meaning or the dictionary meaning.

CONVENTIONS   Agreement within an art community that allows designers/artists to communicate with that community through learned, imitated, and codified social constructs that are intrinsically rhetorical, according to Kostelnick and Hassett; accepted customs or practices with shared meaning for that community of delegates, artists, or communicators.

COUNTERATTITUDINAL ADVOCACY   When speakers advocate a position that they are opposed to, it tends to influence their attitudes in that direction, e.g., smoking pot and speaking to children against pot smoking; a communication theory explored by Gerald Miller.

CREATION NARRATIVE   The biblical story that explains the beginning of the universe when God created the Heavens and Earth in seven days and placed Adam and Eve in the Garden of Eden where they ate from the tree of knowledge and fell from the state of grace and innocence.

CREDIBILITY   Believability; the reputation of the speaker, which includes many components such as attractiveness, expertise, trustworthiness, similarity to the audience, and past performances.

CRYSTAL, DAVID   (2007) Wrote *The Fight for English: How Language Pundits Ate, Shot, and Left*, which traces the evolution of English from Latin through the Anglo-Saxon era.

CULTIVATION THEORY   Based on the work of George Gerbner, which showed that heavy television viewing led to the cultivation of distorted values, or the "Mean World Syndrome."

DECODE   To interpret or decipher a message to derive meaning from it.

DELIBERATIVE RHETORIC   Political communication that supports the democratic process by generating legitimacy through opinion and will formation, publicity and transparency for the deliberative process with inclusion for participation, and a presumption for reasonable outcomes based on rational arguments; one of the three forms of rhetoric Aristotle identified that addressed four forms of government—democracy, oligarchy, aristocracy, and monarchy.

DEMAGOGUE   A speaker who uses unethical methods to appeal to the people to achieve their own selfish ends, generally power and wealth.

DEMOGRAPHICS   The general characteristics of the audience such as age, income, ethnicity, politics, and education; data used to target consumers, voters, or audience members for persuasive messages.

DENOTATION   The direct, explicit meaning of a word or term; the dictionary meaning agreed on by educated people.

DEVIL-TERMS   A concept introduced by Kenneth Burke to analyze language that had a negative connotation and presented evil to the receiver, such as war, recession, racism; the opposite of a god-term.

DIDACTIC NARRATIVE A story that makes a point or teaches some lesson.

DIGITAL ADVERTISING Marketing that uses the Internet to reach consumers, which has claimed market shares from traditional channels of mass communication like newspapers and television.

DOUBLE BIND A situation where two alternatives are offered, but both lead to the same conclusion or consequence; a persuasion strategy, according to D. T. Jacobs (1995), used by Rush Limbaugh.

EFFECT(S) The impact that a message has immediately and through time.

EFFORT JUSTIFICATION PARADIGM General acceptance that if a person has to earn something then he or she appreciates it more.

EIGHT HIDDEN NEEDS Vance Packard (1957) offered these as sources of persuasion—emotional security, reassurance of worth, ego gratification, creative outlets, love objects, sense of power, sense of roots, and immortality.

ELABORATION LIKELIHOOD MODEL An information-processing theory that posits that there are two routes to persuasion—the central processing route, which uses logical elaboration to examine ideas, and the peripheral route, which uses more rule-of-thumb reasoning, like the appearance or expertise of the speaker to evaluate ideas.

ENCODE To create a message from words or symbols that have shared meaning.

ENDORSEMENTS Testimonials or advertisements that generally feature celebrities like Tiger Woods, Kobe Bryant, or Michael Jordan as part of an ad campaign to promote a product or service.

ENTERTAINMENT FUNCTION One of the functions of mass media; the entertainment industry has increasingly become part of public discourse influencing attitudes, values, and beliefs in serious ways.

ENTHYMEME An argument in which one of the premises or sometimes the conclusion is not stated but implied; an example where the audience fills in the essential details to reach a conclusion.

EPIDEICTIC RHETORIC One of three types of rhetoric that Aristotle identified; speech that is largely ceremonial, offering eulogies or tributes to the deceased or offering accolades to the living.

ESCHATOLOGY The branch of theology that deals with end things like death, resurrection, immortality, and Judgment Day; mysteries known through belief or faith that explain what is beyond human experience during life.

ESTABLISHMENT CLAUSE That portion of the First Amendment that guarantees that there will be no government-established church or religion but freedom to practice the religion of personal choice.

ETHOS The image, credibility, and character of the speaker; one of the three classical appeals Aristotle identified as most influential in persuasion. There are three stages of ethos: initial—audience assessment of speaker based on speaker's reputation before the speech; derived—audience assessment speaker earns during the speech; and terminal—assessment based on interaction between initial and derived ethos.

EVANGELISTS Any of the four writers of the gospel; a preacher who spreads the gospel and attempts to convert others to Christianity by holding revivals, using mass media platforms, or traveling place to place as a missionary.

EVIDENCE Supporting material or forms of proof, such as analogies, examples, narratives, statistics, testimony, artifacts, or audiovisual aids, to support an argument or claim.

EXAMPLE A form of proof that can be a real historical reference or a hypothetical construction to clarify an idea, to elaborate on an idea by offering specific details, for instance, the 1936 Johnstown flood or Hurricane Katrina.

EXCELLENCE STUDY An investigation conducted on public relations intended to discover what theories and practices best exemplified excellence in the field by Professors James E. Grunig and Larissa A. Grunig from the University of Maryland

EXPECTANCY VIOLATION THEORY (EVT) Deals with audience expectations regarding language, nonverbal behavior, gender roles, and social norms and the reaction when those expectations are violated or are not met by persuaders.

EYE BEHAVIOR The nonverbal code that focuses on eye contact, gaze, staring, or eye avoidance, which can be interpreted as showing honesty, attention, confidence, or regard for the other party or audience. Eye behavior functions to regulate, monitor, reflect cognitive activity, express emotions, or show communication in relationships.

FALLACY An error in reasoning that leads to incorrect conclusions by avoiding the real issues, attacking the speaker rather than analyzing the arguments, diverting attention through emotional appeals, or selectively presenting only a partial truth.

FALSE DILEMMA A fallacy in reasoning which only offers either/or options, when social political issues generally are multidimensional, e.g., "America, love it or leave it."

FAULTY ANALOGY Comparisons that are not logically constructed, e.g., comparing apples to oranges, offering a comparison that lacks the similarity to support the claim or argument.

FEDERAL COMMUNICATIONS COMMISSION (FCC) A federal regulatory agency established in 1934 that issues licenses to stations and monitors them to assure that they serve the public interest, convenience, and necessity and may take corrective action such as fines or denial of license renewal.

FEDERAL FOOD AND DRUG ADMINISTRATION (FDA) A federal agency established 1906 to monitor foods, drugs, medicines, and liquors to assure public safety.

FEDERAL TRADE COMMISSION (FTC) The federal agency established 1914 by Congress to prevent unfair methods of competition in commerce, which includes deception in advertising, to protect consumers' interests.

FEEDBACK The response given to a message which informs the source that the idea was transmitted successfully, interpreted, and understood by the receiver, an essential part of communication.

FEEDBACK LOOP Means simply that the message went from the speaker to the receiver and the receiver responded to complete the loop.

FEMININE MYSTIQUE A malady identified by Betty Friedan (1963) as a loss of identity and power in the book *The Feminine Mystique*, which became a touchstone book for the feminist movement that demanded not just voting power, but parity in corporations and in sexual politics.

FIDELITY Faithfulness to truth and duty; accuracy in reproduction.

FIELD OF EXPERIENCE Common ground or diverse views that each sender and receiver has that can either facilitate or obstruct communication efforts.

FIRST AMENDMENT "Congress shall make no law respecting an establishment of religion, or prohibiting the free exercise thereof; or abridging the freedom of speech, or of the press; or the right of the people peaceably to assemble, and to petition the Government for a redress of grievance." Part of the Bill of Rights added to the Constitution of the United States (1791).

FORENSIC RHETORIC From the Latin *forensis*, meaning public or marketplace, suitable for public debate; focused on the legal system where prosecution and defense of individuals occur, one of the three forms of speech Aristotle identified.

FOURTH ESTATE A term applied to mass media that elevates the function of journalism to a fourth branch of government alongside the executive, legislative, and judicial, to serve the people by reporting on government.

FREE-CHOICE PARADIGM Deals with the psychological doubts that a person feels after making a decision; buyer's remorse

FREE WILL The capacity to choose freely; in theology, according to Kenneth Burke, free will allows humankind to follow the Covenant or to disobey God with action that is freely chosen.

FREEDOM OF INFORMATION ACT (FOIA) A law passed in 1966 to make it easier for scholars or journalists to gain access to information from the government or other sources of evidence, a statute intended to broaden public access to information often concealed through classification or proprietary means.

FUNCTIONS OF WORDS The cognitive, affective, and behavioral jobs that words perform, they transmit ideas, evoke emotions, and call people to action.

GENDER STYLES Characteristics such as anecdotes, self-disclosing speech with hedges or qualifiers has been attributed by analysts as "feminine speech" or powerless speech, while "masculine speech" is identified with logic and powerful arguments; stereotypes associated with gender communication.

GENERAL SEMANTICS The study of the relations between language, thought, and behavior; between how we talk, therefore how we think, and therefore how we act.

GOD-TERMS Powerful terms for which people are willing to sacrifice or to die, according to Kenneth Burke, e.g., liberty, justice, peace, progress, etc.; the opposite of devil-terms.

HAPTICS The nonverbal code that focuses on touch and distinguishes between professional touch (such as a doctor examining a patient), social touch (the handshake), and intimate touch (caressing or body contact between lovers, parent–child, or trusted others).

HARD NEWS A report of an event that happened or that was disclosed within the previous 24 hours and treats an issue of ongoing concern, for example, a crime story or a political upset.

HAYAKAWA, S. I A language scholar who defined general semantics as the study of language to analyze the relationship between language, thought, and behavior to understand how we talk, how we think, and how we act.

HERMENEUTICS Explanation and interpretation of scripture or texts.

HOMILETICS The art of writing and preaching sermons.

HOMOEROTICA Literary or artistic works characterized by or portraying sexual desire for one of the same sex.

IDENTIFICATION Communication wherein the receiver's ideas are in alignment with those of the source; the ability to fully understand the position, beliefs, and attitudes of another.

IDEOLOGY A system of beliefs that express a worldview according to doctrines, ideas, or practices of an individual or group.

IDIOSYNCRATIC Mannerisms, customs, or views peculiar to the individual or group.

IMAGE RESTORATION A public relations function that attempts to restore confidence or credibility in a government, organization, or individual when there has been a scandal, accident, or event that created negative perceptions regarding the reputation or performance of these entities or participants.

INARTISTIC PROOFS Means of persuasion that are not invented by the orator's knowledge or creativity, but merely used, Aristotle said, like laws, witnesses, contracts, tortures, and oaths.

INDICES OF CREDIBILITY An index constructed by Robert and Dale Newman in their book *Evidence* (1969) that consisted of 14 points that could be applied to test the quality of evidence according to situational and documentary characteristics as well as the expertise and record of the writer.

INDUCED COMPLIANCE PARADIGM Also called the *forced choice paradigm*; if a person is forced to engage in actions contrary to their attitudes or self-image, they find it easier to accept than doing it for rewards or of their own free will—e.g., defending a heinous criminal pro bono.

INDUCTIVE Statements that can be proven by collecting or analyzing data. Reasoning that goes from a claim or assertion to evidence that supports the claim.

INFORMATIVE SPEECH Speech that transmits facts and has comprehension as the goal for the receiver.

INOCULATION In persuasion, the practice of making audiences immune to the damaging information of an adversary by controlling how the message is released, explained, or framed beforehand.

INTEGRATED COMMUNICATION MODEL (ICM) A model that coordinates all research, education, and communication functions intended to seamlessly serve the goals of the organization.

INTEGRATED MARKETING COMMUNICATION (IMC) The process of building and reinforcing mutually profitable relationships with employees, customers, and other stakeholders through a coordinated communications program.

INTERPRETATION FUNCTION One of the functions of media wherein journalists or broadcasters offer background or commentary on culture, policies, events, or relationships in journalism.

JARGON Incoherent speech or gibberish; language from a specialized field such as medicine or science that is not readily understood by others.

KINESICS The nonverbal code that focuses on body movement, commonly called "body language," which includes posture, gait, gestures, and behaviors that indicate orientation toward another, or nervousness through fidgeting, or comfort through a relaxed demeanor.

KORAN The holy book of Muslims based on reported revelations to Mohammed by Allah.

KORZYBSKI, ALFRED A physicist who started the semanticist movement when he wrote the book *Science and Sanity: An Introduction to Non-Aristotelian Systems and General Semantics* (1933).

LA TECHNIQUE The process of propagandizing the masses; Jacques Ellul's theory that the masses are propagandized daily by the immersion of individuals continuously by indoctrination from technological society's myths and ideology.

LAKOFF, GEORGE A language scholar who has written widely about the nature of metaphors and how conceptual systems of thought influence philosophical discourse by framing arguments.

"LETTER FROM BIRMINGHAM JAIL" The letter that Dr. Martin Luther King Jr. wrote to critics to explain his active participation in the civil rights movement through demonstrations, sit-ins, and marches to confront the established power structure in Alabama.

LINKAGE FUNCTION A media function that links or connects products to consumers through advertising, or makes political, economic, or social issues available to the masses.

LOGOLOGY The study of words, speech, or discourse.

LOGOS The logic of the arguments created by the source; one of Aristotle's three classical appeals used in persuasion.

MEDIA BIAS The belief that traditional media shows a liberal bias because the practitioners have lost touch with the American people; a critique by Bernard Goldberg (2002) and others.

MERE EXPOSURE THEORY (MET) Also called "mere exposure effect," the repeated exposure to an unfamiliar stimulus can have a positive effect toward the stimulus, e.g., name or face recognition.

MESSAGE The ideas or thoughts that a source creates to send to a receiver in oral or written form.

METAPHORS A figure of speech where one thing is likened to another, for example, "the mind is like a computer"; an implied comparison.

MILLENNIUM A period of a thousand years; in theology, the period when Satan will be bound on earth and Christ will return to reign, bringing peace and prosperity.

MISOGYNISTIC Characterized by a hatred of women; a characteristic attributed to gangsta rap music.

MODERNITY Of or characterized by modern influences; in theology, a challenge to orthodox Judeo-Christian beliefs and practices through pluralistic culture and secular influences.

MOPS Memory organization packages, which consist of context-dependent memories of common experiences that conjure up immediate visual and auditory recollections, like going on a date or to the dentist's office; Roger Schank stated that attorneys should elicit these MOPs to persuade jurors.

MORTIFICATION The control of physical desires or passion by self-denial, fasting, confession; to be humiliated or shamed.

MYTH A traditional story of unknown authorship handed down for generations that explains some phenomenon of nature, generally involving gods or heroes; a story, legend or tribal belief. Ellul (1965) defined *myth* as "an all encompassing image".

NARRATIVE A story that has characters, action, and a logical structure—a beginning, middle, and end—that resonates with the oral tradition of humans; a form of communication that dramatizes or relates to the human condition.

NARRATIVE THEORY Walter Fisher's (1984) paradigm that synthesizes two strands in rhetorical theory—the argumentative, persuasive theme and the literary, aesthetic theme premised on the persuasive power of narratives.

NATURALISM A worldview that embodies the beliefs that matter exists and that is all there is, death is the extinction of individuality, history has no purpose, and ethics are derived from people.

NICHE Derived from the Latin word for "nest," meaning a place built exclusively for the inhabitants of it; a specialized and narrowly defined market segment that fills a unique selling position; a narrowed field of consumers or audience members.

NOISE Any interference that impedes the transmission or reception of a message, which may include physical noise, like a factory, or psychological noise, which includes prejudices and biases for or against another.

NOMOS The relationship between custom and law, according to philosophers Leucippus and Democritus in fifth-century Greece.

NONARTISTIC PROOFS Proofs used to persuade that included five kinds of evidence—laws, witnesses, contracts, tortures, and the oath, according to Aristotle; those proofs not created but used by the orator.

NONVERBAL CODES The categories of nonverbal communication that have been studied for meaning that include affect displays, chronemics, eye behavior, haptics, kinesics, proxemics, territoriality, olfactics, and vocalics.

NONVIOLENT RESISTANCE The philosophy that Dr. Martin Luther King Jr. taught during the civil rights movement, based on the writings of Mahatma Ghandi and Henry David Thoreau, combining peaceful resistance and civil disobedience to demonstrate a need for change.

NON SEQUITUR A fallacy in argument; means simply "does not follow; an idea out of sequence or an illogical statement that does not pertain to the topic being discussed.

OLFACTICS The nonverbal code that focuses on smell, such as baked goods that stimulate hunger or body odor that stigmatizes a person socially.

PARADIGM A pattern, example, or model; the accepted view of an idea or situation.

PARADIGM SHIFT A challenge to existing perceptions or practices, for example, liberal ideology challenges conservative ideology, Muslim ideology challenges Judeo-Christian ideology.

PATHOS Emotions or psychological appeals to arouse compassion, pity, or outrage; one of the three classical appeals used in persuasion, according to Aristotle.

PEJORATIVE Depreciatory; in linguistics, applies to words whose basic meaning has been changed for the worse; for example, "propaganda" used to mean to propagate the Catholic faith, now it means to use deceptive means or to mount a campaign to control, as in the Nazi regime.

PERSUASION A form of communication that employs both verbal and nonverbal symbols that intend to influence receivers to voluntarily change attitudes, values, beliefs, and behaviors to agree with those supported by the advocate of the message.

PHAEDRUS A dialogue by Plato that discusses the nature of rhetoric through the use of characters like Socrates and others who distinguish between emotional appeals and truth or logic; contains an allegory that represents the dual nature of man as being both an appetitive beast and one capable of rationality.

POLITICAL RHETORIC Communication that involves deliberation offering arguments for or against public policies; debates focusing on topics such as war and peace, treaties, foreign and domestic welfare.

PORNOGRAPHY Writing, images, or art intended to arouse sexual desire; the criteria to identify pornography was set forward by the *Miller* v. *California* case (1973), which established that a work taken as a whole had to appeal to prurient interests, violate community standards, and lack social, literary, artistic, or political value to be defined as pornography.

POST HOC ERGO PROPTER HOC A fallacy in reasoning that concludes that just because one thing precedes another the first caused the second event to occur; means literally "after this therefore because of this," for example, "Every time I wash my car it rains."

POSTMODERNISM A worldview that rejects metaphysical considerations that make anything or anyone divine, reject belief in a predetermined purpose for life, which then liberates people to create their own purpose and to find meaning for themselves.

PRESIDENTIAL RHETORIC A genre of rhetorical study that analyzes the strategies and tactics used by the president to win consent or to administer the executive office; communication from the "bully pulpit" of the presidency with the authority of that office in the United States.

PRESS AGENTRY One of the four models of public relations identified by Grunig and Grunig (2001) that uses one-way communication to disseminate information to various publics from the organization.

PRIMACY-RECENCY EFFECT In communication theory; the findings that the beginning and the end of a message are the most memorable places for ideas, so the speaker should put their strongest arguments in either of these places.

PRODUCT PLACEMENT The practice of paying a fee to have a product written into a movie, game, or show where the actor wears or uses the brand, for example, *American Idol* displays Coke prominently on drink cups that the judges use.

PRODUCT POSITIONING The stage of the life cycle of a campaign when a product is classified and differentiated from all other products.

PRODUCT PROMOTION All communication means used to reach consumers with information about the goods or services being offered—mailings, coupons, samples, advertisements, and special events.

PROPAGANDA The deliberate, systematic attempt to shape perceptions, manipulate cognitions, and direct behavior to achieve a response that furthers the desired intent of the propagandist.

PROXEMICS The nonverbal code that focuses on how humans use personal space. Anthropologist Edward Hall broke this code into four distances: intimate = 0 to18 inches; personal = 18 inches to 4 feet; social = 4 to 12 feet; and public distances = 12 feet and farther. This code is culturally and personally defined.

PSYCHOGRAPHICS Consumer or audience profiles that aim to reveal their lifestyles and mindsets, e.g., veterans, baby boomers, generation Xers, and millennials.

PUBLIC PHILOSOPHY Walter Lippmann's term meaning a civility in language and in deeds based on natural law which guaranteed certain rights to all humans.

PUBLIC RELATIONS A management function that includes press agentry; education; image creation, maintenance, and repair; lobbying; special events; and communication with all publics; according to Edward Bernays, engineering of public consent.

PUBLIC RELATIONS SOCIETY OF AMERICA (PRSA) A professional society headquartered in New York City with 109 chapters and 20 different professional interest groups that represent business and industry, counseling firms, independent practitioners, military, government, associations, hospitals, schools, professional services firms, and nonprofit organizations.

PYGMALION EFFECT A transformation based on charm or linguistic expertise, named for the play *Pygmalion* by George Bernard Shaw, who wrote how Professor Higgins transformed a vulgar flower girl into a refined lady by teaching her proper speech and genteel manners; in court, a confident behavioral style that attorneys use to influence jurors to support the attorney's case or findings.

PYRAMID OF NEEDS A. H. Maslow's theory that people have needs arranged in a pyramid—physiological, safety, belonging, and esteem needs, called deficit needs, and at the top self-actualization needs.

RAPIST–SEDUCER–LOVER RELATIONSHIP A sexual metaphor used by Wayne Brockriede to demonstrate the various types of persuaders, with the rapist manipulating and using the audience, the seducer using charm and deceit, and the lover who respects and enlightens or tries to empower the audience.

RECEIVER The person or audience who is targeted to get the message.

RECEIVER-CENTERED Rhetorical discourse is receiver-centered because the response to the message depends on the audience's, or receiver's, response to it.

RELUCTANT TESTIMONY A form of testimony that is damaging to the witness or self-indicting and believed to be highly credible because of the consequences; the credibility of such reluctant testimony has been questioned more recently.

RHETOR A speaker; a master teacher of communication, according to the Greeks, that combined politics and public speaking.

RHETORIC The faculty of observing in any given case the available means of persuasion according to Aristotle; the foundations of persuasion.

RHETORIC OF COMMUNION One of five forms of rhetoric described by Quentin J. Schultze (2003) that supports the need for unity amid growing cultural and ethnic diversity by Christian groups.

RHETORIC OF CONVERSION One of five forms of rhetoric described by Quentin J. Schultze (2003) that preaches turning away from the sinful ways of the world and toward the path of righteousness.

RHETORIC OF DISCERNMENT One of five forms of rhetoric described by Quentin J. Schultze (2003) that urges religious groups to differentiate their brand from others as the tensions and disagreements grow in our multicultural society.

RHETORIC OF EXILE One of five forms of rhetoric described by Quentin J. Schultze (2003) that reflects the core values of Christians who believe that the cultural environment is hostile to their faith community, which has led to the "naked public square" where there is an absence of God or religion; the conflict between materialism and the life of faith or Judeo-Christian religions.

RHETORIC OF PRAISE One of the five forms of rhetoric described by Quentin J. Schultze (2003) that capitalizes on mass media to gain success, legitimacy, and market share for religious enterprises that turns pundits and celebrities into icons of praise.

ROKEACH'S BELIEF SYSTEM Milton Rokeach stated that beliefs were like the layers of an onion, with central beliefs at the core about one's self, then beliefs that are socially derived, beliefs from authority figures, and more peripheral beliefs that are easier to influence; central beliefs are most resistant to change.

ROLE-PLAYING Taking the role of another has been used in couples' counseling and other settings to change attitudes and behavior.

SCAPEGOAT A person, group, or thing that bears the blame for others' mistakes or crimes; to transfer the blame to another agency or person for misfortunes or scandal.

SECULARIZATION The absence of any religious character, influence, or significance; to turn to worldly enterprise.

SECURITIES AND EXCHANGE COMMISSION (SEC) A federal regulatory agency that was established after the stock market crash of 1929 to protect the public from fraudulent advertising for stocks and bonds.

SELECTIVE EXPOSURE People generally avoid messages or information that is inconsistent with their beliefs, values, and customs, and they seek out people, messages, or customs that are consistent with their own.

SELF-FULFILLING PROPHESY A form of wish fulfillment wherein one works, hopes, and is motivated to reach a particular goal or outcome, i.e., to fail because one believes one will fail, or conversely to triumph because one has faith and works to succeed.

SIGN An indication of a condition or event, like smoke is a sign of fire; a symbol that conveys meaning, like a stop sign regulates traffic or a black armband indicates mourning.

SLAP TEST Criteria applied to determine if a work taken as a whole lacks Social, Literary, Artistic, or Political value to qualify as pornography.

SLIPPERY SLOPE A fallicy in reasoning that assumes that one event will give rise to a series of events that will lead inevitably to a bad outcome.

SOCIAL JUDGMENT THEORY Positions exist along a continuum from strong opposition to acceptance on issues with an anchor point that identifies an individual's stand on that issue, and persuaders attempt to change the anchor position through various strategies of communication.

SOCRATIC METHOD Employs the use of leading questions to make a point or to elicit the correct answer.

SOPHIA The Greek word meaning "wisdom, intelligence, or skill"; the root for "sophisticated."

SOPHISTS The first teachers in ancient Greece, who taught rhetoric, law, and public speaking for a fee.

SOURCE Also known as the **speaker**; the person who creates the message.

SPIN A derogatory term applied to communication that is perceived to manipulate, conceal, or obfuscate facts to diminish consequences at the expense of transparency or full disclosure to interested parties or the public; propaganda.

STATISTICS Numerical representations for many entities studied; a form of proof that relies on numbers to present facts; commonly seen in polls, economic forecasts, or any quantitative analysis.

STEREOTYPE A prejudicial characterization or mold that does not allow for any individuality; when applied to people, the image is generally negative.

STIGMATIZED Characterized or marked as disgraceful or shameful.

STONE AGE BRAIN THEORY In evolutionary psychology, the theory that our brain is composed of certain functions that enable us to adapt to the specific tasks of our ancestors; in advertising the belief that ads should represent sex or reproduction, power, speed, and survival themes.

SUBLIMINAL Messages that are below the conscious level but still are believed to be received and influential, e.g., embedded pictures in ads, hidden graphics or messages.

SUBLIMINAL ADVERTISING Ads that contain covert images or messages; a practice that most marketing experts deny having used or discredit as unethical and ineffective.

SURVEILLANCE FUNCTION A media function that is based on the belief that it is media's role to keep an eye on government, to inform citizens, and to give warnings about matters that threaten public welfare.

SYLLOGISM A form of argument that offers first a claim, then a subclaim, and finally a conclusion, or major premise, minor premise, and conclusion.

SYMBIOTIC RELATIONSHIP A biological relationship between two entities where each is dependent upon the other for survival; in politics, although the media and government have an adversarial relationship, each is dependent upon the other to survive or to function optimally.

SYMBOL A sign that stands for another thing, as words represent the thing referred to; a token, sign, or image that stands for another, e.g., a cross represents Christianity or a dove represents peace; a vehicle to convey meaning through verbal, written, or graphic form.

SYMMETRICAL Having correspondence in form, size, or arrangement; in public relations, a two-way model that involves communication between an organization and the public that it serves; contrasted with asymmetrical communication, like press agentry that is one-way.

SYNECDOCHE A figure of speech or a person who stands for the whole, like bread represents all food.

TANAKH The Hebrew Bible.

TECHNOLOGICAL DARWINISM Survival of the fittest, through the neural networks that join consumers and providers of goods and services around the globe; social Darwinism expanded through technology.

TERRITORIALITY The nonverbal code that deals with the possession and defense of a given space; part of the code of proxemics, for example, our feeling of ownership of a favorite chair, bar stool, or library table; nonverbal messages we send to defend territory include dirty looks, spreading our things about, or attacks on intruders.

TESTIMONY Data offered by experts in a particular field, e.g., medicine, or law, or the sworn version of truth offered in a courtroom by either laypersons or experts.

THEISM A worldview based on the beliefs that God exists, created the cosmos, created people in His image, serves as the foundation for ethics, and that there is life after death.

THEORY OF REASONED ACTION Addresses the process of an individual weighing the benefits and risks of taking a course of action and also taking into consideration what friends or family will think of their action.

THIRD-PERSON EFFECT The common belief that media affects other people's attitudes, behaviors, and values, but denial that we are influenced by media also.

TOWER OF BABEL A tower that the Babylonians built to represent their power and ingenuity; in the Bible, God divided the Babylonians by language as punishment for their hubris, which introduced foreign tongues and disunity.

TRANSMISSION OF VALUES A media function that subtly informs readers, viewers, and followers, through socialization, what values and behaviors are appropriate; a powerful effect that some cultures resist from U.S. media, which is seen as characterized by sex and violence.

TRANSPARENCY Open and full disclosure in an organization that supports honesty and instills public confidence; lack of concealment.

UNILATERAL COMMUNICATION Communication that is one way.

UNIQUE SELLING POSITION (USP) A marketing goal to establish a niche for a good or service that differentiates it from all others through design, price, brand, or novelty.

UNITED STATES POSTAL SERVICE A federal agency that not only delivers mail but also enforces some regulations regarding pornography, deception in advertising, and public safety.

UNIVERSALS OF COMMUNICATION Joseph DeVito's communication model, which consists of 10 parts: communication context, source, encode, message, noise, channel, receiver, decode, feedback, and effect.

UTOPIAN The word "utopia" was created by Thomas More, drawn from two Greek prefixes with one meaning "no-place" and the other meaning "good place"; "utopian" means ideal, like paradise.

VIRAL VIDEO A video that spreads across the Internet with great speed, for example, the political spoof *This Land* featuring George W. Bush and John Kerry, or the Obama Girl video in 2008.

VISUAL RHETORIC Communication that uses graphics, art, cartoons, or other visual symbols designed to be interpreted by an audience; visual symbols that communicate meaning to an intended audience. To qualify as visual rhetoric, the image must be symbolic, involve human intervention, and be presented to an audience for the purpose of communicating with that audience, according to Sonja Foss.

VOCALICS Also called "paralanguage," the nonverbal code that includes all vocal qualities—pitch, rhythm, resonance, dialect, volume, and rate.

VOIR DIRE (French *voir*—truthfully; *dire*—to say). The jury-selection process wherein the witness swears to answer truthfully questions about his or her ability to serve on a jury.

WATCHDOG OF THE PEOPLE A reference to mass media and the role it plays to protect the public by keeping them informed so they can make enlightened decisions.

WEAK PROPAGANDA A term Kevin Maloney used to describe public relations that seeks advantage for its principals and uses many promotional techniques, both visible and invisible, outside of paid advertising.

CREDITS

INDEX

Note: page numbers in *italics* refer to figures; those followed by t refer to tables.

Printed in the USA/Agawam, MA
August 26, 2020

760400.018